Gender Politics at Home and Abroad

Hyaeweol Choi examines the formation of modern gender relations in Korea from a transnational perspective. Diverging from a conventional understanding of "secularization" as a defining feature of modernity, Choi argues that Protestant Christianity, introduced to Korea in the late-nineteenth century, was crucial in shaping modern gender ideology, reforming domestic practices and claiming new space for women in the public sphere. In Korea, Japanese colonial power – and with it, Japanese representations of modernity – was confronted with the dominant cultural and material power of Europe and the US, which was reflected in Korean attitudes. One of the key agents in conveying ideas of "Western modernity" in Korea was globally connected Christianity, especially US-led Protestant missionary organizations. By placing gender and religion at the center of the analysis, Choi shows that the development of modern gender relations was rooted in the transnational experience of Koreans and not in a simple nexus of the colonizer and the colonized.

HYAEWEOL CHOI is a scholar of gender history. She is the C. Maxwell and Elizabeth M. Stanley Family and Korea Foundation Chair in Korean Studies at the University of Iowa.

Gender Politics at Home and Abroad

Protestant Modernity in Colonial-Era Korea

Hyaeweol Choi

CAMBRIDGE
UNIVERSITY PRESS

University Printing House, Cambridge CB2 8BS, United Kingdom

One Liberty Plaza, 20th Floor, New York, NY 10006, USA

477 Williamstown Road, Port Melbourne, VIC 3207, Australia

314–321, 3rd Floor, Plot 3, Splendor Forum, Jasola District Centre, New Delhi – 110025, India

79 Anson Road, #06–04/06, Singapore 079906

Cambridge University Press is part of the University of Cambridge.

It furthers the University's mission by disseminating knowledge in the pursuit of education, learning, and research at the highest international levels of excellence.

www.cambridge.org
Information on this title: www.cambridge.org/9781108487436
DOI: 10.1017/9781108766838

© Hyaeweol Choi 2020

This publication is in copyright. Subject to statutory exception and to the provisions of relevant collective licensing agreements, no reproduction of any part may take place without the written permission of Cambridge University Press.

First published 2020

A catalogue record for this publication is available from the British Library.

Library of Congress Cataloging-in-Publication Data
Names: Choi, Hyaeweol, author.
Title: Gender politics at home and abroad : Protestant modernity in colonial-era Korea / Hyaeweol Choi.
Description: Cambridge, United Kingdom ; New York, NY : Cambridge University Press, 2020. | Includes bibliographical references and index.
Identifiers: LCCN 2020014620 (print) | LCCN 2020014621 (ebook) | ISBN 9781108487436 (hardback) | ISBN 9781108766838 (ebook)
Subjects: LCSH: Women – Korea – Social conditions – 20th century. | Sex role – Korea – History – 20th century. | Feminism – Korea – History – 20th century. | Protestantism – Korea – Influence. | Transnationalism. | Korea – Civilization – Western influences. | Korea – History – Japanese occupation, 1910–1945.
Classification: LCC HQ1765.5 .C4453 2020 (print) | LCC HQ1765.5 (ebook) | DDC 305.409519–dc23
LC record available at https://lccn.loc.gov/2020014620
LC ebook record available at https://lccn.loc.gov/2020014621

ISBN 978-1-108-48743-6 Hardback

Cambridge University Press has no responsibility for the persistence or accuracy of URLs for external or third-party internet websites referred to in this publication and does not guarantee that any content on such websites is, or will remain, accurate or appropriate.

Contents

List of Illustrations	*page* vi
Notes on Romanization and Translations	viii
Preface and Acknowledgments	ix
Introduction	1
1 Ideology: "Wise Mother, Good Wife"	36
2 Materiality: The Experience of Modern House and Home	73
3 Crossing: Selfhood, Nation, and the World	109
4 Labor: Searching for Rural Modernity	149
Conclusion	190
Bibliography	208
Index	232

Illustrations

1.1	The opening scene of *Mimong* (Illusive Dream) Source: Korean Film Archive (1936)	*page* 69
2.1	Missionary home interior Source: The Reverend Corwin & Nellie Taylor Collection, Korean Heritage Library, University of Southern California, Los Angeles	78
2.2a	A cradle roll party at the home of Mrs. W. A. Noble Source: Photograph courtesy of the Noble family	80
2.2b	The cradle roll in the South Mountain Church, Pyeng Yang Source: Photograph courtesy of the Noble family	80
2.2c	Cradle roll babies for baptism by W. A. Noble at the Hallusu Church, Manchuria Source: Photograph courtesy of the Noble family	80
2.3	*"Home, sweet home"* Source: *Sin kajŏng* 1 (1933)	84
2.4	"Culture house" (文化住宅)? or "annoying house" (蚊禍住宅)? Source: *Chosŏn ilbo*, April 14, 1930	95
3.1	Barbour Scholarship recipients: Martha Choy, Katherine Kim, and Mary Kim (third, eighth, and tenth from the left in the last row), 1930–1931 Source: HS835, UM Barbour, photograph by Rentschler, Bentley Historical Library, University of Michigan	137
3.2	The Candle Ceremony of the Intercollegiate Cosmopolitan Club, Columbia University, circa 1921 Source: Harry Edmonds, "A New Endowment for International Friendship," Educational Interests, 1921–1922 (Rockefeller Family, R62, Series G, Box 10, Folder 68A), Rockefeller Archive Center	141
3.3	Kim Hwallan at the International Missionary Council, Jerusalem, 1928 Source: LC-DIG-matpc-07146 (digital file from original photograph) LC-M361-888 (b&w film copy negative), G. Eric and Edith Matson Photograph Collection, Library of Congress	146

4.1	Women's collective farm Source: *Samch'ŏlli* 4, no. 3 (March 1932): 55	150
4.2	Early members of the Korea YWCA Source: Courtesy of the Korea YWCA	173
4.3	Korea YWCA Rural Revitalization Campaign Source: Courtesy of the Korea YWCA	177
5.1	New woman	192
Panel 1	She makes full use of the limited time given to her, reading until midnight	192
Panel 2	She composes poems while cooking	192
Panel 3	She thinks about the successful future of *Sin yŏja* while mending clothes	192
Panel 4	She works on an article throughout the night until dawn Source: *Sin yŏja* 4 (1920): 53–6	192
5.2	Ava Milam with her Korean students during her visit to South Korea in 1948 Source: Ava Milam Clark Papers, Oregon State University Libraries Special Collections & Archives Research Center	198
5.3	Ch'oe Isun Source: *The Beaver* (1937), Ava Milam Clark Papers, Oregon State University Libraries Special Collections & Archives Research Center	203
5.4	Barbour Scholarship recipients: Kim Meri and Ko Hwanggyŏng (third and eighth from the left in the first row), 1933–1934 Source: HS838, UM Barbour, photograph by Rentschler, Bentley Historical Library, University of Michigan	204
5.5	Ch'oe Yŏngsuk Source: *Tonga ilbo*, November 29, 1931	204

Notes on Romanization and Translations

Korean words in the text are rendered using the McCune-Reischauer system, with the exception of proper names, for which alternative spellings are well-established. Korean names follow the standard order – family name first – unless a particular name is traditionally rendered in Western order. Unless a source is specified, all translations of Korean texts are mine.

Preface and Acknowledgments

One of the perks of being an academic is having opportunities to travel far and wide for a variety of professional reasons. We go to archives, attend conferences, or present research at various locations – domestic and international. When I launched this book project, "travel" itself became a focus of the analysis as I was tracing the footsteps of Korean women (mostly elite women) who traveled overseas as students or speakers in the 1920s and 1930s. Their experience of travelling and living abroad resonated with me. Sixty years after these women undertook their journeys, I myself became an international student, coming from South Korea to the United States to embark on my graduate studies. Having been in this situation myself and thinking about my predecessors, I became fascinated by the question: What does it mean to cross borders and leave "home," and how does that border-crossing experience shape subjectivity, work and life? Separated by a century from my foremothers, I wondered how our ventures compared: What did it mean to travel overseas as a colonized woman in the late-nineteenth and early-twentieth centuries? How was it possible for them to travel overseas? What did they see and experience? What inspired them? What discouraged them? How was their experience translated in the local and national context when they returned home?

This book takes up a transnational perspective to examine the formation of modern gender relations in Korea under Japanese colonial rule. It focuses on the flow of people, materials, and images to investigate the ways in which transnational encounters played a role in shaping modern gender ideology, reforming domestic practices, coming to grips with a sense of locality and the world, and claiming new space for women in the public sphere. The analysis centers particularly on the role of the global Christian network as a key facilitator in the education of women, travel, and socioeconomic reforms. Diverging from the conventional understanding of modernity as "secularization," the book foregrounds the thesis that Protestant Christianity, introduced into Korea in the late-nineteenth century, was crucial in shaping modern gender relations along with nationalism and colonial influences. Furthermore, the analysis recognizes the historical context in which Japanese colonial power – and with it, Japanese representations of modernity – was confronted with the dominant cultural and material power of Europe and the US that Koreans considered the origin of modernity. One of the key agents in conveying "Western modernity" was globally interconnected Christianity, particularly in the form of US-led missionary organizations. By placing gender and religion at the center of the analysis, the book traces the roots of the development of modern gender relations through the *transnational* experience of Koreans rather than in the simple nexus of the colonizer and the colonized, and discusses how such transnational contact helped advance indigenized ideas and reform activities in modern Korea.

This book has been a long time in the making, and there were several momentous occasions and opportunities that significantly shaped it. So many scholars, friends, archivists, and librarians generously shared their time, knowledge, and helpful feedback. Shortly after I finished the manuscript for the book *Gender and Mission Encounters in Korea: New Women, Old Ways* (2009), Timothy Lee invited me to join a panel he was organizing for the annual conference of the American Academy of Religion. The paper I presented at that AAR meeting was about the modern construction of the gender ideology, "wise mother, good wife," and it eventually became Chapter 1 of the present book and the jumping-off point for many of the other issues covered in this volume. I thank Tim for offering me a "launching pad" for a new book project.

Relocating to the Australian National University in 2010 was an important turning point in my intellectual journey and especially in developing a transnational outlook. The sheer fact of relocating to the southern hemisphere and a region that has a fundamentally different relationship to Asia and the Pacific provided an eye-opening shift in perspective. Furthermore, it gave me opportunities to interact and work with a whole new slate of colleagues in East Asian, South Asia, Southeast Asia, and the Pacific studies. Tessa Morris-Suzuki, Narangoa Li, Shameem Black, Robert Cribb, Ariel Heryanto, Geremie Barmé, and Simon Avennell were excellent interlocutors in helping me rethink what "Asian studies" or "area studies" are. I am grateful for the constant support and collegiality of my fellow Koreanists at ANU, Roald Maliangkay and Ruth Barraclough, who saw the evolution of the book project from its earliest stages. I am also forever thankful for my interactions with Kim Rubenstein, Margaret Jolly, Hilary Charlesworth, Fiona Jenkins, Carolyn Strange, and my fellow feminists at the ANU Gender Institute. Their curiosity and commitment to intellectual investigation continue to be a great source of inspiration. Precious friendships with Sora Park, Eunro Lee, and Kyungja Jung have been like an oasis – a wellspring of pure joy, comfort, and wisdom.

The University of Iowa became my new home institution in 2018. My department, Religious Studies, has been a very collegial community and the Obermann Center for Advanced Studies has been an ideal site for intellectual collaboration with public engagement. I am especially thankful to Morten

Schlütter, Diana Cates, Jenna Supp-Montgomerie, Bob Gerstmyer, Paul Dilley, Roxanna Curto, John Finamore, Cynthia Chou, Jiyeon Kang, Alyssa Park, Teresa Mangum, and Leslie Schwalm for welcoming me into the UI community and extending their friendship. Beyond the campus, my yogi friends in the "hot room" have helped me find regular doses of fun and camaraderie.

The book project was generously funded by three grants. A Fulbright grant afforded me the opportunity to stay in South Korea for several months to conduct preliminary research. In preparing the Fulbright grant proposal I benefited from conversations with Theodore Jun Yoo, Hwasook Nam, and Seoungsook Moon, who helped me rethink a set of questions related to gender and modernity in colonial-era Korea. As a Fulbrighter, I was affiliated with the Korean Women's Institute at Ewha Womans University. Its director, Jae Kyung Lee, and other fellow scholars at KWI provided me with an intellectually stimulating community to be part of. I also received a three-year grant from the Australian Research Council (DP140103096) that enabled me to travel globally (Asia, Europe, the US, and Australia) and helped me spend time not only in conventional archives but also a number of rare sites that I would never have had the means to otherwise visit. Many colleagues read and gave me helpful comments on my ARC grant proposal, including Tessa Morris-Suzuki, Robert Cribb, Margaret Jolly, Carolyn Strange, and Tamara Jacka. Finally, a five-year grant from the Academy of Korean Studies Overseas Leading University Program for Korean Studies (AKS-2011-BAA-2016), for which I was the project director, provided additional support for the research that went into this book. The grant supported a number of conferences and speakers that further stimulated and fostered my exploration of transnational history. None of the international travel that I undertook to visit various archives in Korea, Japan, China, the US, Sweden, Denmark, Germany, and Australia would have been possible without these generous grants.

While conducting research in Korea, I benefited greatly from conversations with scholars and librarians who shared their time and knowledge. I would particularly like to extend my thanks to Yu Sŏnghŭi, Yi Yunhŭi, and Ch'oe Susanna of the Korea YWCA, Chang Kyusik of Chungang University, Kim Sanghŭi of Induk University, Ko Aeran, Cho Han Hyejŏng, Kim Hyŏnmi, and Pak Chinyŏng of Yonsei University, Chŏng Chiyŏng and Lee Jaegyŏng of Ewha Womans University, Pak Ch'ansŭng, Yun Haedong, Hong Yanghŭi, and Im Chihyŏn of Hanyang University, Kim Kyŏngil of the Academy of Korean Studies, Mun Kyŏnghŭi of Changwon University, Yi Songhŭi of Silla University, and Kim Chinsuk of Pusan University. Librarians at the National Institute of Korean History, National Library of Korea, National Assembly Library of Korea, and Korean Film Archive were also very helpful in identifying source materials. For decades now it has been a sacred ritual for me to get together with Ko Chŏng Kaphŭi, Yi Sugin, Chŏng Chiyŏng, and Kim Hyŏnmi when I am in Korea. I greatly admire their feminist scholarship, and I have derived countless insights and ideas from our conversations. During trips to Tokyo, Kyoto, and Nagoya in Japan, I received invaluable support from Mori Rie of Japan Women's University, Takahashi Yuko of Tsuda College, Tazuke Kazuhisa of the Korea YMCA in Japan, Watanabe Naoki of Musashi University, Ryuta Itagaki and Michael Shapiro of Doshisha University, and Pak Sŏnmi of Tsukuba University. In China, mostly in Shanghai, I received assistance from Yun Zou, a PhD student at ANU, and Liuya Zhang of Fudan University to conduct research at the Shanghai Municipal Archives and historic sites, including the site of the Korean Provisional Government. I also want to express my sincere appreciation to the scholars in Europe who generously gave me their time and guided me in searching sources. I am especially grateful to Sonja Häussler of Stockholm University, Anders Riel Müller of the University of Copenhagen, Geir Helgesen of the Nordic Institute of Asian Studies, Andrew Jackson of the University of Copenhagen, Søren Launbjerg of the International People's College in Helsingør, Koen De Ceuster and Remco Breuker of Leiden University, Alain Delissen, Isabelle Sancho, and Valérie Gelézeau of L'École des Hautes Études en Sciences Sociales, Florence Galmiche of Université Paris 7-Diderot, and Jong Chol An and You Jae Lee of the University of Tübingen.

During trips to the US to visit various archives, I was generously granted the time and assistance of archivists and librarians at Oregon State University, University of Southern California, University of Michigan, Columbia University, Union Theological Seminary in the City of New York, Rockefeller Archive Center, Boston University, Harvard University, Vanderbilt University, and Wesleyan College. A sabbatical semester in the fall of 2017 gave me much needed time to concentrate on writing chapters. I was affiliated with Columbia University at that time, and I am especially grateful to Ted Hughes and Jungwon Kim for their generosity and friendship in making my sabbatical such an enjoyable and productive time.

At various stages of the current project, a number of research assistants helped me compile literature and identify sources: Alison Darby, Narah Lee, Yonjae Paik, Joowhee Lee, Younghye Suh, Bo Kyung Seo, Lee Hanbit, Liuya Zhang, and Malin Adolfsson. I thank them for their excellent work.

I also greatly benefited from the questions and comments from audiences when I presented elements of the research in this book at various institutions. For those opportunities, I would especially like to thank Ksenia Chizhova and Steven Chung of Princeton University, Jesook Song, Jennifer Chun, Judy Han, and Andre Schmid of the University of Toronto, Alison Bashford of the University of Cambridge, John Lie of UC-Berkeley, Jisoo Kim of George Washington University, Joe Cutter of Arizona State University, Jong Chol An and You Jae Lee of the University of Tübingen, Alain Delissen, Isabelle

Sancho, and Valérie Gelézeau of L'École des Hautes Études en Sciences Sociales, Theodore Hughes and Jungwon Kim of Columbia University, Wonjung Min of Pontificia Universidad Católica de Chile, Changzoo Song of Auckland University, Sunyoung Park and David Kang of the University of Southern California, Lawrence Wang of the Chinese University of Hong Kong, Dafna Zur and Kären Wigen of Stanford University, Hyunjung Lee of Nanyang Technological University, Yunghee Kim of the University of Hawai'i, Ellen Widmer of Wellesley College, Daniel Bays of Calvin College, Sun Joo Kim of Harvard University, Heejin Lee of Yonsei University, and Nancy Abelmann of the University of Illinois. I would like to pay special homage to the late Daniel Bays and the late Nancy Abelmann, who were rare gems in academe for both their brilliance and generosity. I miss them dearly.

In thinking and writing about the book project, I have enormously benefited from working together with scholars across disciplinary and area specialization, which further stimulated my thinking about transnational perspectives. I am thankful for the opportunity to collaborate with Barbara Molony and Janet Theiss, with whom I coauthored the book *Gender in Modern East Asia: An Integrated History*. The experience was a gift in so many ways. I have also enjoyed the chance to engage in interregional dialogue at various conferences, and it has been my great delight to participate in conference panels with Ellen Widmer of Wellesley College, Stefan Hübner of the National University of Singapore, Paola Zamperini of Northwestern University, Gal Gvili of McGill University, Margaret Tillman of Purdue University, Jan Bardsley of the University of North Carolina, Rebecca Copeland of Washington University in St. Louis, Laura Prieto of Simmons University, Helen Schneider of Virginia Tech, Vera Mackie of the University of Wollongong, and Tsui Kai Hin Brian of Hong Kong Polytechnic University.

I would like to acknowledge that Chapter 1 is based on the earlier version that appeared first in the *Journal of Korean Studies* and Chapter 2 in the *Journal of Women's History*, both of which were significantly revised with additional analysis. I also thank various archives for giving me permission to use images in this book.

It has been such a joy to work with my editor, Lucy Rymer, who embraced my proposed book project from the outset and provided me with constant support and guidance at every stage. I have also been impressed by editorial team members, Emily Sharp, Natasha Whelan, Jayavel Radhakrishnan, Lauren Simpson, and Helen Baxter, at Cambridge University Press, who were always ready to answer questions and helped me navigate each stage toward publication. I would also like to express my deepest appreciation to the anonymous reviewers of my manuscript for insightful and constructive feedback that helped me clarify and elaborate my arguments.

I want to express special thanks to three friends and colleagues whose generosity and friendship have been crucial in completing the book. Robert Eskildsen has been a wonderful interlocutor in helping me develop and articulate research ideas, especially in relation to colonialisms. His incisive questions and comments, always peppered with humor, pushed me to go deeper. Our virtual "meetings" via Skype and our annual foodie outing to find the best restaurant in the host city of the AAS conference were precious occasions for stimulating dialogue and lots of laughter. Theodore Jun Yoo is a rare talent whose creativity, intellectual acuity, and endless energy inspire me in so many ways. He read my full book manuscript and offered incredibly helpful feedback that helped me reframe and improve my arguments. Tessa Morris-Suzuki, whose singular brilliance and generosity has enriched my intellectual and personal life from the time I arrived at ANU, has helped me in ways she is far too modest to take credit for. Our conversations at numerous seminars and conferences in Canberra, hikes around in Bateman's Bay, and discovery walks through Seoul and Tokyo make up a significant part of the tapestry of my work and life.

In the long journey that makes up the writing of a book, it is vital to find small happinesses in everyday life to keep moving onward and put things in perspective. I have had the great good fortune to find a partner who helps me discover new delights in what happens day to day. As we enter our twenty-fifth year of marriage, I am reminded again of my exceptional luck in sharing a life with Dan. He is a constant source of happiness, nurture, and wisdom. Even magical words would not suffice to express enough my admiration and gratitude to him. Hugs and kisses will have to do.

Introduction

In April 1932, the popular magazine *Samch'ŏlli* reported on a roundtable discussion featuring three prominent women intellectuals who had studied overseas: Ch'oe Yŏngsuk (B.A. from Stockholm University), Pak Indŏk (B.A. from Wesleyan College and M.A. from Columbia University), and Hwang Aesidŏk (M.A. from Columbia University).[1] These women were asked to share their observations on a variety of topics, such as childcare facilities, opportunities for employment, birth control, marriage, and divorce. The panelists frequently offered illustrative examples from Sweden and the United States, since they had studied in those countries, but they also referred to Russia, India, Britain, and France, places in which they had traveled briefly.[2] Although some of their observations were overstated, the time they had spent in the United States or Europe gave them a certain authority on foreign models and practices. Capitalizing on this newly acquired status, they presented the legal, economic, and social arrangements in those countries that, as they observed them, treated women as equal participants in society. For example, with respect to the workplace, the three women agreed that European and US societies offered women treatment equal to that of men. They stated that women were free to choose any profession they wanted, limited only by their individual merit and interests. Pak described Russia's state-run childcare centers, which provided reliable and professional childcare, a boon to working mothers. Ch'oe and Hwang made note that in Sweden and the United States divorce and child custody were handled in a way that did not make women vulnerable or put them at a disadvantage.[3]

---

[1] "Oeguk taehak ch'ulsin yŏryu 3haksa chwadamhoe" (Roundtable Discussion with Three Women Notables Who Graduated from Universities Overseas) *Samch'ŏlli* 4, no. 4 (April 1932): 32–38. Hwang Aesidŏk is also known as Hwang Aedŏk.

[2] It is significant to note that Japan, Korea's colonizing power, was conspicuously absent in the discussion.

[3] This type of "roundtable" discussion was fairly common in popular magazines. See Sin Chiyŏng, *Pu/chae ŭi sidae: kŭndae kyemonggi mit singminjigi Chosŏn ŭi yŏnsŏl, chwadamhoe* (The Age of Absence: Speeches and Roundtable Talks in Korea during the Enlightenment and Colonial Periods) (Seoul: Somyŏng, 2012).

1

Although their observations of the West contain some inaccuracies, the main point is that their transnational experience gave these women some cultural capital. The opportunity to travel abroad was an exceptional privilege, especially for women, and more and more Koreans sought out those opportunities. By the early twentieth century, a number of Korean women and men were traveling globally as students, representatives of international organizations, social reformers, performers, or tourists.[4] In their travels, they interacted with and learned from a wide range of thinkers, reformers, and activists, including Sarojini Naidu, the Indian nationalist; Rosa Luxemburg, the Polish-born German revolutionary; Alexandra Kollontai, the Russian communist; Hiratsuka Raichō and Yosano Akiko, Japanese feminists; Mary Lyon, the founder of Mount Holyoke College; John R. Mott, a leader of the YMCA and World Student Christian Federation; Jane Addams, the pioneering social worker; and Ava Milam, a leading home economist.[5] In addition, beginning in the late-nineteenth century a significant number of Protestant Christian missionaries from the United States, Canada, Australia, and Britain came to Korea, establishing modern institutions such as schools and clinics through which they disseminated modern knowledge and novel ways of life as well as Christian faith. These Christian institutions created a pipeline for Koreans to gain experience with foreign languages and culture. Some of the protégés of missionary teachers received advanced training in Japan, China, the United States, Canada, Sweden, and Australia. Furthermore, the flow of modern ideas, cultural icons, and material cultures into Korea from Japan, Europe, and the United States began to refashion gender identity and the practices of everyday life. Women were reading newspaper reports of world and local events and foreign literature in translation, largely Euro-American, watching Hollywood movies, and browsing the latest Western fashions in department stores.[6] In this way, Koreans began to experience modernity either directly through contact

---

[4] Yi Sunt'ak, *Ch'oegŭn segye ilchugi* (Record of the Recent Global Tour) (Kyŏngsŏng: Hansŏng tosŏ chusik hoesa, 1934); "Ryundon, P'ari ro kanŭn muhŭi Ch'oe Sŭnghŭi" (Dancer Ch'oe Sŭnghŭi Going to London and Paris), *Samch'ŏlli* 7, no. 11 (1935): 77–88; "T'aep'yŏngyang hoeŭi esŏ han hoeŭi yŏnsŏl" (Address given at the Pacific Conference), *Samch'ŏlli* 6, no. 8 (1934): 42–44.

[5] For example, see Chŏng Ch'ilsŏng, "Amnal ŭl parabonŭn puin nodongja" (Women Laborers Looking Ahead), *Tonggwang* 29 (December 1931): 70; Pak Indŏk, "6-nyŏnman ŭi na ŭi pando, Amerik'arobut'ŏ torawasŏ yŏjang ŭl p'ulmyŏnsŏ nyet hyŏngje ege" (Returning from the United States to my Homeland after Six Years, To Brothers and Sisters While Unpacking), *Samch'ŏlli* 3, no. 11 (1931): 89–91.

[6] Theodore Jun Yoo, *The Politics of Gender in Colonial Korea: Education, Labor, and Health, 1910–1945* (Berkeley and Los Angeles: University of California Press, 2008); Hanmee Na Kim, "'America' in Colonial Korea: A Vantage Point for Capitalist Modernity," *positions* 26, no. 4 (November 2018): 647–85; Kim Chinsong, *Sŏul e ttansŭhol ŭl hŏhara* (Permit Dance Halls in Seoul) (Seoul: Hyŏnsil munhwa yŏn'gu, 1999). Hollywood movies, in particular, captured the imagination of Korean moviegoers to the extent that "practically there was no distance between Hollywood and Kyŏngsŏng [Seoul, Keijō]" in terms of sharing news about movie stars and films.

and travel overseas, or secondhand, through exposure mediated by printed and visual materials at home.

However, Korea's pursuit of modernization, which began in the late-nineteenth century when Korea opened its doors to foreign countries, got much more complicated once Korea became a colony of Japan (1910–1945). Japan was a colonial power, and it was the dominant route through which modern knowledge and materials were introduced to Korea. Even before Korea was annexed to the Japanese empire, Japan served as the main conduit for modern knowledge, technology, and institutions exemplified by the dispatch of "Chosa Sich'aldan" (Korean Couriers' Observation Mission), comprised of Korean high-level officials, students and translators, to Japan in 1881.[7] Korea became a Protectorate of Japan in 1905, a "virtual annexation," and the Japanese began to exert their legal, diplomatic, and administrative power over Chosŏn Korea.[8] A great many Japanese texts as well as Japanese translations of foreign texts were translated into Korean at this time as useful sources for "modern" reforms.[9] However, Koreans were not looking for Japanese thought or style in these works; rather, Japanese "translations and adaptations" were viewed as an access point for Euro-American ideas and practices, which had been part of the construction of the modern Japanese nation-state.[10] In other words, Japanese sources were expedient samples of "trial and error" process Japan had gone through, demonstrating how Japan had apprehended modern Western civilizations for its own modernization, while reinterpreting the past history of Japan.[11] Just like reformers in China and Japan, who "were simultaneously drawn by Western wealth and power and repelled by aspects of the Western social ethos," Korean reformers were concerned about the potential risks of adopting certain unsavory aspects of Western social practice, and

---

See Chang Tusik, "Ilsang sok ŭi yŏnghwa" (Films in Everyday Life), in *Kŭndae Han'guk ŭi ilsang saenghwal kwa midia* (Everyday Life and Media in Modern Korea), ed. Tan'guk taehakkyo tongyang yŏn'guso (Seoul: Minsogwŏn, 2008), pp. 121–52, quoted on pp. 126–7. See also Dong Hoon Kim, *Eclipsed Cinema: The Film Culture of Colonial Korea* (Edinburgh: Edinburgh University Press, 2017).

[7] Chosa Sich'aldan (aka Sinsa Yuramdan) was not an official but informal envoy with a secret mission from King Kojong to observe modern developments in Meiji Japan. Donghyun Huh, trans. Vladimir Tikhonov, "The Korean Courtiers' Observation Mission's Views on Meiji Japan and Projects of Modern State Building," *Korean Studies* 29 (2005): 30–54.

[8] "The Annexation of Korea to Japan" (editorial comment), *American Journal of International Law* 4, no. 4 (1910): 923–25, quoted on 923.

[9] Pak Chinyŏng, *Pŏnyŏk kwa pŏnan ŭi sidae* (The Age of Translation and Adaptation) (Seoul: Somyŏng ch'ulp'an, 2011); Theresa Hyun, *Writing Women in Korea* (Honolulu: University of Hawai'i Press, 2004); Heekyoung Cho, *Translation's Forgotten History: Russian Literature, Japanese Mediation, and the Formation of Modern Korean Literature* (Cambridge: Harvard University Press, 2016).

[10] Michael D. Shin, "Yi Kwang-su: The Collaborator as Modernist Against Modernity," *Journal of Asian Studies* 71, no. 1 (February 2012): 116.

[11] Pak Sŏnmi, *Kŭndae yŏsŏng cheguk ŭl kŏch'ŏ Chosŏn ŭro hoeyu hada* (Modern Women Return to Korea via Empire) (Seoul: Ch'angbi, 2005), pp. 63–9, quoted on p. 65.

they believed that understanding the Japanese experience with Western civilizations would save them from such risks.[12] In the end, Japan was seen as a mediator that had learned, experimented with, and adjusted Euro-American models in its modern nation-building. Koreans' perception of Japan as a "mediator" or "translator" of Western modernity continued even after Japan officially annexed Korea into its empire in 1910, although the colonial state and its affiliated institutions made persistent efforts in presenting Japan's prowess as a leading modern power through a plethora of colonial policies on the Koreans.[13]

When it comes to gender relations, the effect of Japanese colonial hegemony in Korea gets even more complicated. Before talking about gender dynamics in colonial Korea under Japanese rule in greater depth, it is worthwhile to discuss some of the unique characteristics of Japanese imperialism. As the historian Andre Schmid points out, unlike the European imperial powers, Japanese empire-building took place simultaneously with its modernizing process, and its colonial engagements had a significant impact on Japanese modernity.[14] In addition, Japan's rise as an imperial power should be understood within the context of Euro-American imperial expansion and Euro-American-centric worldviews and racial conceptions that viewed Caucasians as superior and Asians as inferior. Japan was a latecomer to the imperial enterprise, and it succeeded in demonstrating its military prowess in the Sino-Japanese War (1894–1895) and the Russo-Japanese War (1904–1905), and yet it struggled to gain status on a par with Euro-American countries when it came to racial, religious, and cultural matters.[15] In this vein, Jordan Sand characterizes the Japanese as "subaltern imperialists," which means that the Japanese were "formally participating in the imperial system yet socially and culturally kept outside it."[16] In other words, Japanese dominance in the political and economic

---

[12] Joan Judge, *The Precious Raft of History: The Past, the West, and the Woman Question in China* (Stanford: Stanford University Press, 2008), p. 112.

[13] In reality, Japanese imperial power was not a simple imitator of Western models. As shown in the cases of medical modernity, Japan was "coeval with the West." See Jin-kyung Park, "Picturing Empire and Illness: Biomedicine, Venereal Disease and the Modern Girl in Korea under Japanese Colonial Rule," *Cultural Studies* 28, no. 1 (2014): 108–41, quoted on 110. See also Kyung Moon Hwang, *Rationalizing Korea: The Rise of the Modern State 1894–1945* (Oakland: University of California Press, 2016); Todd A. Henry, *Assimilating Seoul: Japanese Rule and the Politics of Public Space in Colonial Korea, 1910–1945* (Berkeley: University of California Press, 2014); Mark E. Caprio, *Japanese Assimilation Policies in Colonial Korea, 1910–1945* (Seattle: University of Washington Press, 2009).

[14] Andre Schmid, "Colonialism and the 'Korea Problem' in the Historiography of Modern Japan: A Review Article," *Journal of Asian Studies* 59, no. 4 (2000): 951–76.

[15] Joseph Henning, *Outposts of Civilization: Race, Religion, and the Formative Years of American-Japanese Relations* (New York: New York University Press, 2000); and Emily Anderson, *Christianity and Imperialism in Modern Japan: Empire for God* (London: Bloomsbury, 2014), pp. 63–6.

[16] Jordan Sand, "Subaltern Imperialists: The New Historiography of the Japanese Empire," *Past and Present* 225, no. 1 (2014): 273–88, quoted on 275.

realms as an imperial power was not necessarily accompanied by cultural dominance. In his analysis of Japan's 1874 Expedition to Taiwan, Robert Eskildsen further elaborates on the ways in which Japan not only "resisted Western notions of Japanese inferiority" in Euro-American-centered discourse on civilization but also appropriated the discourse of civilization to justify its imperial ambition overseas. Eskildsen proposes the concept of "mimetic imperialism" to describe Japan's efforts in modernization as it adopted, adapted, and appropriated Western imperialism and its accompanying discourse on civilization.[17]

A concept that has been productive in understanding the complex history of colonial Korea under Japanese rule is "colonial modernity." Since the publication of the book, *Formations of Colonial Modernity in East Asia* (1997),[18] the concept has been usefully deployed to go beyond the Euro-American-centered framework by critiquing the modernization theory that relies on a linear and hierarchical view of history. It also shows the limitations of the binary approach to colonial power as violent oppressors and the colonized as hopeless victims. More importantly, the concept of colonial modernity attends to the contributions and agency of the colonized in perceiving, experiencing and appropriating what the modern meant (as it focuses on everyday life and material culture) within the context of a transnational dynamic beyond the confines of metropole and colony.[19]

In their highly influential book, *Colonial Modernity in Korea* (1999), the editors Gi-Wook Shin and Michael Robinson posit that Japan "as a latecomer to the business of imperialism had the advantage of learning from Western colonialism and thus created uniquely effective control strategies," and they suggest considering "Japanese domination within the broader lens of *cultural hegemony*" [emphasis added] in part because modern forms of colonial domination are felt not only in the political and economic domains but even in mundane, cultural, and personal life.[20] Here Antonio Gramsci's notion of "hegemony" is important as it "helps to explain how political and civil society, with institutions ranging from education, religion, and family to the microstructures of the practices of everyday life, shapes the meaning and values that produce, direct, and maintain the 'spontaneous' consent of the various strata of

---

[17] Robert Eskildsen, "Of Civilization and Savages," *The American Historical Review* 107, no. 2 (April 2002): 388–418. See also Robert Eskildsen, *Transforming Empire in Japan and East Asia: The Taiwan Expedition and the Birth of Japanese Imperialism* (Singapore: Palgrave Macmillan, 2019).

[18] Tani Barlow, ed., *Formations of Colonial Modernity in East Asia* (Durham: Duke University Press, 1997); Gi-Wook Shin and Michael Robinson, eds., *Colonial Modernity in Korea* (Cambridge: Harvard University Press, 1999).

[19] Tani Barlow, "Debates over Colonial Modernity in East Asia and Another Alternative," *Cultural Studies* 26, no. 5 (2012): 617–44.

[20] Shin and Robinson, *Colonial Modernity in Korea*, pp. 6–7.

society to domination."[21] Shin and Robinson take the Japanese-initiated Rural Revitalization Campaign in the 1930s as an example of success in cultural hegemony. That movement was designed not only to save increasingly devastated rural households but to encourage "mental awakening" and "friendly feelings and hearty cooperation between Japanese and Koreans."[22]

Whether the Japanese succeeded in gaining "cultural hegemony" in Korea is still an open question. In her study of Japanese settlers in colonial Korea, Jun Uchida describes a telling story of how one of the Japanese settlers, the journalist Aoyagi Tsunatarō, saw "Japan as still 'a second- or third-class inferior country' lagging behind the West," and he says that he "implicitly concurred with his 'close Korean friends' that unless Japan defeated the United States, the Japanese effort to capture Korean minds might forever be doomed."[23] Indeed, as a Korean commentator put it in 1921, Japan had been trying to adopt from the West "new trends" (*sin sajo*) or "new morality" (*sin todŏk*), such as class equality and gender equality, but it was far from being reformed.[24] In this comparison of Japan with the West, Koreans assumed that these new trends and the new morality for the modern era originally came from the West. While Japan played a key role in mediating and distributing knowledge about Western modernity to its colonies, Koreans considered Euro-American societies to be a more authentic source of modernity, and that attitude tended to diminish Japan's influence, especially in social and cultural domains, in spite of its political dominance in Korea.

The question of Japanese cultural hegemony is especially pertinent to understanding modern gender relations. In colonial studies, the analysis of gender has been fruitfully used to shed new light on dynamic formations of imperial culture.[25] Often informed by postcolonial theories, these studies illuminate the complex power dynamics and multidirectional flow of influence between the

---

[21] Shin and Robinson, *Colonial Modernity in Korea*, p. 7.
[22] Shin and Robinson, *Colonial Modernity in Korea*, p. 8.
[23] Jun Uchida, *Brokers of Empire: Japanese Settler Colonialism in Korea, 1876–1945* (Cambridge: Harvard University Press, 2011), p. 219. See also Leo Ching, "Yellow Skin, White Masks: Race, Class, and Identification in Japanese Colonial Discourse," in *Trajectories: Inter-Asia Cultural Studies*, ed. Kuan Hsing Chen (Routledge, 1998), pp. 65–86.
[24] Sŏng Kwanho, "Na ŭi pon Ilbon sŏul" (The Capital of Japan from my Viewpoint), *Kaebyŏk* 12 (June 1921): 66–71, quoted on 67.
[25] Anne McClintock, *Imperial Leather: Race, Gender, and Sexuality in the Colonial Contest* (New York: Routledge, 1995); Ann Laura Stoler, *Carnal Knowledge and Imperial Power: Race and the Intimate in Colonial Rule* (Berkeley: University of California Press, 2002); Nupur Chaudhuri and Margaret Strobel, eds., *Western Women and Imperialism* (Bloomington: Indiana University Press, 1992); Clare Midgley, ed., *Gender and Imperialism* (Manchester: Manchester University Press, 1998); Frederick Cooper and Ann Laura Stoler, eds., *Tensions of Empire: Colonial Cultures in a Bourgeois World* (Berkeley: University of California Press, 1997); and Mary Taylor Huber and Nancy Lutkehaus, eds., *Gendered Missions: Women and Men in Missionary Discourse and Practice* (Ann Arbor: University of Michigan Press, 1999).

Introduction 7

colonizer and the colonized that took place in the "contact zone," to use Mary Louise Pratt's term.[26] However, most of that research has been focused on European colonialism and its colonial subjects. A much less explored question is how racial and gender dynamics played out in the contact zone when the colonial power was not Euro-American. As a non-Western, non-Christian colonial power, Japan is an interesting case to consider due to its geographic proximity to and its "racial, cultural and religious affinities" with Korea, including gender ethics stemming from Chinese Confucianism.[27]

Needless to say, their shared history does not mean that Japanese and Korean women lived under the same conditions. For instance, in spite of the overall disregard for "educated women" in Confucian teachings,[28] the level of education for Japanese women was much higher than that of Koreans.[29] The Meiji government (1868–1912) made public education for boys and girls compulsory in 1872. Even before that, during the Edo period (1603–1867), Japanese girls had access to local schools (*terakoya*) and private academies (*shijuku*).[30] There were no such educational institutions for Korean girls during the Chosŏn dynasty (1392–1910) until the first girls' school, Ewha Haktang, opened in 1886. In Chosŏn Korea, education for girls and women took place only informally and at home.

Nonetheless, Japanese women in society did not necessarily fare better than did the colonized women of Korea. The pioneering Japanese feminist Kishida Toshiko (1863–1901) points out that Japanese women themselves struggled with, "evil teachings and customs" inherited from the past. In her article in 1884, she wrote, "In ancient times there were various evil teachings and customs in our country, things that would make the people of any free, civilized nation terribly ashamed. Of these, the most reprehensible was the practice of 'respecting men and despising women'," a notion that was also prevalent in

---

[26] Mary Louise Pratt, *Imperial Eyes: Travel Writing and Transculturation* (London: Routledge, 1992). See also Tony Ballantyne and Antoinette Burton, eds., *Bodies in Contact: Rethinking Colonial Encounters in World History* (Durham: Duke University Press, 2005).

[27] Park, "Picturing Empire and Illness," 108; Ramon H. Myers and Mark R. Peattie, eds., *The Japanese Colonial Empire, 1895–1945* (Princeton: Princeton University Press, 1984); Ch'anghae kŏsa, "Kajok chedo ŭi ch'ŭngmyŏn'gwan" (Opinion on Aspects of Family System), *Kaebyŏk* 3 (August 1920): 23–8.

[28] Yi Sugin, trans., *Yŏ sasŏ* (The Four Books for Women) (Seoul: Yŏiyŏn, 2003); Martina Deuchler, "Propagating Female Virtues in Chosŏn Korea," in *Women and Confucian Cultures in Premodern China, Korea, and Japan*, eds. Dorothy Ko, Jahyun Kim Haboush, and Joan R. Piggott (Berkeley: University of California Press, 2003), p. 150.

[29] "Che myŏngsa ŭi Chosŏn yŏja haebanggwan" (Experts' View on the Liberation of Korean Women), *Kaebyŏk* 4 (September 1920): 28–45, quoted on 42.

[30] Those local schools and private academies were managed and taught by women. Martha Tocco, "Made in Japan: Meiji Women's Education," in *Gendering Modern Japanese History*, eds., Barbara Molony and Kathleen Uno (Cambridge: Harvard University Press, 2005), pp. 39–41; Elizabeth Knipe Mouer, "Women in Teaching," in *Women in Changing Japan*, eds. Joyce Lebra, Joy Paulson, and Elizabeth Powers (Stanford: Stanford University Press, 1976), p. 161.

8 Introduction

Korea.[31] In her study of Japanese colonial literature, Kimberly Kono illustrates how Japanese women had privileges as colonizers and how colonial territories functioned as "sites *outside* of the moral and social restrictions of the Japanese archipelago, identifying the *gaichi* [colony] as a place of liberation for Japanese women." And yet in spite of certain privileges they enjoyed as colonizers, the actual lives of Japanese women were significantly restricted by "discourses of femininity" and "[t]he reality of patriarchal colonial governments and male-dominated communities in the colonies."[32] Colonial textbooks, especially the subject of *"susin"* (morality), clearly reflect such discourses of femininity. While Japanese women were featured as exemplary models whom Korean girls were expected to emulate, the central component of that model image heavily focused on Confucian ethics stemming from the Five Moral Imperatives (*oryun*) one of which is the "distinction/separation between husband and wife" (*pubu yubyŏl*). Through this distinction a woman's domestic duties and responsibilities are stressed, primarily in her capacity as daughter-in-law, wife, and mother.[33] In spite of the colonial discourse that portrayed the Japanese as "advanced" and "civilizing forces" for the presumably inferior Koreans, the shared Confucian legacy of "evil teachings and customs" deeply shaped the gender and racial dynamics in colonial Korea.

Here we need to return to the example of the roundtable discussion described at the beginning of the chapter. In spite of Japanese colonial dominance, it was not Japanese but Euro-American sources that were most frequently hailed as the most exemplary models for modern womanhood. The Western images were the ones that were circulated in the print media up until mid-1930s. The conspicuous absence of Japanese models and the omnipresent influence of Euro-American models in the discourse of modern womanhood in Korean print media lead to a question: To what extent did the Japanese colonial state exert its cultural hegemony in shaping gender relations? To put it differently, if the colonial state was a "mobilizing agent of modernity,"[34] how effective was it, especially when it had to face other competing forces – Euro-American cultural influences – in the emerging discourse on modern womanhood in Korea?

---

[31] Barbara Molony, Janet Theiss, and Hyaeweol Choi, *Gender in Modern East Asia: An Integrated History* (Boulder: Westview, 2016), p. 145; "Che myŏngsa ŭi Chosŏn yŏja haebanggwan," 29; Mark Peterson, "Women without Sons: A Measure of Social Change in Yi Dynasty Korea," in *Korean Women: View from the Inner Room*, eds., Laurel Kendall and Mark Peterson (New Haven: East Rock Press, 1983), p. 33.

[32] Kimberly Kono, *Romance, Family and Nation in Japanese Colonial Literature* (New York: Palgrave Macmillan, 2010), pp. 34–5.

[33] Kim Sunjŏn and Chang Migyŏng, "'Pot'ong hakkyo susinsŏ' rŭl t'onghae pon yŏsŏng myosa" (Portrayal of Women Reflected in "Book of Moral Education for Common School"), in *Cheguk ŭi singminji susin* (Empire's Moral Cultivation of the Colonized), ed. Kim Sunjŏn (Seoul: Cheiaenssi, 2008), pp. 304–24.

[34] Hwang, *Rationalizing Korea*, p. 253.

There are a number of areas in which the Japanese colonial state had a far-reaching impact on Korean women and their lives and work. Arguably, the most prominent colonial policy that significantly affected the domestic sphere is the "household-registry system" (J: *koseki*, K: *hojŏk*).[35] It clearly defined the legal boundaries of the "household" (*ie* in Japanese) with exclusive rights given to the male head of the family. This "household-registry system" differed significantly from the family system of the Chosŏn dynasty. Although family structure was still patriarchal in Chosŏn, it focused on the extended family lineage as well as all cohabitants, including slaves. A distinctive impact of the colonial "household" system was to weaken the extended family network and move toward the proliferation of nuclear families – parents and their children.[36] In her analysis of the colonial legal system with particular focus on civil disputes, Sungyun Lim challenges the long-held assumption that women were victimized by both Korean patriarchy and Japanese colonial oppression. Instead, she demonstrates how Korean women as colonized subjects proactively used the legal system to defend or claim their rights. Lim even suggests that Korean women were more at odds with Korean men than they were with the Japanese in the civil dispute cases.[37] Beyond the legal system, the colonial state's influence is also evident in education. As Chapter 1 shows, the Meiji gender ideology of "good wife, wise mother" (*ryōsai kenbo*) was effectively incorporated into girls' education under the topic of morality (*susin*).

In spite of the markers of colonial influence in shaping modern womanhood in Korea, a competing and sometimes more powerful source of "modernity" in the construction of modern womanhood in Korea was the Protestant missionaries, especially those from the United States, who began to arrive in the late-nineteenth century. Much research demonstrates that East Asian countries had some common experiences in terms of the significant role of Protestant missionaries in modern gender politics.[38] The missionary impact was particularly evident in the areas of women's education, medicine, and social work. At the

---

[35] Sungyun Lim, *Rules of the House: Family Law and Domestic Disputes in Colonial Korea* (Oakland: University of California Press, 2019). See also Kim Hyegyŏng, *Singminji ha kŭndae kajok ŭi hyŏngsŏng kwa chendŏ* (Gender and the Formation of the Modern Family under Colonial Rule) (Seoul: Ch'angbi, 2006).

[36] Hong Yanghŭi, "Singminji sigi hojŏk chedo wa kajok chedo ŭi pyŏnyong" (Transformation of the Family System through the Family Registrar during the Japanese Colonial Era), *Sahak yŏn'gu* 79 (2005): 167–205.

[37] Lim, *Rules of the House*. For the history of women engaging in legal system during the Chosŏn dynasty, see Jisoo Kim, *The Emotions of Justice: Gender, Status, and Legal Performance in Chosŏn Korea* (Seattle: University of Washington Press, 2017); Jungwon Kim, "'You Must Avenge on My Behalf': Widow Chastity and Honour in Nineteenth-Century Korea," *Gender & History* 26, no. 1 (2014): 128–46; Sun Joo Kim and Jungwon Kim, comp. and trans., *Wrongful Deaths: Selected Inquest Records from Nineteenth-Century Korea* (Seattle: University of Washington Press, 2014).

[38] Karen K. Seat, *"Providence Has Freed Our Hands": Women's Missions and the American Encounter with Japan* (Syracuse: Syracuse University Press, 2008); Rebecca Copeland, "All

same time, however, the differing political situations of the East Asian countries – Japan as an imperial power, China as a semi-colonized country and Korea as a colony of Japan – had an impact on the dynamics of the missionary work. Although it is not to precisely summarize the missionary dynamics in East Asia, as E. Taylor Atkins observes: "Protestant missionaries from North America and Europe had a deeper impact on notions and experiences of modernity in Korea than they did in either China or Japan."[39] In spite of the fact that there were fewer missionaries in Korea than there were in China and Japan, the success of the mission in Korea was remarkable. The phenomenal success seen in the evangelical activities in Korea cannot be divorced from the particular political situation especially after the Sino-Japanese War (1894–1895) and the Russo-Japanese War (1904–1905), both of which took place on Korean territory. It was at that time that many Koreans "sought refuge in the church," and the number of Korean converts rapidly increased from 4,356 in 1896 to 106,287 in 1907 to nearly 300,000 by the early 1920s.[40]

What is at work here is not only Koreans' perception of the "West" as the origin of modernity. Even though Euro-American countries actually were colonizers elsewhere, they were not colonizing Korea. In the eyes of Koreans under Japanese colonial rule, these Westerners represented the strength of the United States or the European nations but did not pose a colonial threat. In fact, they were viewed as potential allies who could support the Koreans in their struggle against the Japanese. This disassociation from colonial ambition in Korea played a significant role in creating the dynamics between various parties involved. In her analysis of the relationship between British women and Pandita Ramabai, an Indian Christian, Antoinette Burton demonstrates how "some Western women's collaboration in the ideological work of empire" placed limitations on "women's international solidarity," as Ramabai found "more sympathy and financial support among American women reformers than among her British 'sisters'."[41] In other words, the imperial power relations

---

Other Loves Excelling: Mary Kidder, Wakamatsu Shizuko and Modern Marriage in Meiji Japan," in *Divine Domesticities: Christian Paradoxes in Asia and the Pacific*, eds. Hyaeweol Choi and Margaret Jolly (Canberra: ANU Press, 2014), pp. 85–112; Helen Schneider, *Keeping the Nation's House: Domestic Management and the Making of Modern China* (Vancouver: UBC Press, 2011); Ellen Widmer, "The Seven Sisters and China, 1900–1950," in *China's Christian Colleges: Cross-Cultural Connections, 1900–1950*, eds. Daniel H. Bays and Ellen Widmer (Stanford: Stanford University Press, 2009), pp. 83–105; Jeesoon Hong, "Christian Education and the Construction of Female Gentility in Modern East Asia," *Religions* 2019, 10, 467.

[39] E. Taylor Atkins, "Colonial Modernity," in *Routledge Handbook of Modern Korean History*, ed. Michael J. Seth (London: Routledge, 2016), pp. 124–40, quoted on p. 131.

[40] Timothy S. Lee, *Born Again: Evangelicalism in Korea* (Honolulu: University of Hawai'i Press, 2010), p. 13; W. Carl Rufus, "The Japanese Educational Policy in Korea," *Korea Review* 2, no. 11 (January 1921): 13–16, quoted on 14.

[41] Antoinette Burton, "Colonial Encounters in Late-Victorian England: Pandita Ramabai at Cheltenham and Wantage 1883–6," *Feminist Review* 49 (Spring 1995): 29–49, quoted on 30.

Introduction 11

tended to undermine the potential for solidarity between colonial and colonized women.

In colonial Korea under Japanese rule, Koreans did not associate Western missionaries directly with any formal colonial power, so a different kind of dynamics emerged in the interactions between the Koreans and missionaries.[42] By way of comparison, one can look at the United States missions in its colony, the Philippines, where the missionaries "worked alongside the federal goal of civilising and 'Christianising' the Philippines" and thus were viewed by the nationalist Filipinos as the "embodiment of American imperialism."[43] In contrast, US missionaries in Korea were not official colonizers, which helped to create the situation where they were most closely associated with the idea of modernity rather than dominance or oppression. In a significant way, "Christianity, civilization, [and] the US" all coalesced under the idea of "modernity," which persisted throughout much of the Japanese colonial period.[44]

It is not a minor point that Protestant missionaries began to work in Korea a quarter century *before* the Japanese colonial authority was established in 1910. As Jun Uchida points out: "Conspicuously absent from these early [Japanese] migrants [to Korea] were religious workers. Whereas missionaries were among the first Europeans to set foot in Africa and Asia, they were, as one Japanese settler bemoaned in 1911, 'the last ones to come' to the peninsula. And when they did come, they were far fewer and less successful than the raft of Western missionaries already active there."[45] Prior to Korea's colonization by Japan in 1910, US and other Western mission schools and hospitals had already been established in Korea. Their precedence in the areas of education and medicine associated them with modern practices and innovation. In the eyes of Koreans, these missionaries represented modernity, and that image of missionaries as the bearers of Western civilization continued even after Japan took control of Korea. That is, Christianity and Western civilization were perceived as aspects of the same thing.[46] Further, as Atkins points out,

---

[42] Hyaeweol Choi, "Christian Modernity in Missionary Discourse from Korea, 1905–1910." *East Asian History* 29 (June 2005): 39–68.

[43] Laura Prieto, "Bibles, Baseball and Butterfly Sleeves: Filipina Women and American Protestant Missions, 1900–1930," in *Divine Domesticities*, pp. 367–96, quoted on p. 380.

[44] John Frankl, *Han'guk munhak e nat'anan oeguk ŭi ŭimi* (The Meaning of the Foreign Reflected in Korean Literature) (Seoul: Somyŏng, 2008), pp. 178–99, 211. See also Kim Ch'ŏl, *Pokhwasulsa tŭl: sosŏl ro ingnŭn singminji Chosŏn* (The Ventriloquists: Reading Colonial Korea through Fiction) (Seoul: Munhak kwa chisŏngsa, 2008), pp. 63–75; Lew Young Ick, "A Historical Overview of Korean Perceptions of the United States: Five Major Stereotypes," *Korea Journal* 44, no. 1 (Spring 2004): 109–51, especially 117–28.

[45] Uchida, *Brokers of Empire*, p. 39.

[46] Kyusik Chang, "Christianity and Civil Society in Colonial Korea: The Civil Society Movement of Cho Man-sik and the P'yŏngyang YMCA against Japanese Colonialism," in *Encountering Modernity: Christianity in East Asia and Asian America*, eds. Albert L. Park and David K. Yoo (Honolulu: University of Hawai'i Press, 2014), pp. 119–20.

Koreans "detected a distinct advantage in learning modern ways and ideas directly from 'the source' [missionaries and the West], rather than secondhand from their imperial overlords."[47]

The role of US Protestant missionaries loomed particularly large in creating and fostering the new class of educated women in Korea as they pioneered in establishing mission schools and opening their doors to the poorest and most disadvantaged girls.[48] Missionary teachers, looking to train the next generation of Christian workers, encouraged and sponsored their most talented students to continue their education overseas, often at mission-run schools in Japan, China, or the United States.[49] In many cases, that overseas education led some to even broader exposure to the world community through the global Christian network, which was comprised of such organizations as the Young Women's Christian Association, the Student Volunteer Movement, the Woman's Christian Temperance Union, the International Missionary Council, and the World Student Christian Federation. Transnational exposure and experience helped these women articulate their gender, national, and racial subjectivities.[50] In particular, some international conferences, such as the meetings of the International Missionary Council and World Student Christian Federation, provided them with rare opportunities to interact with other non-Western, colonized people from all over the world and gain insights into local particularities as well as global issues. Such experiences greatly sharpened their sense of the local and the national and guided their vision of the aspects of modernity that were appropriate to conditions in Korea.

In a significant way, Korean women's encounters with Western women missionaries, largely from the United States, often served as a catalyst in imagining and experiencing modernity, and in mapping out their gendered, racialized, and nationalized status in the face of the Western-centered world hierarchy. As much research demonstrates, Western women missionaries were largely conservative because they generally embraced the deeply entrenched patriarchal ideology and practices of "separate spheres," in the form of "woman's work for woman" in churches and mission organizations. However, in reality, Western women, who constituted the majority of the

---

[47] Atkins, "Colonial Modernity," p. 131.

[48] All three women intellectuals at the roundtable discussion mentioned in the beginning of this chapter were graduates of mission schools, and their international journey was closely linked with global Christian network.

[49] Pak, *Kŭndae yŏsŏng cheguk ŭl kŏch'ŏ Chosŏn ŭro hoeyu hada*; Hyaeweol Choi, "In Search of Knowledge and Selfhood: Korean Women Studying Overseas in Colonial Korea," *Intersections: Gender and Sexuality in Asia and the Pacific* 29 (May 2012) http://intersections.anu.edu.au/issue29/choi.htm (online access).

[50] For examples of Chinese students overseas, see Chih-ming Wang, *Transpacific Articulations: Student Migration and the Remaking of Asian America* (Honolulu: University of Hawai'i Press, 2013); and Weili Ye, *Seeking Modernity in China's Name: Chinese Students in the United States, 1900–1927* (Stanford: Stanford University Press, 2002).

missionary personnel by the late-nineteenth century, actively participated in building not only churches but also other essential elements of the modern infrastructure, such as hospitals and schools. Their ability to travel globally and exercise power and authority in their mission fields created unusual opportunities for these Western women to explore the rapidly changing modern world.[51] Thus, as Susan Thorne argues, "part of the transformative power of the missionary project was its sanctioning of transgressive behavior as religious exceptions to the standard rules for women. It was, after all, the pious woman's 'duty' to overcome her 'natural diffidence' in order that she might better serve the mission cause."[52] Under the banner of Christian faith and its propagation on a global scale, traditional gender rules were bent as women missionaries actively engaged in public and global life as professionals.[53]

In the minds of the local women converts, Christian mission schools, hospitals, and social welfare centers were, for the most part, their only entry into the modern world. This was especially true for women who had been denied access to education and other aspects of the modern world due to poverty or the stigma attached to their low social status. In the world of Korean women in the late-nineteenth and early-twentieth centuries, affiliation with Christianity was often the only route to modernity, a means by which women could become educated and even cross boundaries beyond domestic and colonial confinement. Under these circumstances, the life trajectories of "educated women" in colonial Korea share a remarkably unifying characteristic: Many of these women were associated at some point in their individual histories with the globally interconnected Christian network through mission schools and various Christian organizations at home and overseas. More importantly, in spite of the tiny number of elite Korean women who had transnational experiences mediated by the global Christian network, their impact on the path of Korean modern womanhood was immense and lasting, for they ushered in a new way of thinking and living through their direct and indirect exposure to the world and played a leading role in the emerging fields of professional work for women in education, medicine, home economics, journalism, art, and music. It is no wonder that Yi Man'gyu (1889–1978),

---

[51] Jane Hunter, *The Gospel of Gentility: American Women Missionaries in Turn-of-the-Century China* (New Haven: Yale University Press, 1984); Dana Robert, *American Women in Mission: A Social History of Their Thought and Practice* (Macon: Mercer University Press, 1996); Barbara Reeves-Ellington, Kathryn Kish Sklar, and Connie A. Shemo, eds., *Competing Kingdoms: Women, Mission, Nation, and the American Protestant Empire, 1812–1960* (Durham: Duke University Press, 2010); Huber and Lutkehaus, *Gendered Missions*.

[52] Susan Thorne, "Missionary-Imperial Feminism," p. 50.

[53] For a more nuanced analysis of the dynamics between gender and Christianity, see Jacqueline DeVries, "Rediscovering Christianity after the Postmodern Turn," *Feminist Studies* 31, no. 1 (Spring 2005): 135–55.

14   Introduction

a prominent male educator, asserted in 1934 that "Christian-influenced women have near complete hegemony (*p'aegwŏn*) in the women's world" in Korea.[54]

Considering the omnipresence of Protestant Christian influence in the lives and work of elite Korean women during the time of Japanese colonial rule, this book examines the formation of modern gender relations in Korea, which were being shaped by the competing forces of Korean nation-building, Japanese colonial imperatives, and global evangelical ambition in the interwar period. Previous studies in the field of Korean studies have elaborated on how nationalism, colonialism, and modernity have been the dominant influence on the discourse and experience of modern womanhood in early-twentieth century Korea.[55] What is much less explored, however, is how the transnational experience of Koreans interacted with and complicated nationalist mandate, colonial imperatives, and the lures of modernity. Informed by perspectives on both transnational history and postcolonial feminism,[56] this book explores three main questions: How did the transnational circulation of knowledge and the mobility of people, fostered by the global Christian network, affect gender norms, domestic material culture, and women's engagement in the public sphere within the specific historical context of colonial Korea? What insights can we gain from the gendered experiences of transnational encounters in the making of modern Korea? And, what new light does Korea's experience shed on wider historical transformations of gender relations under colonialism?

---

[54] Yi Man'gyu, "Chosŏn samdae chonggyo konggwaron: Kidokkyohoe ŭi kong kwa kwa" (Discussion of the Contribution and Shortcomings of Three Major Religions in Korea: The Contribution and Shortcomings of Christianity), *Kaebyŏk* sin'gan 1 (November 1934): 27–31, 42, quoted on 28. The historian Don Baker observes that "Christians were overrepresented among the modernizing elite in the early twentieth century." See Don Baker, "Creating the Sacred and the Secular in Colonial Korea," unpublished paper presented at a workshop on secularism in Japan held at University of Oslo, Norway, June 19, 2015, p. 6.

[55] Yoo, *The Politics of Gender in Colonial Korea*; Kyeong-Hee Choi, "Neither Colonial nor National: The Making of the 'New Woman' in Pak Wansŏ's 'Mother's Stake 1'," in *Colonial Modernity in Korea*, pp. 221–47; Kenneth M. Wells, "The Price of Legitimacy: Women and the Kŭnuhoe Movement, 1927–1931," in *Colonial Modernity in Korea*, pp. 191–220; Sheila Miyoshi Jager, *Narratives of Nation Building in Korea: A Genealogy of Patriotism* (Armonk: M.R. Sharpe, 2003); Yung-Hee Kim, "Under the Mandate of Nationalism: Development of Feminist Enterprises in Modern Korea, 1860–1910," *Journal of Women's History* 7, no. 4 (1995): 120–36; Vladimir Tikhonov, "Masculinizing the Nation: Gender Ideologies in Traditional Korea and in the 1890s-1900s Korean Enlightenment Discourse," *Journal of Asian Studies* 66, no. 4 (2007): 1029–65.

[56] Kwak Pui-lan, *Postcolonial Imagination and Feminist Theology* (Louisville: Westminster John Knox Press, 2005); Angela Woollacott, *To Try Her Fortune in London: Australian Women, Colonialism, and Modernity* (New York: Oxford University Press, 2001) and "Postcolonial Histories and Catherine Hall's Civilising Subjects," in *Connected Worlds: History in Transnational Perspective*, eds. Ann Curthoys and Marilyn Lake (Canberra: ANU Press, 2005), pp. 63–74; and Fiona Paisley, *Loving Protection? Australian Feminism and Aboriginal Women's Rights 1919–1939* (Carlton South: Melbourne University Press, 2000).

Gender and Protestant Modernity

In this book, I use the concept of "Protestant modernity" as a heuristic device to unpack the complex dynamics found in the formation of modern gender relations fostered by the global Christian network within the specific historical context of colonial Korea. I define "Protestant modernity" as a composite of religious morality, historical outlook, and material practices that could mean different things to different historical subjects.[57] From the perspective of Euro-American evangelical groups, it is an ideology that advocates the linear movement in history toward modernity in material and technological aspects but that also places the moral and spiritual role of Christianity at the core of that enterprise.[58] However, for the newly converted Koreans, the centrality of religious spirituality may have sometimes been secondary to the material progress and mundane advantages that were afforded to people who affiliated themselves with Christianity. Christian affiliation tended to provide opportunities for education, employment, leadership, and even lifestyle.[59] It is in this coalescing dynamic between the sacred and the secular, and between discourse and experience, that the concept of Protestant modernity can be fruitfully understood within the particular historical context of Korea during the years it was colonized by Japan. As a way to articulate the concept in relation to the competing forces of Japanese colonial imperatives, Korean nationalism and Western modernity in shaping modern gender relations, I will examine two related characteristics that provide us with analytical advantages: one is the transnational dynamic and the other is the significant place of religion in the discourse and experience of "modernity."

---

[57] Rodney Stark uses the term, "Protestant Modernity," in his book, *Bearing False Witness: Debunking Centuries of Anti-Catholic History* (West Conshohocken: Templeton Press, 2016), pp. 209–29. However, he does not provide a precise definition. In his critique of Max Weber's thesis that Protestant ethics provided a basis for the development of capitalism and modernity, he offers numerous examples of "capitalist" elements in the history of Catholicism long before the Reformation.

[58] The term "modern" itself has close ties with Christianity as it derives from the fifth-century Latin term *modernus*, which distinguished a "Christian present" from a "pagan past." In the nineteenth century, however, Western modernity was defined by much more complex philosophical, sociopolitical, and aesthetic terms that were not always mutually compatible and were often in competition. As the historian Prasenjit Duara points out, during the nineteenth century "the singular conception of Civilization based originally upon Christian and Enlightenment values came not only to be dominant but to be the only criterion where sovereignty could be claimed in the world." See Barry Smart, "Modernity, Postmodernity and the Present," in *Theories of Modernity and Postmodernity*, ed. Bryan S. Turner (London: Sage, 1990), pp. 14–30; Prasenjit Duara, "The Discourse of Civilization and Pan-Asianism," *Journal of World History* 12, no. 1 (2001): 99–130; and Choi, "Christian Modernity."

[59] Hunter, *The Gospel of Gentility*, p. 26; Prieto, "Bibles, Baseball and Butterfly Sleeves," pp. 376–77.

16   Introduction

(1)   Transnational Flow

The idea of "Protestant modernity" is firmly grounded in a transnational perspective. The rise of evangelical activities overseas, especially from the mid-nineteenth century, went hand in hand with various forms of Euro-American colonialisms that are essentially transnational.[60] Seemingly detached from the political and economic branches of colonial administration, the missionary work was an integral part of the colonial governance, focused on Euro-American-centered moral and spiritual reform. Further, missionaries were present not only in their formal colonies but also in non-colonies throughout the world, exemplified by US Protestant missionaries in Korea under Japanese rule.

It is important to note that the concept of "transnational" as I use it in this book is not a unitary but rather a fluid and adaptive concept. Although scholars continue to debate whether "transnational history" is a perspective or a method, there are at least two points on which many agree.[61] One is that transnational history concerns the movement of people, ideas, materials, institutions, and technologies across national boundaries. Unlike "global history," transnational history allows us to focus on worlds connected by agents, networks, and organizations that are not necessarily global in scope.[62] In this book, when I discuss "transnational" encounters and network, those encounters encompass neither the entire world nor all domains of transnationalism. Rather, with specific focus on evangelical missionary organizations and personnel, I connect scattered places, people, and ideas to make sense of the invisible network that was formed across national boundaries. In this connected world, as I demonstrate throughout the book, there are some leading players, such as US Protestant missionary organizations, as well as minor but still significant players, like the Danish models for rural reform, in facilitating and prompting the mobility of people, ideas and materials.

The other consensus view is that transnational history does not deny the category of "nation-state"; rather, it aims to highlight the transnational forces in

---

[60] Huber and Lutkehaus, *Gendered Missions*; Barlow, "Debates over Colonial Modernity."
[61] "AHR Conversation: On Transnational History," *American Historical Review* 111, no. 5 (December 2006): 1441–64; Ian Tyrrell, "What is Transnational History?" A paper given at the Ecole des Hautes Etudes en Sciences Sociale, Paris, in January 2007 (https://iantyrrell.wordpress.com/what-is-transnational-history/); Ian Tyrrell, "New Comparisons, International Worlds: Transnational and Comparative Perspectives," *Australian Feminist Studies* 16, no. 36 (2001): 355–61; Bernhard Struck, Kate Ferris, and Jacques Revel, "Introduction: Space and Scale in Transnational History," *International History Review* 33, no. 4 (December 2011): 573–84; David Thelen, "The Nation and Beyond: Transnational Perspectives on United States History," *Journal of American History* 86, no, 3 (Dec. 1999): 965–75; Matthew Pratt Guterl, "Comment: The Futures of Transnational History," *American Historical Review* 118, no. 1 (2013): 130–39; and Curthoys and Lake, *Connected Worlds*.
[62] "AHR Conversation: On Transnational History," 1446.

the making of a nation-state.[63] Recent research studies attend to the dynamic interplay between home and empire, illuminating how colonial projects overseas shaped domestic culture and society.[64] Amy Kaplan demonstrates the close linkage between middle-class domesticity in mid-nineteenth century US and US imperial expansion in the world. Taking two examples of writing by Catherine Beecher and Sarah Josepha Hale, Kaplan offers an acute analysis of how US domesticity was intimately embedded in the discourse of US imperialism and how women writers and activists contributed to that link.[65] Similarly, Ian Tyrrell's *Reforming the World: The Creation of America's Moral Empire* exemplifies a transnational history when he analyzes the work of American Protestant missionaries and moral reformers, especially those who were involved in the Woman's Christian Temperance Union. He demonstrates how those who deeply engaged in creating "America's moral empire" at home and overseas had impact not only on the people they interacted with but on US domestic issues.[66]

In the field of Korean studies, a growing body of research has taken a transnational approach, looking specifically at such things as the role of translation of foreign literature in shaping new gender subjectivities and national literatures,[67] the experiences of women studying in Japan during the colonial period,[68] the impact of transpacific encounters with East Asia and Asian America on the disciplinary development of US academia,[69] borderland membership politics in Northeast Asia,[70] transnational forces and network in transforming modern Buddhism in colonial-era Korea,[71] biopolitics and medical modernity,[72] and rural modernity at the intersections of colonialism,

---

[63] Tyrrell, "What is Transnational History?"
[64] Susan Thorne, *Congregational Missions and the Making of an Imperial Culture in Nineteenth-Century England* (Stanford: Stanford University Press, 1999); Cooper and Stoler; and Bernard S. Cohn, *Colonialism and Its Forms of Knowledge* (Princeton: Princeton University Press, 1996).
[65] Amy Kaplan, "Manifest Domesticity," *American Literature* 70, no. 3 (1998): 581–606.
[66] Ian Tyrrell, *Reforming the World: The Creation of America's Moral Empire* (Princeton: Princeton University Press, 2010).
[67] Hyun, *Writing Women in Korea*; Cho, *Translation's Forgotten History*.
[68] Pak, *Kŭndae yŏsŏng cheguk ŭl kŏch'ŏ Chosŏn ŭro hoeyu hada*.
[69] Robert Oppenheim, *An Asian Frontier: American Anthropology and Korea, 1882–1945* (Lincoln: University of Nebraska Press, 2016).
[70] Alyssa M. Park, *Sovereignty Experiments: Korean Migrants and the Building of Borders in Northeast Asia, 1860–1945* (Ithaca: Cornell University Press, 2019); and Jaeeun Kim, *Contested Embrace: Transborder Membership Politics in Twentieth-Century Korea* (Stanford: Stanford University Press, 2016).
[71] Hwansoo Ilmee Kim, *The Korean Buddhist Empire: A Transnational History, 1910–1945* (Cambridge: Harvard University Press, 2018).
[72] Sonja M. Kim, *Imperatives of Care: Women and Medicine in Colonial Korea* (Honolulu: University of Hawai'i Press, 2019); Theodore Jun Yoo, *It's Madness: The Politics of Mental Health in Colonial Korea* (Berkeley: University of California Press, 2016); Jin-Kyung Park,

nationalism, and transnational networks.[73] While recognizing the penetrating impact of the Japanese colonial governance on the colonized, these studies illuminate how the nexus of the metropole and the colony got further complicated by the workings of transnational forces. This book is in line with those attempts to go beyond the metropole–colony network. It specifically concerns the politics of gender and its deep connections with the extensive global Christian network that was instrumental for Korean women – largely elite class of women – to develop a modern, national, and cosmopolitan identity and participate in the construction of modern Korea.

In her discussion of the promise and challenges of the transnational historical approach, Marilyn Lake argues that "feminist scholarship is an international enterprise, and feminism has a transnational history." She explains that: "[I]f I were to understand feminists' ideas and strategies, their aspirations and victories, as well as the ambiguities of their achievements and the tensions in their thinking, then I must locate them in the transnational community of which they were a part and pursue them on their travels beyond Australia to London, Geneva, Paris, Rome, San Francisco, and New York. Despite the time invested and the difficulty endured in travel by boat and rail in the 1920s and 1930s, these women drew inspiration from international encounters."[74] As Chapter 3 details, for Korean women, who had for centuries been expected to reside in the inner quarters of their houses, leaving home and crossing national borders for study or professional meetings was an extraordinary step on a new path for life and work. In their journeys, they observed and interacted with intellectuals, politicians, activists, religious leaders, artists, journalists, and educators as well as with ordinary citizens on the street, in train stations, at churches, and in markets. Along with the spectacular advances of modernity, they also witnessed the despair and agony brought by modern developments, racial tensions, and class disparity.

Furthermore, transnational encounters did not necessarily undercut national concerns. On the contrary, I argue that transnational encounters were highly instrumental in developing a sharper perspective on local and national particularities, and in gaining a new appreciation of Korea's national heritage as a source for constructing a modern nation.[75] In her analysis of gender politics

---

"Yellow Men's Burden: East Asian Imperialism, Forensic Medicine, and Conjugality in Colonial Korea," *Acta Koreana* 18, no. 1 (June 2015): 187–207.

[73] Albert Park, *Building A Heaven on Earth: Religion, Activism, and Protest in Japanese Occupied Korea* (Honolulu: University of Hawai'i Press, 2015).

[74] Marilyn Lake, "Nationalist Historiography, Feminist Scholarship, and the Promise and Problems of New Transnational Histories: The Australian Case," *Journal of Women's History* 19, no. 1 (Spring 2007): 180–86, quoted on 181–82. See also Angela Wollacott, *To Try Her Fortune in London*, and *Race and the Modern Exotic: Three "Australian" Women on Global Display* (Clayton, Victoria: Monash University Publishing, 2011).

[75] Recent research argues that the flow of influences between the East and the West was never unidirectional; rather, modernity should be understood as a dynamic process involving constant

in Indonesia under Dutch colonial rule, Elsbeth Locher-Schoten demonstrates how Indonesian women (mainly Javanese) deployed an Indonesian idiom (*iboe jang sedjati*), which means "the true women," to invoke new gender perceptions as opposed to the perceived "immorality of Dutch colonial and Western culture." In addition, Locher-Schoten characterizes the Indonesian women's movement as "companionate feminism" because they emphasized harmony and unity in their support of men and the nation.[76] In this way, the nation and nationalism continue to be a constitutive part of gender politics. The histories of colonized women amply demonstrate that "the struggle for women's emancipation occurred in tandem with anticolonial nationalist struggles" at the height of imperialism.[77] In addition, unlike the predominant view of modernity as "the rise of 'individualism' at the expense of 'community,'"[78] we can point to the emphasis on the family, community, and the nation as a particularly expedient strategy that colonized women used to claim new status in the making of the nation. As I demonstrate in Chapter 1, "wise mother, good wife" – the prevailing gender ideology of twentieth-century Korea – centered on the communal and national well-being while providing women with new space in which they could pursue self-empowerment in the domestic and even public spheres. In this vein, while the traditional notion of separate spheres for men and women continued, nationalist mandates enabled some women to go beyond the domestic in the name of the nation. Studying overseas was the most dramatic deviation from the traditional gender norms, becoming a rite of passage that women could undertake to equip themselves with modern knowledge in order to better equip themselves to contribute to the family and the nation. There was a synergy between nationalism and transnationalism as mutually constitutive forces.

---

negotiations between the old and the new, between Asian and Western values. See Judge, *The Precious Raft of History*, and *Republican Lens: Gender, Visuality, and Experience in the Early Chinese Periodical Press* (Stanford: Stanford University Press, 2015); and Karen Thornber, *Empire of Texts in Motion: Chinese, Korean, and Taiwanese Transculturations of Japanese Literature* (Cambridge: Harvard University Press, 2009).

[76] Elsbeth Locher-Schoten, "Morals, Harmony, and National Identity: 'Companionate Feminism' in Colonial Indonesia in the 1930s," *Journal of Women's History* 14, no. 4 (Winter 2003): 38–58, quoted on 39.

[77] Mrinalini Sinha, "Gender and Nation," in *Women's History in Global Perspective*, ed. Bonnie Smith (Bloomington: University of Illinois Press, 2004), pp. 229–74. Cited from *The Feminist History Reader*, ed. Sue Morgan (London: Routledge, 2006), p. 325. See also Chŏng Chinsŏng, "Minjok mit minjokjuŭi e kwanhan Han'guk yŏsŏnghak ŭi nonŭi: Ilbon kun wianbu munje rŭl chungsim ŭro" (A Debate on Nation and Nationalism in Korean Feminism: The Issue of Comfort Women during the Japanese Colonial Era), *Han'guk yŏsŏnghak* 15, no. 2 (1999): 29–53; Ella Shohat, "Area Studies, Transnationalism, and the Feminist Production of Knowledge," *Signs* 26, no. 4 (Summer 2001): 1269–72.

[78] Charles Taylor, *Modern Social Imaginaries* (Durham: Duke University Press, 2004), pp. 17–18.

20   Introduction

(2)   Religion in Gendered Modernity

The concept of "Protestant modernity" is useful in shedding new light on the complex relationship between gender and modernity. Gender has been a crucial tool for reexamining the multifaceted nature and process of modernity.[79] However, in that reanalysis, very little attention has been paid to the role of religion because religion was often understood not only "as a hopelessly patriarchal institution and a primary source of oppressive domestic ideology" but also "a social relic no longer relevant (or interesting) in the contexts of modern, industrialized cultures."[80] Indeed the expectation was that religion would be relegated to the private sphere in the age of modernity. Yet, as recent scholarship demonstrates, that did not happen. Religion has never lost its power. To be sure, modern nation-states (although not all of them) often claim to abide by the "separation of church and state," but religion has always been intertwined with virtually all aspects of modern life.[81] Christianity is a case in point. A range of theologies falls under the label "Christianity," but they all share the dictate to spread the tenets of the religion, which is at the heart of the missionary enterprise both at home and abroad. Significantly, at the height of Euro-American imperialisms in the nineteenth century, a global Christian network emerged that incorporated Christianity into the discourse of enlightenment, civilization, and modernity.[82] Missionaries often shared the "crusading optimism" to "bring about God's kingdom on earth."[83] Focusing on foreign missionary enterprise undertaken by American Christians, William Hutchison characterizes that enterprise as a "moral equivalent for imperialism" with its civilizing emphasis.[84] Although such characterization tends to

---

[79] Rita Felski, *The Gender of Modernity* (Cambridge: Harvard University Press, 1995).

[80] DeVries, "Rediscovering Christianity after the Postmodern Turn," 136.

[81] Talal Asad, *Genealogies of Religion: Discipline and Reasons of Power in Christianity and Islam* (Baltimore: Johns Hopkins University Press, 1993); José Casanova, *Public Religions in the Modern World* (Chicago: University of Chicago Press, 1994); Peter van der Veer, ed., *Conversion to Modernities: The Globalization of Christianity* (New York: Routledge, 1996); Linell E. Cady and Tracy Fessenden, eds., *Religion, the Secular, and the Politics of Sexual Difference* (New York: Columbia University Press, 2013); Janet Jakobsen and Ann Pellegrini, eds., *Secularisms* (Durham: Duke University Press, 2008).

[82] Tomoko Masuzawa, *The Invention of World Religions: Or, How European Universalism Was Preserved in the Language of Pluralism* (Chicago: University of Chicago Press, 2005); Dana Robert, ed., *Converting Colonialism: Visions and Realities in Mission History, 1706–1914* (Grand Rapids: William B. Eerdmans Publishing Company, 2008); Kwok, *Postcolonial Imagination & Feminist Theology*; and Duara, "The Discourse of Civilization and Pan-Asianism."

[83] Robert, *American Women in Mission*, p. 136.

[84] William R. Hutchison, "A Moral Equivalent for Imperialism: Americans and the Promotion of 'Christian Civilization,' 1880–1910," in *Missionary Ideologies in the Imperial Era: 1880–1920*, eds. Torben Christensen and William R. Hutchison (Aarhus: Forlaget Aros, 1982), pp. 167–77. For a critique on Hutchison's notion of "moral equivalent for imperialism," see Choi, *Gender and Mission Encounters*, footnote 56, pp. 196–7.

Gender and Protestant Modernity 21

downplay the power and agency of the missionized who accepted, rejected, or appropriated the newly introduced religion for their own interest, it brings into sharp focus the close linkage between imperialism and evangelical Christianity and its moral claim in the modern age.

In the history of modern Korea, Christianity, especially Protestantism, has played a significant role in shaping the Korean elite's perception of modernity. Christianity was seen as an essential marker of an advanced civilization that adhered to a new moral order, including gender equality, and helped develop modern institutions.[85] Both the rhetoric of the new moral order and the work of missionary institutions, especially in education and medicine, assisted Korean women and men in finding pathways to modernity within and beyond Korea. This book aims to demonstrate that the foreign missionary network, most especially that of the United States, was a powerful, pervasive, and far-reaching force in fashioning gendered modernity by facilitating transnational encounters with people of disparate backgrounds, new ideas, and novel bodily practices.

The role of Protestantism in shaping gendered modernity should be understood within the specific historical context of Japanese rule in Korea. In his investigation of the rise of the modern state in Korea, Kyung Moon Hwang takes "religion" as one of the social spheres, along with economy, education, population, and public health, in understanding the process, mechanisms and effects of the modern state from the late Chosŏn dynasty to Japanese colonial rule. Deploying the term "state secularization" to conceptualize "the rationalities of the state's relationship to an evolving realm of modern religion," Hwang demonstrates how the Japanese colonial state classified religions as either legitimate or pseudo and tightly regulated them in the name of religious pluralism. He argues that: "At one level, secularization through pluralism represented a reification of religion itself through classification and bureaucratization, but it also aimed to bolster the state's claims as an entity that served all religious interests through its commanding authority."[86] Christianity was one of the three legitimate religions along with Shinto and Buddhism. However, the colonial state suspected Christians, especially Protestant groups as a possible "bastion of Western-inspired, anti-Japanese nationalism" and "as examples of a non-Japanese path toward civilizational advancement."[87] In the eyes of the Japanese, "Western missionaries represented the most painful thorn in the side of the regime, which had to tread carefully before attempting any

---

[85] Hyaeweol Choi, "A New Moral Order: Gender Equality in Korean Christianity," in *Religions of Korea in Practice*, ed. Robert E. Buswell Jr. (Princeton: Princeton University Press, 2006), pp. 409–20.
[86] Hwang, *Rationalizing Korea*, see chapter 5, "State and Religion," pp. 146–67, quoted on pp. 147, 149.
[87] Hwang, *Rationalizing Korea*, p. 161.

crackdown on Westerners' activities in an era when the Japanese remained sensitive to perceptions and pressures from the outside."[88] In fact, there were numerous incidents in which tension between the colonial state and Western missionaries broke out. One of the most notorious cases of such tension was the "105 Incident" in 1911, in which a large number of Christians, especially in the regions of Hwanghae and P'yŏngan, were arrested on the charge that they had allegedly conspired to assassinate the Governor-General, Terauchi Masatake. An even more volatile incident occurred between the two parties when the March First Independence Movement broke out in 1919 with Christians playing a prominent role. On March 12, a Japanese daily in Korea reported that "the stirring up of the mind of the Koreans is the sin of the American missionaries. This uprising is their work ... They take the statement of Wilson [Woodrow Wilson] about the self-determination of nations and hide behind their religion and stir up the people ... from the part that even girl students in Christian schools have taken it is very evident that this uprising has come from the missionaries."[89] In reality, however, as Timothy Lee points out, "the demonstrations surprised the missionaries no less than the Japanese." They strongly denied their involvement in Koreans' anti-Japanese movement, proclaiming their political neutrality. The American Consulate stepped in to mediate with the Japanese colonial authority, and the missionaries received public exoneration from the Government-General of Korea.[90] The rocky relationship between the missionaries and the colonial state changed after the colonial policy shifted to "Cultural Rule" (*munhwa chŏngch'i*) as the result of the 1919 March First Independence Movement, and up until the mid-1930s, "a working truce ensued between Protestant organizations and the colonial state."[91]

While the colonial state constantly suspected that American missionaries could potentially subvert Japanese authority and threaten their colonial governance of Korea, there were attempts to bring Japanese and Korean Christians together under the banner of Christian universalism. The Government-General sponsored Japanese Christian groups, which envisioned their mission to be building "God's kingdom on earth through the Japanese empire."[92] In particular, the "Korea mission," which lasted almost a decade (from 1911 to 1920), is noteworthy. As Emily Anderson shows, the Government-General made annual contributions to the Korea mission that was "founded on a logic sympathetic to Japanese imperial policy that claimed that a common lineage and familial affinity among Koreans and Japanese legitimized Japanese rule of Koreans." The mission had dual goals: "to convert Koreans to a specifically Japanese form of Christianity and to convince them of the legitimacy of Japanese rule in

---

[88] Hwang, *Rationalizing Korea*, p. 161.   [89] Lee, *Born Again*, p. 39.
[90] Lee, *Born Again*, p. 40.   [91] Hwang, *Rationalizing Korea*, p. 163.
[92] Anderson, *Christianity and Imperialism in Modern Japan*, p. 6.

Gender and Protestant Modernity 23

Korea."[93] Although the mission ended after the 1919 March First Independence Movement, it illustrates "how the colonial government incorporated Christians into the colonial infrastructure as mediators between the colonial government and colonized subjects as part of a multilayered strategy of implementing a policy of assimilation."[94] In this complex religious landscape in colonial Korea, however, any evidence of influence from Japanese Christians in the lives of Korean converts is scarce.[95]

In contrast, foreign missionaries, especially those from the United States, played a prominent role in shaping modern gender relations. In understanding the central role that Protestant Christianity had in shaping gendered modernity in Korea, it is crucial to pay attention to the dynamic working relationships between foreign missionaries and Korean converts. Uneven power relations under a Western-centered racial hierarchy – in which missionaries were deemed superior to local converts – and the solidly conservative gender norms embedded in mission organizations sometimes caused tension and outright conflict.[96] In this book, I emphasize the agency of the missionized, who were far from being passive recipients of the new religion. To many of the converts, Protestantism was a platform on which they could conceive, experience, and sometimes resist new ideals of womanhood in the modern era. As the story of Pak Indŏk in Chapter 3 demonstrates, it is important to recognize the local agency that was at work, in the sense that Korean converts selected, rejected, or appropriated what missionaries aimed to deliver.

Even more importantly, the gap between what missionaries intended and what converts drew from missionary contact is best exemplified in the tensions between the spiritual and moral versus the secular and material. While spiritual commitment was the mainstay of the work of the missionaries, for many

---

[93] Anderson, *Christianity and Imperialism in Modern Japan*, p. 23.
[94] Anderson, *Christianity and Imperialism in Modern Japan*, p. 23.
[95] There has been very little understanding of Japanese women in colonial Korea with a few exceptions, such as Fuchizawa Noe, who was actively engaged in women's education and also Christian temperance movement in colonial Korea during her stay from 1905 until her death in 1936, and Tsuda Setsuko, who was the head of the women's section of *Ryokki renmei* (Green Flag Association), Japanese settlers' organization based in Keijō (Seoul). See Helen J. S. Lee, "Eating for the Emperor: The Nationalization of Settler Homes and Bodies in the Kōminka Era," in *Reading Colonial Japan: Text, Context, and Critique*, eds. Michele M. Mason and Helen J. S. Lee (Stanford: Stanford University Press, 2012), pp. 141–77.
[96] A number of strikes at mission schools and hospitals demonstrate ongoing tension between missionaries and Korean converts. See *Kijŏn 70-nyŏnsa* (The Seventieth History of Kijŏn) (Chŏnju: Kijŏn 70-nyŏnsa p'yŏnch'an wiwŏnhoe, 1974), pp. 47–48; Songdo Mangin, "Hosŭdon yŏgo kyojang ege" (To the Principal of Holston Girls' School), *Sin yŏsŏng* 2, no. 10 (1924): 68–70; "Sungŭi yŏgyosaeng tonghyu" (Students at Sungŭi Girls School on Strike), *Tonga ilbo*, October 18, 20, 27, 28, 29, 30, and November 4, 10, 14, 19, 24, and 25, 1923; see also *Kaebyŏk* 41 (November 1923): 113–14; Cho Sanghang, "Sŏyang sŏn'gyosa tŭl ŭi hakkyo tanggukja ege" (To the Authorities of Western Missionary Schools), *Sin yŏsŏng* 2, no. 10 (1924): 81–82; "Mogyo e taehan pulp'yŏng kwa hŭimang" (Complaints and Hopes about Alma Mater), *Sin yŏsŏng* 4, no. 4 (1926): 45–49; Kim, *Imperatives of Care*, pp. 92–3.

Korean girls and women the conversion to Christianity was instrumental, and in many cases the only way to gain access to "secular modernity" in the form of modern education, scientific home management, economic independence through paid work, opportunities to travel, and a new lifestyle, all of which were available through missionary organizations and personal networks.[97] This "secular orientation to the sacred," to use Craig Calhoun's words,[98] blurred the boundary between the religious and the secular in the pursuit of modernity.[99] Such fluid boundaries, I would argue, can be better understood when we bring to light the agency and contribution of the converted in shaping modernity within colonial and global contexts. The notion of "colonial modernity" is also better understood when we acknowledge the "greater contribution and agency from colonized populations" rather than focusing on "a unilateral imposition by omnipotent imperial regimes."[100] Likewise, the concept of "Protestant modernity" takes into serious consideration the agency of the converted, who were not simply passive recipients of the new religion but rather proactive adopters who critically evaluated various aspects of the religion.

The dynamic and wide-ranging exposure that Koreans had beyond domestic and colonial boundaries via the Christian network calls for a transnational approach in order to reveal the divergent roots and agencies that helped shape Korea's modern gender relations. The nature of modern gender relations mediated by the global Christian network also offers important insights into the ways in which patriarchy in crisis manages to adapt to a changing milieu.[101] The foreign missionary enterprise spurred global mobility among women, which, in turn, had a far-reaching impact on the shape of gendered modernity in both the Western and non-Western world. The tension between what was expected of women and what women actually experienced within the specific political, economic, and cultural contexts of colonial Korea reveals an important gap between intended and unintended outcomes of the missionary enterprise. As illustrated throughout the book, having the space to negotiate within that gap enabled women – both the missionaries and the converted – to open up a new path to self-realization. At the same time the conservative gender ideology embedded in the local cultures and the missionary organization continued to hinder women from pursuing rights that were equal to those of men. Women often had to tread a delicate balance between their own agency

---

[97] Hunter, *The Gospel of Gentility*; Choi and Jolly.
[98] Craig Calhoun, "Rethinking Secularism," *The Hedgehog Review* (Fall 2010): 35.
[99] Much research has been devoted to inquiries into the complex relationship between the religious and the secular in the modern era. To mention just a few: Janet Jakobsen and Ann Pellegrini, eds., *Secularisms* (Durham: Duke University Press, 2008); José Casanova, *Public Religions in the Modern World* (Chicago: University of Chicago Press, 1994); Talal Asad, *Formations of the Secular: Christianity, Islam, Modernity* (Stanford: Stanford University Press, 2003).
[100] Atkins, "Colonial Modernity," p. 127.
[101] Judith Bennett, "Feminism and History," *Gender & History* 1, no. 3 (Autumn 1989): 263.

and male superiority, navigating traditional demands and new opportunities. Thus, it was rare to see women missionaries or Korean women converts explicitly challenge the male-centered church and mission organizations; however, there are a few cases in which women missionaries publicly questioned unfair treatment of women in the mission field.[102] On the part of Korean converts, their relationship with missionaries was not always harmonious. Korean girl students, for example, criticized rigid, illiberal, and even oppressive educational policy at mission schools, demanding more freedom and revision of the curriculum to better prepare students for the rapidly changing modern era.[103] It is important to acknowledge that conformity and resistance are not necessarily separate. More often than not, they happen simultaneously, reproducing uneven power relations and the patriarchal structures but also creating cleavages.

Scope and Organization of the Book

The current book is essentially a sequel to my earlier book, entitled *Gender and Mission Encounters in Korea: New Women, Old Ways*. In that book, I trace the genealogy of the idea of "modern womanhood" in Korea through a close examination of the encounters between Koreans and Protestant missionaries from the United States. Focusing on the decades immediately after Korea opened its doors in 1876 to the eve of Japanese colonial rule beginning in 1910, the book complicates the longstanding Korean historiography that regards US missionary women as pioneers in shaping modern womanhood in Korea. While that claim is valid to a degree, one of the main arguments in that book is that the majority of missionary women cherished a conservative Victorian gender ideology that valued domesticity, purity, and piety, and also held a hierarchical (and racist) view of non-Western people. However, the most fascinating aspect of the story may be that the experiences missionary women had while in the mission field challenged the conventional, male-centered gender domains as they had unprecedented opportunities to exercise power and authority as teachers, doctors, and social workers in the "woman's work for woman" that they undertook as part of the mission. In turn, the presence and activities of missionary women, especially in the areas of education and

---

[102] Hyaeweol Choi, "Claiming Their Own Space: Australian Women Missionaries in Korea, 1891–1900," *Australian Historical Studies* 48, no. 3 (August 2017): 416–32; Sandra Taylor, "Abby M. Colby: The Christian Response to a Sexist Society," *New England Quarterly* 52, no. 1 (March 1979): 68–79; Robert, *American Women in Mission*, pp. 184–8; Jane Haggis, "Ironies of Emancipation: Changing Configurations of 'Women's Work' in the 'Mission of Sisterhood' to Indian Women," *Feminist Review* 65 (Summer 2000): 108–26; Thorne, *Congregational Missions*.

[103] Choi, *Gender and Mission Encounters*, pp. 104–6.

medicine, were rare sources of inspiration for Korean girls and women in their pursuit of modern knowledge and life opportunities.

In this book, I shift the focus from the missionary women to the Korean women who were educated at mission schools from the late-nineteenth century and emerged as the first generation of "educated women" under Japanese colonial rule. This "elite" class of women in colonial Korea, that is women who received any education, was tiny. In 1912 the rate of enrollment in public common (elementary) schools was barely 1 percent, and by 1942 it had increased to only 34 percent.[104] At the level of higher common schools for girls (high school), by the 1930s there were only ten schools and six of those were Christian mission schools.[105] Opportunities for women to receive college-level education (*chŏnmun hakkyo*, professional schools) were even rarer.[106] This miniscule cohort of educated women, however, played a leadership role in the various professions open to women, especially in education and medicine, in the 1920s and 1930s.

The March First Independence Movement of 1919 had a far-reaching impact on the political and sociocultural milieu of the 1920s and 1930s. Inspired in part by US President Woodrow Wilson's doctrine of self-determination, the independence movement was a watershed event that mobilized millions of people – men and women, young and old, educated and uneducated – seeking "the independence of Korea and the liberty of the Korean people." Approximately one out of every ten people living in the country participated in some form of protest on the streets. According to official reports by the Japanese colonial authorities, 46,948 were arrested, 15,961 injured, and 7,509 killed.[107] The immediate response to the demonstration was harsh and punitive, and the movement failed to bring about the political changes its organizers had hoped for. However, it also led to a shift in colonial policy. The new model, "Cultural Rule" (J: *bunka seiji*, K: *munhwa chŏngch'i*) signaled greater openness and more liberal and democratic governance, in contrast to the earlier approach known as "Military Rule" (J: *budan seiji*, K: *mudan chŏngch'i*).[108] To be sure, "Cultural Rule" took a much more sophisticated and discreet approach, ensuring a tighter grip on colonial subjects by increasing bureaucratic and police

---

[104] Kim Puja, *Hakkyo pak ŭi Chosŏn yŏsŏng tŭl* (Korean Women Outside the School) (Seoul: Ilchogak, 2009), p. 380.
[105] Kim Kyŏngil, *Yŏsŏng ŭi kŭndae, kŭndae ŭi yŏsŏng* (Modernity of Women, Women of Modernity) (Seoul: P'urŭn yŏksa, 2004), p. 302.
[106] Kim, *Yŏsŏng ŭi kŭndae, kŭndae ŭi yŏsŏng*, p. 286.
[107] Ki-baik Lee, *A New History of Korea*, trans. Edward W. Wagner with Edward J. Shultz (Seoul: Ilchogak, 1984), pp. 341–44.
[108] Michael Robinson, *Cultural Nationalism in Colonial Korea, 1920–1925* (Seattle: University of Washington Press, 1988).

surveillance.[109] Nonetheless, it still opened up new space for Koreans to engage in socioeconomic, political, and cultural activities more freely than before.[110]

Within this political and social context, numerous women's organizations were founded. They advocated for a greater role for women in society. As noted earlier, it was also during this Cultural Rule era that the colonial state had "a working truce" with Protestant Christian organizations.[111] There was a rise in the publication of popular magazines, newspapers, and literary pieces. These print outlets served as a forum in which rapid changes in world affairs were introduced, competing claims for the future direction of Korea were discussed, and old and new norms of gender relations for modern Korea were debated.[112] At the same time, the Japanese colonial government's policies on studying overseas were loosened, making it easier for more Korean students to go overseas for advanced study.[113] Upon returning to Korea, these foreign-educated elite played a crucial role in introducing, interpreting, and adapting foreign knowledge and practices for the Korean context, contributing to the shaping of new perspectives on gender identity and quotidian practices. It was within this specific historical milieu that elements of Protestant modernity were manifest in gender ideology, material cultures, and public engagement.

"Cultural Rule" lasted about a decade. The Japanese imperial war efforts were set in motion with the Manchurian Incident in 1931, and were further escalated with the outbreak of the second Sino-Japanese War in 1937. Korea became the crossroads for Japan's military ambitions throughout Asia and the Pacific. The *kōminka* (imperialization) period (approximately 1937–1945) brought the Korean people under much tighter control by the colonial power under the slogan of "Japan and Korea as One Body" (*naisen ittai*). Much stricter regulations were imposed not only at the level of political, economic, and military policies but also in the minutiae of daily life, such as diet, clothing, birth control, and even the use of language. The Korean language, a symbol of Korean identity, was eliminated as the medium of instruction in schools and was replaced by Japanese. In addition, all colonial subjects were required to attend Shinto ceremonies, and Koreans had to adopt Japanese surnames. All these forceful assimilation policies during the *kōminka* period were designed to

---

[109] Kŏmyŏl yŏn'guhoe, *Singminji kŏmyŏl: chedo, t'eksŭt'ŭ, silch'ŏn* (Censorship in Colonial Korea: System, Text, Practice) (Seoul: Somyŏng ch'ulp'an, 2011).
[110] Kyung Moon Hwang, *A History of Korea* (London: Palgrave Macmillan, 2010), p. 164.
[111] Hwang, *Rationalizing Korea*, p. 163.
[112] Yoo, *The Politics of Gender in Colonial Korea*; and Hyaeweol Choi, *New Women in Colonial Korea: A Sourcebook* (New York: Routledge, 2013), pp. 1–2.
[113] Pak, *Kŭndae yŏsŏng, chegug ŭl kŏch'yŏ chosŏn ŭro hoeyuhada*, pp. 28–32; Pak Ch'ansŭng, "1920-nyŏndae toIl yuhaksaeng kwa kŭ sasang chŏk tonghyang" (The Ideology of Korean Students Studying in Japan in the 1920s), *Han'guk kŭnhyŏndae yŏn'gu* 30 (2004): 99–151, quoted on 101.

annihilate Korean roots and identity and turn Koreans into loyal servants of imperial Japan.[114] Under this milieu, the transnational flow of people and ideas was also significantly restricted, the role of the Protestant missionary network was seriously curtailed, and some women leaders channeled their energies into Japan's war effort, resulting in tarnished reputations as "collaborators" with Japanese imperial power (*ch'inilp'a*). Given the immensity and complexity of this *kōminka* period, the current book leaves that topic for future study.

In this book, I focus on the historical period from the late-nineteenth century to the 1930s, just prior to the *kōminka* period. Centering on the concept of Protestant modernity, the book probes four topics to illuminate the divergent, multisited sources of influence beyond the Japanese empire in shaping modern womanhood in Korea. Chapter 1 focuses on the most powerful gender ideology in twentieth-century Korea: The concept of the "wise mother, good wife" (*hyŏnmo yangch'ŏ*). That ideology has become so pervasive and naturalized that Koreans often believe it to be an authentic Korean "tradition"; however, I trace the genealogy of "wise mother, good wife" and demonstrate the diachronic, multivalent, and transcultural sources that contributed to this enduring gender ideology. Specifically, I examine the dynamic interactions between the Confucian tradition of womanly virtue (*pudŏk*) from the Chosŏn dynasty, the Japanese Meiji gender ideology (*ryōsai kenbo*, "good wife, wise mother") that gained prominence during the Japanese colonial era, and the Victorian notion of domesticity introduced by Protestant missionaries from the United States. I argue that the prevailing notion of "wise mother, good wife" as the ideal for womanhood in Korea was a modern construct that grew out of these transcultural interactions. It was also an expedient framework that redefined domesticity in a way that was appropriate for the changing national and global milieu of modern times.

The gender ideology of "wise mother, good wife" was embodied in material, symbolic, and bodily practices in the domestic sphere, informed by the transnational flow of knowledge, people, and material cultures. Taking the idea of the "modern home" as a key concept on which national, colonial, and missionary projects converged, Chapter 2 explores a wide range of issues that went into the discourse about the "modern home": Architectural features, scientific management of the household, proper domestic routines, cultured family life, rational budgeting, and healthy child development. It specifically investigates the role of American missionaries, colonial authorities, and foreign-educated Korean intellectuals in introducing what constitutes the ideal house and home through examples of the "missionary home," the 1915 Home Exhibition organized by the Japanese colonial government, and Korean elite's observations of the models of Euro-American domestic life. This chapter also analyzes

---

[114] Caprio, *Japanese Assimilation Policies in Colonial Korea*, pp. 141–70.

the institutionalization of "home economics" as an academic discipline in women's higher education, viewing it as the culmination of the transpacific flow of ideas and people in fashioning modern domesticity in Korea. In doing so, it demonstrates how the intimate sphere of the domestic space became one of the most dynamic sites for uncovering the confluence of the local, the national, and the global.

Chapter 3 turns our attention to travel overseas and its impact on modern womanhood. In late-nineteenth- and early-twentieth-century Korea, it was not uncommon for people to leave the Korean peninsula to seek a better life or simply to survive, whether on their own initiative or by force.[115] In this chapter, I focus on Korean women intellectuals and reformers who crossed domestic boundaries to study or attend international conferences to gain firsthand knowledge from "advanced" countries. Their life trajectories share one remarkable unifying characteristic: Many of these women were associated at some point with the globally interconnected Christian network, through mission schools and various Christian organizations at home and overseas. Retrieving rare records of some of these Korean Christian women, Chapter 3 examines the gender politics of overseas travel with a particular focus on the crucial role of the global missionary network, which served as a channel through which young women could experience the world beyond the metropole and the colony. Tracing the footsteps of these women through Asia, North America, Europe, and Australia, this chapter demonstrates how their travel experiences provided

---

[115] For example, beginning in the late-nineteenth century, many Koreans began migrating to Manchuria in search of new life opportunities. By 1945 there were 1.5 million Koreans in Manchuria. Women were a significant part of the Korean exile communities in Shanghai, North Kando (Chien-tao), the United States, and the Russian Maritime Territory during the colonial period. More than 1,000 Korean women went to Hawai'i as "picture brides" for Korean laborers working on the sugar plantations, beginning in 1903. And thousands of Korean women were forcibly drafted into service in military brothels for Japanese soldiers throughout Asia and the Pacific. See Kwangmin Kim, "Korean Migration in Nineteenth-Century Manchuria: A Global Theme in Modern Asian History," in *Mobile Subjects: Boundaries and Identities in Modern Korean Diaspora*, ed. Wen-hsin Yeh (Berkeley: Institute of East Asian Studies, 2013), pp. 17–37; Hyun Ok Park, *Two Dreams in One Bed: Empire, Social Life, and the Origins of the North Korean Revolution in Manchuria* (Durham: Duke University Press, 2005); Hyun Ok Park, "Ideals of Liberation: Korean Women in Manchuria," in *Dangerous Women: Gender and Korean Nationalism*, eds. Elaine H. Kim and Chungmoo Choi (New York: Routledge, 1998), pp. 229–48; Hŏ Ŭn, *Ajikto nae kwi en Sŏgando param sori ka* (I Still Hear the Sound of the Wind in Sŏgando) (Chŏngusa, 2008; first edition in 1995); Chŏng Chŏnghwa, *Changgang ilgi* (Diary of Changgang) (Seoul: Hangminsa, 1998); Alice Yun Chai, "Women's History in Public: 'Picture Brides' of Hawai'i," *Women's Studies Quarterly* 16, no. 1/2 (Spring–Summer 1988): 51–62; Wayne Patterson, *The Ilse: First-Generation Korean Immigrants in Hawai'i, 1903–1973* (Honolulu: University of Hawai'i Press, 2000), pp. 80–99; Keith Howard, ed., *True Stories of the Korean Comfort Women: Testimonies* (New York: Cassell, 1995); Sarah Soh, *The Comfort Women: Sexual Violence and Postcolonial Memory in Korea and Japan* (Chicago: University of Chicago Press, 2008). See also the special issue, "The Comfort Women: Colonialism, War, and Sex," in *positions: East Asia Cultures Critique* 5, no. 1 (Spring 1997).

them with new ideas about selfhood, racial and national identity, and cosmopolitanism, and created the context for the growth of a women's movement. In my analysis, I emphasize the dialectical process of representations in the "contact zone" when those women travellers encountered diverse people, customs, protocols, and daily practices in foreign countries. In a significant way, the representation of the Other – in this case the West – found in travel writing and memoirs of Korean women offers not simply a description of what they saw in their travels but a meditation on their awakening to the patterns of their own thoughts, which, in turn, allowed them to see Korea in a new light. After all, a sense of oneself is reshaped by a greater understanding of others.[116] I argue that their direct exposure to Western and Japanese modernity sharpened their sense of locality, which, in turn, shaped their vision for social reforms that were locally grounded while also informed by theories and practices developed in foreign nations.

One of the major reform activities drawn from the transnational experiences of Korean women was the rural revitalization movement, which was prominent from the late-1920s to the mid-1930s, when the worsening economic situation caused a spike in poverty and despair in rural communities. Chapter 4 offers a detailed history of the role of women reformers in the rural revitalization movement. At the core of these efforts was an interdenominational, global Christian network that brought people, resources, and information together, and linked the urban elite with the rural populace. A particular source of inspiration for Korean reformers in their pursuit of the restoration of Korea was the Danish rural model, which emphasized national spirit, folk cultures, manual labor, and democratic education. This chapter argues that these women reformers were pursuing an alternative modernity that was inspired by their transnational experience in Europe and the United States but adapted for the local conditions in Korea.

Untraceable Traces: The Politics of the Archive

In postcolonial feminist studies, bringing in the voices of indigenous women is a significant task, but in reconstructing gendered colonial history, the sheer

---

[116] To highlight the traveler's agency in accruing data and representing Korea and foreign societies and cultures, I find it useful to borrow the concepts of "ethno-Orientalism" and "ethno-Occidentalism" coined by James Carrier. "Ethno-Orientalism" means "essentialist renderings of alien societies by the members of those societies themselves" and "ethno-Occidentalism" refers to "essentialist renderings of the West by members of alien societies." The fact that these concepts were originally conceived of with relation to European colonialism needs to be born in mind when applied to the Asian context. Still, the premise of those concepts can be productively utilized in articulating the nature of narrative strategies used by Korean women travellers in representing themselves and foreign cultures. James G. Carrier, "Occidentalism: The World Turned Upside-down," *American Ethnologist* 19, no. 2. (May 1992): 195–212.

Untraceable Traces: The Politics of the Archive   31

paucity of archival materials has been a major challenge.[117] The voices of less-educated, poor, rural women have too often been left out entirely. The class of educated women do not necessarily fare any better. In doing research on gender history in modern Korea, it is still a reality that the records of women in the conventional "archives" in Korea are sparse and incomplete.[118] Certainly some women left writings of various kinds, ranging from opinion pieces in popular magazines and newspapers to travelogues and autobiographies. However, the vast majority left very little in the way of documentation or narrative description. The tradition of "writing women" was not unheard of in Korean history. During the Chosŏn dynasty women wrote poetry, letters, diaries, injunctions, song lyrics, lineage novels, and even legal petitions.[119] With the dawn of modern times, women writers and translators emerged, putting forward "new feminine ideals."[120] Still, a woman voicing her opinions in public invited social criticism, especially if she advocated women's rights, challenged patriarchal norms, or expressed a desire for selfhood. The male-led discourse on the "New Woman" (*sin yŏsŏng*) in the 1920s and 1930s often presented the newly emerging class of educated women as selfish, luxury-seeking, morally loose, and Westernized.[121] Although some of the "New Women" tried to correct these misrepresentations by describing for readers how actual "New Women" led their lives, they faced fierce scrutiny and were often the subjects of unfounded rumors.[122] In this atmosphere, some women intellectuals may have exercised

---

[117] See a special issue, "Revising the Experiences of Colonized Women: Beyond Binaries," *Journal of Women's History* 14, no. 4 (Winter 2003).

[118] Even the enterprise of digitalizing historical data in South Korea has conspicuously marginalized gender-, women-related historical documents. The most representative digitalizing enterprise of historical data can be found in Han'guksa teit'ŏbeisŭ (Korean History Database) conducted by Kuksa p'yŏnch'an wiwŏnhoe (http://db.history.go.kr/). A number of magazines that were published in the colonial period have been digitalized, but almost none of the women's magazines that were published in that era are as yet digitized. The only women's magazine included in that digital library is *Man'guk puin* (1932), which produced only one issue.

[119] Ksenia Chizhova, "Bodies of Texts: Women Calligraphers and the Elite Vernacular Culture in Late Chosŏn Korea (1392–1910)," *Journal of Asian Studies* 77, no. 1 (February 2018): 59–81; Kim, *The Emotions of Justice*; Kim, "You Must Avenge on My Behalf"; Jahyun Kim Haboush, ed., *Epistolary Korea: Letters in the Communicative Space of the Chosŏn, 1392–1910* (New York: Columbia University Press, 2009); Sonja Häussler, "Kyubang kasa: Women's Writings from the Late Chosŏn," in *Creative Women of Korea: The Fifteenth Through the Twentieth Centuries*, ed. Young-Key Kim-Renaud (Armonk: M. E. Sharpe. 2004), pp. 142–62; and Lady Hyegyŏng, *The Memoirs of Lady Hyegyŏng: The Autobiographical Writings of a Crown Princess of Eighteenth-Century Korea*, compiled and annotated by JaHyun Kim Haboush (Berkeley: University of California Press, 1995).

[120] Hyun, *Writing Women* in Korea, pp. 42–59.   [121] Choi, *New Women in Colonial Korea*.

[122] Kim Hwallan wrote an essay in which she urged men to reflect on their own hypocrisy before they acted as watchdogs for women's bad behavior. See "Namsŏng ŭi pansŏng ŭl ch'ok ham" (Urging Men to Critically Reflect on Themselves), *Sin yŏja* 4 (June 1920): 38–40; and Choi, *New Women in Colonial Korea*, pp. 1–15.

32   Introduction

self-censorship and chosen not to air their ideas in public in order to avoid the critical male gaze.

The voices and experiences of less-educated women are even harder to trace. According to the census conducted by the Japanese Government-General of Korea, the overall literacy rate in 1930 was approximately 22 percent, and the literacy rate for women was even lower.[123] Those figures foretell the scarcity of any written records we face today. Non-elite women left very little writing of their own to record their perspectives and experiences. As Chapter 4 illustrates, some rare sources exist in the form of feedback or reflections on workshops that rural women attended, but what we have often consists of representations of their lives written by members of the elite class or the colonial state.

In this vein, feminist historians critically probe "what counts as an archive," while exploring alternative sources that could help recuperate the little that is known about the lives and experiences of women and ultimately shed new light on colonial histories.[124] In my earlier work, which focused on American women missionaries, various "mission archives" provided me with relatively rich data about mission policies and the lives and activities of individual missionaries. In the mission archives, more often than not, indigenous women's voices are absent or elusive, as they were typically presented as "girls," "women," or "Bible women" without much acknowledgement of them as individuals. In her analysis of American missionaries in the Philippines, Laura Prieto argues that for the promotion of evangelical work, "they [the converted] mattered in the aggregate, but did not figure as individual human beings."[125] In this sense, it is challenging to find any direct evidence of "native agency" which isn't screened and represented by the missionaries.

During the preparation of this book in search of native voices in whatever traceable forms, I constantly wondered why and in what ways certain materials were preserved while others were conspicuously absent; what such absences tell us about the politics of knowledge, which cannot be separated from gender

---

[123] Ji Yeon Hong and Christopher Paik, "Colonization and Education: Exploring the Legacy of Local Elites in Korea," *The Economic History Review* (2017): 1–27; Mitsuhiko Kimura, "Standards of Living in Colonial Korea: Did the Masses Become Worse off or Better off under Japanese Rule?" *Journal of Economic History* 53, no. 3 (September 1993): 629–52.

[124] Focusing on three Indian women, Antoinette Burton examines the ways in which they "made use of memories of home in order to claim a place in history at the intersection of the private and the public, the personal and the political, the national and the postcolonial." Burton uses the term "archive" in two ways: 1) in its conventional, disciplinary meaning – "as the source of evidence" and 2) "a text like the 'Family History' [which] is itself an enduring site of historical evidence and historiographical opportunity in and for the present." Antoinette Burton, *Dwelling in the Archive: Women Writing House, Home, and History in Late Colonial India* (Oxford: Oxford University Press, 2003), pp. 4–5. See also Antoinette Burton, "Archive Stories: Gender in the Making of Imperial and Colonial Histories," in *Gender and Empire*, ed. Philippa Levine (New York: Oxford University Press, 2004), pp. 281–93.

[125] Prieto, "Bibles, Baseball and Butterfly Sleeves," p. 368.

politics; and what alternative sources I could and should consult. To collect material for this book, I traveled to various archives in Korea, Japan, China, the United States, Sweden, Denmark, Germany, and Australia. The book draws on a wide range of sources I collected from major and minor archives (e.g., local genealogy societies, grade books, campus magazines, alumni records), from museums and universities in those countries, and from visual and literary material such as photographs, film clips, postcards, handicrafts, and creative writing, in order to tease out how the transnational flow of ideas and material cultures was instantiated in both discourse and everyday life.

The long, transnational sojourn I undertook with this research was something of a "treasure hunt" in search of the traces of Korean women who crossed domestic and international borders in pursuit of new knowledge and new lives. Excavating photos, theses, and academic transcripts from various campus archives was an exhilarating process of discovery, bringing to light what had been buried and forgotten. My archival search, however, was not always successful. For example, I was disappointed (indeed, almost saddened) not to find any direct evidence related to Ch'oe Yŏngsuk, who travelled to Sweden for her college education. During visits to the archive at Stockholm University and the National Archive of Sweden I was unable to uncover any details of her time in that country. However, in a way, just being there and finding out what exists and what does not was helpful. I was still able to gather indirect but crucial information that helped me contextualize her student life in Stockholm. Those small nuggets of information helped me fill in the puzzle, make connections to other facts, and make sense of the lives and work of these women. Still, there are many gaps that need to be filled in. As the historian Susan Mann demonstrates in her book, *The Talented Women of the Zhang Family*, it is incumbent on us to "reconstruct" the lives of women not only from conventionally accepted materials but also from anything else that "might help to unlock the secrets they chose to keep to themselves."[126] In this book, my overall strategy in reconstructing the gender history of colonial-era Korea is to pay attention to the tensions between "discourse" and "experience" not as "opposing domains but as a vast, interdependent archive," in Antoinette Burton's words.[127] To do that, I have chosen texts, images, materials, and individual lives that provide us with some clues as to the scale and depth of the life experiences of Korean women, especially those that went beyond the local and the national and were interconnected with the global web of ideas, people, organizations, and material cultures.[128]

---

[126] Susan Mann, *The Talented Women of the Zhang Family* (Berkeley: University of California Press, 2007), p. xv.
[127] Burton, *Dwelling in the Archive*, p. 5.
[128] Struck, Ferris, and Revel, "Introduction: Space and Scale in Transnational History," 577.

The handful of elite women that this book largely focuses on made up only a tiny proportion of the adult female population of Korea before and during Japanese rule. Nevertheless, their exceptional lives provide clues to how modern gender identity and politics formed in Korea within the context of the increasingly interconnected world, through imperial encounters, capitalist developments, print and visual media, overseas study, and the Christian foreign missionary enterprise. Historians who advocate "micronarrative" or "microhistory" pay special attention to the exceptional, the deviant, or the marginal as indicators of what may lead to a larger, but hidden or unknown, structure. The concept of "exceptional typical," elaborated by Matti Peltonen, captures a key methodological strategy in the new microhistory by taking unusual cases as a prospect, or viewpoint, onto the broader structure.[129] Similarly, following "C. Wright Mills's idea of the sociological imagination – to make sense of the biographical against the larger contexts of history and social structure," John Lie argues that: "Personal anecdotes can illuminate larger historical, structural, or theoretical points, which in turn cannot possibly exist without them."[130] In other words, personal anecdotes and other marginalia serve as a window to larger historical contexts and sociocultural structures. Furthermore, in a longer historical outlook, as Charles Taylor posits in his discussion of modernity through his concept of "social imaginaries," there was a long march into the modern era that was first incubated by a few thinkers whose ideas gradually became "integral to our social imaginary, that is, the way our contemporaries imagine the societies they inhabit and sustain."[131] Thus, despite their exceptional life experiences, the significance of this pioneering group of Korean women elite lies in their having ushered in a new way of thinking and living through their exposure to the wider world.

Overall, this book aims to offer a new perspective on gender and colonial history by examining cross-border movements and networks of women and men that went beyond the nexus of the metropole and colony from the late-nineteenth to early-twentieth centuries. Through analysis of archival and visual materials, I explore the ways in which Korea's broader interactions with foreign countries, especially the United States, transformed gender norms, domestic practices, and public engagements during Japanese rule. I investigate the exceptional lives of a few elite women as an entry point for detecting the zeitgeist of the era and its reach into the everyday lives of ordinary

---

[129] Matti Peltonen, "Clues, Margins, and Monads: The Micro-Macro Link in Historical Research," *History and Theory* 40 (October 2001): 347–59. One of the best-known examples of microhistory is Natalie Zemon David, *The Return of Martin Guerre* (Cambridge: Harvard University Press, 1984).
[130] John Lie, *Zainichi (Koreans in Japan): Diasporic Nationalism and Postcolonial Identity* (Berkeley: University of California, 2008), p. xii.
[131] Charles Taylor, *Modern Social Imaginaries* (Durham: Duke University Press, 2004), p. 6.

women and men in terms of ideology, material practices, and public participation in socioeconomic and cultural reforms. Also, I argue that the development of modern gender relations finds its roots in the transnational experience of Koreans, far beyond the nexus of the colonizer-colonized. Korea's interactions with the United States, and to a less extent with Europe and other Asian countries, transformed (and reinforced) the idea of domesticity, gender norms, bodily practices, socioeconomic and cultural reform efforts, and everyday life within the context of Korea's colonization by Japan. Throughout the book I illustrate the critical role of the global Christian missionary network as a platform that enabled and sometimes disabled women to pursue modern life. Here I understand the global Christian missionary network at the intersection of the hegemonic power of Western modernity, Japanese colonial imperatives, Korean nationalist mandates, and secular modern aspirations, and demonstrate the crucial role of globally connected Protestant individuals and groups in inducing tensions between the old and the new and between patriarchal undercurrents and modern transformations. Ultimately, the book addresses a question the feminist historian Judith Bennett raised decades ago: How did patriarchy persist, get challenged, and then get adjusted at a particular historical juncture?[132] Situating particular local and national circumstances of colonial-era Korea, the following chapters trace the modern transformations of patriarchy that women participated in or resisted, as manifested in the narratives, lives, and images of women in colonial Korea.

---

[132] Bennett, "Feminism and History."

1   Ideology: "Wise Mother, Good Wife"

On November 5, 2007, the Bank of Korea announced that it had decided to include a portrait of Lady Sin Saimdang (1504–1551) on the new 50,000 *wŏn* note.[1] The announcement listed a number of reasons for choosing Lady Sin for this honor. One was that she was the most renowned female artist from the Chosŏn dynasty (1392–1910). Indeed, her paintings are presumed to be the earliest examples of extant work by a Korean woman painter.[2] However, perhaps her greatest claim to fame is the fact that she was the mother of one of Korea's most prominent Confucian scholars, Yi I (1536–1584). Eulogized as the quintessential example of a "wise mother, good wife" (*hyŏnmo yangch'ŏ*), she has long been celebrated as the ideal Korean woman.[3]

The selection of Sin Saimdang stirred lively debates among women's organizations that reflected mixed emotions about her. On the one hand, many women welcomed that, for the first time, a woman was considered significant enough to have her portrait printed on Korean currency. On the other hand, some were troubled by the selection of Sin Saimdang over other, perhaps more preferable, candidates, such as Yu Kwansun (1902–1920), who had become a symbol of female patriotism during Japanese colonial rule (1910–1945).[4] In

---

[1] *Han'gyŏre*, November 5, 2007. *Wŏn* refers to the basic unit in Korean currency.
[2] Martina Deuchler, "Propagating Female Virtues in Chosŏn Korea," in *Women and Confucian Cultures in Premodern China, Korea, and Japan*, eds. Dorothy Ko, JaHyun Kim Haboush, and Joan R. Piggott (Berkeley: University of California Press, 2003), p. 163; Yi Sŏngmi, "Sin Saimdang: The Foremost Woman Painter of the Chosŏn Dynasty," in *Creative Women of Korea: The Fifteenth through the Twentieth Centuries*, ed. Young- Key Kim-Renaud (Armonk, New York: M. E. Sharpe, 2004), pp. 58–77.
[3] Yi, "Sin Saimdang," p. 59; Yung-Chung Kim, *Women of Korea: A History from Ancient Times to 1945* (Seoul: Ewha Womans University Press, 1979), p. 158; and Kim Sujin, "Chŏnt'ong ŭi ch'ang'an kwa yŏsŏng ŭi kungminhwa: Sin Saimdang ŭl chungsim ŭro" (The Invention of Tradition and the Nationalization of Women with a Focus on Sin Saimdang), *Sahoe wa yŏksa* 80 (2008): 215–55.
[4] When the nationwide March First Independence Movement took place in 1919, Yu Kwansun was a student at Ewha Girls' School. Her leadership role in the movement landed her in jail, where she died. In popular imagination, she was tortured to death and her body was mutilated, reinforcing the idea of the brutality of the Japanese colonial authority. However, Jeannette Walter, who was a missionary teacher at Ewha at that time who helped bring Yu's body back to the school for burial, confirmed that "her body was not mutilated. I had dressed her for burial."

a public forum organized by the feminist group "If," Kim Kyŏngae argued that Sin Saimdang was selected due to her status as the ideal of the "wise mother, good wife," and that that choice was primarily motivated by a desire to maintain the anachronistic patriarchal order of Korean society. Another participant, Kim Sin Myŏngsuk, further pointed out that the notion of "wise mother, good wife" associated with Sin Saimdang was in actuality a modern product of the Japanese colonial education system in Korea, which tried to suppress critical consciousness and propagate obedient female colonial subjects.[5] Despite the concerns expressed by women's organizations about the negative impact that such a conservative female role model might have on women in contemporary Korean society, the Bank of Korea issued the new bill with her portrait on it on June 23, 2009.[6]

What is most noteworthy in this controversy is the fact that, in spite of her status as a pioneering sixteenth-century woman artist, Sin Saimdang has been, perhaps first and foremost, the most potent symbol of the "wise mother, good wife" ideology in modern Korea, an ideology that continues to shape gender discourse even in the twenty-first century.[7] In 2007, a TV drama, *Sin hyŏnmo yangch'ŏ* (*New Wise Mother, Good Wife*), aired in Korea, envisioning a twenty-first-century woman who was physically beautiful, exceptionally devoted to her children and husband, and highly resourceful in terms of managing the family finances. Another popular TV drama, *Saimdang, pit ŭi ilgi* (*Saimdang, a Diary of Light*), broadcast in 2017, presented Saimdang's "womanly virtues" (*pudŏk*), such as moral integrity, purity, diligence, and endurance, while creatively imagining her artistic passion and tender emotions, including romantic feelings. The huge popularity of these dramas shows the everlasting currency of the idea of "wise mother, good wife," and the continuing fascination with the figure of Sin Saimdang.

Given the ongoing influence of the image of Sin Saimdang as "wise mother, good wife," a series of questions arises: What is the genealogy of that influential gender ideology? What exactly constitutes a "wise mother, good wife"? To what extent have women exercised their agency in accepting, resisting, or appropriating the dominant gender ideology? And what does the persistent invocation of a historical figure as the ideal "wise mother, good wife" tell us about resilient patriarchal systems? Feminist historian Judith Bennett has

---

Jeannette Walter, *Aunt Jean* (Boulder: Johnson Publishing Company, 1968), pp. 142–3. Cited in Donald N. Clark, *Living Dangerously in Korea: The Western Experience 1900–1950* (Norwalk, CT: EastBridge, 2003), p. 183.

[5] *OhmyNews*, October 15, 2007.
[6] *Chosŏn ilbo*, October 15, 2008; *OhmyNews*, February 25, 2009.
[7] Hong Yanghŭi, "Sin Saimdang, 'hyŏnmo yangch'ŏ' ŭi sangjing i toeda'" (Sin Saimdang Becomes the Symbol of "Wise Mother, Good Wife") in *Sin Saimdang, kŭ nyŏ rŭl wihan pyŏnmyŏng* (Sin Saimdang: In Her Defense), eds. Ko Yŏnhŭi, Yi Kyŏnggu, Yi Sugin, Hong Yanghŭi, and Kim Sujin (Seoul: Tasan Kihoek, 2016), pp. 166–213.

suggested that one strategy for bringing about a better understanding of the mechanisms of persistent patriarchy is to undertake case studies with an especial focus on historical times of exceptional crisis, and to examine how historical "transitions challenged patriarchies, how patriarchies changed in response to these challenges, and how patriarchies nevertheless endured."[8] In exploring these questions within the Korean historical context, the concept of "wise mother, good wife" is a particularly expedient target for analysis because it has been extremely influential in (re)shaping gender discourse and practices in Korea. Furthermore, an analysis of the formation, maintenance, and rupture of "wise mother, good wife" sheds light not only on the complex mechanisms of patriarchy at the structural level but also on women's own complicity in and resistance to these patriarchal arrangements.

Feminist scholars in Korea have probed the legacy of Sin Saimdang and the implications of that legacy for the changing gender dynamics in Korean history and society.[9] In her analysis of the various discourses on Sin Saimdang that took place between the sixteenth and nineteenth centuries, Yi Sugin (aka Sookin Lee) illuminates the male-dominated Confucian politics of knowledge that invoked Sin as the model of ideal motherhood and the bearer of Confucian "womanly virtues."[10] In an article focusing on the invention of tradition and the nationalization of women as citizens, Kim Sujin demonstrates that an array of social and political forces, including enlightenment-oriented Korean intellectuals of the early twentieth century, the Japanese colonial authority, the regime of President Park Chung Hee in the 1960s and 1970s, and various women's groups, presented selected images of Sin Saimdang to promote their own distinctive and disparate agendas.[11] Hong Yanghŭi also offers an insightful analysis of the ways in which the status of Sin Saimdang as a symbol of "wise mother, good wife" has been used as a disciplinary tool to reinforce traditional gender roles and control women's sexuality.[12] What these studies suggest is that for the past five centuries the imagery of Sin Saimdang as "wise mother, good wife" has been historically and discursively constructed, in some ways even fabricated, in accordance with the particular political and cultural

---

[8] Judith M. Bennett, "Feminism and History," *Gender & History* 1, no. 3 (Autumn 1989): 259. See also the book forum in the *Journal of Women's History* 20, no. 2 (2008), which focuses on Judith Bennett's book, *History Matters: Patriarchy and the Challenge of Feminism* (Philadelphia: University of Pennsylvania Press, 2006).

[9] Ko et al., *Sin Saimdang*.

[10] Yi Sugin, "Sin Saimdang tamnon ŭi kyebohak (1) kŭndae ijŏn" (The Genealogy of the Discourse on Sin Saimdang in pre-Modern Korea), *Chindan hakpo* 106 (2008): 1–31.

[11] Kim, "Chŏnt'ong ŭi ch'ang'an kwa yŏsŏng ŭi kungminhwa," 215–55.

[12] Sin's image as an ideal woman has been contrasted with the demonized image of "New Woman" (*sin yŏsŏng*) in colonial Korea and "soybean paste girl" (*toenjangnyŏ*) in contemporary South Korea. See Hong, "Sin Saimdang." For details about a "soybean paste girl," see Jee Eun Regina Song, "The Soybean Paste Girl: The Cultural and Gender Politics of Coffee Consumption in Contemporary South Korea," *Journal of Korean Studies* 19, no. 2 (2014): 429–48.

Ideology: "Wise Mother, Good Wife" 39

demands of different historical agents. They have also elucidated the complex ways in which the norm of "wise mother, good wife" was deployed for the purpose of the Korean nationalist mandate, on the one hand, and Korean women's desire for a new ideal in the form of an "empowered" and "educated" mother and wife in the modern, nuclear family, on the other.[13]

What has been less explored, however, is the ways in which conservative Western gender ideology was enmeshed in the making of "wise mother, good wife," especially through the personnel and institutions of Protestant Christianity. The fact that the vast majority of educated Korean women in the late-nineteenth and early-twentieth century had either direct or indirect connections with American, Canadian, or Australian missionaries through education at mission schools or job opportunities in Christian organizations makes it impossible to talk about the evolution of a new ideal for women in modern Korea without considering the crucial influence of Protestant Christian groups.[14] Beyond the simple fact of the Western missionaries' influence, we must consider what ideals were elevated through their influence. In typical Korean historiography, Western missionary women have often been portrayed as pioneers of modern womanhood who delivered progressive notions of gender freedom and equality. However, their legacy is more complex than what that triumphant rhetoric would suggest.[15] As this chapter demonstrates, Western women missionaries in Korea held up a largely conservative ideal of Victorian womanhood that transpired in their educational and religious work. Significantly, their emphasis on domesticity and purity was quite compatible with Korea's traditional gender norms and became an integral part of the idea of "wise mother, good wife" in modern Korea.

In this chapter, I provide a fuller and more nuanced picture of the modern gender ideology of "wise mother, good wife," detailing how it evolved through a number of forces – national, colonial, and Protestant Christian – in turn-of-the-

---

[13] Kawamoto Aya, "Han'guk kwa Ilbon ŭi hyŏnmo yangch'ŏ sasang" (Ideology of Wise Mother and Good Wife in Korea and Japan), in *Mosŏng ŭi tamnon kwa hyŏnsil*, ed. Sim Yŏnghŭi (Seoul: Nanam Ch'ulp'an, 1999), pp. 221–44; Hong Yanghŭi, "Ilche sigi Chosŏn ŭi yŏsŏng kyoyuk: hyŏnmo yangch'ŏ kyoyuk ŭl chungsim ŭro" (Korean Women's Education during the Japanese colonial era: with a Focus on Education for Wise Mother and Good Wife), *Han'gukhak nonjip* 35 (2001): 219–57. [The journal *Han'gukhak nonjip* changed its title to *Tong Asia munhwa yŏn'gu* in 2010.] For an in-depth analysis of the discourse on filiality in Chosŏn dynasty, see JaHyun Kim Haboush, "Filial Emotions and Filial Values: Changing Patterns in the Discourse of Filiality in Late Chosŏn Korea," *Harvard Journal of Asiatic Studies* 55, no. 1 (June 1995): 129–77.

[14] According to Pak Sŏnmi, in 1935, about 65.4 percent of girls in high school were attending mission schools and 60 percent of those who enrolled in professional schools for women had attended mission-run institutes. Pak Sŏnmi, *Kŭndae yŏsŏng cheguk ŭl kŏch'ŏ Chosŏn ŭro hoeyuhada* (Modern Women Return to Korea via Empire) (Seoul: Ch'angbi, 2007), p. 53.

[15] For a critical approach to the missionary legacy in gender history in modern Korea, see Hyaeweol Choi, *Gender and Mission Encounters in Korea: New Women, Old Ways* (Berkeley: University of California Press, 2009).

twentieth century Korea. The late nineteenth and early twentieth centuries comprised arguably the most turbulent era in Korea's history, one that contained unprecedented challenges to the Korean patriarchal system. The era was characterized by foreign aggression and the influx of new and modern ideas from other countries. During this unsettled era,[16] not only were the traditional political and economic systems shaken but the Confucian moral and cultural values that had been the foundation of the Chosŏn dynasty came under critical scrutiny.[17] In particular, inspired by the Western notion that the status and treatment of woman reflects the level of civilization, the "woman question" emerged as a theme in the critique of Confucian-prescribed gender norms. Intellectuals and reformers endeavored to reconfigure the role women would play in the domestic, familial sphere as an integral part of a modern nation-state. The concept of "wise mother, good wife" came about within this particular historical moment, shaped by regional and transnational forces.

In her analysis of the construction of the concept of "good wives and wise mothers" (*liangqi xianmu*) in late Qing China, Joan Judge argues that the concept of "good wives and wise mothers" (*liangqi xianmu*) should be understood "as a product of its own transnational moment in history."[18] As she notes, the notions of *liangqi* (good wife) and *xianmu* (wise mother) are found in Chinese texts as early as the first century BCE.[19] However, it was Meiji Japan (1868–1912) that first developed a combined notion, *ryōsai kenbo* (good wife, wise mother), which Japanese historian Koyama Shizuko characterizes "as an ideology that made women into members of the modern state, while at the same time assigning them to an existence within the boundaries of the home with their primary roles being those of wife and mother."[20] That concept of *ryōsai kenbo* subsequently traveled to China and Korea in the early twentieth

---

[16] The period between 1876 and 1910 is broadly known as the "enlightenment period" (*kaehwagi*). In his analysis of modern political thought, the Korean historian Pak Ch'ansŭng terms the particular period after Korea became a Japanese Protectorate (1905–1910) as the "self-strengthening movement era" (*chagang undonggi*) to capture the wide variety of social movements that came about during that time. See Pak Ch'ansŭng, *Han'guk kŭndae chŏngch'i sasangsa yŏn'gu* (A Study of the History of Modern Political Thought in Korea) (Seoul: Yŏksa Pip'yŏngsa, 1993). See also Peter Lee, ed., *Sourcebook of Korean Civilization*, vol. 2, *From the Seventeenth Century to the Modern Period* (New York: Columbia University Press, 1996), pp. 337–60.

[17] Key-Hiuk Kim, *The Last Phase of the East Asian World Order: Korea, Japan, and the Chinese Empire, 1860–1882* (Berkeley: University of California Press, 1980); Vipan Chandra, *Imperialism, Resistance, and Reform in Late Nineteenth-Century Korea: Enlightenment and the Independence Club* (Berkeley: Institute of East Asian Studies, University of California, Berkeley, Center for Korean Studies, 1988); and Andre Schmid, *Korea between Empires 1895–1919* (New York: Columbia University Press, 2002).

[18] Joan Judge, *The Precious Raft of History: The Past, the West, and the Woman Question in China* (Stanford: Stanford University Press, 2008), p. 113.

[19] Judge, *The Precious Raft of History*, p. 112.

[20] Koyama Shizuko, *Ryōsai Kenbo: The Educational Ideal of "Good Wife, Wise Mother" in Modern Japan*, trans. Stephen Filler (Boston: Brill, 2013), p. 8.

century.[21] The evolution and circulation of the concept of "good wife, wise mother" or its reversal "wise mother, good wife" in East Asia should be understood within a historical context in which the onslaught of Western imperial powers prompted reformers in East Asian countries to overhaul the role of women in pursuit of a strong nation-state.[22] In the Eurocentric, masculinist discourse on gender and civilization, "a society's treatment of women was frequently held up as evidence of its degree of civilization, with 'rude' societies cruel to their womenfolk and 'advanced' ones respectful of them."[23] Although Western women themselves were, in reality, struggling to improve their status within their own "civilized" societies, reformers in East Asia were compelled to react to the prevailing perception in the West that Asian women were ignorant, oppressed, and superstitious. Thus, reforming the role and status of women became a national imperative. Significantly, Western-dominated representations of women do not necessarily mean that the direction of influence was unidirectional, moving from the West to the rest of the world. The concept and utility of "wise mother, good wife" illustrate how "traditional" gender norms interacted with the global flow of ideas and discourses, helping create a *localized* gender ideology with significant imprint of other societies and cultures whether it was through force or volition.

Focusing on divergent sources of influence, I argue that the ideology of "wise mother, good wife" in Korea was a transcultural modern construct. I demonstrate how it came about at the turn of the twentieth century through a convergence of the Chosŏn dynasty's Confucian ideal of *pudŏk* (womanly virtues), Japan's Meiji gender ideology of *ryōsai kenbo* (good wife, wise mother), which transpired through Japanese colonial policies in Korea, and American Protestant women missionaries' Victorian ideology of domesticity in mission schools.[24] To be sure, *pudŏk*, *ryōsai kenbo*, and the Victorian notion of domesticity were shaped by their respective indigenous cultures and histories, and, as a result, the specific details of their particular notions of ideal

---

[21] In China, the phrase *liangqi xianmu* (good wife, wise mother) was most common, but we also find *xianmu liangqi* (wise mother, good wife), and *xianqi liangmu* (wise wife, good mother), while in Korea, the expression *hyŏnmo yangch'ŏ* (wise mother, good wife) was most commonly rendered.

[22] Barbara Molony, Janet Theiss, and Hyaeweol Choi, *Gender in Modern East Asia: An Integrated History* (Boulder: Westview, 2016), p. 139.

[23] Philippa Levine, "Introduction: Why Gender and Empire?," in *Gender and Empire*, ed. Philippa Levine (Oxford: Oxford University Press, 2007), pp. 1–13, quoted on p. 6.

[24] Kim Sujin notes that, although the order changed in the literal translation from Japanese *ryōsai kenbo* (good wife and wise mother) to Korean *hyŏnmo yangch'ŏ* (wise mother and good wife), it does not mean that Koreans gave greater emphasis to motherhood. In colonial-era Korea, *hyŏnmo yangch'ŏ* (wise mother, good wife) and *yangch'ŏ hyŏnmo* (good wife, wise mother) were used interchangeably. See Kim Sujin, "1920–30-nyŏndae sin yŏsŏng tamnon kwa sangjing ŭi kusŏng" (Excess of the Modern: Three Archetypes of the New Woman and Colonial Identity in Korea, 1920s to 1930s) (PhD, Seoul National University, 2005), p. 344.

womanhood varied.[25] However, they all placed high value on the idea that women should occupy the domestic sphere in which they were expected to contribute to the family and society in their capacity as mothers and wives. More importantly, the dynamic interactions among these various concepts took place in the specific historical context in which Korea was colonized by Japan, a non-Western and non-Christian imperial power, and Western missionaries in Korea were perceived by Koreans not as imperialists, but as allies in their struggle against the Japanese colonial power and harbingers of Western modern civilization.[26] It is within these complex historical and political dynamics that indigenous, Japanese, and Western gender beliefs and practices interacted to shape the new modern gender ideology.

I further argue that the promotion of this modern gender ideology of the "wise mother, good wife" was not simply a continuation of traditional patriarchal gender relations. Rather, it was a "transcultural discursive construct" that served as an expedient, flexible, and contested ideology that a diverse collection of sociopolitical and cultural agents – Korean intellectuals, the Japanese colonial authority, and American Protestant missionaries – all embraced, challenged, or strategically appropriated for their own unique mandate, whether it was for the reconstruction of the nation, efficient colonial governance, or the Christianization of the world. These groups actively participated in the rearticulation of this particular gender discourse, which was based on their own primary objectives and readjusted to reflect local particularities. In spite of the uneven power relations among these groups, I underscore the creative engagement of different agencies in promoting or challenging the emerging new gender ideology. An examination of the complexity of the idea of "wise mother, good wife" within this transcultural context helps us articulate major fissures and challenges that patriarchal systems faced; but, more importantly, it illustrates the paradoxical nature of the evolving patriarchies in which both oppressive and liberating forces were embedded.[27]

A Modern Discursive Construct of Gender

Korean intellectuals and reformers were keenly aware of the emergence of "woman" as a visible category in the discourse of "civilization and enlightenment"

---

[25] In this book, "Victorian" refers to American Victorian culture and society. See Thomas Schlereth, *Victorian America: Transformations in Everyday Life, 1876–1915* (New York: HarperCollins, 1991).

[26] Hyaeweol Choi, "Christian Modernity in Missionary Discourse from Korea, 1905–1910," *East Asian History* 29 (June 2005): 39–68.

[27] Line Nyhagen Predelli and Jon Miller, "Piety and Patriarchy: Contested Gender Regimes in Nineteenth-Century Evangelical Missions," in *Gendered Missions: Women and Men in Missionary Discourse and Practice*, eds. Mary Taylor Huber and Nancy C. Lutkehaus (Ann Arbor: University of Michigan Press, 1999), pp. 67–112.

(K. *munmyŏng kaehwa*, J. *bunmei kaika*) that was dominated by Euro-American politicians and Christian groups at that time. In his 1895 book *Sŏyu kyŏnmun* (*Observations of My Travels to the West*), Yu Kilchun (1856–1914), a leading enlightenment-oriented reformer who was educated in Japan and the United States, noted that valuing women's education and treating them better were signs of an advanced civilization. He wrote that Westerners treated their women fairly well because they believed that the "woman is the foundation of human society and the girder of the house and thus if she is weak or ignorant, she would not be able to fulfill her central role."[28] He further noted that since children are the foundation of the country, their having well-informed and knowledgeable mothers is crucial to the well-being of the country.[29] It is important to note that Yu's writing about gender relations in Western countries is not so much an advocacy as a report based on his observations. He wrote: "The manners with which Westerners treat their women are quite different from those in Korea. I am not sure what preferences readers might have, but I am writing about the subject only based on what I saw and will reserve my judgment whether those Western manners are good or bad."[30] Yu's cautious statement about Western practices was relatively common among reformers in East Asia, who were "simultaneously drawn by Western wealth and power and repelled by aspects of the Western social ethos."[31] One of the strategies for dealing with this dilemma was to adopt Western material civilizations but to preserve Eastern morality, expressed in such terms as "*Tongdo sŏgi*" (literally meaning "Eastern Way, Western Method").[32]

A much harsher critic on "Eastern morality," including Confucian-prescribed gender relations, was Yun Ch'iho (1864–1945), who was another prominent reformist intellectual and politician with education in Japan, China, and the United States. From his point of view, the "doctrine of inferiority of women" that prevailed in Chosŏn Korea was deeply embedded in Confucianism – a root cause of Korea's backwardness – that "has made Corea [Korea] a hell."[33] In contrast, Yun believed that one of the features of advanced civilization was women having enhanced status in society. His discourse significantly echoes how Euro-Americans described Korean and Asian women at that time. It is evident that Yun's intellectual trajectory was significantly influenced by Young J. Allen (1836–1907). Allen was the founder of the Anglo-Chinese Southern Methodist School in Shanghai and ran an influential monthly magazine, called *Wanguo gongbao* (*Review of the Times*,

---

[28] Yu Kilchun, *Sŏyu kyŏnmun* (Observations of my Travels to the West), trans. Hŏ Kyŏngjin (Sŏul: Hanyang Ch'ulp'an, 1995), p. 350.
[29] Yu, *Sŏyu kyŏnmun*, pp. 326–27, 349–53.   [30] Yu, *Sŏyu kyŏnmun*, p. 350.
[31] Judge, *The Precious Raft of History*, p. 112.
[32] Kuksa p'yŏnch'an wiwŏnhoe, *Sŏgu munhwa waŭi mannam* (Encounters with Western Cultures) (Kwach'ŏn: Kyŏngin munhwasa, 2010), pp. 28–34.
[33] Yun Ch'iho, *Yun Ch'iho ilgi* (Diary of Yun Ch'iho), December 12, 1893.

1889–1907) that was well-known and circulated among Korean reformers as well as the late Qing reformers.[34] In his book, *A Survey of Female Customs in the Five Continents*, Allen suggests using "the status of women and their treatment in every country as the yardstick for judging the degree of civilization of each culture." He further argued that "no country could ever hope to flourish without elevating and educating its women."[35] Allen's view was squarely in line with his contemporary Euro-Americans, who placed Europe and the United States at the top of the hierarchy of "civilizations." Yun was a protégé of Allen when he studied at the Anglo-Chinese Southern Methodist School in Shanghai between 1885 and 1888. Allen was also instrumental in Yun's further education at Vanderbilt University and Emory University.

The "doctrine of inferiority of women," as Yun disparagingly referred to the prevailing practices, was related to the fact that there were no formal institutions of education for women in the Chosŏn dynasty. However, education was still of great importance in Chosŏn, especially for women of the upper class, for the purpose of maintaining and advancing the prestige of the family as well as distributing Confucian gender ethics.[36] Such education was done exclusively through informal instruction from family members within the domestic sphere, primarily emphasizing filial piety (*hyo*), chastity (*yŏl*), serving the ancestors (*pongjesa*), and domestic skills, such as sewing and cooking.[37] The government as well as illustrious families also published instructional books for women, often based on Chinese works. For example, Queen Sohye (1437–1504) published a book entitled *Naehun* (*Instructions for Women*), drawing selected passages from Chinese texts, such as *Elementary Learning* (*Xiaoxue*), *Notable Women* (*Lienü*), *Lessons for Women* (*Nüjiao*), and *Mirrors of Sagacity* (*Mingjian*).[38] King Yŏngjo (1694–1776) ordered the translation into Korean of the Chinese works, *The Four Books for Women* (*Nü sishu*) – a collection that includes "Lessons for Women" (*yŏ kye*), "Analects for Women" (*yŏ nonŏ*), "Teachings for the Inner Court" (*naehun*), and "Short

---

[34] Yi Kwangnin, *Han'guk kaehwasa yŏn'gu* (A Study of the History of Korean Enlightenment) (Seoul: Ilchogak, 1981), pp. 45–6.
[35] Cited from Hu Ying, *Tales of Translation: Composing the New Woman in China, 1899–1918* (Stanford: Stanford University Press, 2000), p. 2.
[36] Han Hŭisuk, "Yŏhakkyo nŭn ŏpsŏtta, kŭrŏna kyoyug ŭn chungyo haetta" (There was no Girl's School, but Education was Important), in *Chosŏn yŏsŏng ŭi ilsaeng* (Lives of Chosŏn Women), ed. Kyujanggak han'gukhak yŏn'guwŏn (P'aju: Kŭrhangari, 2010), pp. 214–41.
[37] Theodore Jun Yoo, *The Politics of Gender in Colonial Korea: Education, Labor, and Health, 1910–1945* (Berkeley and Los Angeles: University of California Press, 2008), pp. 38–40; Kim, *Women of Korea*, p. 154; Hong, "Ilche sigi Chosŏn ŭi yŏsŏng kyoyuk," p. 223.
[38] Molony, Theiss, and Choi, *Gender in Modern East Asia*, pp. 65–6; John Duncan, "The Naehun and the Politics of Gender," in *Creative Women of Korea: The Fifteenth through the Twentieth Centuries*, ed. Young-Key Kim-Renaud (Armonk: M. E. Sharpe, 2004), pp. 26–57.

Records of Models for Women" (*yŏbŏm ch'ŏmnok*).[39] Centering on "womanly virtues," these instructional works taught girls and women how to cultivate wisdom, morality, prudence, and resourcefulness within the domestic realm. For women to aspire to training beyond the domestic sphere was considered inappropriate. A prominent Confucian scholar, Yi Ik (1681–1763) noted that "teaching women scholarship (*hangmun*) will lead to disaster."[40]

However, when Korea was thrown into competition with modern countries beginning in the late nineteenth century, the idea of "educated women" began to take on new meaning. At that time, male reformers and intellectuals began to advocate for a "modern" form of schooling for all, including girls and women, in the spirit of distributing new learning (*sin hangmun*) appropriate for the new era.[41] Women also urged the government to establish schools for girls. Most notably, a group of "learned women from the north village in Seoul" distributed a circular letter entitled "After Five Hundred Years," dated September 1, 1898, to gain support for the establishment of a girls' school.[42] They also submitted a "Petition for a Girls' School" to the king, signed on October 10, 1898, urging him to understand the necessity of girls' formal education in strengthening the nation. They referred to "America and many countries in Europe" that "have reached enlightenment and progress by establishing schools for women to teach the various kinds of skills and arts," and asked "why is our country the only one neglecting women's education?"[43] The Korean government (The Taehan Empire, 1897–1910) was not able to establish a public girls' school in response to the above-mentioned petition. It was only in 1908 that the first public school for girls, Hansŏng Kodŭng Yŏhakkyo, was established.[44]

---

[39] Yi Sugin, trans. *Yŏ sasŏ* (The Four Books for Women) (Seoul: Yŏiyŏn, 2003). See also *The Confucian Four Books for Women: A New Translation of the Nü Sishu and the Commentary of Wang Xiang*, ed. and trans. Ann A. Pang-White (Oxford: Oxford University Press, 2018).

[40] Deuchler, "Propagating Female Virtues in Chosŏn Korea," p. 150.

[41] Chŏng Kyŏngsuk, "Taehan cheguk malgi yŏsŏng undong ŭi sŏnggyŏk yŏn'gu" (Characteristics of the Women's Movements in the Late Taehan Empire) (PhD dissertation, Ewha Womans University, 1989), p. 197.

[42] The circular was published with a somewhat paraphrased title, such as "A Circular for the Establishment of a Girls' School" in *Tongnip sinmun*, September 9, 1898.

[43] The petition and the king's written response to that petition were published in several newspapers. Se-mi Oh points to a significant shift in the "the dialogue between the monarch and the people" in the traditional form of petition "from government sector to public sphere as the king came into direct contact with the public through newspapers." See Se-mi Oh, "Letters to the Editor: Women, Newspapers, and the Public Sphere in Turn-of-the-Century Korea," in *Epistolary Korea: Letters in the Communicative Space of the Chosŏn, 1392–1910*, ed. Jahyun Kim Haboush (New York: Columbia University Press, 2009), pp. 157–67, quoted on p. 162.

[44] According to Sonja Kim, in response to the 1898 petition by women, the Korean government "did set aside money in its budget for a girls' school and instituted its Regulation on Girls' Schools in 1899," and this Regulation "laid the groundwork by establishing the purpose and recommending the curriculum of girls' schools." See Sonja Kim, *Imperatives of Care: Women and Medicine in Colonial Korea* (Honolulu: University of Hawai'i Press, 2019), p. 33.

46   Ideology: "Wise Mother, Good Wife"

Before then, it was mostly Western missionaries who opened the schools for girls.[45]

The emerging print media, especially from the 1890s onward, also served as a vehicle for challenging Confucian-prescribed hierarchical gender relations and advocating the critical importance of "educated" women for the family and the nation.[46] Some prominent newspapers, such as the *Tongnip sinmun* (1896–1899) and the *Cheguk sinmun* (1898–1910), and women's magazines, including *Kajŏng chapchi* (1906–1908), *Yŏja chinam* (1908), and *Chasŏn puinhoe chapchi* (1908), chose to publish in the Korean vernacular (*han'gŭl*) rather than in Chinese – the language of the elite for centuries – in order to reach out to as many women as possible and distribute new knowledge (*sin chisik*). Christian magazines and newspapers, such as *Sinhak wŏlbo* (1900–1909), were also important media for the dispersal of new perspectives on both the role of educated women in Korea's advancement to the status of a civilized country and the new ethics of gender relations in the Christian family.[47] Furthermore, after the first appearance of "New Fiction" (*sin sosŏl*)[48] in 1906, when Yi Injik (1862–1916) published the novel *Hyŏl ŭi nu* (Tears of Blood), that genre, along with other print media, engaged in the "woman question" by contributing new imagery of "educated women" at the intersection of enlightenment, nationalism, modernity, and selfhood.[49]

At the core of the new gender discourse during this era was the idea of the "wise mother, good wife" – a new, idealized image of woman who would be

---

[45] For the contribution of American missionaries to women's education in Korea, see Choi, *Gender and Mission Encounters in Korea*, pp. 86–120.

[46] *Tongnip sinmun*, April 21, 1896, September 5, 1896, September 29, 1896, May 18, 1897, May 31, 1899; *Cheguk sinmun*, January 11, 1898; and *Taehan maeil sinbo*, July 2, 1907.

[47] Editorial, *Sinhak wŏlbo* 4, no. 7 (July 1904); "Pubugan chikpun" (Duties and Responsibilities of Husbands and Wives), *Kŭrisŭdo sinmun*, January 10, 1901. Other key pieces that appeared in Christian magazines and newspapers discuss "The Custom of the Inside-Outside Rule," *Sinhak wŏlbo* 3, no. 7 (1903): 187–90, "Education for Women," *Kŭrisdo sinmun*, February 28, 1901, "Questions and Answers about Marriage," *Kŭrisdo sinmun*, August 8, 1901, "The Ways of Husbands and Wives," *Sinhak wŏlbo* 1, no. 3 (1901): 101–4; and "The Vice of the Concubine System," *Sinhak wŏlbo* 1, no. 11 (1901): 437–41. For the translation of some of these articles, see Hyaeweol Choi, "A New Moral Order: Gender Equality in Korean Christianity," in *Religions of Korea in Practice*, ed. Robert E. Buswell Jr. (Princeton: Princeton University Press, 2006), pp. 409–20.

[48] The label *sin sosŏl* first appeared in *Taehan maeil sinbo* (February 1, 1906) in the advertisement of Yi Injik's fiction, *Hyŏl ŭi nu*. For the role of *sin sosŏl* in the formation of new modern subjectivities, see Yoon Sun Yang, *From Domestic Women to Sensitive Young Men: Translating the Individual in Early Colonial Korea* (Cambridge: Harvard University Press, 2017); Susie Jie Young Kim, "The Ambivalence of 'Modernity': Articulation of New Subjectivities in Turn of the Century Korea" (PhD dissertation, University of California Los Angeles, 2002).

[49] It should be noted that not all *sin sosŏl* have the theme of enlightenment and modernity. Although expected to play a key role in educating the public, the *sin sosŏl* also drew criticism because it failed to focus on nationalist-bent agendas and instead explored private, individual, and lascivious emotions. Yi Injik's *Kwi ŭi sŏng* was singled out as an example of bad literature. *Taehan maeil sinbo*, March 14, 1909.

instrumental in creating a strong, modern nation-state. The terminology "wise mother, good wife" (*hyŏnmo yangch'ŏ*) first appeared in Korea in 1906 when Korea was a protectorate of Japan (1905–1910) and Japan was rapidly expanding its control over Korean affairs, including the educational system.[50] The mission statement of Yanggyu Ŭisuk, a private Korean girls' school that followed the Japanese model, stated that the school aimed to "cultivate and perfect the qualifications for a wise mother, good wife (*hyŏnmo yangch'ŏ*) by educating girls with academic work, dexterous skills for craft-making, and womanly virtues of compliance and wisdom (*pudŏk sunch'ŏl*)."[51] The board of directors of Yanggyu Ŭisuk, including the principal, Kwŏn Chunghyŏn, had studied in Japan, and thus it is feasible that they were aware of the discourse of *ryōsai kenbo* that had circulated throughout East Asia. In the case of China, as Joan Judge shows, one of the earliest uses of the term, *liangqi xianmu* (good wives and wise mothers) appeared in 1903 in "a translated excerpt from a treatise by the prominent Japanese educator Yoshimura Toratarō (1848–1917), *Contemporary Japanese Education* (*Nihon genji kyōiku*)." Yoshimura believed that "through their moral and intellectual influence on their children, 'good wives and wise mothers' in all nations are 'the mothers of national enlightenment and civilization'."[52] Those views on the role of women in "civilization and enlightenment" were clearly embedded in the mission statement of Yanggyu Ŭisuk.[53] The first public school for girls, Hansŏng Kodŭng Yŏhakkyo, was the first tangible product of the Japanese colonial policy on women's education pursuant to the Edict of High Education for Girls in April 1908.[54] The goals of Hansŏng Kodŭng Yŏhakkyo also echoed those of Yanggyu Ŭisuk in that the school aimed to train each student to become a "wise companion, benevolent mother" (*hyŏnbae chamo*) by teaching them morality, reading, art, hygiene, nursing skills, childcare, and home economics.[55] These goals significantly reflect the Confucian ideals represented by "womanly

---

[50] For Japanese educational policies during the protectorate era, see Yun Kŏnch'a, *Han'guk kŭndae kyoyuk ŭi sasang kwa undong* (The Ideology of Korean Modern Education and Its Social Movements), trans. Sim Sŏngbo (Seoul: Ch'ŏngsa, 1987), pp. 299–329.

[51] "Chappo" (Miscellaneous), *Taehan maeil sinbo* May 9, 1906, 3; Han'guk yŏsŏng yŏn'guso yŏsŏngsa yŏn'gusil, ed., *Uri yŏsŏng ŭi yŏksa* (Our Women's History) (Seoul: Ch'ŏngnyŏnsa, 1999), p. 264.

[52] Judge, *The Precious Raft of History*, p. 111.

[53] *Taehan maeil sinbo* May 9, 1906, 3. Since its first appearance, enlightenment-oriented national organizations began to use the term, *hyŏnmo yangch'ŏ*. See *T'aegŭk hakpo* 2, September 24, 1906, 12; *Taehan hyŏphoe hoebo* 4, July 25, 1908, 43; *Kiho hŭnghakhoe wŏlbo* 12, July 25, 1909, 11.

[54] The comment of the Japanese vice-minister of education captures the essence of women's education at the time: "It is not necessarily important to offer education to girls. When we do, we offer it only to the extent that facilities are available, and its curriculum should be rudimentary and practical." As a result, girls' education centered on "sewing, embroidery, and homemaking," tasks that were considered appropriate and practical for girls. See Yun, p. 310.

[55] Kim, *Women of Korea*, p. 225; Pak, *Kŭndae yŏsŏng*, pp. 192–3.

virtue," which was systematically propagated, especially after patrilineal social and economic arrangements were adopted and implemented during the Chosŏn dynasty.[56] At the same time, they also exemplified the beginning of the Japanese colonial imprint based on the Meiji gender ideology of *ryōsai kenbo*.

After Korea became a colony of Japan in 1910, the Japanese government systematically promoted the ideology of *ryōsai kenbo* through women's education in colonial Korea.[57] The most consistent and emphatic focus was on the cultivation of "womanly virtue" (*pudŏk*) and good character as a *national* subject (J: *kokumin*; K: *kungmin*). In 1911, the first Edict of Korean Education (1911–1922) proclaimed that girls' higher common schools should educate students "to cultivate 'womanly virtues' (*pudŏk*), build the character as a national subject, and learn knowledge useful to everyday life."[58] In the second Edict of Korean Education (1922–1938), the goals remained very similar to the 1911 Edict with the addition of "physical development" and "proficiency in the national language [Japanese]."[59] The consistent use of the term *pudŏk* as an educational goal makes it clear that, as Theodore Jun Yoo argues, colonial education "promoted a cult of domesticity not for the purpose of fostering modern middle-class womanhood in the Western sense, which included cultivation of moral sensibilities, cultural refinement, and aesthetic taste [*bildung*], but with the sole intent of maintaining Korean women, who were knowledgeable about 'modern ideals,' within the traditional constraints of domesticity."[60] Thus, it is no wonder that graduates of Hansŏng Kodŭng Yŏhakkyo (later Kyŏnggi Yŏja Kodŭng Hakkyo), one of the premier schools for girls during the colonial era, remember the emphasis that was placed on "wise mother, good wife," giving the impression that it was the central theme of their education.[61]

---

[56] Martina Deuchler, *The Confucian Transformation of Korea* (Cambridge: Harvard University Press, 1992); and Kim, *Imperatives of Care*, pp. 17–22.

[57] The connection between Japan's *ryōsai kenbo* and Korea's *hyŏnmo yangch'ŏ* is relatively well-known, especially in the area of Japanese colonial education for women. See Hong, "Ilche sigi Chosŏn ŭi yŏsŏng kyoyuk"; Chang Migyŏng, "Kŭndae Ilbon susin kyogwasŏ e nat'anan yŏsŏng ŭi kŭndaesŏng kwa pan-kŭndaesŏng" (The Modern and Anti-modern Nature of Womanhood Reflected in Ethics Textbooks in Modern Japan), *Ilbon'ŏ munhak* 25 (2005): 219–37; Chŏn Migyŏng, "1920–30-nyŏndae hyŏnmo yangch'ŏ e kwanhan yŏn'gu" (A Study of Wise Mother, Good Wife in the 1920s and 1930s), *Han'guk kajŏng kwalli hakhoeji* 22, no. 3 (2004): 75–93.

[58] The original text reads: "女子高等普通學校ハ女子ニ高等ノ普通教育ヲ爲ス所ニシテ婦德ヲ養ヒ國民タルノ性格ヲ陶冶シ其ノ生活ニ有用ナル知識技能ヲ授ク"; http://contents.history.go.kr/front/hm/view.do?treeId=010704&tabId=01&levelId=hm_141_0010; and An T'aeyun, *Singmin chŏngch'i wa mosŏng* (Colonial Politics and Motherhood) (P'aju: Han'guk haksul chŏngbo, 2006), p. 93.

[59] The original text reads: "女子高等普通學校ハ女生徒ノ身體ノ發達及婦德ノ涵養ニ留意シテ之ニ德育ヲ施シ生活ニ有用ナル普通ノ知識技能ヲ授ケ國民タルノ性格ヲ養成シ國語ニ熟達セシムルコトヲ目的トス"; http://contents.history.go.kr/front/hm/view.do?treeId=010704&tabId=01&levelId=hm_141_0010.

[60] Yoo, *The Politics of Gender*, p. 70.   [61] An, *Singmin chŏngch'i wa mosŏng*, pp. 184, 194.

At the same time, it is also important to recognize that the emphasis on *pudŏk* was not a simple repetition of Confucian prescriptions for women. In particular, there was a significant shift in emphasis in the modern era away from wifely duties and toward motherly ones. In her analysis of distinctive traits of "womanly virtue" in the Chosŏn dynasty, Sonja Kim argues that *pudŏk* was oriented "primarily toward their husband's affines ... the role prioritized for them [women] was that of daughter-in-law and not necessarily mother." Furthermore, "[w]omen may have performed some of the tasks that contributed to the operations of a household but the main targets of *kajŏng* [governing the household] instructions were men."[62] A quite similar phenomenon is also found in the Edo period (1603–1867). Based on analysis of instructional texts for girls (*jokunsho*) from the Edo period, Koyama Shizuko notes that "the ideal woman portrayed in the *jokunsho* of the Edo period was mainly that of a good wife and daughter-in-law, and the main virtue demanded of her in that respect was that of submission to her husband and parents-in-law." She goes on to point out that "it was fathers who were responsible for children's education."[63] What took place in the transition into the modern era was a shift in emphasis from the role of wife and daughter-in-law to the role of mother, and particularly to the role of mother as caregiver and educator of the next generation. Koyama points out that the novel and distinctive aspect of *ryōsai kenbo* in the Meiji era lies in the cultivation of women as "citizens of the nation" in their capacity as educators of children. Women were assigned this new responsibility for the good of the nation-state, and that is what justified formal education for girls.[64]

One of the central goals of the Japanese colonial educational policy was to build character "as a national subject" (*kungmin*). It meant learning how to be loyal and obedient imperial subjects of the Japanese empire. From the beginning, Japanese colonial authorities were keenly aware of the critical role women would play in bringing about social harmony as the foundation of colonial governance. They believed that turning Korean women into loyal Japanese subjects would be the fastest way to achieve social integration.[65] "Womanly virtue" was promoted in this broader context of assimilation policy. To prepare them for their roles as mothers, women were trained in the basic knowledge appropriate for them to reproduce and raise children to be industrious, obedient imperial subjects, with knowledge of the Japanese language, Japanese ethics, and practical skills.[66]

---

[62] Kim, *Imperatives of Care*, pp. 19, 21, 22.   [63] Koyama, *Ryōsai Kenbo*, p. 21.
[64] Koyama, *Ryōsai Kenbo*, pp. 23–6, 49.
[65] Hong, "Ilche sigi Chosŏn ŭi yŏsŏng kyoyuk," 236.
[66] Kumamoto Shigekichi, "Kyohwa ŭigyŏnsŏ" (An Opinion on Education), September 8, 1910, quoted in *Ilche kangjŏmgi chonggyo chŏngch'eksa charyojip* (A Sourcebook of the Religious Policies during the Japanese Colonial Era), ed. Kim Sŭngt'ae (Seoul: Han'guk kidokkyo yŏksa yŏn'guso, 1996), pp. 29–41. For a comparative study of the Japanese colonial education system in Taiwan and Korea, see E. Patricia Tsurumi, "Colonial Education in Korea and Taiwan," in *The Japanese Colonial Empire, 1895–1945*, eds. Ramon H. Myers and Mark R. Peattie (Princeton: Princeton University Press, 1984), pp. 275–311.

However, in spite of the rhetoric about the importance of education for girls and women, educational opportunities for the colonized Koreans was exceedingly limited.[67] The vast majority of girls and women received no education at all. In 1919, only 2.2 percent of girls entered public elementary schools (compared to 10.2 percent for boys). Ten years later, the percentage had increased to only 7.9 percent (compared to 30.9 percent for boys).[68] Out of this small number of elementary school graduates, roughly one-fifth advanced to middle school. The scarcity of "educated" female students throughout the colonial era is in drastic contrast to the higher rate of school attendance among Japanese female students. Japan mandated primary education for both boys and girls beginning in 1872, and by 1920, 98.8 percent of Japanese girls were enrolled in primary school.[69]

Although a similar gender ideology was in place in both Korea and Japan, the significant disparity in educational opportunities for girls led to different outcomes. While the Japanese gender ideology of *ryōsai kenbo* "gradually replaced the premodern differentiation of women by class,"[70] the ideology of *hyŏnmo yangch'ŏ* that transpired in colonial education in Korea evolved into a marker of middle-class women, serving to distinguish them from the vast majority of women, who were low-income urban dwellers, factory workers, or peasants. In this vein, socialist intellectuals criticized the bourgeois nature of "wise mother, good wife." For example, Chŏng Ch'ilsŏng (1897–1958) contrasted well-educated bourgeois women and their presumably decadent lifestyle with working-class women in the cigarette and textile factories, who had little or no education and had to labor in terrible conditions merely to survive.[71] In a similar fashion, Kim Ŭnhŭi details the miserable lives of proletarian women, noting that "in their family life mired in poverty, every day proletarian women (*musan puin*) struggle to provide meals and wood for heating. They do not even have enough time to nurse their children crying out from hunger." In contrast, bourgeois women are described as "housewives who lead leisurely lives without shedding a drop of sweat." Although "educated mothers" were publicly lauded, Kim urged people to see the reality in which proletarian women could not even afford the opportunity to gain basic literacy because

---

[67] Yun, *Han'guk kŭndae kyoyuk*, p. 310.
[68] Kim Kyŏngil, *Yŏsŏng ŭi kŭndae, kŭndae ŭi yŏsŏng* (Modernity of Women, Women of Modernity) (Seoul: P'urŭn yŏksa, 2004), p. 281.
[69] Elizabeth Knipe Mouer, "Women in Teaching," in *Women in Changing Japan*, eds. Joyce Lebra, Joy Paulson, and Elizabeth Powers (Stanford: Stanford University Press, 1976), p. 161.
[70] Sharon H. Nolte and Sally Ann Hastings, "The Meiji State's Policy Toward Women, 1890–1910," in *Recreating Japanese Women, 1600–945*, ed. Gail Lee Bernstein (Berkeley: University of California Press, 1991), pp. 172–3.
[71] Chŏng Ch'ilsŏng, "Amnal ŭl parabonŭn puin nodongja" (Woman Laborers and their Vision for the Future), *Tonggwang* 29 (December 1931): 70.

they had to struggle daily just to sustain themselves.[72] Despite the growing criticism of "educated" women and their complacent, privileged lifestyle, the Korean model of "wise mother, good wife" remained a gender ideology closely associated with the middle class, accepted by and expected of those women who had garnered formal education in colonial Korea. Significantly, when there were few jobs for women, becoming a "wise mother, good wife" represented the most realistic "career option" available to the small cohort of educated women.[73] In this vein, "home economics" became the most coveted and competitive major field for talented women in colonial Korea.[74]

Together with the influence from Japanese gender ideology, Western Protestant women missionaries, largely from the United States, also shaped the modern gender ideology of "wise mother, good wife." Mary F. Scranton (1832–1909), the first American Methodist woman missionary, landed in Korea in 1885 and founded Ewha Haktang, the very first school for girls in Korean history, in 1886, and ever since that time American Protestant women missionaries (largely Methodists and Presbyterians) have had a significant impact on the lives of Korean women, particularly in the field of women's education.[75] Mission schools represented part of a larger strategy to spread the Gospel. Furthermore, education was regarded as "women's work" and thus became a major focus for women missionaries, not only in Korea but elsewhere.[76] Since Korean reformers established girls' schools relatively slowly, despite their rhetoric about the value of women's education, Korea proved to be a fertile ground for the mission to have lasting impact.[77] Further, as Horace G. Underwood (1859–1916), a Presbyterian missionary from the United States, wrote, during the colonial era, the "Japanese government in Korea avowedly does not propose to provide much beyond the grammar grade

---

[72] Kim Ŭnhŭi, "Musan puin undongnon" (On the Movement of Proletarian Women), *Samch'ŏlli* 4, no. 2 (1932): 64–7.
[73] Song Yŏnok, "Chosŏn 'sin yŏsŏng' ŭi naesyŏnŏllijŭm kwa chendŏ" (Gender and Nationalism of the "New Woman" in Korea) in *Sin yŏsŏng*, ed. Mun Okp'yo (Seoul: Ch'ŏngnyŏnsa, 2003), pp. 83–117.
[74] Hong, "Ilche sigi Chosŏn ŭi yŏsŏng kyoyuk," 252–53. The middle-class orientation of "wise mother, good wife" has been perpetuated, moreover, in the activities of the Korean Federation of Housewives' Clubs (Taehan Chubu K'ŭllŏp Yŏnhaphoe), which was founded in 1966 with the goal of enlightening middle-class housewives. The group even instituted an annual award, the Sin Saimdang prize, in 1968. See Kim, "Chŏnt'ong ŭi ch'angan kwa yŏsŏng ŭi kungminhwa," 240. Furthermore, in the aforementioned 2007 TV drama, "New Wise Mother, Good Wife," the first episode begins with a classroom scene at an elementary school. A girl student presents in front of her class that her dream is to become a "wise mother, good wife." The almost naturalized and taken-for-granted image of ideal womanhood embedded in the term, "wise mother, good wife" embodied by the historical figure, Lady Sin Saimdang, has been a "career option" for women from the colonial era into the twenty-first century.
[75] Choi, *Gender and Mission Encounters in Korea*.
[76] Dana L. Robert, *American Women in Mission: A Social History of Their Thought and Practice* (Macon: Mercer University Press, 1996), pp. 81–124, 160–62.
[77] Editorial, *Tongnip sinmun*, May 12, 1896.

alleging that the mentality of the Koreans is of such a low grade that the few exceptionally bright ones can secure their higher education in Tokyo."[78] Because there were very few institutions of higher education, especially ones open to women, mission schools took the lead in educating the next generation of women beginning in the late-nineteenth century and continuing through the first half of the twentieth century.[79] As a result, at the turn of the twentieth century the vast majority of Korean women who had modern education up to the level of middle school were linked with Christianity because they attended and/or taught at mission schools or became involved in Christian organizations, such as the Korea YWCA.[80] Chu Yosŏp (1902–1972), a public intellectual during the colonial era, regarded the opportunity to receive a "modern education" as a criterion that distinguished "new women" (*sin yŏsŏng*) from "old-fashioned women" (*ku yŏsŏng*). According to his definition, the vast majority of "new women" had ties with Christian schools and societies.[81] In her discussion of the women's movement in Korea, Hwang Sindŏk (1898–1983), a graduate of Sungŭi Yŏhakkyo, a mission school in P'yŏngyang, commented that since the opening of Korea to other countries in the late-nineteenth century, "almost all women over thirty who were educated and had worked in society had been exposed to Christianity, even if it was only minor contact."[82] In this way, Christian-educated women often took center stage in setting agendas and activities for the women's movement in Korea.

Given the prominence of Christian-educated women in modern Korean history, it is not surprising to find American women missionaries hailed in Korean historiography as pioneers who ushered in new models of gender

---

[78] October 12, 1911, letter of H.G. Underwood to Arthur Brown, Record Group 140, pp. 11–26, Presbyterian Historical Society (hereafter PHS), Philadelphia. See also Tsurumi, "Colonial Education in Korea and Taiwan," pp. 294–308.

[79] Especially for education at the middle school level, the oppressive policy of the colonial government resulted in the greater role of mission schools in meeting the demand of Koreans. Kim, *Yŏsŏng ŭi kŭndae, kŭndae ŭi yŏsŏng*, pp. 280–85.

[80] Ch'ŏn Hwasuk, *Han'guk yŏsŏng kidokkyo sahoe undongsa* (History of the Social Movement of Korean Christian Women) (Seoul: Hyean, 2000).

[81] Chu Yosŏp, "Sin yŏsŏng kwa ku yŏsŏng ŭi haengno" (The Ways of the New Woman and the Old-fashioned Woman) *Sin yŏsŏng* 7, no. 1 (January 1933): 32–5. The definition of the "new woman" (*sin yŏsŏng* or *sin yŏja*) in Korea varies. Kim Sujin detects two major trends in defining the "new woman" in Korea: one uses the label for an actual, collective group. In the popular imagination, the concept of the "new woman" often refers to a small number of elite women represented by Na Hyesŏk, Kim Myŏngsun, Kim Wŏnju, Yun Simdŏk, Kim Hwallan, and Pak Indŏk, who became prominent figures in art, literature, education, or journalism in the 1920s. The other trend focuses on the discursive formation of the image of the "new woman," largely through the print media. However, it should also be noted that within each trend, one can see subtle variations on the "new woman," depending on characteristics of education, attitude, ideology, and occupation. See Kim, "1920-30-nyŏndae sin yŏsŏng," pp. 1–19.

[82] Hwang Sindŏk, "Chosŏn puin undong ŭn ŏttŏk'e chinaewanna" (How has the Korean Women's Movement Developed), *Sin kajŏng* (April 1933): 22–3, quoted in *Yŏsŏng ŭi kŭndae, kŭndae ŭi yŏsŏng*, p. 74.

roles based on conceptions of Christian gender equality and Western modernity.[83] However, the imagined role of Christianity and Western modernity in constructing a new gender ideology should be examined within the context of the prevailing gender norms in both American society and foreign missionary organizations at the time. It is also important to keep one key question in mind: What constituted modern womanhood in the minds of American women missionaries? One way to answer this key question is to examine the significance of the notion of "woman's work for woman," a motto prominent among women missionaries.

"Woman's work for woman" identified a separate sphere for women missionaries within the foreign mission enterprise, one in which women were precluded from the right to ordination and were channeled into the care of women and children.[84] This work assignment grew out of the prevailing gender ideology in the United States, which privileged religious piety, domesticity, purity, and submissiveness.[85] Significantly, this gender ideology of domesticity went hand in hand with the nineteenth century's singular notion of civilization being primarily informed by a worldview based in Christian and Enlightenment ethics.[86] In her analysis of American missionaries in Ottoman Europe, historian

---

[83] Yi Paeyong with the cooperation of Son Sŭnghŭi, Mun Sukchae, and Cho Kyŏngwŏn, "Han'guk kidokkyo yŏsŏng kyoyuk ŭi sŏnggwa wa chŏnmang – Ihwa Yŏja Taehakkyo rŭl chungsim ŭro" (Accomplishment and Prospect of Korean Christian Education for Women – With a Focus on Ewha Womans University), *Ihwa sahak yŏn'gu* 27 (2000): 9–36.

[84] Jane Hunter, *The Gospel of Gentility: American Women Missionaries in Turn-of-the-Century China* (New Haven: Yale University Press, 1984); Patricia R. Hill, *The World Their Household: The American Woman's Foreign Mission Movement and Cultural Transformation, 1870–1920* (Ann Arbor: University of Michigan Press, 1985); Leslie A. Flemming, ed., *Women's Work for Women: Missionaries and Social Change in Asia* (Boulder: Westview Press, 1989); Kwok Pui-lan, *Chinese Women and Christianity 1860–1927* (Atlanta: Scholars Press, 1992); Gael Graham, *Gender, Culture, and Christianity: American Protestant Mission Schools in China 1880–1930* (New York: Peter Lang, 1995); Dana Robert, *American Women in Mission: A Social History of Their Thought and Practice* (Macon: Mercer University Press, 1996); Susan Thorne, *Congregational Missions and the Making of an Imperial Culture in Nineteenth-Century England* (Stanford: Stanford University Press, 1999); Mary Taylor Huber and Nancy Lutkehaus, eds., *Gendered Missions: Women and Men in Missionary Discourse and Practice* (Ann Arbor: University of Michigan Press, 1999); Maina Chawla Singh, *Gender, Religion, and "Heathen Lands": American Missionary Women in South Asia (1860s–1940s)* (New York: Garland Publishing, Inc., 2000); Karen K. Seat, *"Providence Has Freed Our Hands": Women's Missions and the American Encounter with Japan* (Syracuse: Syracuse University Press, 2008); Barbara Reeves-Ellington, Kathryn Kish Sklar, and Connie A. Shemo, eds., *Competing Kingdoms: Women, Mission, Nation, and the American Protestant Empire, 1812–1960* (Durham: Duke University Press, 2010); and Hyaeweol Choi and Margaret Jolly, eds., *Divine Domesticities: Christian Paradoxes in Asia and the Pacific* (Canberra: ANU Press, 2014).

[85] Barbara Welter, "The Cult of True Womanhood: 1820–1860," *American Quarterly* 18, no. 2 (Summer 1966): 151–74; "She Hath Done What She Could: Protestant Women's Missionary Careers in Nineteenth-Century America," *American Quarterly* 30 (Winter 1978): 624–38.

[86] Prasenjit Duara, "The Discourse of Civilization and Pan-Asianism," *Journal of World History* 12, no. 1 (2001): 99–130.

Barbara Reeves-Ellington notes that: "Evangelical Christian Americans believed that the United States was at the pinnacle of progress as a Protestant Republic where Christian women were educated and charged with the responsibility of shaping the character of the home and the nation by raising future generations. Domestic discourse established the moral authority of white, middle-class Protestant women within the home as the household became the 'empire of the mother'."[87] Women missionaries shared a sense of urgency about the need to spread Christian civilization to the entire world to rescue "heathen" women and children and create "Christian homes."[88] Especially in those countries that maintained the custom of keeping the genders separate, the role of women missionaries became vital in distributing the Gospel to local women because male missionaries did not have permission to interact with them. In the case of Korea, the culturally prescribed gender roles, expressed in the Confucian norm of the "distinction between man and woman" (*namnyŏ yubyŏl*), assigned women to the domestic arena and men to the public domain. This distinction manifested itself spatially in the architecture of the home – women stayed in inner chambers (*anbang*), and men in outer chambers (*sarangbang*).[89] William Scranton, the son of Mary F. Scranton, reported that "the seclusion of women in Korea has made this temporary separation in the places of worship necessary," and that the mission work for Korean women was "in the hands of the ladies of the WFM [Woman's Foreign Missionary] Society."[90] As Chapter 2 details, the creation of a "Christian home" became a central goal of "woman's work for woman" in which the role of the woman was valorized as the "moral arbiter" in nurturing children and fostering a loving conjugal relationship.[91] Women missionaries actively engaged in distributing and articulating the ideal of "domesticity" and "Christian home" in their interaction with Korean women. They largely succeeded in their primary goal, as affirmed by Yang Chusam (aka J. S. Ryang, 1876–?), a leading

---

[87] Barbara Reeves-Ellington, "Embracing Domesticity: Women, Mission, and Nation Building in Ottoman Europe, 1832–1872," in *Competing Kingdoms*, pp. 269–92, quoted on p. 270.

[88] After World War I, the gendered division of labor in the foreign mission came to be challenged for the first time. See Ruth Compton Brouwer, *Modern Women Modernizing Men: The Changing Missions of Three Professional Women in Asia and Africa, 1902–69* (Vancouver: University of British Columbia Press, 2002); Hill, *The World Their Household*.

[89] Laurel Kendall and Mark Peterson, eds., *Korean Women: View from the Inner Room* (New Haven: East Rock Press, 1983). See especially "Introduction" by Kendall and Peterson (pp. 5–21) and "Women, Men, Inside, Outside" by Clark Sorensen (pp. 63–79).

[90] W. B. Scranton, "Report of Pastor, Baldwin Chapel and Ewa Hak Tang – 1893," Minutes of the Ninth Annual Meeting of the Korea Mission of the Methodist Episcopal Church (1893), pp. 44–6. See also Huldah A. Haenig, "From West Gate to East Gate," *Woman's Missionary Friend* 43, no. 1 (January 1911): 9–11.

[91] Dana Robert, "The 'Christian Home' as a Cornerstone of Anglo-American Missionary Thought and Practice," in *Converting Colonialism: Visions and Realities in Mission History, 1706–1914*, ed. Dana Robert (Grand Rapids, Michigan: William B. Eerdmans Publishing Company, 2008), pp. 134–65.

Korean Christian of that time, who praised the role of women missionaries in bringing forth "true Christian homes" that "dignified the wife and raised the mother to a higher plane."[92]

The ways in which Confucian "womanly virtue," Meiji Japan's *ryōsai kenbo*, and the American gender ideology of domesticity intersected with one another in Korea should be understood within the context of Japan's burgeoning colonialism, Korea's struggle to modernize itself and regain national sovereignty, and the height of Western imperialism in political, economic, and moral spheres. Although they were rooted in different historical circumstances, these gender ideologies found both comparable and distinctive practices in one another's notions of ideal womanhood, and, ultimately, they each contributed to what would come to constitute ideal modern womanhood. In the next section, I delve into the ways in which the interactions among Korean, Japanese, and American gender ideologies in the contact zone challenged, reinforced, or appropriated gender rules, and discuss how the ideal of "wise mother, good wife" possessed both oppressive and liberating traits, depending on each woman's particular perspective on "modern" womanhood.

Modern Cult of Domesticity

When American women missionaries first arrived in Korea, they criticized the "oppressive" nature of the Confucian gender rules imposed on Korean women. They were shocked by the confinement of Korean women to the inner chambers, the lack of formal educational opportunities, and the practice in which individual women did not even receive names. They described a "heathen" womanhood that rendered the woman "unworthy of a name, a creature without rights or responsibilities, only a convenient adjunct to some man – his daughter, his wife, his mother."[93] They often characterized Korean women pejoratively as deeply ignorant and superstitious.[94] Women missionaries certainly felt much more liberated in comparison. After all, they were educated, had the freedom to work in public, and traveled overseas. However, despite being proud of this "liberated" status, women missionaries largely embraced the idea of having a separate sphere of "woman's work for woman," centered on domesticity and with particular emphasis on religious piety. This orientation toward "domestic

---

[92] J. S. Ryang, "Foreword," in *Fifty Years of Light*, prepared by the Missionaries of the Woman's Foreign Missionary Society of the Methodist Episcopal Church in Commemoration of the Completion of Fifty Years of Work in Korea (Seoul, 1938).

[93] Mrs. E. W. Rice, "A Woman of Korea," *Heathen Woman's Friend* 17, no. 8 (February 1886): 182–3; Mrs. T. J. Gracey, "Something about the Koreans," *Heathen Woman's Friend* 23, no. 12 (June 1892): 282–3; Ellasue Wagner, "Girls and Women in Korea," *Korea Mission Field* 4, no. 6 (June 1908): 82; Haenig, "From West Gate to East Gate," 9–11.

[94] Josephine Paine and Lulu Frey, "Ewa Haktang, Seoul," Annual Report of the Korea Woman's Conference of the Methodist Episcopal Church (May 1903), pp. 7–9.

Ideology: "Wise Mother, Good Wife"

feminism," which meant "women using domestic credentials to enhance their position in the family or in the society,"[95] provided a link with Korean reformers, who were keenly interested in the enlightenment of Korean women to the benefit of the nation but envisioned a "new" role for women as educated wives and mothers in the domestic sphere. The overall Japanese colonial policy on girls' education also centered on domesticity and practical knowledge with special focus on "morality" (*susin*) in order to assimilate Koreans into the Japanese empire. Through the curriculum of *susin*, the ideals of "wise mother" and "good wife" were actively promoted, often with Japanese women featured as exemplary models whom Korean girls were expected to emulate.[96] Ultimately, missionary women's advocacy of the "divine art of home-making,"[97] the Korean reformers' vision of the modern ideal Korean women as educated mothers, and the Japanese state's policies designed to produce obedient female imperial subjects converged to construct a gender ideology that placed a heavy emphasis on domesticity for women.[98]

This emphasis on the domestic proved to be a strategic advantage for the Korea mission. In the beginning of the mission in the late-nineteenth century, the Korean public feared that American women missionaries and their educational work would turn Korean girls into "American ladies" who would defy Korean customs and be uninterested in learning domestic skills. In response to this anxiety, the missionaries publicly emphasized the elements of domesticity in their curriculum for Korean girls. Emily Haynes (1877–?), a Methodist missionary, reported in 1910: "Having heard the fear expressed on more than one occasion that if the girls were educated they would not learn to sew, cook, and do other household tasks, we decided to put it to the test. Accordingly on the last half day of the winter term we had an exhibit of the girls' sewing.... Not a hint have we heard since that the girls would not know how to sew."[99] In addition, missionaries stressed that they came to Korea to help produce "better Koreans" with "home-grown Christian characters."[100] Annie Baird (1864–1916), a Presbyterian missionary, precisely expressed this caution.

---

[95] Daniel Scott Smith, "Family Limitation, Sexual Control, and Domestic Feminism in Victorian America," in *Clio's Consciousness Raised*, eds. Mary Hartman and Lois W. Banner (New York: Harper & Row, 1974), quoted in Glenna Matthews, *"Just a Housewife": The Rise and Fall of Domesticity in America* (New York: Oxford University Press, 1987), p. 28.

[96] Kim Sunjŏn and Chang Migyŏng, "'Pot'ong hakkyo susinsŏ' rŭl t'onghae pon yŏsŏng myosa" (Portrayal of Women Reflected in "Book of Moral Education for Common School"), in *Cheguk ŭi singminji susin* (Empire's Moral Cultivation of the Colonized), et al. Kim Sunjŏn (Seoul: Cheiaenssi, 2008), pp. 304–24.

[97] Mary Swale Wilkinson, "The Place of the Missionary Training School," *Woman's Missionary Friend* 35, no. 11 (November 1903): 384–85.

[98] Yoo, *The Politics of Gender*, pp. 58–94.

[99] Emily Irene Haynes, "Union Academy School and Evangelistic Work on Pyeng Yang District," Annual Report of the Korea Woman's Conference of the Methodist Episcopal Church (1910), pp. 55–60.

[100] Annie Baird, "Higher Education of Women in Korea," *Korea Mission Field* 8, no. 4 (1912): 113–16.

She wrote: "We want a system which will train young women and yet leave them indigenous, their thoughts and affections deep in Mother Korea, who can reach out on all sides and draw to themselves other girls and young women in whom they can instill their own home-grown Christian characters, and to whom they can impart the training they have themselves received."[101]

The focus on domesticity and indigenous Korean character is most clearly manifested in the curriculum of mission schools that put particular emphasis on domestic science as a key subject, in addition to the Bible and Christian teachings. Josephine Paine and Lulu Frey, teachers at Ewha Girls' School in Seoul, stated that the aim of their school "is not only to educate the girls and lift them out of the ignorance and superstition in which the Korean woman is found, but also to teach them to be good house wives with cleanly habits."[102] Velma Snook (1866–1960), the principal of Pyeng Yang Academy for Young Women (P'yŏngyang Sungŭi Yŏhakkyo), proudly reported that "amid many discouragements and trials our hearts are made glad when we hear that Koreans say 'When you want a good cook for a wife go to the Women's Academy in Pyeng Yang,' and that the 'graduates of the Kindergarten Training Dep't are in great demand both as teachers and wives'."[103] The establishment of the "Self Help Department" at mission schools, which was originally designed as a work-study program to help poor students pay tuition by selling sewing and embroidery, also served as a platform for displaying the domesticity and femininity of their students to the public through regular exhibitions of the students' needlework.[104] The schools invited patrons and the general public to see that girl students "were learning to use their hands as well as their heads."[105] In addition to domestic skills, students received "lessons in neatness and cleanliness and obedience," and "their going and coming, receiving of visitors and such things [at the dormitory] have been given closer oversight."[106]

---

[101] Baird, "Higher Education of Women in Korea."

[102] Josephine Paine and Lulu Frey, "Ewa Haktang, Seoul," Annual Report of the Korea Woman's Conference of the Methodist Episcopal Church (May 1903), pp. 7–9, quoted on p. 7.

[103] Velma Snook, "Annual Report for 1928–29," Record Group 360, PHS.

[104] "Self Help Departments" at mission schools functioned as a financial device to support poor students by selling their needle work and crafts overseas. See Elizabeth M. Campbell, *After Fifty Years: A Record of the Work of the P.W.M.U. of Victoria* (Melbourne: Spectator Publishing, 1940), pp. 21–22.

[105] Velma Snook, letter (no exact date indicated but it was filed on June 26, 1913), Record Group 140, pp. 11–13, PHS. To some students, earnings from their embroidery or sewing were crucial for continuing to study because they could muster no other financial resources. Missionary teachers "supervised, bought materials for, found a market for, and managed the business end of the work in the self-help department, which provided board and a little extra money for needy students." Anna Bergman managed the department particularly well with "a lot of thinking and planning to get the work ready for them and to sell it fast enough." Anna Bergman, March 28, 1931, Record Group 360, PHS.

[106] Velma Snook, "Pyeng Yang Union Academy for Women, 1911–1912," Record Group 140, pp. 7–28, PHS.

The displays of domesticity and strict discipline not only reassured a skeptical public but were also an important tool in recruiting future students. Missionary teachers proudly noted that "we have already heard of some of the women who went home [after viewing the exhibit] saying that they had thought that girls who went to school did not know how to sew, but they had found out that they could do even better than others so they were going to send their daughters to us."[107] In 1940, a half-century after the introduction of Protestantism into Korea, a Methodist missionary teacher, Ellasue Wagner (1881–?), claimed that "the ideal woman of Korea to-day is, as it should be, the ideal wife and mother. We believe that there is no higher destiny than this. We remember the old saying that 'the hand that rocks the cradle rules the world.' In Korea to-day, however, there is a new realization of the fact that the woman who wields this influence needs the best of education and training. We have heard it said over and over lately that the best families now demand an educated daughter-in-law."[108]

In this way, by consistently extolling the model of good wife and wise mother, the mission schools offered a model of female education that went hand in hand with Korean reformers' emphasis on the sacred role of mother as the core of a good female education.[109] Yi Kwangsu (1892–1950), a novelist and leading reformer, asserted that "the only duty that women have to humankind, to the nation and to society is to become good mothers and raise good children, and only women can do this. If a nation wants to produce good citizens, it first has to cultivate good mothers. Especially in a case like Korea, where the population urgently needs to reform its national character, there is a particular need for many good mothers."[110] A prominent Christian woman intellectual, Hwang Sindŏk (1898–1983), echoed Yi's call to center women's education on motherhood when she envisioned a new model of the mother in colonial Korea. She wrote that Korea is "waiting for strong-willed mothers ... to raise children who could transform Korea from its miserable condition to the glorious future."[111] In this way, the "good mother," a model appropriate for the reconstruction of the nation, deeply resonated with the missionary emphasis on the role of mother as the moral arbiter in creating a "Christian home" that would raise "better Koreans."

---

[107] Velma Snook, letter (no exact date but was filed on June 26, 1913), Record Group 360, PHS.
[108] Ellasue Wagner, "Then and Now Founders' Day at Holston Institute May 15th, 1940," *Korea Mission Field* 36, no. 8 (1940): 133–5, quoted on 134.
[109] Yi Kwangsu, "Mosŏng chungsim ŭi yŏja kyoyuk" (Women's Education Centering on Motherhood), *Sin yŏsŏng* 3, no. 1 (1925): 19–20; "Mosŏng ŭro ŭi yŏja" (Woman as Mother), *Yŏsŏng* 1, no. 3 (June 1936): 8.
[110] Yi, "Mosŏng chungsim ŭi yŏja kyoyuk," 19–20.
[111] Hwang Sindŏk, "Chosŏn ŭn irŏhan ŏmŏni rŭl yoguhanda" (Korea Demands This Type of Mother), *Sin kajŏng* (May 1933): 12–15.

The connection between domesticity and modern education put the focus on scientific homemaking and childrearing. The "modern" version of the "wise mother, good wife" should know how to raise children and manage the home scientifically. Since the opening of the nation in the late-nineteenth century, hygiene, nutrition, and scientific childrearing had come to be viewed as hallmarks of modernity and a necessary step on Korea's path to becoming an advanced civilization. To that end, a set of women's magazines, such as *Kajŏng chapchi* and *Chasŏn puinhoe chapchi*, provided a variety of information, ranging from ways to prevent disease and hygienically preserve food to the proper care of children.[112] In the 1920s and 1930s, women's magazines such as *Sin yŏsŏng*, *Sin kajŏng*, and *Yŏsŏng* poured out detailed information about scientific homemaking and childrearing, reinforcing the new mandate that women raise healthy children to be the future citizens of the modern nation-state.[113] Hwang Sindŏk urged Korean women to carefully observe their children. She wrote: "A mother who does not know her son's physical constitution, personality, taste, and goals in life is no different from a wet nurse. She must know what kind of exercise is good for his body, what kinds of toys suit his taste, and what pedagogical methods would maximize his ability to learn."[114] Like Hwang Sindŏk, an emerging group of experts, trained overseas and armed with modern scientific knowledge, played a crucial role in shaping the new modern family and the role of women within the family. Chapter 2 further probes the emergence of "home economics" as a scholarly discipline, describing how the transpacific network of Christian organizations played a key role in distributing the ideology of modern domesticity that brought with it new, scientific ways of managing the home and caring for children, the aesthetics of home interior design, and advice on how best to use family leisure time.

In addition, the modern perspective on domesticity included a denouncement of "superstitions." Western pundits commenting on "Eastern civilization" regarded the "ignorance and superstition of the women" as "the one insurmountable obstacle to the improvement of society in those countries."[115] The link between women and superstition came to bear connotations of backwardness and inferiority as problems to overcome.[116] Among the traditional Korean

---

[112] *Kajŏng chapchi* 1, no. 3 (1906): 6–8; *Chasŏn puin hoe chapchi* 1 (August 1908): 23–5.
[113] Yi Hwayŏng et al., *Han'guk kŭndae yŏsŏng ŭi ilsang munhwa* (The Everyday Life and Culture of the Korean Modern Woman), vol. 8 (Seoul: Kukhak Charyowŏn, 2004).
[114] Hwang, "Chosŏn ŭn irŏhan ŏmŏni rŭl yoguhanda."
[115] Susan B. Anthony and Elizabeth Cady Stanton, "The Kansas Campaign, 1867," quoted in Sharon L. Sievers, *Flowers in Salt: The Beginnings of Feminist Consciousness in Modern Japan* (Stanford: Stanford University Press, 1983), p. 10.
[116] Kim Yunsŏng, "1920-30-nyŏndae Han'guk sahoe ŭi chonggyo wa yŏsŏng tamnon: 'misin t'ap'a' wa 'hyŏnmo yangch'ŏ' rŭl chungsim ŭro" (Religion and Gender Discourse in 1920s and 1930s Korea: With a Focus on "Eradication of Superstition" and "Wise Mother, Good Wife"), *Chonggyo munhwa pip'yŏng* 9 (2008): 164–90. What is fascinating about this analysis is that regardless of race, women are often lumped together as the inferior gender easily subjected to

religious beliefs and practices, shamanism was viewed as the quintessential example of superstition. Numerous missionary articles testified to the phenomenon of "demon possession" and to shamanist rituals performed to drive evil spirits away. Missionaries decried shamanism and portrayed shamans as evil, greedy, manipulative, and the "obedient servant[s] of Satan."[117] Annie Baird offered a vivid portrait of a "heathen" woman in a fictionalized story, entitled *Daybreak in Korea*. In the story, the female protagonist resorts to the "magical power" of a greedy shaman when her baby daughter contracts smallpox, and, ultimately, the daughter dies.[118] Another missionary, Ellasue Wagner, condemned the horror that ignorance and superstition brought upon children:

Where ignorance and superstition prevail the burden is always heaviest on the helpless children. The fact that mother and father are devoted to their children and would give their very lives for them does not make any less dangerous the unsanitary conditions of the home, nor can that devotion mitigate their disobedience to every law of hygiene and common sense.... To whom can the mother go for help when the baby is sick? Probably, unless she is a Christian, she will think first of the sorceress, the mudang, for she has been taught all her life that sickness is the work of evil spirits and these must be driven out before there can be any relief.[119]

Offering a clear contrast between educated Christian women and ignorant "pagan" women, Wagner suggests that motherly devotion and love are no longer sufficient for good childrearing. A mother had to be educated, equipped with scientific knowledge for childrearing, and steered away from old practices based on the recommendations of shamans. In their attempt to encourage Korean women to use Christian childrearing techniques, women missionaries offered formal and informal lessons about the "care of children" at mission schools and local churches.[120] As the number of educated women in Korea increased, Korean women themselves began to identify superstition as a marker of backwardness. Kim Sŏkcha, managing director of the woman's magazine *Chasŏn puinhoe chapchi*, criticized Korean women's tendency to rely on the power of ghosts for luck and waste their resources on visiting shamans. She urged women to relinquish this "evil practice" (*p'yedan*) in favor

---

the temptation of superstition. Kim further notes that while Protestant missionaries assailed Korea's superstitions from the beginning, other Korean religions, including Buddhism and the indigenous Ch'ŏndogyo (Religion of the Heavenly Way) also began to do so from the 1920s.

[117] Annie Baird, *Daybreak in Korea: A Tale of Transformation in the Far East* (New York: Fleming H. Revell Company, 1909); L. A. Miller, "The Conversion of a Sorceress," *Korea Mission Field* 2 (February 1906): 65.

[118] Baird, *Daybreak in Korea*, pp. 25–39.

[119] Ellasue Wagner, *Korea: The Old and the New* (New York: Fleming H. Revell Company, 1931), p. 107.

[120] Esther L. Shields, "Nursing in Mission Stations: Work in Korea," *The American Journal of Nursing* 8, no. 5 (February 1908): 368–72.

of joining civilized forces.[121] In the words of Bible woman Song Myŏngsa, conversion to Christianity meant that a woman had become "a born-again new person" and had broken away from a life drenched in superstition.[122] In this way, condemning superstition became an important criterion for distinguishing the educated modern wife and mother from the uneducated old-fashioned woman.

Cherished and Rebuked Ideology of Domesticity

The meaning of the modern form of domesticity has been neither singular nor unchallenged. Women often found strategic utility in largely complying with the dominant gender ideology while appropriating power and authority within the patriarchal family structure. Nancy Cott argues that American women cherished and strengthened the ideology of domesticity out of their own self-interest because the separate "woman's sphere opened to women (reserved for them) the avenues of domestic influence, religious morality, and child nurture."[123] American women missionaries – both single and married – and their interaction with Korean women precisely reflected the complex nature of this ideology of domesticity. In line with the global trend toward the "feminization of the mission force" that started in the late-nineteenth century,[124] women missionaries constituted the majority of personnel in the Korea mission field. In 1901, for example, women comprised 56.5 percent of the mission force in Korea. Among the women missionaries, 52 percent were unmarried and held leadership positions in "woman's work for woman."[125] The fact that single women held these leadership roles was at odds with the idealized gender image of the home-bound mother and wife that was common in the United States at the turn of the twentieth century. Nonetheless, unmarried women became

---

[121] Kim Sŏkcha, "Kwisin ege kidohaesŏ pok pilji malgo pulssanghan saram ege chasŏn ŭl pep'ul il" (Do Not Pray to Ghosts for Luck But Rather Exercise your Benevolence for Poor People), *Chasŏn puinhoe chapchi* 1 (1908): 3–5. See also Kim, "1920-30-nyŏndae han'guk sahoe ŭi chonggyo wa yŏsŏng tamnon," 164–90.

[122] Mattie Noble, ed. *Victorious Lives of Early Christians in Korea: The First Book of Biographies and Autobiographies of Early Christians in the Protestant Church in Korea* (Sŭngni ŭi saenghwal) (Seoul: The Christian Literature Society, 1927), pp. 20–22. A "Bible woman" (*chŏndo puin*) was generally defined as "a Christian woman employed in the distribution of Christian literature, and in biblical instruction" and was "supported by foreign funds who is the personal helper of one of the foreign women, and works under her personal supervision." See Mrs. Herbert Blair, "Women's Work in Kang Kai," *Korea Mission Field* 7, no. 11 (1911): 314–17.

[123] Nancy Cott, *The Bonds of Womanhood: "Woman's Sphere" in New England, 1780–1835* (New Haven: Yale University Press, 1977), p. 200.

[124] Hunter, *The Gospel of Gentility*, p. 14.

[125] Sung-Deuk Oak, "The Indigenization of Christianity in Korea: North American Missionaries' Attitudes towards Korean Religions, 1884–1910" (ThD dissertation, Boston University, 2002), p. 484.

a vital component in the mission's plan to spread Christianity, and thus these women were able to actively participate in the foreign mission enterprise, where they had exceptional opportunities to exercise power and authority in their own "woman's work for woman."

These unmarried women became powerful role models for young Korean women to emulate. Korean girls and women encountered women teachers in mission schools, women doctors in hospitals, and women social workers in city centers.[126] Indeed, some of the most prominent Christian "new women" in Korea remained unmarried, two prominent examples being Kim Hwallan (1899–1970), the first Korean woman to obtain a PhD and one of the most influential female educators of that time, and Kim Maria (1892–1944), whose commitment to national independence was so inspirational to the general public that she came to be called "Korea's Joan of Arc."[127] Many of these women later stated that the pressures of Korean society made it difficult to remain single, but that their work in education or the national independence movement helped ratify their unusual choice and even enabled them to pave the way into new territory for women. It could be argued that, although these women defied the prevailing conception of the ideal Korean woman by remaining unmarried, they were accepted because they devoted their lives and careers to the fulfillment of the nationalist mandate of modernization and political independence. Although Kim Hwallan's history of collaboration with the Japanese authorities during World War II has made her a controversial figure,[128] the significant role she played in women's education has never been questioned. In her capacity as a leading educator, she declared in 1927 that "marriage is not necessarily an absolute thing to do if a woman has the will to pursue an important task."[129] The global mission to Christianize the world was seen as validating the work of single women missionaries. In parallel, Koreans were willing to tolerate the work of unmarried Korean women professionals as long as they contributed to the nation and future generations of educated women.

Just as unmarried women missionaries provided their students with a model of women as professionals, so married women missionaries exemplified the proper duties and behavior of wives and mothers. In her discussion of the role of missionary wives, Annie Baird presented the dual aspect of the woman's domain. Baird strongly believed in the clear division of roles between men and

---

[126] Induk Pahk, *September Monkey* (New York: Harper & Brothers, 1954).
[127] Pak Yongok, *Kim Maria* (Seoul: Hongsŏngsa, 2003), p. 339.
[128] For a feminist critique on the public accusations against Kim Hwallan for her "collaboration" with the Japanese colonial power, see Insook Kwon, "Feminists Navigating the Shoals of Nationalism and Collaboration: The Post-Colonial Korean Debate over How to Remember Kim Hwallan," *Frontiers* 27, no. 1 (2006): 39–66.
[129] "Ilmun ildap, Kim Hwallan ssi pangmungi" (Question and Answer, Visiting Ms. Kim Hwallan), *Pyŏlgŏn'gon* 9 (October 1927): 49–54.

women and felt that no one should try to blur gender boundaries. However, she also believed in the power of women. As she put it, a "good wife ought to influence a good husband and a good husband ought to be neither afraid nor ashamed to be influenced by a good wife; and by the use of this influence there are some ways, I am convinced, by which we may prove that we not only do not impede but do actually accelerate the promotion of the missionary enterprise."[130] To Baird, a woman's role as helpmate did not erode her influence; on the contrary, a woman was indispensable in advocating the evangelical mission from her own position within the domestic sphere as a good wife and mother.

The idea that the power of women resided primarily within the domestic arena had significant appeal to Korean converts. Mattie Noble (1872–1956), a Methodist missionary wife, described how the missionary home and family had become a model for Koreans in bringing about an enhanced role and status for wives and mothers:

They [Korean students] have watched us in the training of our children and have seen our companionship with them. Different ones have told me how wonderful it appeared to them to see a mother in her home, educated and capable, able to enter into the fuller life experiences with her husband, and to be a real companion, mentally and physically, with her children, even with the grown-up ones.... I would like to tell of the scores of things material that have been improved in and around the homes of this land, of which a great deal has been due to the precept and example of the members of the missionary home – father, mother and children, (missionaries' children have a great part also in this out-going influence.) ... let me just say, that love through Christ gradually but surely brings cleanliness, purity and beauty.... The modern Korean woman, in many cases, is no longer the subservient one but the co-serving one; she no longer remains aside while her master, (the husband), and her sons eat; she no longer walks behind her husband with downcast eyes and covered by a cloak thrown over her head and held closely so as to nearly cover her face and form; no longer does she have to give to the mother-in-law complete authority in the raising of her child.... She is learning, and she sees the bearing out of this truth in concrete, tangible form in the missionary home, by observing the wife and mother – her freedom, her love, her authority ... this missionary mother has met people who have told her how, in the raising of the children, they have taken pattern after some methods they had seen used in the raising of children in the missionary home.[131]

Mattie Noble attributed the enhanced role and status of Korean women to Christian belief and practice. Indeed, the ideal "Christian home" drew Korean women to the new religion. For example, Kim Sedŭi, one of the early converts and a well-known Bible woman in the P'yŏngyang area, decided to join the church because she was told that if she became a Christian, "her family

---

[130] Annie Baird, "The Relation of the Wives of Missionaries to Mission Work," *Korean Repository* (November 1895): 417.
[131] Mattie Wilcox Noble, "The Missionary Home," *Korea Mission Field* 27, no. 4 (1931): 75–7.

would be in peace, her husband would give up womanizing and her relationship with her husband would be harmonious."[132] The missionary family served as a new model, inspiring the Korean woman to become educated, pious, resourceful, and morally upright. She would have "her freedom, her love, her authority" in an idealized family in which she would be a true companion to her husband, would have control over the household free from her in-laws' intervention, and would practice clean, pure, and beautiful housekeeping.

This allegedly upgraded power of women within the modern Korean family constituted the core of the discourse on the "wise mother, good wife" in the 1920s and 1930s.[133] In her study of "new women" (*sin yŏsŏng*) in 1920s and 1930s Korea, Kim Sujin argues that, contrary to the common assumption that "new woman" was the polar opposite of the "wise mother, good wife," the discourse on "wise mother, good wife" constituted a crucial part of the discourse on "new woman."[134] She further suggests that in the late 1920s and early 1930s, there was a major shift in emphasis away from "wise mother" toward "good wife." The notion of *chubu* (house mistress) emerged as "a complex system of standard knowledge to be mastered to secure the role of good wife" in the new family.[135] In a similar vein, Chŏn Migyŏng distinguishes the role of "wise mother," a socially expected virtue, from that of "good wife," a virtue desired by new women who aspired to have modern love and equal companionship.[136] In an example of "Camera Art," the daily newspaper *Tonga ilbo* published a photograph in 1930 of a nest with two birds, taken in the city of Phoenix, Arizona. The title of the photograph is "sŭwit'ŭ hom (*tallanhan kajŏng*)" (sweet home – happy and harmonious family), signifying the new modern family.[137] The contemporary domestic sphere based on modern love became an integral part of the imagery of new womanhood. Indeed, this conception of the new family (*sin kajŏng*) provided an expedient platform on which the "new woman" could safely create a noble space for her own empowerment and individual subjectivity.

However, the association between the "new woman" and "wise mother, good wife" remained flimsy and contingent. Na Hyesŏk (1896–1948), one of the prominent new women, made comments critical of the notion of "wise mother, good wife" in a 1914 essay entitled "Isang chŏk puin" (The Ideal Woman):

---

[132] Noble, *Victorious Lives of Early Christians in Korea*, pp. 34–49.
[133] Yoo, *The Politics of Gender*; Kim, "1920-30-nyŏndae sin yŏsŏng tamnon kwa sangjing ŭi kusŏng," pp. 323–74.
[134] Kim, "1920-30-nyŏndae sin yŏsŏng tamnon kwa sangjing ŭi kusŏng," p. 323.
[135] Kim, "1920-30-nyŏndae sin yŏsŏng tamnon kwa sangjing ŭi kusŏng."
[136] Chŏn Migyŏng, "1920-30-nyŏndae hyŏnmo yangch'ŏ e kwanhan yŏn'gu" (A Study of Wise Mother and Good Wife in the 1920s and 1930s), *Han'guk kajŏng kwalli hakhoeji* 22, no. 3 (2004): 75–93.
[137] *Tonga ilbo*, February 15, 1930.

We need to acquire all the strength we can muster and elevate our consciousness daily. By doing so, we can progress toward the best ideal. We cannot say that a woman has achieved an ideal if she is a moral woman by virtue of habit alone or by merely fulfilling her secular duties. I believe that she has to go one step farther and prepare herself to fulfill future ideals. I also believe that it is not wise only to pursue the customary ideal of "good wife, wise mother" (yangch'ŏ hyŏnmo). It seems to me that that ideal is one of the favorite marketing strategies that teachers have used. The man is both husband and father; however, I have never heard of any curriculum that emphasizes "good husband, wise father" (yangbu hyŏnbu). It is only women whose conduct as good spouses and wise parents is reinforced through our education, and this makes women into mere appendages of men. Such education does not develop our minds. In addition, the idea of warm and compliant womanhood, which has been a necessary point of the propaganda to turn women into slaves, cannot be an ideal for women.[138]

Na's interpretation of "good wife, wise mother" pointed to a patriarchal mechanism that continued to subjugate women to slavish bondage under men. After her highly publicized divorce in 1930, which had been prompted by an extramarital affair she had had during her sojourn in Europe, Na made an even bolder and more controversial comment on chastity, a thorny topic that often drew heated debate in the print media. She argued: "Chastity is neither morality nor law. It is merely a matter of taste. Just as we eat rice when we want to eat rice (pap), and we eat rice cake (ttŏk) when we want to eat rice cake, chastity depends on our will and usage. We should not be constrained.... In order to keep chastity, we often suppress our natural laughter, our irresistible passion, and our point of view. How ironic is that? Therefore, our liberation begins with our liberation from the requirement of chastity."[139] Na's rejection of the "requirement of chastity" directly affronted the order of the patrilineal Confucian society that valorized women's purity and fidelity.[140] In this context, society portrayed Na as uncontrollable and unconstrained, subject to the whims of her passions, while her husband, who was a lawyer, represented the safety of rules and convention. There is no doubt that the divorce greatly shook Na, but she publicly announced in her essay "Confession about my Divorce" that she was "going to willingly take all the ridicule and criticism from people and go on silently with the cross on my back. I am determined to continue my journey for renewal, listening to the gentle whisper of life coming from profound agony."[141] After her divorce, she continued to pen her challenges to the conventional male-centered moral codes and lifestyles.[142] Na's continuing

---

[138] Na Hyesŏk, "Isang chŏk puin" (The Ideal Woman), *Hakchigwang* 3 (December 1914): 13–14.
[139] Yi Sanggyŏng, ed., *Na Hyesŏk chŏnjip* (The Complete Works of Na Hyesŏk) (Seoul: T'aehaksa, 2000), pp. 432–3.
[140] "Pyŏnhosa p'yŏngp'angi" (A Lawyer's Comment), *Tonggwang* 31 (March 1932): 65–68.
[141] Na Hyesŏk, "Ihon kobaekchang" (Confession about my Divorce), *Samch'ŏlli* 6, no. 8 (August 1934): 85.
[142] Na Hyesŏk, "Sin saenghwal e tŭlmyŏnsŏ" (Starting a New Life), *Samch'ŏlli* 7, no. 1 (January 1935): 70–81. See also "Manhon t'agae chwadamhoe, aa, ch'ŏngch'un i akkawŏra" (Debate on

public discourse received unsympathetic responses from the public. One critic went so far as to suggest that Na suffered from a form of madness that drove her to publish these exhibitionistic essays in which she talked openly about her intimate private life and divorce in the print media. The same critic argued that Na's justification of her free-love lifestyle by using examples of Western practices was a mere delusion.[143]

The public's fear of the instability of the family as the fundamental social unit was further demonstrated when a prominent Christian woman intellectual Pak Indŏk (aka Induk Pahk, 1896–1980) filed for divorce in 1931. Her divorce became a national sensation and ignited heated debate on the tensions between selfhood and motherhood. On returning from studying in the United States, Pak sought to end her unhappy marriage, placing the blame for its failure on her husband's infidelities. She became the "first woman to divorce her husband for infidelity under new laws introduced by the colonial authorities."[144] In her autobiography, she wrote that "unless ills were cured they would go on hurting. I would rather have an arm amputated and live than to die because it was diseased.... Being bound by age-old concepts and traditions was the worst burden of all. I had learned that the most precious thing in the world is freedom to do what one believes is right and now I must choose between the Korean custom of remaining with my husband 'no matter what,' or starting out on an independent way of life."[145] Keenly aware of the scorn and notoriety her divorce would surely bring, Pak nonetheless ended her marriage. She claimed that the divorce was her sacrifice for the younger generation of women, providing them with a model of a woman opting for independence rather than remaining in a marriage where she would have to be subservient.[146]

And just as Pak had predicted, her divorce made her a social outcast, the target of harsh public criticism. Referring to Pak as "Korea's Nora Who Left the Doll's House," the media condemned her "selfish and irresponsible" decision to end her marriage as well as her justification for leaving. Here the invocation

---

How to Solve Deferred Marriage: Alas! The Blossom of Youth Lost!), *Samch'ŏlli* 5, no. 10 (October 1933): 84–9. In her response to a question asking why marriage-aged women remained single, she told the reporter at *Samch'ŏlli* that "it is because they have observed the unhappy married lives of their senior women friends ... Indeed, how many couples lead a happy married life among the educated class of people? Statistically speaking, there are more unhappy couples than happy couples."

[143] *Sin kajŏng* (October 1934), quoted in Yi Sanggyŏng, *In'gan ŭro salgo sipta* (I Want to Live as a Human Being) (Seoul: Han'gilsa, 2000), pp. 425–6.

[144] Kenneth Wells, "Expanding their Realm: Women and Public Agency in Colonial Korea," in *Women's Suffrage in Asia*, eds. Louise Edwards and Mina Roces (London: Routledge Curzon, 2004), p. 160.

[145] Pahk, *September Monkey*, pp. 162–3.

[146] For the criticism of Pak, see "Chosŏn ŭi Nora ro inhyŏng ŭi chip ŭl naon Pak Indŏk ssi" (Pak Indŏk: Korea's Nora Has Left the Doll's House), *Samch'ŏlli* 5, no. 1 (January 1933): 73–4; "Pak Indŏk konggaejang: Ihon sodong e kwanhayŏ" (Open Letter to Pak Indŏk: Regarding her Divorce Fiasco), *Sin yŏsŏng* 5, no. 11 (1931): 30–35.

of the figure of Nora from Henrik Ibsen's *A Doll's House* was significant. Ever since a translation of the play had first appeared in *Maeil sinbo* in 1921,[147] the character of Nora had fascinated and inspired the new class of educated women and men in Korea just as it had elsewhere.[148] One literary critic asserted that Nora was not only a symbol of "new romance" (*sin yŏnae*) or "individualism" (*kaeinjuŭi*) but an icon of "self-awakening" (*cha'gak*).[149] Indeed, in her 1921 song lyric, "A Doll's House" (*Inhyŏng ŭi ka*), written nine years prior to her own divorce, Na Hyesŏk expressed her desire not to live as a doll for her father and husband but to live as a human being with full self-determination.[150] The self-awareness of such women as individuals and their desire to pursue the "freedom to do what one believes is right" was a continuing source of great anxiety and public criticism.[151]

A growing fear of the breakdown of the family transpired, with the public suspecting educated "new women" of causing deterioration of the family in the name of their own independence and self-realization. In the divorces and love affairs of these prominent women intellectuals, the public came to know this unexpected outcome of women's education. Theodore Jun Yoo notes that while members of the new class of educated women were expected to serve as "symbols of modernity, civilization, and nationalism," some social critics and commentators feared that these women were "undermining the stability of the family, compromising sexual morality, and denigrating national character."[152] Within this context, the idealized "wise mother, good wife" was regarded as the antithesis of the liberal womanhood of the West, which was understood to produce selfish, irresponsible, and extravagant women. In particular, various scandals involving high-profile women intellectuals who had had significant exposure to liberal ideas through their overseas education in the West and Japan functioned as powerful cautionary tales in warning of the danger of the modern.

---

[147] *Maeil sinbo*, January 25–April 3, 1921.
[148] Focusing on the Chinese adaption of *A Doll's House*, Yang Lianfen argues that "the project of woman's emancipation was more often than not unintentionally omitted in the course of the 'liberation of the human,' ... most May Fourth literary works neglect the fact that Nora's discovery of her humanity is realized through reflection on her gender position." Rather, a more concerted focus was on "the generation gap between young people and their parents." Yang Lianfen, "The Absence of Gender in May Fourth Narratives of Women's Emancipation: A Case Study of Hu Shi's *The Greatest Event in Life*," *New Zealand Journal of Asian Studies* 12, no. 1 (June 2010): 6–13, quoted on 9–10.
[149] Hyŏn Ch'ŏl, "Kŭndae munye wa Ipssen" (Modern Literature and Ibsen), *Kaebyŏk* 7 (January 1921): 129–38.
[150] *Maeil sinbo*, April 3, 1921.
[151] Hŏ Yŏngsuk, "Puin munje ŭi ilmyŏn – namja hal il, yŏja hal il" (One Aspect of the Woman Question: Men's Work, Women's Work), *Tonga ilbo*, January 1, 1926 and January 4, 1926; "Myŏngil ŭl yaksok hanŭn sin sedae ŭi ch'ŏnyŏ chwadamhoe" (Talk with Promising Single Women of the New Era), *Sin yŏsŏng* 7, no. 1 (January 1933): 26.
[152] Theodore Jun Yoo, "The 'New Woman' and the Politics of Love, Marriage and Divorce in Colonial Korea," *Gender and History* 17, no. 2 (August 2005): 296.

As Christine Marran argues in her book *Poison Woman: Figuring Female Transgression in Modern Japanese Culture*, the transgressive figure of the "undesirable woman" functions to reinforce what is considered ideal and desirous.[153]

Cautionary tales about "undesirable woman" prevailed not only in stories about women such as Na and Pak but also in the images of the ideal modern family and the role of the modern woman in it that were portrayed in the literary and visual arts. Two representative examples are the 1933 novel by Ch'ae Mansik (1902–1950) entitled *Inhyŏng ŭi chip ŭl nawasŏ* (After the Doll's House),[154] and the 1936 feature film, *Mimong* (Illusive Dream). Both works contemplate "what happened after Nora left home." Ch'ae's novel literally takes up the story of Nora Helmer as she slams the door in the final scene of Ibsen's play, while *Mimong* presents a Nora-like figure named Aesun, who mirrors Nora's dramatic rejection of the traditional home life. The two works, however, differ starkly in the outcomes they imagine for their respective Noras. The Nora in Ch'ae's novel experiences all manner of humiliation and deprivation, but she is ultimately redeemed and reborn as a factory worker, reflecting Ch'ae's interest in socialist realism at that time. In contrast, Aesun, the Nora figure in *Illusive Dream*, commits suicide as a final act of regret over her vainglorious desire for luxury, fashion, and bodily pleasure. It should also be noted that literary works like Ch'ae Mansik's novel could be enjoyed only by those who were literate, whereas films had much greater potential for far-reaching impact on the wider population. The consumption of films did not require literacy, and ticket prices were quite reasonable, so that even low wage earners (e.g., daily manual workers) could afford admission.[155] Although there are no records indicating how popular the film was, let alone the reception of the film, the plot of *Illusive Dream* sharply reflects a growing sense of despair over the temptations of modernity and the presumed consequence – the instability of the modern family.

---

[153] Christine L. Marran, *Poison Woman: Figuring Female Transgression in Modern Japanese Culture* (Minneapolis: University of Minnesota Press, 2007).

[154] For detailed analysis, see Hyaeweol Choi, "Debating the Korean New Woman: Imagining Henrik Ibsen's 'Nora' in Colonial Era Korea," *Asian Studies Review* 36 (March 2012): 59–77.

[155] Roald Maliangkay, "Dirt, Noise, and Naughtiness: Cinema and the Working Class during Korea's Silent Film Era," *Asian Ethnology* 70, no. 1 (2011): 1–31; No Chisŭng, "Na Ungyu yŏnghwa ŭi kwan'gek tŭl hogŭn musŏng yŏnghwa kwangek e taehan han yŏn'gu" (A Study on the Change of Spectatorship and the Meaning of the Na Ungyu's Films from the Late 1920s to the Late 1930s), *Sanghŏ hakpo* 23 (2008): 185–224.

Figure 1.1 The opening scene of *Mimong* (Illusive Dream)
Source: Korean Film Archive[156]

The opening scene of the film sets the tone and theme. A bird cage dangling under the eaves of a tile-roofed house signifies this middle-class family home as a "modern prison with gold bars."[157] In the main room (*anbang*), while her husband reads a newspaper, Aesun is sitting in front of a mirror applying powder to her face. He asks her where she is going. She tells him that she is going to the department store to shop for some new Western-style suits because what she has is out of fashion. He complains about how frequently she goes out, and she retorts: "Do you want to keep me locked up in this room? I am not a bird in a cage!" He calmly reminds her of her duties as a housewife, scolding her for neglecting the housework. Upset by that comment, she shouts: "Why don't you find some little woman [concubine] who'll keep your house clean for you? You don't have to be stuck with me. Should I just leave?" In disbelief, her husband asks, "How could you say that?" to which she replies, "I am serious. I am leaving." The scene ends with her slamming the door as she leaves her "cage," mirroring the final act of Nora in *A Doll's House*.

Aesun's life after the "cage" is one of luxury, indulgence, and deceit. She takes up with a man and stays with him at a Western style hotel, drinking,

---

[156] The film is available for viewing online, provided by the Korean Film Archive. https://www.youtube.com/watch?v=tmd_OBPFll8.
[157] Emma Goldman, *Anarchism and Other Essays* (New York & London: Mother Earth Publishing Association, 1911), pp. 201–202.

smoking, and frequenting cafés, theaters, and the beauty salon. She indulges in modern luxuries and shows no hint of concern about her daughter or husband. Her daughter, in contrast, longs so desperately for her mother that she cannot study or sleep, and she finally falls ill. Aesun's life begins to fall apart when she discovers that her boyfriend is actually a con man and quite possibly a murderer. In the tragic climax of the film, she is rushing to get to the train station, trying to catch a male dancer for whom she has developed romantic feelings (although he has no feelings for her). She presses the taxi driver to go faster and faster, and, as the cab speeds through the city of Seoul, it hits a young girl, who turns out to be Aesun's daughter. She goes to the hospital with the child, and as she watches the doctors and nurses work to save her daughter, Aesun is filled with remorse. She despairs at her behavior and the emptiness of her pursuits, and ultimately she commits suicide.

The message is clear. A woman who would dare to abandon her family, who would conduct her life in a way that might bring harm to her own child, must pay the ultimate price. Her bold choice to leave the "cage" and her subsequent life filled with decadence and deceit are predictable plot points in a cautionary tale meant to instruct viewers on the consequences of not complying with the role of "wise mother, good wife" in a modern family. However, it is also important to note another aspect of the message conveyed through the irresistible temptations of the modern, as embodied in the fancy department store, the chic café, the seductive movements of the male dancer at the theater, the beauty salon, and the bustling urban landscape. In particular, Aesun's mad dash to catch the train – a symbol of modernity representing mobility, novelty, and infinite possibility – and her failure to achieve her goal reflect the tensions between what modernity promises and what the reality is.[158] Her relentless pursuit of a modern self ends abruptly when she causes devastating injury to her own child. She sees her daughter lying in the street, her body broken, nearly dead, and suddenly Aesun is filled with maternal concern. Yet the close-up shot of her weeping in remorse and her eventual suicide together convey a certain ambivalence as to what is expected of a woman in the modern family. In this connection, the alternative title of the film, *Chugŭm ŭi chajangga* (Lullaby in Death), is quite telling. Certainly the invocation of a "lullaby" is compelling, in that it invokes maternal love and care – the image of a mother singing her baby to sleep may be the quintessential image of motherly love. But what, then, does the suicide mean? Does Aesun commit suicide out of despair over what she has done to her daughter? Or does she commit suicide because she can't face the prospect of returning home, living like a caged bird, and denying her desire for

---

[158] Todd Presner, *Mobile Modernity: Germans, Jews, Trains* (New York: Columbia University Press, 2007); and Marian Aguiar, *Tracking Modernity: India's Railway and the Culture of Mobility* (Minneapolis: University of Minnesota Press, 2011).

the modern? Although we cannot know what audiences of the film felt at the time, it is likely that many viewers condemned Aesun as a dangerous woman deserving only of condemnation for her failure to fulfill her duty and responsibility as a "wise mother, good wife."

Conclusion

The origin and evolution of the modern gender ideology of "wise mother, good wife" demonstrates the complex intersections of patriarchy, colonialism, nationalism, and Western modernity in which women conformed to, resisted, or appropriated the existing male-dominant structures. Various social agents strategically promoted this gender ideology. Korean nationalists actively utilized the ideology to revitalize the nation, emphasizing the sacred role of educated mothers in the modern scientific training of children as future citizens, and the crucial duty of educated wives in assisting their husbands. This ideology served as a central aspect of Japan's gender policy to discipline colonial subjects to be obedient and efficient with practical knowledge for the Japanese empire. The American missionaries' primary goal of spreading the Gospel went hand in hand with their emphasis on the vital role of the pious mother and wife as a moral guide in the Christian family.

It is significant that both Korean women reformers, including "new women," and American women missionaries strategically employed this domestic gender ideology as a way to empower women within a certain circumscribed domain. Even though the centrality of domesticity and "woman's work for woman" continued to restrict women to the domain of the private and the informal spheres, these factors also worked to extend the scope of lives and work of women into the public and even the global sphere. Those who benefited from an education that was focused on domesticity paved the way for the next generation of career women, especially in the fields of teaching and nursing, and empowered modern housewives (*chubu*). However, limited openings within the overall patriarchal system did not provide sufficient opportunities for those few pioneering new women to move beyond the confining roles of mothers and wives. Some of these women openly questioned and directly challenged the very roots of patrilineal social arrangements in discourses on chastity, marriage, divorce, and motherhood.[159] It is no surprise, then, that these pioneering women came under relentless criticism and antagonism. In a significant way, the self-righteous condemnation of these "new women" (and of fictional representations of them in literary works and films) was simply the

---

[159] For a comprehensive analysis of the phenomenon of "new woman" and the translation of major archival materials on the topic, see Hyaeweol Choi, *New Women in Colonial Korea: A Sourcebook* (London: Routledge, 2013).

expression of a collective fear about the subversion of the basis of patriarchy and a deliberate effort to tame and discipline women.

It is important to note that even those "new women" who publicly resisted the gender-specific, discriminatory roles in their families and society did not necessarily deny the value of "wise mother, good wife." Motherhood in particular was often extolled as a glorious fulfillment for women. Kim Wŏnju (aka Kim Iryŏp, 1896–1971), the founder of the first feminist magazine, *Sin yŏja* (New Woman), praised motherhood (*mosŏng*) as the most beautiful and grand thing a woman could do.[160] Confucian-prescribed "womanly virtue" and the Japanese colonial regime's gender ideology of "*ryōsai kenbo*," combined with American missionaries' "true womanhood," had indeed produced a particular version of the "wise mother, good wife" ideal in these pioneering women. As I detail in Chapter 2, the scientification of the domestic and the enhanced power of women within the family added a significant flavor of the modern to the new ideal of wife and mother.[161] It can be argued that what the early feminists primarily refuted was the singular, confining role of women that suppressed intellectual, artistic, and sensual desires. Many of them also consciously distanced themselves from the caricature of the new woman who "wore a fox hair shawl and strong perfume,"[162] or the "contemporary woman" (*hyŏndae yŏja*) whose presumed vanity, carelessness, and conspicuous consumption often drew public criticism in the print media.[163] Nonetheless, the largely defamed personal lives of some of the best-known new women generated heated debates that were often led by male intellectuals. The public debates criticizing the scandalous lives of "new women," while intended as a way to tame and discipline them, ironically helped cleave the solid building-blocks of patriarchy by publicly addressing the unconventional life choices made by these women – choices that undermined male-centered social arrangements. In this sense, the promotion and critique of the modern gender ideology of "wise mother, good wife" in the pages of the male-dominated print and visual media and in the life experiences of actual "new women" demonstrated the complex formation of a new ideal womanhood. This new ideal constantly interacted – and continues to interact – with the resilient, ever-changing patriarchy that continues to evolve and accommodate the new demands of particular historical realities.

---

[160] Kim Wŏnju, "Chaehon hu ilchunyŏn ŭi hoego: in'gyŏk ch'angjo e" (Reflections on the Occasion of the First Anniversary of my Remarriage: on the Creation of Character), *Sin yŏsŏng* 2, no. 6 (August 1924): 40–43.
[161] Theresa Hyun, *Writing Women in Korea: Translation and Feminism in the Colonial Period* (Honolulu: University of Hawai'i Press, 2004), pp. 9–22; and Hyaeweol Choi, "Women's Literacy and New Womanhood in Late Choson Korea," *Asian Journal of Women's Studies* 6, no. 1 (2000): 88–115.
[162] Hwang, "Chosŏn ŭn irŏhan ŏmŏni rŭl yoguhanda," 12–15.
[163] Kim, "Chaehon hu il chunyŏn ŭi hoego," 40–43.

2 Materiality: The Experience of Modern House and Home

In the original outline for his book on Korean village life, Jacob Robert Moose, a Southern Methodist missionary in Korea (1899–1927), included a chapter entitled "The Village Home." He later changed the title of that chapter to "The Village Family," explaining that Korean did not have a translation equivalent for "home," a single word that conveys "the true idea of home" with all the connotations and nuance that the English word carries. The nearest equivalent he and other missionaries could find was the word *chip* (literally, "house"). When missionaries needed to translate the phrase "Home, Sweet Home" for a hymn book, they opted for *chip, chip, ch'ŏndang chip* ("House, House, Heavenly House").[1] According to Ellasue Wagner, a Southern Methodist missionary in Korea (1904–1940), the typical Korean house was a hut with a straw-thatched roof, mud walls, no windows, and very small rooms – "all is dingy, dark, and generally very dirty … we say that *a Korean woman has no home, only a house*."[2] To the white American Protestant middle-class sensibility, the Korean *house* was unattractive and unhygienic in its structural and material aspects. But beyond those tangible and practical considerations, missionaries were more troubled by the absence of Christian spirituality, which they presumed to be the foundation for a true *home* life, along with Victorian ideals of companionate marriage, scientific homemaking, and childhood discipline. This idea was conveyed by Moose when he wrote: "The real reason for there being no word for home in the language is the very good one that there is not a home in the land."[3] Thus, as elsewhere, the creation of the "Christian home" in "heathen" Korea became a central project for American missionaries.[4]

---

[1] Jacob Robert Moose, *Village Life in Korea* (Nashville: Publishing House of the M.E. Church South, Smith & Lamar, Agents, 1911), p. 73.
[2] Ellasue Wagner, "A Korean home," *The Korea Mission Field* 4, no. 6 (1908): 90, emphasis added.
[3] Moose, *Village Life*, p. 73.
[4] Dana Robert, "The 'Christian home' as a cornerstone of Anglo-American missionary thought and practice," in *Converting Colonialism: Visions and Realities in Mission History, 1706–1914*, ed. Dana Robert (Grand Rapids: William B. Eerdmans, 2008), pp. 134–65. See also Dipesh Chakrabarty, "The Difference – Deferral of a Colonial Modernity: Public Debates on Domesticity in British Bengal," in *Tensions of Empire: Colonial Cultures in a Bourgeois*

In the missionary discourse, the rhetorical distinction between "house," the material and profane domain, and "home," the cultural and spiritual realm, meant to promote the idealized "Christian home" as an integral part of their "civilizing" mission. As much research demonstrates, Euro-American colonialisms and the foreign missionary enterprise played a crucial role in shaping modern domesticities as part of European and US empire-building and the propagation of Christianity worldwide.[5] Beginning especially in the second half of the nineteenth century, the discourse on domesticity and its accompanying material cultures were circulated at an unprecedented level through the globally connected imperial and missionary network. International trade and industrial development further accelerated the transnational flow of artifacts, knowledge, and print materials that began to reshape domestic practices and cultures. Not only did colonialists and missionaries promote their Euro-American-centered and highly racialized concepts of ideal modern house and home into the colonies and the mission field, but the colonized also began to travel overseas, observe domestic practices in other societies, and adapt them to the local conditions at home. For the colonized, the domestic site presented double-edged challenges when the "conditions of domesticity often become markers that distinguish civilization from savagery."[6] On the one hand, it symbolized the foundation of the nation to preserve, but, on the other hand, it also needed to be reformed and modernized to strengthen the nation.[7] What emerged was an eclectic mosaic of ideas from a variety of sources that were subject to local conditions within the context of imperial expansion, nationalist desire, and cosmopolitan sensibility.[8]

World, eds. Frederick Cooper and Ann Laura Stoler (Berkeley: University of California Press, 1997), pp. 373–405.

[5] Amy Kaplan, "Manifest Domesticity," *American Literature* 70, no. 3 (1998): 581–606; A special issue, "Domestic Frontiers: The Home and Colonization," *Frontiers: A Journal of Women Studies* 28, no. 1–2 (2007); Hyaeweol Choi and Margaret Jolly, eds., *Divine Domesticities: Christian Paradoxes in Asia and the Pacific* (Canberra: ANU Press, 2014); and Barbara Reeves-Ellington, Kathryn Kish Sklar, and Connie A. Shemo, eds., *Competing Kingdoms: Women, Mission, Nation, and the American Protestant Empire, 1812—1960* (Durham: Duke University Press, 2010).

[6] Kaplan, "Manifest Domesticity," 582.

[7] Yi Ki, "Kajŏng haksŏl" (Discussion of Home Economics), *Honam hakpo* 1 (June 25, 1908): 27–37; Paektu sanin, "Tongyang sik ŭi yulli sasang pyŏnch'ŏn kaegwan (sok): kajŏng yulli ŭi iltan" (An Overview of the Changes in the Ethics in the East: An Aspect of Family Ethics), *Kaebyŏk* 17 (November 1921): 32–39.

[8] For examples, see Kristin Hoganson, "Cosmopolitan Domesticity: Importing the American Dream, 1865–1920," *The American Historical Review* 107, no. 1 (2002): 55–83; Judith E. Walsh, *Domesticity in Colonial India* (Lanham: Rowman & Littlefield Publishers, 2004). See also Jordan Sand, *House and Home in Modern Japan: Architecture, Domestic Space, and Bourgeois Culture, 1880–1930* (Cambridge: Harvard University Press, 2003); and Karen Transberg Hansen, ed., *African Encounters with Domesticity* (New Brunswick: Rutgers University Press, 1992).

The added complexity in the formation of modern domesticity in colonial Korea under Japanese rule lies in the ambiguous status of imperial Japan as a cultural force. As I demonstrate in this chapter, the Japanese domestic models that were presented in public exhibitions in colonial Korea were often Western in style and origin. Furthermore, in the discourse on modern domesticity, Korean intellectuals rarely made reference to those Japanese models, at least until 1937, when the *kōminka* era (imperialization of colonial subjects; K. *hwangminhwa*) began. The conspicuous absence of domestic models of the Japanese colonizers is contrasted with the predominance of Euro-American models, which raises the question of cultural hegemony in shaping the domestic. As Jordan Sand vividly illustrates in his study of house and home in modern Japan, the concept of "home" was actually alien to Japan. Through missionary influences and Anglo-American texts, Meiji-era Japanese reformers came to be exposed to "the rich Victorian language of domesticity, something without parallel in Japan" and "home" was "among the new ideas fertilized by contact with the West after the Meiji Restoration."[9] Initially contrasted with the Japanese family system, *ie sei*, however, the notion of "home" (initially called *hōmu* and later translated as *katei*) became "part of a Japanese discourse on women, family, and dwelling."[10] This Western origin in the genealogy of modern house and home in Japan has significant implications for the Japanese colonial project, which took domesticity to be part of its "civilizing mission" in its colonies.

Taking the idea of the "modern house and home" as a key point of convergence for national, colonial, and missionary projects, this chapter explores the ways in which ideals, material forms, and the performance of modern domesticity emerged from the multivalent encounters Koreans had with Japanese powers and Western missionaries through examples and modeling, formal schooling, and overseas travel. It specifically traces the evolution of the modern home as embodied in the various images and models presented by Western missionaries (mostly Americans), the Japanese colonial power, the Korean popular media, and foreign-educated Korean intellectuals.[11] It also analyzes the institutionalization of "home economics" (*kajŏnghak* or *kasa*) in women's higher education, viewing it as the culmination of the transpacific flow of ideas and people in fashioning modern domesticity in Korea. I argue that although there was significant impact from the Japanese colonial authority, particularly

---

[9] Sand, *House and Home in Modern Japan*, p. 22.
[10] Sand, *House and Home in Modern Japan*, pp. 21–4.
[11] There was a significant gap between the reality and "object lessons" as ideals put forward by American missionaries, Japanese colonialists and Korean elite. In addition, negotiations and adaptations among the participating parties were crucial in shaping modern domesticity. See Jane Simonsen, "'Object Lessons': Domesticity and Display in Native American Assimilation," *American Studies* 43, no. 1 (Spring 2002): 75–99; Sand, *House and Home in Modern Japan*, p. 7.

evident in the late-colonial period (1937–1945), the dominant sources of modern domesticity came from Europe and the United States. In particular, American missionaries and their global network were a crucial vehicle through which Koreans learned about, observed, or directly experienced the ideal modern home and grappled with what an indigenous form of modern domesticity might be like. I further argue that a transnational approach brings the private sphere into sharper focus as a dynamic site of interplay between the local and the global. In its position at the forefront of the radical transformation of gender roles, the traditionally female domain of house and home thus served as a springboard into the public and global spheres, in the name of the scientific, rational domesticity of the modern era.

"Home, Sweet Home" as Modern Sensibility

The genealogy of the "modern home" in Korea can be traced to the arrival of Western Protestant missionaries in the late-nineteenth century and with them the "missionary home."[12] In contrast to the thatched roofs and earth walls of the typical Korean houses, missionary homes stood out for their Western-style, two-story brick structures filled with imported furnishings. In the early period of the mission, missionaries often lived in Korean houses with some minor renovations to the interior, such as glass windowpanes, which did not exist in traditional Korean houses.[13] However, it was not long before the missionaries began to build Western-style residences. These were typically funded through an appropriation from the foreign mission board, but some missionaries used their own private funds to build rather grandiose structures, which sometimes drew criticism from Western visitors.[14] In general, American Protestant missionaries lived in houses that were substantial and reasonably comfortable.

Often located on highly desirable sites, missionary houses were prominent amid the humble, thatched-roofed Korean dwellings.[15] It was not only the

---

[12] For an extended analysis of the role of the missionary home in Korea, see Hyaeweol Choi, "The Home as a Pulpit: Domestic Paradoxes in early Twentieth-Century Korea," in *Divine Domesticities: Christian Paradoxes in Asia and the Pacific*, eds. Hyaeweol Choi and Margaret Jolly (Canberra: ANU Press, 2014), pp. 29–55.

[13] *The Gospel in All Lands* (August, 1888): 373.

[14] Katherine Ahn, *Chosŏn ŭi ŏdum ŭl palk'in yŏsŏngdŭl* (Awakening the Hermit Kingdom: Pioneer American Women Missionaries in Korea), trans. Kim Sŏngung (Seoul: P'oiema, 2009), p. 174. The prolific nineteenth-century world traveler Isabella Bird Bishop reported that French Catholic missionaries lived "in the wretched hovels of the people, amidst their foul surroundings, and shar[ing] their unpalatable food and sordid lives." See Dae Young Ryu, "Understanding Early American Missionaries in Korea (1884–1910): Capitalist Middle-Class Values and the Weber Thesis," *Archives de sciences sociales des religions* [online], 113 (January–March 2001): 93–117.

[15] Annie Baird, *Inside Views of Mission Life* (Philadelphia: Westminster Press, 1913), p. 26; Ahn, *Chosŏn ŭi ŏdum ŭl palk'in yŏsŏngdŭl*, p. 26. One photograph that dramatically illustrates the distinctiveness of missionary houses in Korean cities was the residence of Arthur and Mattie

grandiose exterior architectural features that stood out. The interiors of these homes were also a matter of note. To maintain their standard of living, missionaries would bring with them or import from the United States the accoutrements of fine Western homes.[16] The missionary homes were typically equipped with modern furniture and artifacts that very few Koreans had ever seen before. The photograph of a Korean woman in a missionary home (see Figure 2.1) shows some details of the interior, which typically included chairs, books, lamps, clocks, framed photographs, rugs, and richly patterned wallpaper. In some instances, one might even find the home equipped with an organ, a furnace, a sewing machine, or a typewriter.[17]

In her seminal work on American women missionaries in China, Jane Hunter asks "why missionaries of this period were so faithful to the artifacts of home that they transported them around the world. The answer lies in the association of the idea of civilization, which was at the heart of the missionary enterprise, with the stuff of the late Victorian woman's sphere."[18] Similarly, in the Korea mission field, as Dae Young Ryu demonstrates, the majority of missionaries came from the middle class or at least strove to obtain the status of the middle class, and most of them "endeavored to retain their American middle-class lifestyle."[19] Their furniture and other household items were very important in maintaining this identity and their standards for "a civilized lifestyle." In addition to the furnishings for home interiors, food and everyday items were imported in bulk from companies such as Montgomery & Ward in Chicago, so that missionaries could continue their Western diet and lifestyle.[20] Arthur Brown, General Secretary of the Presbyterian Board of Foreign Missions from 1895 until 1929, viewed American products as important mechanism for introducing Western civilization to mission fields. The furnishings and

---

Noble, Methodist missionaries from the United States, who spent decades in P'yŏngyang. See Herbert Henry Austin, *A Scamper Through the Far East* (London: E. Arnold, 1909), p. 180.

[16] Baird, *Inside Views of Mission Life*, p. 27.

[17] Baird, Inside Views of Mission Life, p. 27; Arthur J. Brown, *The Mastery of the Far East: The Story of Korean's Transformation and Japan's Rise to Supremacy in the Orient* (New York: Charles Scribner's Sons, 1919), p. 471.

[18] Jane Hunter, *The Gospel of Gentility: American Women Missionaries in Turn-of-the-Century China* (New Haven: Yale University Press, 1984), p. 129. See also Mary Taylor Huber and Nancy C. Lutkehaus, eds., *Gendered Missions: Women and Men in Missionary Discourse and Practice* (Ann Arbor: University of Michigan Press, 1999), p. 3.

[19] Ryu, "Understanding early American missionaries in Korea," 98. See also A. Deacon and M. Hill, "The Problem of Surplus Women in the Nineteenth Century: Secular and Religious Alternatives," in *A Sociological Year Book of Religion in Britain*, no. 5, ed. D. Martin (London: SCM Press, 1972), pp. 87–102.

[20] *The Journals of Mattie Wilcox Noble*, October 22, 1892, June 22, 1897, and December 6, 1897, General Commission on Archives and History, The United Methodist Church, Drew University, Madison, New Jersey. American missionaries also celebrated the Fourth of July, gathering together and enjoying "fireworks, we shot off a few fire crackers ... sang patriotic songs, and were treated with ice cream & cake." *The Journals of Mattie Wilcox Noble*, July 15, 1893.

78   Materiality: Experience of Modern House and Home

Figure 2.1 Missionary home interior
Source: The Reverend Corwin & Nellie Taylor Collection, Korean Heritage Library, University of Southern California, Los Angeles

goods that could be found in the missionary household offered Koreans a glimpse of the modern home that would have been attractive to them and thereby helped to develop a "desire" for these modern material products and for the lifestyle with which they were associated.[21]

As the Presbyterian missionary Annie Baird (1891–1916) suggested, the furnishings and the practices were so peculiar and so exotic that Korean visitors took the missionary home to be the fanciful residence of "mountain spirits."[22] To missionaries, the things commonly found in their homes – chairs, tables, rugs, lamps, clocks, sewing machines – were everyday household items; local people, however, had never seen such paraphernalia and, for the most part, did not have the means to possess such things. Baird noted that "the plainest

---

[21] Brown, *The Mastery of the Far East*, p. 471.
[22] Annie Baird, *Daybreak in Korea* (New York: Fleming H. Revell Company, 1909), p. 60. When Western missionaries arrived in Korea in the late-nineteenth century, they encountered largely polytheistic practices in Korea. People believed that gods, goddesses, spirits, and ghosts were everywhere. Mountain spirits were part of this polytheistic tradition.

missionary home is still a palace in the eyes of the native."[23] The furnishings were more than the object of simple curiosity; they were exotica coveted by Korean visitors. Many Koreans made spontaneous "sightseeing" visits to the homes of missionaries to see all those extraordinary objects.[24] Rather than seeing these visits as an inconvenience, the missionary women looked on them as opportunities to introduce the new religion to their captive audience. In 1908 a Methodist missionary in Korea, Mattie Noble (1892–1934), wrote in her diary that "a Christian home in a non-Christian land is a great object lesson."[25] That idea formed the basis for a strategy in which the missionaries were able to take advantage of the Koreans' curiosity about the missionaries, their lifestyle, their dwellings and furnishings, and use their homes as models to illustrate the virtues of a Christian household.

In addition to welcoming these spontaneous "sightseeing" visits from the Koreans, the missionaries invited local Koreans to planned events, such as Christmas celebrations or a "cradle roll parties" (see Figure 2.2a, b, and c).[26] Mattie Noble, who kept a diary over the forty-two years of her missionary work in Korea (1892–1934), describes in a December 1893 entry her first attempt to introduce local women to the meaning of the Christmas holiday by inviting them to her house. She writes that she had her Korean teacher "write me a nice invitation to my neighbor women to come in the afternoon." To her surprise, "more than I invited heard of my plan" and "more than fifty women besides children" came. She prepared a table "well loaded with nuts, oranges and cakes" and borrowed from her missionary colleague a "baby organ." She describes how none of the Korean visitors had heard about Christmas or Jesus, and writes: "What an opportunity to tell them the story.... I wanted to win their hearts for Jesus and let them see that we foreigners loved them." To Noble, the Koreans' overwhelming response to her invitation was a sure sign of how the missionary home could serve as an informal pulpit.

It is important to note that the missionaries' desire to tell Koreans the story of Christ was not always successful. In her 1909 book entitled *Daybreak in Korea*, Baird vividly describes how polytheistic Koreans responded to the monotheistic Christian belief. In that book, a group of local women, led by a female shaman, ask to peek inside the missionary home, having heard about all the exotic things that could be found in foreigners' houses and the new "doctrine" (read Christianity) that the missionaries had brought to Korea. The missionary woman invites the local women into her home, allowing them free rein to examine the household items. However, when she tries to introduce the new

---

[23] Baird, *Inside Views of Mission Life*, p. 25.   [24] Baird, *Daybreak in Korea*, pp. 58–63.
[25] *The Journals of Mattie Wilcox Noble*, vol. 4, p. 3a. The entry is entitled "Pyeng Yang School April 1908," in which Noble makes a plea to potential donors in the United States for the establishment of a foreign school for missionary children in Korea.
[26] A cradle roll is a list of the names of young children, especially those of church members.

80   Materiality: Experience of Modern House and Home

Figure 2.2a A cradle roll party at the home of Mrs. W. A. Noble
b The cradle roll in the South Mountain Church, Pyeng Yang
c Cradle roll babies for baptism by W. A. Noble at the Hallusu Church, Manchuria
Source: Photograph courtesy of the Noble family

religion, to her dismay, the Korean visitors continually interrupt her to ask questions such as "How old are you?" "How many children do you have?" or "Are your parents living?," which she describes as "irrelevant."[27] What's more, the Koreans don't sit and listen compliantly. When the missionary woman says, "You all know about God, of course?," the Korean shaman reacts "with strong traces of resentment," saying, "Who doesn't know about God? ... Do you take us for animals?"[28] In the end, the missionary's tenet that Jesus Christ is the only "Lord and Savior" is challenged by the Koreans' polytheism. In Baird's account, for the Koreans, "The more objects of worship, the better," and thus the local women decided to "just worship him (Jesus Christ) along with all the rest."[29] Such interactions indicate that the missionary home was a kind of "contact zone" in which vastly different material, religious, and cultural thoughts and practices were dynamically assessed and negotiated for use in the local context.[30]

The missionary home served many other purposes as well. For instance, when Noble held classes at her home, Korean women often brought their children. She found that Korean children were "left untrained," breaking things and acting like tyrants with their mothers. Noble "gave them [the mothers] a little talk on the government of children," and she saw it begin to have some effect as Korean mothers started to discipline and punish children for their unruly behavior.[31] Noble sums up the gradual impact of the missionary home on the Korean woman and family: "She [the Korean woman] is learning, and she sees the bearing out of this truth in concrete, tangible form in the missionary home, by observing the wife and mother, – her freedom, her love, her authority ... this missionary mother has met people who have told her how, in the raising of the children, they have taken pattern after some methods they had seen used in the raising of children in the missionary home."[32] In this way, missionaries considered their home as a site not only for evangelizing but also for "teaching them [Koreans] cleanliness, care of their own health, and that of their children, of making their homes attractive."[33]

What Koreans observed at the missionary home was a Euro-American ideal of modern domesticity and "culture life" (*munhwa saenghwal*) therein. At the

---

[27] Baird, *Daybreak in Korea*, pp. 62–3. [28] Baird, *Daybreak in Korea*, p. 62.
[29] Baird, *Daybreak in Korea*, p. 63.
[30] Mary Louise Pratt, *Imperial Eyes: Travel Writing and Transculturation* (London: Routledge, 1992); Don Baker, "A Slippery, Changing Concept: How Korean New Religions Define Religion," *Journal of Korean Religions* 1, no.1/2 (September 2010): 57–92.
[31] *The Journals of Mattie Wilcox Noble*, February 1, 1897.
[32] Mattie Noble, "The Missionary Home," *The Korea Mission Field* 27, no. 4 (1931): 75–7.
[33] Mattie Wilcox Noble, "Evangelistic Work and Day Schools, Pyeng Yang circuit," Annual Meeting of the Woman's Conference of the Methodist Episcopal Church in Korea (Seoul, May 13–19, 1899), p. 10. See also Jennie Fowler-Willing and Mrs. George Heber Jones (Margaret Bengal Jones), *The Lure of Korea* (Boston: Woman's Foreign Missionary Society, Methodist Episcopal Church, 1910), p. 7.

heart of this "culture life" was music. Lillias Horton Underwood's letter to the *Woman's Work for Woman and our Mission Field*, dated September 3, 1889, captures how the pump organ was an object of great fascination to Korean converts. She wrote: "Large numbers of them [Korean women] come to my house as women at home go to the museum. They marvel over the organ, the music-box, sewing machine, foreign chairs, pictures, mirrors and beds. Miss Hayden and I often sing some bright, striking hymn, which always pleases them."[34] In such visits, resembling more or less excursions, the woman missionary would lead her visitors in songs and prayer,[35] and those visitors would observe the missionary family singing hymns together, which served to introduce them not only to Christian spirituality but to a new sensibility about modern home life in which playing music and singing figured prominently. American missionaries brought the pump organ to Korea mainly for use in church services and music education at mission schools.[36] Introducing hymns and group singing proved an effective way to draw in potential converts, in part because it was presented (and perceived) as part of the modern experience. One of the early converts, Kim Sedŭi, recalled the overwhelming emotional reactions of church members at their first encounter with the sound of the pump organ at the Namsanjae Church in P'yŏngyang in 1897. Entranced by the sound, she noted, they sang hymns and danced to the music with great joy.[37] William C. Kerr, a Presbyterian missionary in Korea, observed commoner women's hymn singing practice as follows:

The music, however foreign it may have been at the beginning, is one of the powerful inspiration features in a large gathering. Old women, who have not gotten so far with their reading that they can fathom the mystery of a page of Scripture, still carry their hymns-books to service and follow the lines with a finger which would say that the owner of the book has made great progress with her letters, while the probability is that she is repeating most of them from memory.[38]

Kerr points out that hymn singing involves an ability to read letters. To those commoner women, who were largely illiterate, reading (or pretending to read) letters was a sign of modernity. The act of singing hymns to the accompaniment of the foreign musical instrument represented a transformation to modernity, which offered the promise of a new modern lifestyle and even upward social

---

[34] "Korea," *Woman's Work for Woman and Our Mission Field* 4, no. 12 (December 1889): 328–9, quoted on 329.
[35] *The Journals of Mattie Wilcox Noble*, December 25, 1893.
[36] Wan Kyu Chung, "An Analysis and Evaluation of Beginning Piano Methods Used in Korea" (PhD dissertation, Texas Tech University, 1992), pp. 60–62.
[37] Mrs. W. A. Noble, comp., *Victorious Lives of Early Christians in Korea* (Seoul: The Christian Literature Society, 1927), pp. 43–4.
[38] William Kerr, "Music in Men's and Women's Bible Classes," *Korea Mission Field* 11, no. 4 (1915): 105, quoted in Hyun Kyong Chang, "Musical Encounters in Korean Christianity: A Trans-pacific Narrative" (PhD dissertation, UCLA, 2014), pp. 50–51.

mobility.[39] Indeed, the popularization of the song "*Home, Sweet Home*," composed by Henry Bishop with lyrics by John Howard Payne, is a feature of this missionary genealogy. In its inaugural issue (1933), the women's magazine *Sin kajŏng* (New Family) published sheet music and lyrics for the song with a detailed biography of Payne (see Figure 2.3).[40] The song was taught and performed at mission schools, concerts, and beyond, contributing to its wider distribution. Here we can see how the idea of "home, sweet home" was promoted through the trio of missionary discourse, materiality, and performativity, which became an integral part of the outlook, style of consumption, and everyday practice of the middle class.[41]

If the "object lesson" of the missionary home were limited to a small segment of the Christian population, the Japanese colonial government engaged in a similar lesson on a grander scale for the wider population. The "Home Exhibition" (Kajŏng Pangnamhoe) in Seoul (September 11–October 31, 1915) was part of the Korean Industrial Exhibition (Chosŏn Mulsan Kongjinhoe), which was held at the site of the Kyŏngbok Palace. With the spectacular demonstration of a plane flying over the exhibition site at the opening ceremony,[42] it was organized to showcase Japan's prowess at achieving modernity and its role in awakening the Korean "people from a hundred years of slumber" and making them realize "the grace of the new rule."[43] Along with the Industrial Exhibition, the colonial government's newspapers, *Kyŏngsŏng ilbo* and *Maeil sinbo*, held the Home Exhibition in their own building near the Kyŏngbok Palace.[44] It is significant that, just as the designers of the Industrial Exhibition "eschewed a recognizably 'Japanese' style of architecture and, instead, drew from an eclectic variety of Renaissance, Secessionist, and other modern aesthetics of Western derivation,"[45] so the "Japanese modern home" at the Home Exhibition showcased primarily Western-style architectural forms, interiors, and objects. The Home Exhibition was a sort of "show and tell" of the modern home. One visitor

---

[39] Nicholas Harkness, *Songs of Seoul: An Ethnography of Voice and Voicing in Christian South Korea* (Berkeley: University of California Press, 2014), pp. 80–111.
[40] *Sin kajŏng* 1 (1933) (no page number). See also *Kajŏng chapchi* 1 (May 1922): 21.
[41] Pang In'gŭn, "Noraehanŭn sŭwitt'ŭhom" (Singing Sweet Home), *Samch'ŏlli* (March 1933): 67.
[42] *Maeil sinbo*, October 5, 1915, p. 3.
[43] Hong Kal, "Modeling the West, Returning to Asia: Shifting Politics of Representation in Japanese Colonial Expositions in Korea," *Comparative Study of Society and History* 47, no. 3 (July 2005): 508.
[44] *Kyŏngsŏng ilbo* was published in Japanese and *Maeil sinbo* was published in Korean.
[45] Todd A. Henry, *Assimilating Seoul: Japanese Rule and the Politics of Public Space in Colonial Korea, 1910–1945* (Berkeley: University of California Press, 2014), p. 99. See also Kal, "Modeling the West, Returning to Asia," pp. 507–10. Kal contrasts the 1915 Exposition, which was characterized by its Western-style architecture as a symbol of modernity and progress, with the 1929 Exposition that "abolished the image of the West as the symbol of modernity" and instead centered on the idea of "co-prosperity" between Japan and Korea as "an effort that was concomitant to the expansion of the Japanese imperial power in Asia."

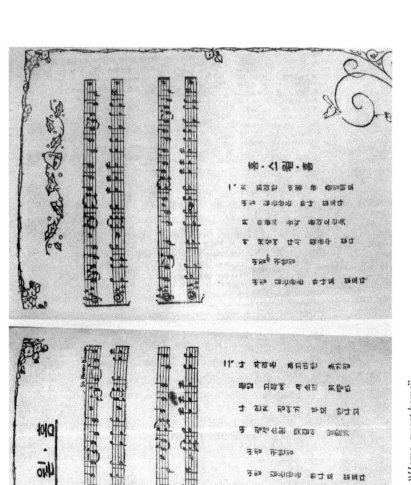

Figure 2.3 *"Home, sweet home"*
Source: *Sin kajŏng* 1 (1933)

advised, "Come and see this exhibition and *reform your home*."[46] It drew the interest of people from all walks of life, and many of those who attended had traveled from faraway provinces to see the exhibits. Schools and various organizations arranged group visits. Every day *Maeil sinbo* ran photographs of scenes from the exhibition, including visits by members of the royal family and other prominent dignitaries. Visitors to the exhibition were presented with displays meant to show the advanced Japanese home, which was rationally designed with separate rooms, each with a specific function and outfitted with modern, often Western-style furniture. In contrast, the model of the Korean home was much smaller, with one big room serving all functions – eating, entertaining, and sleeping – which seemed to represent the backwardness of the past.[47] This juxtaposition seemed to be designed to dramatize the gap between Japan's success in achieving modernity and Korea's failure to do so.[48]

Ironically, what the Japanese colonial government promoted at the Home Exhibition was not Japanese design but largely a Western-style modern home. In this connection, it is important to note that the Home Exhibition in Korea closely replicated the "Home Exhibition" (*katei hakurankai*) that had been mounted in Ueno Park in Tokyo just months earlier, in the spring of 1915, which was also a kind of "object lesson" for the Japanese public, presenting the ideal modern house and home.[49] One of the sponsors of the Tokyo exhibition was the *Kokumin shinbun* (*People's Newspaper*).[50] Significantly, its president Tokutomi Sohō (aka Tokutomi Iichirō) served from 1910 to 1918 as the superintendent of *Kyŏngsŏng ilbo*, which was known as a Keijō (Seoul) branch of *Kokumin shinbun*. In this vein, the Home Exhibitions in Tokyo and Seoul were closely coordinated by the *Kokumin shinbun*.[51] To accompany the Home Exhibition in Tokyo, the publisher of the *Kokumin shinbun* produced a volume entitled *The Ideal Home* (*Risō no katei*), with contributions from experts in home economics, architecture, and related fields. For the volume, the Home Exhibition committee invited experts (and their students) to submit model house plans. In creating those plans, the invitees reflected critically on the traditional Japanese domicile as well as Western models and ways to adapt and adopt elements of Western design into the Japanese home. For example, Itō Chūta, a professor of engineering at Tokyo Imperial University, argues in *The Ideal Home* that the "house" and the family cannot be separated from one

---

[46] "Yangin ŭi an e yŏng han kajŏngbak" (The Home Exhibition Viewed by a Westerner), *Maeil sinbo*, September 26, 1915, p. 3.
[47] Kim Myŏngsŏn, "1915-nyŏn kajŏng pangnamhoe chŏnsi chut'aek ŭi p'yosang" (Representation of "Modern Housing" Exhibited at Home Exposition of *Keijō* in 1915), *Taehan kŏnch'ukhoe nonmunjip* 28, no. 3 (2012): 155–64.
[48] Kal, "Modeling the West, Returning to Asia," 508.
[49] *Pusan ilbo* reported on the Home Exhibition in Tokyo. April 8, 1915, p. 4.
[50] Sand, *House and Home in Modern Japan*, p. 164.
[51] Kim, "1915-nyŏn kajŏng pangnamhoe chŏnsi chut'aek ŭi p'yosang," 155–6.

another, and that the happiness of the family significantly relies on the design and function of the house. He notes that most Japanese homes had been built before the Meiji era and were fundamentally unsuited to modern family life. Even some reformed houses, he points out, show only superficial or partial reform by changing a living room to the Western style or adding Western-style furniture. Itō and his junior colleague Endō Arata designed a model house based on an ideal middle-class family composed of parents, two children, and a housemaid. Their "family-centered" plans were decidedly Western in style, with "innovative details represented in interior perspectives."[52] Another expert, Inoue Hideko, a home economist from Japan Women's College (Nihon Joshi Daigaku) who had been educated at Columbia University and the University of Chicago, discussed the characteristics of Japanese- and Western-style interiors in terms of their function and aesthetics and presented an eclectic design for what would work best in particular rooms. Inoue offered a comparative perspective that was sensitive to social class, and she suggested that a Western-style home interior might be an appropriate option for those who are economically well-to-do, have lots of guests, and want to lead an "orderly and disciplined" life.[53] These examples reflect how the Home Exhibitions in both Japan and Korea largely showcased an idealized Western-style modern home as the ultimate reference point against which Japanese or Korean homes were to be measured and reconfigured.

Whereas the 1915 Home Exhibitions in Tokyo and Seoul were largely based on artificially constructed small-scale models presented with blueprints, the Peace Memorial Exhibition in Tokyo from March to July 1922 featured full-sized model houses. Labeled the "Culture Village" (*bunka mura*), the exhibition site featured fourteen "culture houses," nine of which were based on Western-style architecture in which the family living room was a central locus to which the other rooms were organically connected to improve efficiency, comfort and harmony. The study and the parlor, which did not exist in traditional Japanese houses, were a distinctively Western feature. Rather than sitting on the floor, as in the old-style home, chairs were placed in all the rooms except the bedrooms, as a sign of "improved life," again inspired mostly by the features of Western-style residences.[54]

In Korea, the full-sized modern model homes were on display at the Chosŏn Pangnamhoe (Korean Exposition) held in the Kyŏngbok Palace in Seoul from August to October 1929. Plans for those models were submitted by the Chosŏn

---

[52] Kokumin shinbunsha, ed., *Risō no katei* (Ideal Home) (Tokyo: Kokumin shinbunsha, 1915), pp. 113–28; and Sand, *House and Home in Modern* Japan, pp. 164–7, quoted on p. 166.
[53] Kokumin shinbunsha, *Risō no katei*, pp. 113–28, 137–53.
[54] Kim Yongbŏm, *Munhwa saenghwal kwa munhwa chut'aek: kŭndae chugŏ tamnon ŭl toedoraboda* (Culture Life and Culture House: Reflecting about the Discourse on Modern Housing) (Seoul: Sallim, 2012), pp. 25–30.

Kŏnch'uk Hakhoe (Korean Architecture Association), which had been founded by the Japanese in Korea in 1922. The Association played an important role in shaping and distributing the ideal "culture house" as the new model for modern times. The three model houses in the 1929 Exposition were very similar to the models selected by the Association in its 1922 call for proposals of "improved house designs" that would be suitable for the cultural life of middle-class (Japanese settler) families in the particular climate conditions of Korea. Here a Western-style house design centered on a living room was a predominant feature in these model homes, as it was in the models on display at the 1922 Peace Memorial Exhibition in Tokyo.[55] At the heart of these exhibits was a sense of hierarchy in the architectural design of houses, with the "Western-style" house, represented by the "culture house," being considered superior to Japanese- or Korean-style houses.[56] More importantly, this sense of hierarchy was not separated from people's perceptions of the level of civilization or modern development in Korea, Japan, and the West.[57] Despite its colonial authority in Korea, Japan was seen as a late comer to the modern imperial race. The representations of modern house and home capture this complex situation of the Japanese colonial power in Korea where it had to deal with or compete with Euro-American influences.

"Hom, Sŭwit'ŭ Hom" for the Nation

If the exotic "missionary home" served as an expedient way for American evangelists to convert Koreans to Christianity, and spectacular "home exhibitions" by Japanese colonial authorities were designed to showcase Japan's prowess in modern development, the Korean home and family were a central site for Korean intellectuals to project their nationalist agenda that would regenerate the Korean nation. Making full use of the thriving print media, especially from the early 1920s on under the "Cultural Rule" of the colonial government, Korean intellectuals and reformers took the initiative in various movements under the banners of "new culture" (*sin munhwa*), "new life" (*sin saenghwal*), and "improving everyday life" (*saenghwal kaesŏn*).[58] Taking

---

[55] Kim, Munhwa saenghwal kwa munhwa chut'aek, pp. 31–8.
[56] *Pyŏlgŏn'gon* 64 (June 1933): 27–8; Kim Sŏng'u, "Saeroun tosijut'aek ŭi hyŏngsŏng kwa saenghwal ŭi pyŏnhwa" (The Formation of New Urban Housing and Changes in Life), in *Ilche ŭi singmin chibae wa ilsang saenghwal*, ed. Yonsei University Kukhak Yŏn'guwŏn (Seoul: Hyean, 2004), pp. 75–121; Yi Kyŏnga and Chŏn Pongŭi, "1920–1930-nyŏndae kyŏngsŏngbu ŭi munhwajut'aekchi kaebal e taehan yŏn'gu" (A Study of the Development of the District of Culture Houses in Seoul in the 1920s and 1930s) *Taehan kŏnch'ukhakhoe nonmunjip* 22, no. 3 (March 2006): 191–200.
[57] Popular literature depicted the height of buildings in New York and London vis-à-vis Tokyo and Seoul as if it were a measure of modernity. See Chŏng Chuhŭi, "Kŭndae chŏk chugŏ konggan kwa chip ŭi sasang" (Modern Residential Space and Ideas about House) (PhD dissertation, Yonsei University, 2012), pp. 10–12.
[58] Chŏng, "Kŭndae chŏk chugŏ konggan kwa chip ŭi sasang," p. 13.

"home" as the foundation for the new nation, they advocated not only the cultivation of stronger, positive, and forward-looking mindset but also specific material improvements and changes in lifestyle, ranging from the renovation of the traditional kitchen and toilet to enhanced hygiene, a reformed diet, and a well-planned household budget.[59]

Journalists featured articles describing the "home, sweet home" of well-known public figures, presenting details of the interior design of the house, the family diet, the daily schedule of the family members, their practices of social etiquette, their approach to childrearing, and examples of family activities such as picnics, all presented as a reflection of modern taste and a step forward in the modern reformation of the nation.[60] One example of such a featured article is the description of the home of Yi Kwangsu (1892–1950) and Hŏ Yŏngsuk (1895–1975) published in *Pyŏlgŏn'gon* magazine in 1930 with the title, "Sweet Home: A Report on Visiting Mr. Yi Kwangsu."[61] Yi was arguably the best-known and most influential writer in Korea at that time, and Hŏ was a pioneering figure as a woman medical doctor. Hŏ had trained at Tokyo Women's Medical College in Japan and opened a clinic (Yŏnghye Ŭiwŏn) in Seoul in 1920 – the first clinic for women established by a Korean woman doctor in history.[62] The female reporter describes Yi and Hŏ's tiled-roof Korean-style house as being in a neighborhood with several Western-style "culture houses." The descriptions in the article reflect a combination of both traditional and modern furnishings and features. For instance, the reporter recounts looking through the glass windows installed in the main-floor room, a decidedly modern feature not found in traditional Korean interiors, but also mentions that the doors to the rooms were covered with rice paper, a standard feature in the Korean-style home. Inside the reporter finds an organ, a record player, and bookshelves filled with literary and medical books – signs of a "cultured life." Hŏ's description of the family's diet emphasizes the husband's taste as the central consideration in preparing menus. Yi is described as being largely vegetarian but having a special fondness for fish dishes prepared in the

---

[59] Some examples include: "Sin saenghwal ŭl haya pon sirhŏm" (Experiments with New Life), *Pyŏlgŏn'gon* 16/17 (December 1928): 36–47; "Hyŏnha munje myŏngsa ŭigyŏn, saenghwal kaesŏnan cheŭi" (Opinion of Renowned People on Current Issues, Proposal for Improving Everyday Life), *Pyŏlgŏn'gon* 16/17 (December 1928): 22–30; and Kim Sŏngjin, "Uri kajŏng ŭi wisaeng chŏk saenghwal kaesŏn, chisang hagi taehak" (Hygiene and Life Improvement in our Family, Summer College in Print), *Tonggwang* 36 (August 1932): 63–9.

[60] Some examples include stories about Chu Yohan's wife Ch'oe Sŏndŏk in *Samch'ŏlli* 5, no. 3 (1933), Pak Hwasŏng's house in *Samch'ŏlli* 8, no. 8 (August 1936), Chang Tŏksu and Pak Ŭnhye's home in *Samch'ŏlli* 10, no. 1 (1938), Pang Ingŭn's home in *Samch'ŏlli* 5, no. 3 (March 1933), and Mo Yunsuk's home in *Kaebyŏk sin'gan* 2 (December 1934): 84–5.

[61] "Sŭwit'ŭ hom, Yi Kwangsu ssi kajŏng pangmun'gi" (Sweet Home: A Report on Visiting Mr. Yi Kwangsu), *Pyŏlgŏn'gon* 34 (November 1930): 110–13.

[62] *Tonga ilbo*, May 1, 1920.

Japanese style because of the years he spent in Japan. She makes the point that red chili peppers are avoided because Hŏ feels that food that is too stimulating is bad for his health. She also notes that garlic is supposed to be good for one's health but that its repellent smell is not good for social life, so she never uses it. The reporter inquires into what the family does for entertainment (*orak*) – another modern feature of "sweet home" – and Hŏ answers that they go on picnics in the suburbs when Yi has days off from work. Finally, when the reporter asks about Hŏ's childrearing philosophy, she describes her belief in maintaining a strict schedule for feeding her children. This is different from the traditional practice in which mothers would nurse children whenever the child seemed to be hungry. Hŏ says that she has raised her children to be disciplined and has trained them not to eat anything without her permission. Although she shares her husband's perspective on gender relations with a central emphasis on motherhood for the family and the nation,[63] her modern "sweet home" is not free from conflict or tension. Hŏ tells the reporter that Yi really doesn't like her to go out, so she stays at home unless she has very important business. The area in which the couple tends to quarrel most is on childrearing, especially when the children are sick. Although Hŏ was a medical doctor who ran her own clinic prior to marrying Yi, her husband does not accept her opinion on the appropriate medical treatment for their children, and this has been something of a sore spot for her in the conduct of the household.

This type of home profile offered readers a glimpse into the modern home and new practices in the modern family. Such an ideal is based on a nuclear family composed of a husband, a wife, and children typically living in an urban area. The wife would have been well-educated and scientifically minded in managing family nutrition and childrearing. Moreover, the well-being of her husband and children was seen to be such an important priority that even a highly trained professional woman like Hŏ was expected to stay at home and refrain from going out. In the end, the overall message of articles like this tends to reinforce the ideal of the "wise mother, good wife" (*hyŏnmo yangch'ŏ*) with a modern twist.

Beyond the peek it provided into the lives of well-known public figures, Koreans were particularly interested in foreign-educated Korean women and men, especially those who had studied in Europe or the United States, and newspapers and magazines frequently invited those individuals with experience of living abroad to share their ideas on the ideal modern home and offer a comparative perspective. Going overseas for advanced study was highly unusual in a society where the majority of the population did not receive even an

---

[63] Hŏ Yŏngsuk published a series of articles in *Tonga ilbo* between 1925 and 1926 with specific focus on family and home hygiene. See Sin Tongwŏn, "Ilche kangjŏmgi yŏ ŭisa Hŏ Yŏngsuk ŭi sam kwa ŭihak" (Life and Works of Hŏ Yŏngsuk, the First Female Medical Practitioner), *Ŭisahak* 21, no. 1 (2012): 25–66.

elementary level of education.[64] Therefore, these foreign-educated elite had significant prestige and credentials for shaping the discourse on modern domesticity.[65]

The vast majority of Korean elite studied in Japan. Only a small number managed to travel to alternative destinations such as the United States, Europe, China, Canada, and Australia to acquire modern knowledge. However, despite the fact that Japan hosted the largest number of Korean students, references to Japanese home are surprisingly scarce in commentaries on domesticity in the print media, at least prior to the *kōminka* era (1937–1945). The policies during *kōminka*, which literally means to "transform [colonial subjects] into imperial subjects,"[66] were implemented to support Japan's imperial wars, and those policies aggressively shaped the discourse of domesticity and presented the Japanese home as the ideal.[67] Until the mid-1930s, however, the predominant models of domesticity introduced in the print media originated in Europe or the United States.[68] This imbalance can be attributed to several factors. First, as Chapter 3 describes in detail, the Korean female students who went to Japan for advanced study often enrolled in American mission schools, where they had ample exposure to US- and Western-style domesticity even within Japan.[69]

---

[64] The enrollment rate in elementary schools throughout the period of Japanese colonial rule remained low. In 1912, 4.4 percent of six-year olds were enrolled in public elementary schools. By 1930 it had risen only to 19.8 percent, and by 1942 the rate still stood at only 50 percent.

[65] O Ch'ŏnsŏk, "Miguk yuhaksaengsa" (History of Studying in the US) *Samch'ŏlli* 5, no. 1 (1933): 26–9.

[66] Helen J. S. Lee, "Eating for the Emperor: The Nationalization of Settler Homes and Bodies in the Kōminka Era," in *Reading Colonial Japan: Text, Context, and Critique*, eds. Michelle M. Mason and Helen J. S. Lee (Stanford: Stanford University Press, 2012), pp. 141–77; Wan-yao Chou, "The Kōminka Movement in Taiwan and Korea: Comparisons and interpretations," in *The Japanese Wartime Empire, 1931–1945*, eds. Peter Duus, Ramon H. Myers, and Mark R. Peattie (Princeton: Princeton University Press, 1996), pp. 40–68. For motherhood during the Asia Pacific War, see An T'aeyun, *Singmin chŏngch'i wa mosŏng* (Colonial Politics and Motherhood) (P'aju: Han'guk haksul chŏngbo, 2006).

[67] For an account of everyday life during the kōminka era, see Michael Kim, "Mothers of the Empire: Military Conscription and Mobilisation in Late Colonial Korea," in *Gender Politics and Mass Dictatorship: Global Perspectives*, eds. Jie-Hyun Lim and Karen Petrone (Basingstoke: Palgrave Macmillan, 2011), pp. 193–212; Lee, "Eating for the Emperor."

[68] Even in Japanese-founded magazines, such as *Uri ŭi kajŏng* (*Our Family*, 1913), models from the United States and Europe predominated. In fact, the dominant influence of Euro-American models is found beyond the discourse of domesticity. For example, in the case of translations of foreign literature into Korean, the majority of translations were of European and American literature, with very few works of Japanese literature being translated into Korean. See Pak Chinyŏng, "Chungguk munhak mit Ilbon munhak pŏnyŏk ŭi yŏksasŏng kwa sangsangyŏk ŭi chŏppyŏn" (Historicity and Imagination of Chinese and Japanese Literature Translations), *Tongbang hakchi* 164 (December 2013): 259–85.

[69] Pak Sŏnmi, *Kŭndae yŏsŏng cheguk ŭl kŏch'ŏ Chosŏn ŭro hoeyu hada* (Modern Women Return to Korea via Empire) (Seoul: Ch'angbi, 2007), pp. 47–60, 176–82. See also Paek Okgyŏng, "Kŭndae Han'guk yŏsŏng ŭi Ilbon yuhak kwa yŏsŏng hyŏnsil insik–1910-nyŏn dae rŭl chungsim ŭro" (Korean Women's Studying in Japan and their Viewpoints on Reality in the 1910s), *Ihwa sahak yŏn'gu* 39 (2009): 1–28.

Second, Japanese home economics had been significantly influenced by US home economics. The University of Chicago and Columbia University were especially prominent as institutions where some of the most influential Japanese home economists received their training.[70] Last, in the eyes of the colonized Koreans, the origin of modernity was firmly rooted in the West. An editorial in *Tonga ilbo*, a major daily newspaper in colonial-era Korea, captures this perception when it encourages students to go to Europe or the United States to learn *authentic* Western civilizations directly in order to help make a modern Korea.[71]

A common feature in this discourse biased toward Euro-American modernity was the presentation of a stark contrast between the dismal culture of the Korean home and the idealized (often exaggerated) image of family life in the Euro-American home.[72] This contrast was presented in the interest of reforming the Korean family, whose transformation was understood to be crucial for regenerating the Korean nation. For example, Kim Up'yŏng, who had studied in the United States, characterized Korean family life as "irrational" and lacking in a spirit of "team work" in comparison to the simplicity and reasonable management that governed the American family.[73] Yi Sŏngyong, a medical doctor who had studied in Germany, proposed that Koreans adopt four specific German practices to improve home life: establish habits that promote cleanliness, keep a well-organized household, maintain a disciplined daily schedule, and adopt scientific childrearing methods.[74] Another commentator, Kim Hamna, who studied home economics in the United States, observed that American parents nurtured children's individuality and self-esteem, and she lauded these American methods as "more civilized" than Korean parenting practices.[75] Undoubtedly, the picture of the modern Euro-American home that these writers presented was often based on rather limited exposure during short sojourns in those societies, and thus their impressions

---

[70] Pak, *Kŭndae yŏsŏng*, pp. 157–65.   [71] *Tonga ilbo*, March 24, 1921.
[72] Some of the most dramatic overgeneralizations about foreign family culture can be found in a series of articles published in *Tonga ilbo* in 1931. The series focuses on "foreign family's lifestyle and appropriate examples to apply to Korean family." It includes cases of German, French, Russian, Chinese, Japanese, American, and English families. The key characteristics of the various countries were: thrift and industriousness (Germany), freedom and equality (France), socialized collective system (Russia), polygamy (China), mutual consultation by couples on public and private matters (Japan), heaven for women (US), and gentility toward both genders (UK).
[73] Interestingly, he argues that a husband's income should be divided equally, with the wife receiving one half for her contribution to the family by providing the domestic labor for cooking, cleaning and childrearing, which, in turn, helps her husband to be productive in his work life. *Pyŏlgŏn'gon* 16/17 (December 1928): 77–8.
[74] *Pyŏlgŏn'gon* 16/17 (December 1928): 73–4. Yi had met his wife, a native of Czechoslovakia, while studying in Germany, and the public was fascinated by their "borderless romance" and their two-story Western-style brick house.
[75] *Pyŏlgŏn'gon* 16/17 (December 1928): 75–6.

were fairly superficial.[76] Very few paid any attention to the diversity and complexity that were present in those societies in terms of class, race, religion, or location. Instead, they typically focused on white middle- or upper-middle-class families and highlighted a more or less idealized prototype of the modern bourgeois family as the standard measure against which the old patterns of Korean family life should be reflected on and reformed.

Although this decidedly elitist discourse on the modern home gained currency for its novelty and cosmopolitanism, some Korean intellectuals engaged the foreign models critically, questioning how relevant or appropriate they were for Korean realities. For example, a magazine called *Urak'i*, published by Korean students in the United States, introduced the idealized American family as the "birthplace, if no other, of American ideals such as democracy, liberty and a truism."[77] At the same time, some found that the "American family is by no means perfect. From the viewpoint of *Asian morality*, one finds things that are unpalatable and not so beautiful," such as the high rate of divorce and an overwhelming desire for material comfort and leisure.[78] More importantly, these intellectuals paid attention to the significant gap between everyday reality in the typical Korean household and the images and material forms of the ideal modern home that had been put forward by elite women and men. They wondered how relevant the highly specific Western ideal was for the average Korean family. The middle-class, urban ideal of a modern home that was managed by an educated housewife did not readily comport with the conditions in most Korean households. The majority of Korean women were illiterate, working under terrible conditions in factories, or laboring on subsistence farms in the countryside within the context of the rapid industrialization and rural poverty in the 1920s and 1930s. Thus, for the overwhelming majority of Koreans, the "sweet home" was a mirage. Intellectuals, especially those who had a socialist orientation or who were committed to the rural revitalization movement, called attention to the significant disparity between the privileged few and the large numbers of rural and urban poor, women and men alike, in terms of having the resources to practice new ideals for the modern family. As Sunyoung Park shows, the socialist woman writer Kang Kyŏngae (1906–1944)

---

[76] Sometimes a writer offers a close-up virtual tour of life in the household of one of these foreign families. One such example came from Na Hyesŏk, a high-profile woman intellectual and painter, who presented a fairly detailed description of the daily life of the French family with whom she stayed for about three months in 1927. See Na Hyesŏk, "Tajŏng hago silchil chŏgin pullansŏ puin," *Chung'ang* (March 1934), quoted in Sŏ Chŏngja, *Chŏngwŏl Na Hyesŏk chŏnjip* (Works of Chŏngwŏl Na Hyesŏk) (Seoul: P'ŭrŭn sesang, 2013), pp. 665–71, 687–90.

[77] *Urak'i* 2 (1926): 7–13. *Urak'i* 3 (1928): 1–11.

[78] Son Chinsil, "Miguk kajŏng esŏ paeul kŏt myŏtkkaji" (Things to Learn from the American Family), *Urak'i* 3 (1928): 108–12, quoted on 108–9; emphasis added; Hŏ Chŏngsuk, "Ulchul anŭn inhyŏng ŭi yŏjaguk, Puk-Mi insanggi" (The Country of a Doll that Knows How to Cry: Observations of North America), *Pyŏlgŏn'gon* 10 (December 1927): 74–77.

fundamentally challenged this idealized hegemonic image of domesticity that glorified motherhood. In her novellas, such as *Sogŭm* (Salt, 1934) and *In'gan munje* (The Human Predicament, 1934), Kang presents the household "in its rawness and physicality, as a place of hard labor for bare survival."[79] In doing so, she offers a competing discourse on the ideal of the "sweet home."

Still, by the early 1930s, the ideals of "home, sweet home" and the "culture house" had become cultural icons through the print media and creative works that signaled progress toward modernity, despite deeply fraught class division and a significant gap between the ideals and realities. As Jordan Sand argues, modern domesticity can be viewed "less as a response to new social conditions reiterated in multiple isolated regional and national contexts than as part of a discursive bundle of interpretations and reinterpretations, carried by imperialism and an accelerating global trade in texts and images."[80] The drastic gap between the actual economic conditions most Koreans lived in and the idealized images of the modern home did not prevent the circulation of the discourse on "home, sweet home." In a significant way, those dire conditions may have made the fanciful modern home an object of desire even though it was unobtainable for the majority of the population. The linguistic adoption of the English term "*hom, sŭwit'ŭ hom*," rather than using a Korean translation captures an emerging sensibility toward Western modernity that signaled new, modern material practices and daily patterns.[81]

As amply demonstrated at the home exhibitions, images of *hom, sŭwit'ŭ hom* were embodied in an architectural transformation of the house into a "culture house." Largely referring to a Western-style, two-story house, the culture house was designed by professional architects – both Korean and Japanese. Unlike the traditional Korean house, or *hanok*, in which inner chambers were separated from outer chambers, the spatial design of the culture house was inclusive, private, and enclosed by walls. For purposes of efficiency, hygiene, and privacy, each room was designed with a distinctive function: parlor, living room, dining room, master bedroom, study, kitchen, and children's playroom. Home interiors were also filled with imported foreign paraphernalia such as pianos, radios, electric fans, and phonographs. Korean literature in the 1920s and 1930s reflects the desire of people to live in such culture houses. For example, in his novel, *Chaesaeng* (Rebirth), Yi Kwangsu offers vivid details of modern Western-style interiors. A wealthy male character, Paek Yunhŭi, tries

---

[79] Sunyoung Park, "Rethinking Feminism in Colonial Korea: Kang Kyŏngae and 1930s Socialist Women's Literature," *positions* 21, no. 4 (2013): 947–85, quoted on 967. For the translation of Kang's novel, *In'gan munje*, see Kang Kyŏng-ae, *From Wonso Pond: A Colonial-period Korean Novel, through the Eyes of its Working-Class Heroes*, trans. Samuel Perry (New York: Feminist Press, 2009).

[80] Sand, *House and Home in Modern Japan*, p. 7.

[81] The terms "home, sweet home" and "sweet home" were used interchangeably in the media.

to seduce a young woman, Kim Sunyŏng, by inviting her to his house, which has a separate "Western suite" (*yangsil*). Sunyŏng is overwhelmed by the grand scale and luxury of this residence with its exotic marble fireplace, silk wallpaper, piano, and bed made up with white sheets and a mosquito net hanging over it.[82]

The obsession with the "culture house" was also reflected in cartoons of the time. These cartoons often poke fun at the vanity and absurdity of those who fell for anything Western, particularly the two-story Western-style "culture house." The cartoon in Figure 2.4 by An Sŏgyŏng creatively exploits the homophony of the Chinese characters for "culture house" (文化住宅) and "annoying house" (蚊禍住宅) to ridicule the vain desire of people to have a fancy "culture house" even though it sets them up for huge debt and economic misery.

In spite of the fact that only a tiny group of wealthy urban residents could afford a "culture house," it is notable that Korean reformers and intellectuals liberally used the concept of "home, sweet home" not just for its association with the privilege available to the urban elite but also as a symbol of the new family, which was open to all, even the poorest and the least educated.[83] Popular literature, in particular, conjured up the idealized image of "home" in pastoral, peaceful farmlands where affection and care govern the family and hard-working farmers gain deep satisfaction even from very modest material comfort.[84] The idea of "home, sweet home" gradually spread not only among people of the middle and upper classes but also to those in poor rural communities. Modern Western ideals of "home" meshed with nationalist demands to renovate the

---

[82] Yi Kwangsu, *Chaesaeng* (Rebirth) (Seoul: Uri munhaksa, 1996), pp. 60–62. This novel was serialized in *Tonga ilbo* from November 9, 1924 to September 28, 1925. Another novel, Y*ŏin sŏngjang* by Pak T'aewŏn, is also an excellent example of the description of "culture house" with Western-style home interiors. It was serialized in *Maeil sinbo* from August 1, 1940 to February 9, 1942.

[83] *Sin Kajŏng* (April 1933): 137; Yi Kwangsu, *Hŭk* (Soil) (serialized in *Tonga ilbo* in 1932–1933); Sim Hun, *Sangnoksu* (Evergreen) (serialized in *Tonga ilbo* in 1935–1936).

[84] For example, a song, "Sin kajŏng" (New Family), written by Pyŏn Yŏngno and composed by Hyŏn Chemyŏng. *Sin Kajŏng* (January 1936): 8. See also "Munye e nat'anan kwinong undong" (The Movement to Return to the Rural, Represented in Literature), *Sin kajŏng* (June 1935): 32–33. A poem entitled "Our Home," published in *Sin kajŏng* (New Family) in April, 1933 (p. 137), reflects the significance of the phrase "sweet home" for the greater population:

> I till the land, she makes clothes.
> We help each other in matters large and small, making a home.
> Isn't this a true life? My family is a sweet home.
> Nothing is more precious in this world than love,
> Love even among the tilling farmers.
> It is out of love that we nurture our sons and daughters.
> Sharing joy and suffering together all the time,
> Tasting the sweetness of our supper after a long day's work,
> A *sweet home* is what this is, and let us live like this ever after.

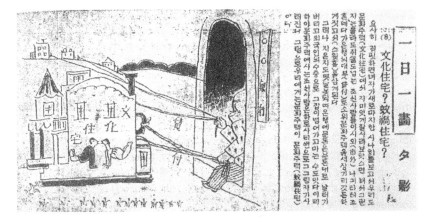

Figure 2.4 "Culture house" (文化住宅)? or "annoying house" (蚊禍住宅)?
Source: *Chosŏn ilbo*, April 14, 1930

Korean home and family, forging reforms that incorporated Western practices moderated by consideration of the impoverished realities of colonial Korea.

Home, a Site of Transpacific Imagination and Adaptation

The models of the "missionary home" and the "culture house," as well as the image of "home, sweet home," were gradually incorporated into the development of "home economics" (*kasa*) as an academic discipline. The Department of Home Economics was established at Ewha Women's Professional School (Ewha Yŏja Chŏnmun Hakkyo) in 1929, and the formal establishment of that program helped to elevate the domestic sphere to a new status by incorporating academic training in economics, biology, bacteriology, physiology, family nursing, and various other fields of science.[85] The notion of "home economics" as a new field of study was introduced to Korea via Japan where the Japanese neologism *kaseigaku* ("the study of household management") began to be used

---

[85] The historian Sonja Kim uses "Domestic Sciences" instead of "home economics" to "highlight the flexibility and permeability of household-related subjects." She argues that the Domestic Sciences "was not a set program of study with a clearly defined syllabus or agenda. Rather, the Domestic Sciences was an amalgam of sometimes disparate, occasionally conflicting, yet overall interconnected subjects that varied depending on the time period, level of education (primary, middle, secondary, vocational, specialized), and particular school." Sonja Kim, *Imperatives of Care: Women and Medicine in Colonial Korea* (Honolulu: University of Hawai'i Press, 2019), p. 16. I use "home economics" in this chapter largely because it was officially used as the name of the department at Ewha and Oregon Agricultural College at the time.

from the early Meiji era in the 1870s.[86] Further, from the late-nineteenth century on enlightenment-oriented Korean intellectuals actively engaged in discourse on women's education and its role at home as part of a social reform agenda for the construction of a strong modern nation-state. Some of the pioneering magazines in early-twentieth-century Korea, including *Sŏu* (*Friends of the West*, 1906–1908), *T'aegŭk hakpo* (*Korean Students' Gazette*, 1906–1908), *Kajŏng chapchi* (*The Home Magazine*, 1906–1908), *Yŏja chinam* (*Women's Guide*, 1908), and *Honam hakpo* (*Honam Newsletter*, 1908–1909), published a number of articles that advocated teaching home economics as a necessity for building healthy, productive families, which would, in turn, help make the nation stronger.[87] As Ji-Eun Lee aptly points out, the "double domestic" view that "a woman's natural and proper place is at home with her family, which in turn is the bedrock of the nation" prevailed in the discourses on modern domesticity in these articles.[88] Largely written by male elites, the articles mostly concentrate on information about better childrearing practices and domestic hygiene, with topics ranging from proper attitudes during pregnancy and the benefits of nursing to the merits of periodic vaccinations, the maintenance of a hygienic environment, the emotional development in children and ideas for keeping children entertained. All these articles point to the key role of the housewife (*chubu*) and mother, who should supervise family members, establish and maintain good family culture, take care of family hygiene and finances, and instill patriotism in their children.[89]

If the print media played a role in advocating modern domesticity at the national level, then schools for girls were the actual training ground where the curriculum trained students systematically in womanly duties and household management. At mission schools, religion was naturally considered to be the foundation of the education they provided, so missionaries took every opportunity to teach about Christianity in various courses. For instance, when students were "engaged in needle-work, the gospel story is read to them and explained."[90] Along with emphasis on Christianity, pioneering missionary educators such as Mary F. Scranton and Lulu Frey made it clear that the training in the missionary schools stressed domestic skills and beyond that "Korean ways" of domesticity. This was done in an effort to dispel local people's suspicion that a foreign education would westernize Korean girls. Scranton

---

[86] Kim, *Imperatives of Care*, pp. 14–50. See also Ch'oe Yunjŏng, "Sŭwit'ŭ hom e taehan hwansang kwa kŭndae adong munhak e nat'anan mosŏng" (A Study on the Illusion of "A Sweet Home" and Motherhood in Modern Children's Literature), *Han'guk adong munhak yŏn'gu* 23 (2012): 225–55.
[87] *Sŏu* 10 (September 1907); and *Honam hakpo* 1 (June, 1908).
[88] Ji-Eun Lee, *Women Pre-Scripted: Forging Modern Roles through Korean Print* (Honolulu: University of Hawai'i Press, 2015), p. 68.
[89] Lee, *Women Pre-Scripted*, pp. 58–81.
[90] H. G. Appenzeller, "Woman's Work in Korea," *The Gospel in All Lands* (September 1891): 424.

wrote: "I emphasize the fact that they [Korean students] are not being made over again after our foreign ways of living, dress, and surroundings.... We take pleasure in making Koreans better Koreans only."[91] One way to appeal to reassure the local people was to emphasize that girls at mission schools were trained to become "model housewives."[92] Louise Rothweiler, teacher at Ewha Girls' School, further articulated the situation as follows:

Whatever may be the private opinion of any one concerning woman's sphere and proper occupation, we must, for the present, at least act under the supposition that in Korea domestic life is her sphere and destiny. Whatever else we may want our girls to do or be, it must be all secondary to this first calling... . They must learn to prepare food, cut, make and repair their clothing, keep themselves and their rooms neat and this all in purely Korean style except where we can improve on that without weaning them from their people, making them discontented with their surroundings or creating demands in them that cannot be supplied when they leave us.[93]

To be sure, domestic skills were not the only subjects included in the curriculum at mission schools. More diverse and advanced subjects were added, including chemistry, physics, English literature, world geography, geometry, algebra, psychology, music, and physical education.[94] However, the emphasis on "Korean ways" and "domesticity" at mission schools continued in the first half of the twentieth century.

Domesticity-centered education for girls was also evident at secular schools supervised by the Japanese colonial government. In high schools for girls, for example, classes on "Household Work" (*kasa*, four hours per week) and "Sewing and Handicrafts" (*chaebong kŭp suye*, ten hours per week) constituted almost 50 percent of the weekly schedule.[95] The emphasis on domesticity at both mission and secular schools was in harmony with the overall vision of conservative Korean intellectuals and reformers who advocated the "wise mother, good wife" as the ultimate goal of educated women.[96]

Whereas domestic skills were incorporated into the curriculum of girls' schools as a matter of practical training for future mothers and wives, the establishment of the Department of Home Economics in 1929 at Ewha

---

[91] *Gospel in All Lands* (August 1888): 373.
[92] George Gilmore, *Korea from Its Capital* (Philadelphia: The Presbyterian Board of Publication, 1892), p. 300.
[93] *The Korean Repository* (March 1892): 90.
[94] Han'guk yŏsŏngsa p'yŏnch'an wiwŏnhoe, *Han'guk yŏsŏngsa* 2 (History of Korean Women) (Seoul: Ewha yŏdae ch'ulp'anbu, 1972), p. 315.
[95] Chŏng Chaech'ŏl, *Ilche ŭi Taehan'guk singminji kyoyuk chŏngch'aeksa* (History of Educational Policy in Korea under Japanese Colonial Rule) (Seoul: Ilchisa, 1985), p. 322. The data about class hours were collected during the First Educational Ordinance, 1911–1922.
[96] Chu Yosŏp, "Yoja kyoyuk kaesinan" (Proposal for Reform of Women's Education), *Sin yŏsŏng* 5, no. 5 (1931): 8–12; Yi Kwangsu, "Mosŏng chungsim ŭi yŏja kyoyuk" (Women's Education Centering on Motherhood), *Sin yŏsŏng* 3, no. 1 (1925): 19–20.

Women's Professional School – the only institution of higher education for women in Korea at that time – was the culmination of ongoing efforts to develop a modern domestic ideology and set of practices and then systematically train skilled home economists. At the heart of this development was a transpacific network fostered by Protestant mission organizations, mission schools, and the students who graduated from them and went on to study overseas. The movement to establish a department of home economics began when Harriett Morris, an American Methodist missionary, joined the faculty of Ewha in 1921. She had received a B.A. in home economics from Kansas State University in 1918 and had taught the subject in Wichita, Kansas, for two years before coming to Korea. At Ewha she began to introduce Western cooking techniques, and for the first time presented Western notions of a balanced diet that took into consideration calorie intake and nutritional value.[97] Morris also learned Korean cooking, primarily from her Korean colleagues, and she later wrote a cookbook, *The Art of Korean Cooking* (1959), for the American public, which was also used to raise funds for Ewha's Department of Home Economics.[98]

The year 1923 is especially significant for understanding the function of transpacific networks in institution-building. It is the year that Ava B. Milam (1884–1976), a professor of home economics at Oregon Agricultural College (present-day Oregon State University; hereafter, OAC), made her first visit to Korea as part of an East Asian tour (1922–1924) to "spread the gospel of home economics."[99] Sponsored by the Women's Foreign Mission Board of the Methodist Church, Milam began a two-year residency in Peking, China, to assist in starting a home economics department at Yenching University. During her stay there she also visited Korea and Japan, conducting surveys and visiting native homes to learn the local "customs in homes, social life, family relationships, child guidance and care, family finance, housing, household management."[100] Short visits to various mission schools in Korea, including Ewha, laid the crucial foundation for her long-lasting involvement in the development of home economics in colonial and postcolonial

---

[97] *Kajŏng taehak, Ewha kajŏnghak 50-nyŏnsa* (The Fiftieth History of Home Economics at Ewha) (Seoul: Ewha yŏja taehakkyo kajŏng taehak, 1979), pp. 173–5.

[98] Harriett Morris, *The Art of Korean Cooking* (Rutland: Charles E. Tuttle Company, 1959); "Furthering Home Economics on a World Wide Basis," 3. fol. Home Economics Students Projects, Box 4, Ava Milam Clark Papers, Oregon State University Archives, Corvallis, Oregon (AMC Papers, hereafter, OSU).

[99] Helen Schneider, "The professionalization of Chinese domesticity: Ava B. Milam and home economics at Yenching University," in *China's Christian Colleges: Cross-Cultural Connections, 1900–1950*, eds. Daniel H. Bays and Ellen Widmer (Stanford: Stanford University Press, 2009), pp. 125–46, quoted on p. 132. Milam is the author of *Adventures of a Home Economist* (Corvallis: Oregon State University Press, 1969).

[100] Ava B. Milam, "A Project in International Friendship, Oct. 1938," 1, fol. Home Economics Students Projects, Box 4, AMC Papers, OSU.

Korea.[101] As detailed below, Milam's East Asian trips and her interactions with local specialists, students, and ordinary citizens proved to be an essential ingredient for transpacific collaborations that effectively linked the local with the regional and the global.

One significant outcome of Milam's first East Asian tour was the creation of a scholarship program at OAC in 1924, called the "International Friendship Scholarship," largely funded with the dues paid by members of the Home Economics Club (fifty cents per quarter per member) and various fund-raising activities, including rummage sales, catering services, and sales of cookbooks.[102] These efforts raised $500 annually to support foreign students. The scholarship was established to train Asian students, generally at the graduate level, with two broad aims: First, that "Westerners could open the way and help in guiding the thinking" of the Asian students; and second, perhaps more importantly, that those students would eventually indigenize home economics.[103] It is interesting that in 1924, the same year the scholarship program was set up, the US government enacted the new Immigration Act, which introduced national origin quotas and completely excluded Asian countries. The 1924 Immigration Act reflected a growing anti-Asian sentiment that took place within the historical contexts of the "yellow peril" and a stratified division between whites and nonwhites.[104] Although this anti-Asian immigration law was largely exclusionary, it did define a class of "non-quota" immigrants that included foreigners whose sole purpose for entering the United States was to study at institutions of higher education.[105] The "non-quota" class was designed to allow the US government, along with educational, religious, and business groups, to strategically recruit talented foreign students who could act as a bridge and "spread U.S. practices and institutions, values and goods."[106] Christian groups such as the Young Men's

---

[101] To encourage further development of the field in Asia, she divided an inheritance she received from her father's estate and donated "a little money" to four women's colleges – Ginling in Nanking, Hwa Nan in Foochow, Yenching in Peking and Ewha College in Seoul – before returning to the US. Milam, *Adventures of a Home Economist*, p. 161.

[102] Milam, "A Project in International Friendship," 2, fol. Home Economics Students Projects, Box 4, AMC Papers, OSU. This is a five-page type-written paper with no date indicated; however, the content of the text suggests that it was written in 1937. See also Milam, "Furthering Home Economics on a World Wide Basis," 3. AMC Papers, OSU.

[103] Milam, "A Project in International Friendship," 2; Milam, "Home Economics: A Basic Need for Democracy in the Orient," August (1949), pp. 7–8, fol. Speeches of the Orient, Box 3, AMC Papers, OSU. Milam notes that the International Friendship Scholarship money "should be used primarily for graduate work," however, "a deserving girl's background was not strong enough for her to undertake advanced study, we accepted candidates for baccalaureate degrees." See Milam, *Adventures of a Home Economist*, p. 167.

[104] Raymond Leslie Buell, "Again the Yellow Peril," *Foreign Affairs* 2, no. 2 (December 15, 1923): 295–309.

[105] "Outstanding Features of the Immigration Act of 1924," *Columbia Law Review* 25, no. 1 (January 1925): 90–95.

[106] Paul A. Kramer, "International Students and U.S. Global Power in the Long 20th Century," *The Asia-Pacific Journal*, 3-3-10, January 18, 2010 (online journal).

Christian Association and Young Women's Christian Association spearheaded efforts to assist foreign students in adjusting to life in the United States, to ensure that their stays in the United States were beneficial. In particular, female foreign students were considered "significant because as home-makers and professional women ... they will mould currents of thought in their own countries."[107] Milam's initiative in setting up the scholarship was part of her vision toward "furthering home economics on a world wide basis," which aligned with broader US policy to expand its political, economic, and cultural power globally through the training of foreign students.[108]

The scholarships were available only to those with recommendations from prominent women's colleges in China, Korea, and Japan, and recipients were required to return to their home countries to teach home economics after receiving advanced training at OAC. To ensure students' success as professionals after returning to their homeland, Milam put a high priority on "adaptation" and "indigenization" of Western knowledge.[109] She wrote:

> Home economics [in East Asia] often is too Westernized. Many of the trained foreign women are unable to adapt the work to the needs of the people of their land and make the work truly indigenous. As a result the public too often regards home economics [as] foreign and not very useful.[110]

Milam's concern about Westernization was not unique. Foreign students themselves were keenly aware of the "danger of estrangement" from their own people and cultures.[111] Missionaries in Korea had also learned that if their students came out of their training "Westernized," those graduates would not be accepted in their local communities, and, as a consequence, the mission would have less influence.

Not only did missionaries worry about "Westernization" but some of them actually considered certain domestic practices in Korea to be better than Western conventions. For example, in an article entitled "What we can learn from our Korean wards," one missionary wrote: "The first thing we can learn from the Koreans is CLEANLINESS." He compared the Western system of dress and clothing with the Korean, describing how Western clothes "particularly those of the men, never got washed or pounded to a pulp at some river side, and then boiled in lye, bleached, and washed again. We wear our sack suits for

---

[107] W. Reginald Wheeler, Henry H. King, and Alexander B. Davidson, eds., *The Foreign Student in America* (New York: Association Press, 1925), p. 186.
[108] Fols. Home Economics Students Projects, "Home Economics on a World Wide Basis," Box 4, AMC Papers, OSU.
[109] To ensure students maintained their native cultures, they were encouraged to "dress in the costume of their native land" while studying at OAC. Milam, "A Project in International Friendship," p. 2.
[110] Ava Milam, "Report from the Field," 1, fol. Speeches of the Orient, Box 3, AMC Papers, OSU.
[111] Wheeler et al., *The Foreign Student in America*, p. xviii.

two or five years without blinking an eye-lash. The Koreans of higher class have their clothes washed every week or so ... Think what *we* could do with their system and at the same time reflect upon the horribleness of their taking up our system, wearing black clothes for five years without washing." Furthermore, the "Koreans leave their shoes outside the doors, we take ours right on in with confident superiority, depositing countless microbes in the recesses of our ingrain carpets, laying ourselves open to disease and disaster." He continued, "Fie upon us, who failing to learn, have even corrupted and perverted a clean and sensible custom, because we stubbornly refuse to take off our own shoes, even when going into their churches!" Even worse, "the unfortunate influence and pernicious example of foreigners" made some Koreans imitate Western practices as they tended to consider those behaviors to be superior and modern.[112] In this way, the mission field was a dynamic site where people perceived, interpreted, adopted or rejected "native" and "Western" domestic practices.

Another important reason for the emphasis on adaptation and indigenization may be related to the desire on the part of the Western experts to collect information on home practices in foreign countries. The American Home Economics Association's *Journal of Home Economics* serves as a major database of domestic practices observed by missionaries, travellers, and diplomats in various societies around the world. Information on practices in the Korean home is surprisingly abundant. For instance, J. D. Van Buskirk, a medical missionary in Korea, reported on the "composition of typical Korean diets." Etta Grimes, a missionary teacher at a girls' school in Korea, discussed widespread malnutrition among girl students that had caused underweight and growth retardation, and reported on local strategies taken to remedy those dietary problems in the poverty-stricken country.[113] A sample syllabus for the introduction to home economics at OAC shows that the course included not only the history of home economics in the United States but also the "development of this field of education in foreign countries," complete with an extensive bibliography.[114] Given Milam's career in East Asia, it is no surprise that the list contains a number of Asian case studies, including Korean examples. However, these articles were written almost exclusively by American experts and missionaries based on their field experiences. Milam's own thinking and writing clearly express the idea that training a generation of

---

[112] "What we can learn from our Korean Wards," *Korea Mission Field* 12, no. 3 (1916): 74–77, quoted on 74–75. See also a short report by W. B. Scranton, a Methodist medical missionary from the United States, in *The Gospel in All Lands* (August, 1888): 373.

[113] J. D. Van Buskirk, "The Composition of Typical Korean Diets," *Japan Medical World* 4, no. 6 (June 1924): 1–4; and Etta Belle Grimes, "Applied Home Economics in Korea," *Journal of Home Economics* 17 (January 1925): 36–37.

[114] "Syllabus for H Ad 101: Introduction to Home Economics (1935)," Record Group (RG) 141, AMC Papers, OSU.

"native" home economists was considered important not only for the purpose of filling gaps in knowledge, but also because it was an expedient way of guaranteeing that the US teachers would have an impact that would last beyond the years of schooling.

In this vein, it is instructive to examine the learning experience and outcomes of Korean students who were trained in home economics at OAC. Two of the first three students from Ewha to be supported by this scholarship – Kim Hamna (grad. 1928) and Ch'oe Isun (grad. 1938) – became leading experts in home economics in Korea.[115] What they learned at OAC became the foundation for the home economics curriculum in Korea, and the work they did as students reflected their conscious effort not only to absorb largely US-based knowledge and practices on domesticity but to adjust it to the local conditions of Korea. The term papers Kim Hamna (called "Hannah Kim" at OAC) wrote in the course of earning her degree reveal her ongoing concerns about the difficulties in applying Western knowledge to the drastically different conditions in Korea. One paper, entitled "Diet of Korean Children Nutrition," discusses how larger structural problems, such as severe poverty and lack of education, are behind the devastatingly high rate of child mortality in Korea. According to a survey in 1923, she writes, "about one fifth of the [Korean] children died within the first six years of age," and the "causes of death were largely infectious diseases such as tuberculosis, measles, smallpox, diarrhea, dysentery, and lack of care."[116] In another paper, "An Adequate Diet for Girls' Boarding Schools in Korea," Kim emphasizes the rather dire dietary situation of schoolgirls in Korea stemming from widespread poverty. She points out that the sources of nutrition that are common in the United States, such as cow's milk, beef, and butter, are much less readily available or too expensive for ordinary Koreans to build a dietary plan around, and calls on teachers to identify cheap, affordable substitute ingredients (e.g., peanut oil and bean curd instead of sesame oil and beef) to enhance the health of the students. As a rule, Kim points out, the greatest obstacle is nevertheless the lack of expertise among school managers regarding food values and a balanced diet, and thus she considers it a matter of some urgency to train Korean experts in modern nutrition.[117]

---

[115] Kim Punok was the third recipient of the scholarship, but unlike Kim Hamna and Ch'oe Isun, Kim Punok was supported for an undergraduate degree. She graduated in 1930. While studying at Oregon Agricultural College, she dated Roy C. Kim, a student at Reed College, Portland, and later married him. When she was one of the hostesses for an open house, Roy C. Kim was on the list of guests. See XV: Guestbooks, Withycombe Home Management House. 1926–1932 – "group VI-1930, April 28th–May 28th, RG 141, AMC Papers, OSU. See also Milam, *Adventures of a Home Economist*, p. 246.

[116] Fol. Korean Diet, Box 3, AMC Papers, OSU.

[117] Ibid. See also Nellie Mary Cowan Holdcroft to "Dear Friends," May 3, 1931, RG 360, Presbyterian Historical Society, Philadelphia.

While keenly aware of the distinctive conditions in Korea, Kim Hamna shared a great deal of her mentor Milam's outlook of "home" as the "nursery of virtues or vices," where parents nurture children's "character, personality and health."[118] In one of her public lectures, Milam wrote:

> School teachers can and do influence children but the character and personality of a child – the child's attitude and values and behavior are largely the product of the example of parents. Parents are the child's most important teachers. It is in the homes where habits are formed, where the first lesson of democracy or autocracy are learned, where respect for personality or lack of it is established, where tolerance or intolerance first develops, where good or poor values are established.[119]

Similarly, troubled by Korean parents' tendency to think of school as the only place where children learn, Kim advocated the idea that the home be treated as an equally important educational site where parents should conduct themselves with great caution and restraint to exemplify good behavior. By way of illustration, she pointed out that the typical pattern in Korean homes was for parents to tell their offspring not to drink alcohol or smoke but continue to indulge in these behaviors in front of the children; in contrast, she noted, American parents are careful to model the behavior at home that they want to instill in their children. Furthermore, she argued, American parents respected their children as human beings, and they were willing to forego parental authority and concede when their children were right. Kim further commented that these attitudes were very important to instill a great sense of individuality (*kaesŏng*) and self-esteem, and that she considered these American methods of childrearing to be "more civilized."[120] Kim's overly generalized and positive view on American family as an ideal and "civilized" model raises the question of social classes, races, religions, and other factors within US society, but, more importantly, it closely resembles missionary and Euro-American discourses on the hierarchy of civilizations wherein the family was a crucial denominator.

Trained in the scientific knowledge of nutrition, hygiene, and home management and with field experience in American homes, Kim Hamna was expected to be a pioneer in reforming the Korean house and home, using what she had learned at OAC while still bearing in mind the particular conditions in Korea. She returned to Korea in 1928 as the first US-educated expert in home economics. Together with her American colleague, Harriett Morris, Kim succeeded in establishing the Department of Home Economics at Ewha Women's Professional School in 1929, where she served as the founding chairperson of the department. In 1932, Ewha opened the Home Management House, which

---

[118] Eva Milam, "What Kind of a Home do you Want?" fol. Speeches of the Orient, Box 3, OSU [five page type-written draft].
[119] Fol. Speeches of the Orient, Box 3, AMC Papers, OSU.
[120] *Pyŏlgŏn'gon* 16/17 (December, 1926): 75–6.

was essentially a home economics lab. All students of the graduating class were required to spend one semester in the house, putting their learning into practice in a real setting. Kim had spent six weeks at the counterpart to the Home Management House at OAC, which was designed to "bring about a greater awareness on the part of the student for a need of basic information and to afford an opportunity to put into practice the principles learned in the classroom."[121] It is likely that her experience there helped to shape Ewha's facility.[122] From 1938 on, graduates of the Department of Home Economics were awarded teacher's certificates, and they went on to teach at girls' schools throughout the country. In addition to training home economics experts, Kim participated in various forms of public education through print media and radio programs that reached out to homemakers.[123] She also used those platforms to spread a new ethos of gender and family relations with an emphasis on gender equality and respect for individuality.[124]

If Kim Hamna played a key role in laying the foundation for the discipline of home economics in Korea, another recipient of the International Friendship Scholarship, Ch'oe Isun (known as "E Soon Choi" at OAC), became a linchpin in the transpacific network that helped shape and reshape modern domesticity in both colonial and postcolonial Korea. Ch'oe was a student of Kim Hamna in the first class of the Department of Home Economics at Ewha. When she was a sophomore in 1931, she was introduced to Milam, who was working "as a consultant in home economics in various universities in the Far East."[125] At that meeting, Ch'oe shared her plans to work in the rural revitalization movement after graduation, but Milam advised her to study further.[126] Ch'oe graduated from Ewha in 1933 and taught home economics at Ewha Girls' School until 1935, when she was awarded the same OAC scholarship her mentor Kim Hamna had received.[127] Like Kim, Ch'oe was keen to indigenize Western knowledge to the specific local conditions in Korea, as indicated by her master's thesis, entitled "A Plan for Adapting Principles of Child Development to Meet

---

[121] "Suggested Material for Mr. Burtner – Vera Brandon," fol. Correspondences 1924–39, Box 1, AMC Papers, OSU. For a similar trend in China, see Helen Schneider, *Keeping the Nation's House: Domestic Management and the Making of Modern China* (Vancouver: UBC Press, 2011), pp. 111–42 (especially pp. 118–19).

[122] Transcript of Hannah Kim, OSU Archives. At OSC, each Home Management House had a baby under one year of age for the practice of child care. Those babies "are usually state wards." OSC "introduced babies into the home management house in 1920." See Milam, "Home Economics in Oregon" (1936), fol. Home Economics at OSU, Box 4, AMC Papers, OSU. A photograph of Ewha's Home Management House shows that it also had a young child.

[123] Milam, *Adventures of a Home Economist*, p. 186.

[124] *Pyŏlgŏn'gon* 16/17 (December, 1928): 75–76; "Miguk kajŏng," *Uri chip* 1 (1931): 13–14.

[125] Ava Milam Clark's Biographical Note, AMC Papers, OSU.

[126] Im Sŏkchae, ed., *Ŏmma p'umsok adŭl maŭm sok* (In Mom's Embrace, in Son's Mind) (Seoul: Yonsei University Press, 2007), p. 34.

[127] By the time Ch'oe finished her M.S. degree, the name of the college had changed from Oregon Agricultural College to Oregon State College in 1937.

the Needs of Korean Children." In chapter 1 of her thesis, she writes: "It is desirable that each nation should retain its own culture which has developed as an outgrowth of the past. It is also desirable and necessary that nations make progress in growth toward better modes of life." She goes on to say that in order to make progress, facts should be collected and distributed through education, and "an interchange of facts among individuals, groups, and nations" would result in maximizing progress. She further notes that after studying for two years in the United States, she will be returning to Korea to teach at Ewha. She intends to select facts and information available in the United States and "evaluate and adapt" what she has learned "in terms of the need of Korean children."[128] Her thesis presents the unique characteristics of Korean home and family life, offering a detailed description of climate, economic conditions, family organization, housing, hygiene, diet, clothing, parenting practices, and the education of women. Based on that, she tried to incorporate what she had learned at OAC to design a curriculum and guidelines for childrearing appropriate to the Korean conditions. For example, she paid attention to the very limited income of the typical Korean family and proposed "to substitute home-made toys for commercial things" by utilizing readily available objects, such as bean bags and gourds. Regarding children's clothing, while she adopted certain principles she had learned at OAC, she proposed to "retain the general characteristics of Korean clothes" rather than taking up Western styles. In a very pointed way, Ch'oe advocated the retention of Korean ways while selectively adopting the more liberal traditions of child development from Western societies.

By the time Ch'oe returned to Korea from OAC in 1938, Korea had become a key avenue for Japan's military ambitions throughout Asia and the Pacific. The outbreak of the second Sino-Japanese War in 1937 and the subsequent Pacific War (1941–1945) had deep ramifications for Korean society. Arguably, the most far-reaching impact of colonial rule on Korean domesticity was manifested during the "*kōminka* era" (1937–1945). The era was marked by policies designed to mobilize the entire population to support Japan's imperial project, and this included measures that emphasized the crucial role of mothers in proliferating subjects who would be loyal to the Japanese emperor. These policies penetrated the minutiae of domesticity, affecting daily habits of diet, clothing, daily rituals, consumption patterns, procreation, and even spirituality. Under the motto of "Japan and Korea as One Body" (*naisen ittai*), the "backward" Korean family was to be transformed to follow the "advanced" Japanese style. Korean women educators who had been trained in Japan and the United States were deployed to participate in a nationwide campaign to support imperial policies. Some of them worked with Japanese women settlers in

---

[128] E Soon Choi, "A Plan for Adapting Principles of Child Development to Meet the Needs of Korean Children" (MS thesis, Oregon State Agricultural College, July 1937), p. 1.

Korea through various associations, most prominently the Green Flag Association (*Ryokki renmei*), an organization founded in 1925 by Keijō Imperial University professor Tsuda Sakae for Japanese civilians who had settled in Keijō (Seoul).[129] Tsuda Setsuko, the wife of Tsuda Sakae, was a particularly prominent member of the association, working closely with Korean home economists and promoting improvements in family life as part of the *naisen ittai* movement.[130]

Under wartime exigencies, the colonial power largely took control of all aspects of the conduct and administration of educational institutions, including personnel and curricula. By the end of the Pacific War educational institutions were greatly diminished.[131] In January 1944, all colleges and universities were designated as one-year training institutes fully dedicated to supporting Japan's war effort. Ewha's Department of Home Economics could not escape the colonial authority's tightening control during the Pacific War. Educational facilities and equipment at Ewha, such as sewing machines, were expropriated to produce goods for the Japanese military.[132] In 1940 Ko Hwanggyŏng (1909–2000), educated in Japan and the United States, was appointed as the new head of the department. In that position, she would comply with Japan's imperial policies.[133] Oral histories from students who were enrolled in Ewha at that time offer a glimpse into what they experienced. For example, students were taught how to sit and behave properly in a (Japanese-style) tatami room in a class on etiquette; yet for many of the students the lessons seemed irrelevant, given that Korean dress and home furnishings were so different from the Japanese style. Some interviewees state that they were able to maintain their Korean identity despite the imposition of *kōminka* policies, largely because their mothers continued to keep Korean values and ways of life at home.

Conclusion

This chapter has examined the multivalent forces that played a role in shaping modern domesticity in Korea under Japanese colonial rule. The centrality of domesticity in both colonial and nationalist discourses is well known within the

---

[129] Lee, "Eating for the Emperor," pp. 141–77.
[130] An T'aeyun, "Singminji e on cheguk ŭi yŏsŏng: chae Chosŏn Ilbon yŏsŏng Tsuda Setsuko rŭl t'onghaesŏ pon singminjuŭi wa chendŏ" (A Japanese Woman in Korea: Gender and Colonialism as Seen through the Eyes of a Korea-based Japanese Woman, Tsuda Setsuko), *Han'guk yŏsŏnghak* 24, no. 4 (2008): 5–33.
[131] An, *Singmin chŏngch'i*, pp. 163–256.
[132] Ewha 70-nyŏnsa p'yŏnjip wiwŏnhoe, ed., *Ewha 70-nyŏnsa* (The Seventieth History of Ewha) (Seoul: Ewha Womans University Press, 1956), p. 34.
[133] Ko Hwanggyŏng contributed a series of essays, entitled "Sin kajŏng tokpon" (A Reader on New Family) to a housewife's magazine, *Kajŏng ŭi u* (Friends of the Family) in 1940 with focus on the role of the family.

context of Euro-American imperial expansion. However, Korea's colonization by Japan, a non-Western power, further complicates the ways in which modern domesticity was constructed. Although Japan was the political and economic hegemon in Korea, its cultural authority was in constant competition with that of the West. Koreans perceived Japanese modernity as being "mediated," and thus as inauthentic; in contrast, Western modernity was represented as original. In this vein, Korean modern domesticity was fashioned from the intersection of the globally influential Western modernity, Japanese colonial imperatives, and Korean nationalist desire.

In this chapter, I specifically focused on the role of the transpacific network that had formed among the Korean elite and American Protestant missionaries who played a crucial role in transmitting, reinterpreting, and performing modern domesticity. From the time they first arrived on the Korean peninsula in the late-nineteenth century, American missionaries built modern schools and hospitals, which linked them to modernity in a very real way. Mission schools trained the next generation of national leaders, some of whom went on to study in the United States and become cornerstones of the transpacific network.

The transpacific flow of people also helps us understand the continuity of modern domesticity in Korea despite the Japanese colonial rule. Prior to Korea's colonization by Japan, the "missionary home" was an exotic and almost fanciful space where Koreans got their first glimpse of a "modern home." Myriad modern household accoutrements imported from the United States, as well as the missionaries' new family dynamics and "cultured" lifestyle, spurred Koreans' imagination about what "home, sweet home" could be. Once colonized, Korea was also subject to colonial imperatives that contributed to the form of the new domesticity. Yet, as illustrated by the 1915 and 1929 Home Exhibitions in Korea, the advanced modern home showcased by the Japanese colonial authorities was largely Western in style, which further reinforced the power of Western modernity. Moreover, Korean intellectuals' and reformers' eclectic ideas about the modern home were predominantly drawn from Euro-American models, which were distributed to the wider population through newspapers, magazines, and creative writing in the 1920s and 1930s. The popular image of the "*hom, sŭwit'ŭ hom*" and the discourse presented in those outlets captured the preference for Western modernity in the creation of a new domesticity, facilitated primarily through the transpacific network of Protestant religious and educational institutions.

The culmination of the transpacific linkage on modern domesticity in Korea occurred when the Department of Home Economics was established at Ewha Women's Professional School in 1929 through the joint efforts of Korean women leaders and American missionaries. Against the background of the foreign missionary enterprise and the US government's strategic recruitment of foreign students as future leaders, a transpacific network enabled students and experts to participate in creating, adjusting, and indigenizing modern knowledge of home economics. There is no doubt that Ava Milam and other missionary teachers were initially engaged in an asymmetrical power dynamic of mentor and mentee with their Korean students, but they nevertheless developed a symbiotic relationship in which the "feminine" domain of home economics served both parties as a platform for pursuing women's education and career aspirations on the national and global stage.

The construction of modern domesticity in colonial-era Korea illustrates the complex interplay among competing forces that defied the typical nexus of the colonizer and the colonized. This shows how the cultural influence of a non-colonial power (especially the United States) was crucial in refashioning the ideals and practices of modern domesticity within the constraints of colonial policies. In particular, the Protestant missionary network played a key role in fostering the transpacific flow of people, images, materials, and knowledge that rendered the most intimate sphere – home and family – one of the most dynamic sites for uncovering the confluence of the local, the national, and the global spheres.

3 Crossing: Selfhood, Nation, and the World

There is perhaps no woman figure in colonial-era Korea who traveled the world more extensively than Pak Indŏk (aka Induk Pahk, 1896–1980). As a child she dreamed of seeing the world, and she grew up to realize that dream, traveling around the globe twice in the 1920s and 1930s as a student, invited speaker, conference participant, and tourist.[1] She was born poor, but her mother, a Christian convert, was so committed to the idea of her daughter's being educated that she dressed the girl in boy's clothing in an attempt to gain her admission to the local school, which was only for boys.[2] Pak eventually enrolled at Ewha, a Methodist mission school for girls, where she became a star student and a protégé of the missionary teachers. She was imprisoned in 1919 for her participation in the March First Independence Movement against Japanese colonial rule. When she was awarded a scholarship to study in the United States, she turned it down and instead married a rich divorced man, much to the disappointment of her missionary teachers. Years later, when another opportunity to receive a scholarship arose, she did go to the United States to further her studies, earning a B.A. from Wesleyan College in 1928 and an M.A. from Columbia University in 1930. Appointed the first "Oriental" Traveling Secretary of the Student Volunteer Movement of the United States, she became an internationally known speaker, logging hundreds of thousands of miles of travel and delivering thousands of lectures in the United States, Europe, and Asia. On returning to Korea from her first global speaking tour, Pak went through a sensational divorce in 1931, after which she became known as "Korea's Nora," a reference to the protagonist of Henrik Ibsen's play *A Doll's House*. In the 1930s, she became deeply involved in the rural revitalization movement, whose activities were funded by individual American Christians and churches. She was eventually labeled a "collaborator" due to her active cooperation with the Japanese imperial power during the Pacific

---

[1] *Urak'i* 4 (1930): 123.
[2] This part of Pak's biography provided the inspiration for *The Girl-Son* (Minneapolis: Carolrhoda, 1992) by the American children's book author Anne E. Neuberger.

109

War.[3] When Korea became independent in 1945, she shifted allegiance back to the United States and acted as a consultant to the US Army Military Government in Korea (1945–1948). Pak was an exceptionally prolific writer, publishing a travelogue, *Segye ilchugi* (*Record of the Global Tour*, 1941), based on her two global tours, and several autobiographical books in English, including *September Monkey* (1954), which was favorably reviewed by the *New York Times* and *Christian Science Monitor* and went into a sixth edition within three years. Her life story was "definitely Hollywood motion picture material"[4] because its dramatic turns and unexpected events were enmeshed with the turbulent political and cultural changes of the first half of the twentieth century.

Pak's life is by no means typical. Although her worldwide travel alone was exceptional even by today's standards, a sketch of her life also provides tantalizing insights into the broader structure and multiple forces that were at play in shaping gendered modernity within the context of Japanese colonial rule.[5] As this chapter highlights, the mobility of Pak and her contemporaries illustrate the centrality of the global Christian network that enabled them to experience the world beyond the boundaries of colonial rule and develop new perspectives on selfhood, nation, and the world.[6] Korea had long practiced the traditional gender ethics of the "inside-outside rule" (*naeoebŏp*), which inculcated a strict sense that women should be both physically and culturally relegated to the private, domestic arena, so it was almost revolutionary for women to transcend the traditional bounds of family and nation to pursue education overseas and travel to experience the world. After Korea opened its doors in 1876 and the process of modernization began in earnest, a small number of women ventured into the new world beyond the home in pursuit of modern knowledge and selfhood.[7] Like their contemporaries elsewhere, Koreans sought inspiration for change from the

---

[3] In this book, I do not cover the issue of "collaboration," one of the most thorny and controversial debates in Korean history, because it deserves a separate, thorough study on its own. As with other contemporary women intellectuals, such as Kim Hwallan, however, there is abundant evidence of Pak's "collaboration." While this part of her history is significant in understanding what she was, it is my contention that her life and work should be understood in a much broader and comprehensive way to do justice to her or, indeed, any historical figure.

[4] "Memorandum" 1996, "deceased folders" for Pahk, Mrs. Induk, AB. 1928: Deceased 4-2-80, The Alumnae Center, Wesleyan College.

[5] Matti Peltonen, "Clues, Margins, and Monads: The Micro-Macro Link in Historical Research," *History and Theory* 40 (October 2001): 347–59.

[6] Angela Woollacott, *Race and the Modern Exotic: Three "Australian" Women on Global Display* (Clayton, Victoria: Monash University Publishing 2011); Ian Tyrrell, *Reforming the World: The Creation of America's Moral Empire* (Princeton: Princeton University Press, 2010).

[7] On April 28, 1909, three pioneering women were publicly celebrated for having completed their study overseas and returning home to work as doctors and teachers. The guests of honor in that public celebration were Pak Esther (aka Kim Chŏmdong) and Ha Nansa who studied in the United States and Yun Chŏngwŏn in Japan. "Hwibo," *Taehan hŭnghakbo* 3 (May 1909): 67; Hwang Hyŏn, *Maech'ŏn yarok* 6 (1909): 45 (from Kuksa p'yŏnch'an wiwŏnhoe, Han'guk saryo ch'ongsŏ); "Yŏja cholŏp," *Mansebo*, August 7, 1906.

transnational community, especially "advanced" modern countries.[8] In the literary genre of "new fiction" (*sin sosŏl*), a common storyline involves the dramatic transformation of a naïve Korean girl into a strong woman who is prepared to devote her life to bringing "civilization and enlightenment" to her fellow women.[9] The protagonists in these stories frequently travel to Japan, the United States, or Europe, where they are exposed to foreign norms, industrial transformation, and new cultural practices. That common plot point has a woman leaving her family home in pursuit of knowledge, and that act generally represents a rite of passage that promises to catapult her inevitably into modern womanhood to fulfill her role for the nation.

Despite growing expectations about the role women would play in the new modern nation, however, there was no systematic effort on the part of the Korean government to provide women with opportunities to study overseas. In contrast, the Korean government did initiate a program to send a group of Korean men to Japan, both to "import foreign civilization" and train future leaders to carry out Korea's modernization projects.[10] In 1895, the Korean government launched a program that provided scholarships and stipends for more than one hundred male students to study in Japan.[11] No such public funding program existed for female students,[12] in marked contrast to Japan and China, where women did receive government support that enabled them to study overseas.[13] In the absence of formal scholarship programs for women, family connections and private funding, primarily among the privileged class,

---

[8] Marilyn Lake, "Nationalist Historiography, Feminist Scholarship, and the Promise and Problems of New Transnational Histories: The Australian Case," *Journal of Women's History* 19, no. 1 (Spring 2007): 180–86.

[9] Yoon Sun Yang, "Enlightened Daughter, Benighted Mother: Yi Injik's Tears of Blood and Early Twentieth-Century Korean Domestic Fiction," *positions* 22, no. 1 (Winter 2014): 103–30.

[10] "Ilbon yuhaksaeng sa" (History of Korean Students Studying in Japan), *Hakchigwang* 6 (July 1915): 10–17; Pak Ch'ansŭng, "1890-nyŏndae huban kwanbi yuhaksaeng ŭi toIl yuhak" (Government-sponsored Students Studying in Japan in Late 1890s), *Kŭndae kyoryusa wa sangho insik* 1 (2001): 75–128.

[11] This government funding program for male students ended in 1903. See Pak, "1890-nyŏndae huban kwanbi yuhaksaeng ŭi toIl yuhak."

[12] An exception was the prominent Christian woman educator Kim P'illye (1891–1983), who did receive a scholarship from the Korean government in 1908, although it was arranged through personal connections that her brother, Kim P'ilsun (1878–1919), had with Yun Ch'io (1869–1950), who was the Minister of Education at the time. Kim P'ilsun was a medical doctor at Severance Hospital in Seoul and had been treating a sister-in-law of Yun. Out of gratitude, Yun offered a government scholarship to Kim P'illye. Yi Kisŏ, *Kyoyuk ŭi kil, sinang ŭi kil* (Path to Education, Path to Faith) (Seoul: Puksanch'ek, 2012), pp. 57–8.

[13] Barbara Rose, *Tsuda Umeko and Women's Education in Japan* (New Haven: Yale University Press, 1992); Paek Okgyŏng, "Kŭndae Han'guk yŏsŏng ŭi Ilbon yuhak kwa yŏsŏng hyŏnsil insik: 1910-nyŏn dae rŭl chungsim ŭro" (Korean Women's Studying in Japan and their Viewpoints on Reality in the 1910s), *Ihwa sahak yŏn'gu* 39 (2009): 1–28; Chŏng Hyejung, "Ch'ŏng mal min ch'o Chungguk yŏsŏng ŭi Ilbon Miguk yuhak" (Chinese Women's Studying in Japan and the US in Late Qing and Early Republican Eras), *Ihwa sahak yŏn'gu* 39 (2009): 101–33.

were crucial for young women who wanted to get higher education.[14] The situation did not improve after Korea became a colony of Japan in 1910. The overall educational policy of the colonial government was to allow Koreans access only to elementary education or practical training (if it offered any educational opportunities at all). To ensure that they would remain loyal and obedient imperial subjects, Koreans were given very few opportunities to engage in advanced study, and that was especially so for girls and women.

Under these stringent circumstances, a closer examination of the first cohort of Korean women who went overseas to study in late-nineteenth and early-twentieth centuries reveals a peculiar pattern. That is, most of them had their contact with Western Protestant missionary organizations, primarily as students at mission schools, and many of them, including Pak Indŏk, came from rather humble families that would not ordinarily have been able to provide such an extraordinary opportunity to their daughters.[15] Widows and concubines were afforded even fewer such opportunities, yet some pioneering women in Korean history came from these backgrounds. Two prominent examples are Ha Nansa (1875–1919), who had been a secondary wife but was educated at Ewha Girls' School and went on to become the first Korean woman ever to be awarded a B.A. degree (in 1906 from Ohio Wesleyan University), and Ch'a Mirisa (1879–1955), who was widowed at the age of nineteen but was able to go to China to study theology (1901–1905) and then to the United States (1910–1912), where she received a degree from Scarritt Bible and Training School.[16] It is a historical irony that some of the most underprivileged young

---

[14] For example, Yun Chŏngwŏn (1894–?), one of the early pioneering women, went to Japan in 1898 with her father Yun Hyojŏng (1858–1939), who had been active in the Independence Club, was charged with conspiring against King Kojong and was sent into exile in Japan. It was through this family tie that Yun was able to study music at the Meiji Girls' School and Tokyo Music School from 1898 to 1909. See Ji-Eun Lee, *Women Pre-scripted: Forging Modern Roles through Korean Print* (Honolulu: University of Hawai'i Press, 2015), pp. 63–70. See also *T'aegŭk hakpo* 3 (October 1906): 55.

[15] One of the prominent examples is Pak Esther (1876–1910). Pak was the first Korean woman to ever study in the United States and became the first Korean woman to receive an M.D. from an American medical school. She had been sent by her father to the first mission school for girls, Ewha, to alleviate some of the burden of trying to keep a large family fed. With the help of her mentor, Rosetta Sherwood Hall, an American medical missionary in Korea, Pak was able to receive some preliminary medical training in Korea and then was given the opportunity to study at the Baltimore Women's Medical School. Sherwood Hall hailed Pak as an exemplary model of "one new life in the Orient," having transformed herself from the abandoned daughter of an impoverished family into a confident medical doctor healing the bodies and minds of her fellow women in Korea. See Rosetta Sherwood Hall, "One New Life in the Orient," *Woman's Missionary Friend* 28, no. 12 (June 1897): 342–43.

[16] When Ha Nansa enrolled at Ewha, she was already an adult and the secondary wife of a government official. Ewha did not allow married women to enroll, but legend has it that Ha's seriousness and determination ultimately convinced the missionary teachers to admit her in 1896 under the condition that she pay tuition and her other educational expenses. See Hyaeweol Choi, "In Search of Knowledge and Selfhood: Korean Women Studying Overseas in Colonial Korea," *Intersections: Gender and Sexuality in Asia and the Pacific* 29 (May 2012);

women in Korea became part of this pioneering group who were able to avail themselves of the highest educational opportunity offered through mission-run schools at that time, and who emerged as a new elite class in Korean society. It is important to note that not all missionary teachers advocated higher learning for women. Indeed, many opposed college education for women because they feared that college-educated Korean women "would be spoiled for service to their own people" and would be inclined to disregard domestic chores and instead seek out modern luxuries.[17] However, some missionary teachers were compelled to train the next generation of Christian workers in Korea, and thus they encouraged their most talented students to continue their study overseas, more often than not at mission-run schools or Christian-affiliated institutions in Japan, China, or the United States.[18]

In this chapter, I examine the gender politics of travel overseas, with a particular focus on the crucial role of the global missionary network, which served as a channel through which Korean women could pursue advanced study and thereby experience the world beyond the boundaries of the domestic sphere.[19] I entitle this chapter "Crossing" to invoke a multitude of ideas: The women I introduce crossed the divide between traditionally prescribed gender roles and new expectations for women in the modern era; in spite of their background as daughters of poor and underprivileged families they overcame the hierarchical order of the social classes; and they also went beyond the nexus of the metropole and colony under Japanese rule as they traveled to China, the United States, Australia, and Europe. As this chapter demonstrates, while Japanese colonial policies tightly regulated opportunities to study overseas, at the center of various "crossings" was the US missionary enterprise and its affiliated organizations and personnel throughout the world. Tracing the paths taken by these women, I analyze some of the key mechanisms that facilitated their study overseas and global experience, such as scholarship programs and international agencies. Taking clues from the fragments of their individual lives,

---

http://intersections.anu.edu.au/issue29/choi.htm. Ch'a Mirisa is also known as Kim Mirisa adopting her husband's last name. See Kim Mirisa, "Ch'unp'ung ch'uu osimnyŏn kan e tarudahan han na ŭi yŏksa" (My Life History Filled with Many Tears and Sorrows for the Past Fifty Years), *Pyŏlgŏn'gon* (February 11, 1928): 54–8. For details about the life of Ch'a, see Han Sanggwŏn, *Ch'a Mirisa chŏnjip I and II* (Compiled Works of Ch'a Mirisa I and II) (Seoul: Tŏksŏng yŏja taehakkyo Ch'a Mirisa yŏn'guso, 2009).

[17] Marie E. Church and Mrs. R. L. Thomas, "Lulu E. Frey: Who Went to Korea," *The One Who Went and the One She Found* (Woman's Foreign Missionary Society, 1929), pp. 150–57; Alice Appenzeller, "Chosŏn yŏja kodŭng kyoyuk munje" (Problems of Higher Education for Women in Korea), *Samch'ŏlli* 4, no. 3 (March 1932): 45–7.

[18] Pak Sŏnmi, *Kŭndae yŏsŏng cheguk ŭl kŏch'ŏ Chosŏn ŭro hoeyu hada* (Modern Women Return to Korea via Empire) (Seoul: Ch'angbi, 2007); and Choi, "In Search of Knowledge and Selfhood."

[19] Pak Sŏnmi's book, *Kŭndae yŏsŏng cheguk ŭl kŏch'ŏ Chosŏn ŭro hoeyu hada*, offers thorough research on Korean women studying in Japan. In this chapter, I focus more on other countries, especially the United States, Europe, and Australia.

I also demonstrate how their travel experiences vaulted them into a sense of self, national identity, and cosmopolitan mindset. While they could never free themselves from various constraints imposed by the Japanese colonial state, the physical and cultural space that transnational mobility afforded them beyond the bounds of colonial rule proved to be temporarily liberating.[20] I further argue that their direct exposure to Western modernity sharpened their perspective on their status as colonized subjects and also on Korea's particular reality, which, in turn, shaped their vision of what kind of social, economic, and cultural reform would bring "enlightenment" (*kyemong*) to the populace. Their stories offer significant insights into the ways in which elite women in colonial Korea navigated their options in life, coped with both old and new challenges, and envisioned a new place for themselves in society and the world.

Missionary Network Beyond the Circuit of Metropole and Colony

During the first decade of the colonial period (1910–1919), studying overseas was strictly regulated by the colonial state regardless of whether the student had secured public scholarships or private funding. The general dictates of educational policy at that time aimed to train "good and loyal subjects of the Empire," as stated in the 1911 Education Ordinance.[21] In that vein, the colonial state largely focused on the provision of basic and practical learning to Korean students rather than higher learning. In the 1910s, there were only four public "professional schools" (chŏnmun hakkyo) and two private professional schools with no college or university.[22] The 1922 Education Ordinance opened opportunities for college education up to Koreans, and the Keijŏ Imperial University (Kyŏngsŏng Cheguk Taehakkyo) was founded in 1924;[23] however, the majority of students and faculty at the University were Japanese expatriates.[24] Going overseas to study was an option for those Koreans who wanted to pursue advanced learning. The 1911 guidelines for studying overseas stipulate that prospective students should know what they are planning to study and when they were admitted to their intended school. Students were required to submit all the necessary documents including a resume to the colonial government through the office of the governor of the province in which they resided. As part

---

[20] Louise Yim, *My Forty Years Fight for Korea* (Seoul: International Cultural Research Center, Chung-ang University, 1951), pp. 162–4.
[21] Mark E. Caprio, *Japanese Assimilation Policies in Colonial Korea, 1910–1945* (Seattle: University of Washington Press, 2009), p. 98.
[22] *Tongnip undongsa charyojip* (The History of Independence Movement: Sourcebook) 13, 1101-2; http://e-gonghun.mpva.go.kr; Chŏng Chaech'ŏl, *Ilche ŭi taeHan'guk singmiji kyoyuk chŏngch'aeksa* (The History of Educational Policy under Japanese Colonial Rule in Korea) (Seoul: Ilchisa, 1985), p. 336.
[23] *Tongnip undongsa charyojip* (The History of Independence Movement: Sourcebook) 13, 1113.
[24] Caprio, *Japanese Assimilation Policies in Colonial Korea*, p. 200.

of the review process, the governor was required to comment on the character of the student, their family background, and financial status.[25] These requirements were loosened after the March First Independence Movement of 1919. The most noticeable change came in 1920 when the guidelines for studying overseas were revised. According to these new guidelines, the regulations applied only to those who planned to study in Japan with public funding (*kwanbi yuhaksaeng*). The result of this change was an immediate increase in the number of privately funded students going overseas.[26]

Japan was by far the most frequent host country for Korean students studying abroad – both male and female. Japan's dominance is understandable because it was the colonial authority in Korea, it was geographically adjacent, and it was economically more affordable than the more distant locations in North America or Europe. Furthermore, as Michael Robinson points out, "attaining Japanese cultural and linguistic skills became *de rigueur* for the ambitious sons of the elite and Korea's tiny middle class if they were to have any chance at even the middle- and low-level, white collar jobs in the cities."[27] For the sake of career advancement, Japan was the most logical option for many male students. For female students, Japan was also the most popular destination. Between 1910 and 1942, 13,417 Korean women went to Japan for some period of time to engage in some level of study.[28] By comparison, during that same period only 148 female students traveled to the United States, the second most frequent destination for Korean students studying abroad.[29]

Despite this great imbalance in where Korean women went to receive further education, a close examination of the details reveals that American mission schools and the regional and global network that they created were the key facilitator in enabling Korean female students to study overseas. For instance, there was a systematic route for studying in Japan through American mission schools and organizations in Korea. Graduates from mission schools in Korea often continued their education at American-run mission schools in Japan, including Doshisha Women's College, Tokyo Women's College, Kobe

---

[25] Pak, *Kŭndae yŏsŏng cheguk ŭl kŏch'ŏ Chosŏn ŭro hoeyu hada*, pp. 23–37; Pak Ch'ansŭng, "1910-nyŏndae toIl yuhak kwa yuhak saenghwal" (Korean Students Studying in Japan in the 1910s and their Lives in Japan), *Yŏksa wa tamnon* 34 (2003): 117.

[26] *Tongnip undongsa charyojip* 13, 1114; Pak Ch'ansŭng, "1920-nyŏndae toIl yuhaksaeng kwa kŭ sasang chŏk tonghyang" (The Ideological Trends of Korean Students Studying in Japan in the 1920s), *Han'guk kŭnhyŏndae yŏn'gu* 30 (2004): 99–151.

[27] Michael Robinson, *Korea's Twentieth-Century Odyssey: A Short History* (Honolulu: University of Hawai'i Press, 2007), p. 46.

[28] Pak, *Kŭndae yŏsŏng cheguk ŭl kŏch'ŏ Chosŏn ŭro hoeyu hada*, p. 41.

[29] Chŏng Pyŏngjun, "Ilcheha Han'guk yŏsŏng ŭi Miguk yuhak kwa kŭndae kyŏnghŏm" (Korean Women's Studying in the US and their Experience of Modernity under Japanese Rule), *Ihwa sahak yŏn'gu* 39 (2009): 29–99. The number of students who went to China and other countries, including Australia, Canada, France, and Sweden, is hard to trace systematically due to lack of extant data.

Women's College, Kwassui Women's College, and Hiroshima Women's College.[30] Some mission schools in Korea and Japan tended to collaborate in an informal chain of training. For instance, Sup'ia Girls School (Speer Girls School) in Kwangju, the first girls' school in Chŏlla Province, founded by the American Southern Presbyterian Church in 1908, often sent its graduates to Kinjo Gakuin in Nagoya, founded in 1889 as Jogaku Senmon Kibokwan (The Home of Hope for Girls), another Southern Presbyterian mission school for women.[31] Likewise, missionary teachers at Ewha Girls' School, the flagship school of the US Methodist Church, encouraged its talented graduates to continue their studies at Kwassui Women's College in Nagasaki, founded in 1879 by an American Methodist Episcopal missionary.[32] Not only Korean students but Japanese graduates from mission schools in Japan also had the opportunity to teach at mission schools in Korea, expanding the ongoing network in the exchange of students and teachers.[33]

While studying in Japan, Korean students aimed to gain the modern Western knowledge that Japan had imported, digested, and (re)interpreted from the time of the Meiji Restoration. Indeed, the curriculum at Japanese schools was filled with works of Western philosophy, literature, and art. Na Hyesŏk, who studied Western painting at the Tokyo Women's Art School, recalled studying the educational theories of Swiss educator Johann Heinrich Pestalozzi and the French philosopher Jean Jacques Rousseau in her preparation for an examination.[34] Some students were completely immersed in the "Western style life" while studying in Japan. Ch'oe Pogyŏng, who was a student of English literature at Tsuda Eigaku Juku (1933–1937), founded by Tsuda Umeko (1864–1929), described her experience of studying in Japan as follows: "Tsuda was completely distant from Japanese authentic culture. All professors were educated overseas and so their perspective was mostly Westernized. We

---

[30] Pak, *Kŭndae yŏsŏng cheguk ŭl kŏch'ŏ Chosŏn ŭro hoeyu hada*, pp. 56–7.
[31] Arlene Woods Kelly, *Educational Institution for Women 1889–1989* (Nagoya: Kinjo Gakuin, 1989), p. 1 (Kinjo Gakuin archives); Sup'ia 100-nyŏnsa kanhaeng wiwŏnhoe, *Sup'ia 100-nyŏnsa 1908-2008* (The Hundredth History of Sup'ia) (Kwangju: Kwangju Sup'ia yŏja chung kodŭng hakkyo, 2008), p. 274.
[32] Ewha 100-nyŏnsa p'yŏnch'an wiwŏnhoe, *Ewha 100-nyŏnsa* (The 100th History of Ewha) (Seoul: Ewha Womans University Press, 1994), p. 71; Karen K. Seat, *"Providence Has Freed Our Hands": Women's Missions and the American Encounter with Japan* (Syracuse: Syracuse University Press, 2008).
[33] Velma Snook, "Annual Report for 1928–29," Presbyterian Historical Society.
[34] Na Hyesŏk, "Na ŭi Tonggyŏng yŏja misul hakkyo sidae," *Samch'ŏlli* (May 1938): 133–8. A male intellectual contemporary of Na, Hyŏn Sangyun, also recalls what he studied when he was a student at Waseda University (1913–1918), listing such Western writers as William Wordsworth, Ralph Emerson, Ivan Turgenev, Rudolf Eucken, and Henri-Louis Bergson. See Hyŏn Sangyun, "Tokyo yuhaksaeng saenghwal" (Days of Studying in Tokyo), *Ch'ŏngch'un* 2 (1914). Quoted in Kim Wŏn'gŭk et al., *Singminji chisigin ŭi kaehwa sasang yuhakki* (Records of Studying Overseas and Enlightenment Thoughts of Intellectuals in Colonial Korea) (Seoul: T'aehaksa, 2005), pp. 43–4.

read books in English and about Christianity. I did not feel any feudal tradition of Japan on campus. It was very liberal and comfortable.... It was a kind of paradise."[35] Modern Japan's experience and success in learning and adopting Western civilization and modern knowledge were inspiring to Korean students, but at the heart of their learning was "the West," which Japan had translated and interpreted. And thus to some students, studying in Japan was an important stepping stone for going to the United States.[36]

In this vein, an editorial in *Tonga ilbo*, a major daily newspaper in colonial-era Korea, explicitly encouraged students to go to the United States or Europe to learn authentic Western civilizations, reasoning that in those locations they would be exposed directly to Western modernity. The central point of the editorial was that Korean students should understand and digest the original form of modernity from the West, which was the cultural hegemon (*p'aekwŏn*) at the time.[37] The United States was held in especially high esteem among Koreans as an advanced modern society. Prior to Korea's colonization by Japan, the print media had strongly advocated studying in the United States as a way to gain confidence in strengthening Korea's national power and protecting its sovereignty from encroaching foreign powers.[38] Even after Korea was colonized by Japan in 1910, that favorable perception of the United States as a destination for further study persisted. As the literary critic Kim Ch'ŏl astutely argues, a discursive formula of "English language = the United States = civilization = the world" is deeply engrained in modern Korean literature.[39] Especially

---

[35] Pak, *Kŭndae yŏsŏng cheguk ŭl kŏch'ŏ Chosŏn ŭro hoeyu hada*, pp. 111–12. In an interview, the writer Pak Sŭngho reflected on her education at Tsuda College, where she mainly read books in English. See "Yŏryu munjangga ŭi simgyŏng t'ajin" (Sounding Out Women Writers' Minds), *Samch'ŏlli* 7, no. 11 (December 1935): 99–102. For the history of Tsuda Eigaku Juku, see Rose, *Tsuda Umeko*.

[36] For example, Kim Aesik (aka Kim Alice), one of the first three graduates of Ewha Women's Professional School (Ewha Yŏja Chŏnmun Hakkyo), studied music at Kwassui beginning in 1917, and then attended the Ellison-White Conservatory of Music in Portland, Oregon, beginning in 1921, becoming the first Korean woman trained in Western music in the United States. When she returned home, she contributed to the founding of the Music Department at Ewha Women's Professional School and served as the first chair of that department. *Ewha 100-nyŏnsa*, pp. 129, 148.

[37] *Tonga ilbo*, March 24, 1921.

[38] Kim Yunsŏn, "Cheguk sinmun e nat'anan Miguk yuhak kwa yuhaksaeng kisŏ (p'yŏnji) yŏn'gu" (A Study of Korean Students Studying in the United States and their Correspondences Reflected in Cheguk sinmun), *Ŏmun yŏn'gu* 38, no. 1 (Spring 2010): 309–33.

[39] Kim Ch'ŏl, *Pokhwasulsa tŭl: sosŏl ro ingnŭn singminji Chosŏn* (The Ventriloquists: Reading Colonial Korea through Fiction) (Seoul: Munhak kwa chisŏngsa, 2008), pp. 63–75. See also Kang Naehŭi, "Yŏngŏ kyoyuk kwa yŏngŏ ŭi sahoe chŏk wisang" (English Education and the Social Status of the English Language), in *Singminji ŭi ilsang, chibae wa kyunyŏl* (Everyday Life in Colony, Dominance and Fissure), eds. Kong Cheuk and Chŏng Kŭnsik (Seoul: Munhwagwahaksa, 2006), pp. 401–32.

after World War I, the United States became the key reference point for socioeconomic and cultural progress.[40]

The hegemonic status of the United States as the destination for advanced study was even stronger by the 1930s. Yi Sunt'ak, a professor of economics at Yŏnhŭi College (present-day Yonsei University) who traveled the globe for ten months in 1933, recorded his impressions of the United States in his travelogue, *Ch'oegŭn segye ilchugi* (Record of the Recent Global Tour):

> Look at the crowds, the luxury, the advertising, and the commodities! Only after I came here [to the United States] did the glorious luxury of Paris look like the remnants of a bygone era. In US society currently, thanks to scientific discovery and invention, you can find the greatest, most advanced civilization on earth, from architecture to transportation to communication to cinema to aviation and military ordinance.... In short, *the present civilization of the United States is the civilization of the world. The United States is the world*.... And there are 600 universities, all with excellent facilities. Three-fifths of the world's universities are in the United States. In other words, in terms of educational development and production of scholars, the United States is at the pinnacle of culture.[41] [emphasis added]

Indeed, US universities witnessed a significant rise in the enrollment of international students in the 1920s, and by the 1930s, the United States had become "a magnetic hub for international students."[42] This represented a major shift in destination for international students, who were choosing to study in the United States rather than in Europe. According to an early census and survey, in 1905 only nine US colleges registered foreign students; by 1930, however, "foreign students attended about 450 colleges and universities; by 1940, the number had grown again to 636," and the number of students "grew from about 600 in 1905 to about 1,800 in 1912 to nearly 10,000 in 1930."[43] In addition, as Randolph Bourne's 1916 essay, "Trans-National America" argues, the United States was already "transnational." That is, the United States "is coming to be, not a nationality, but a trans-nationality, a weaving back and forth, with the other lands, of many threads of all sizes and colors."[44] Foreign students from all over the world played an important intellectual and cultural part in creating "trans-

---

[40] Hanmee Na Kim, "'America' in Colonial Korea: A Vantage Point for Capitalist Modernity," *positions: asia critique* 26, no. 4 (November 2018): 647–85.

[41] Yi Sunt'ak, *Ch'oegŭn segye ilchugi* (Record of the Recent Global Tour) (Kyŏngsŏng: Hansŏng tosŏ chusik hoesa, 1934), pp. 264–7. Yi compares US educational style with Japanese. He observes that Japanese education emphasizes rote memory, formalistic, desktop theory and rigid pedagogy, while US education stresses self-driven learning, practical knowledge and voluntary participation.

[42] Paul A. Kramer, "International Students and U.S. Global Power in the Long 20th Century," *The Asia-Pacific Journal*, 3-3-10, January 18, 2010 (online journal).

[43] Kramer, "International Students and U.S. Global Power in the Long 20th Century."

[44] David Thelen, "The Nation and Beyond: Transnational Perspectives on United States History," *The Journal of American History* 86, no, 3 (December 1999): 965–75, quoted on 967–68.

national America." Internationally renowned writers, politicians, and reformers, such as Rabindranath Tagore (1861–1941), visited the United States and gave talks on college campuses.[45] In particular, US Christian groups played a crucial role in making "trans-national America" through their local, national, and global network, the YMCA/YWCA, and scholarship programs for international students who would become future leaders in their home countries.[46]

According to *Sinhan minbo* (People's Newspaper of New Korea), published by Koreans residing in the United States, there were approximately fifty-four Korean students enrolled in US colleges and universities in 1917, and that number included both men and women.[47] The first volume of *Urak'i* (The Rocky), the official organ of the Korean Student Federation of North America, founded in 1925, lists the names of all of the Korean students who graduated from American institutions from the late-nineteenth century to 1924. There were 106 names on that list, including nine women. One of those women was Esther Pak (aka Kim Chŏmdong, 1876–1910), a protégé of the American medical missionary Rosetta Sherwood Hall. She became the first Korean female doctor, earning a medical degree from the Baltimore Women's Medical College in 1900.[48] Based on reports in contemporary newspapers and magazines, there were approximately 148 Korean female students in the United States between 1895 and 1940.[49] This estimate includes students who had come directly to the United States from Korea as well as the children of Koreans who had immigrated to Hawai'i. The number seeking masters or doctoral degrees was much smaller. Using information compiled by the *Korean Student Bulletin* (1922–1940; hereafter, the *KSB*), Horace H. Underwood (1890–1951), a Presbyterian missionary, reported that fifty-four Korean students received advanced degrees from US colleges and universities between 1912 and 1929, only six of whom were women. He notes: "Doubtless this fact will bring home to many of us still more clearly the necessity for further emphasis on the higher education of women both abroad and in Korea."[50]

One of the most important forces in the rising number of Korean students in the United States was the connection between Protestant missionaries in Korea and institutions of higher education in the United States.[51] Korea was not

---

[45] Induk Pahk, *September Monkey* (New York: Harper & Brothers, 1954), p. 135.
[46] W. Reginald Wheeler, Henry H. King, and Alexander B. Davidson, eds., *The Foreign Student in America* – a Study by the Commission on Survey of Foreign Students in the United States of America, under the auspices of the Friendly Relations Committees of the Young Men's Christian Association and the Young Women's Christian Association (New York: Association Press, 1925).
[47] *Sinhan minbo*, June 21, 1917.   [48] *Urak'i* 1 (1925): 156–63.
[49] Chŏng, "Ilcheha Han'guk yŏsŏng ŭi Miguk yuhak," 29–99.
[50] H. H. Underwood, "Korean Students in America and What They Bring Back," *Korea Mission Field* 26, no. 4 (April 1930): 67–72, quoted on 67.
[51] Yu Hyŏngsuk, "Yŏja wa Miguk yuhak" (Women and Studying in the United States), *Tonggwang* 18 (February 1931): 73–4.

unique in this respect. Ellen Widmer has demonstrated that Protestant Christian colleges for women in China had productive working relationships with single-sex colleges in the United States, exemplified by the close ties between Smith College and Ginling College in Nanjing.[52] In his analysis of the global politics of studying overseas, Paul Kramer notes that Protestant missionaries from the United States "connected promising students and converts from far-flung mission schools to denominational colleges throughout the United States. The goal here was to funnel talented 'native' would-be missionaries to centers of theological intensity and fervor in the United States and then to cycle them back to their home societies to spread both the Gospel and Americanism."[53] In addition, the absence of tertiary educational institutions in Korea made it inevitable that missionaries would send and support their promising Korean students to the United States to pursue further study. As a result, the vast majority of Korean students in the United States were Protestant Christians. According to a survey by the Friendly Relations Committees of the Young Men's Christian Association and the Young Women's Christian Association, of the fifty-seven Korean students who responded to questionnaires, 100 percent were Christian (forty-nine had become Christian in Korea; one had converted to Christianity in Hawai'i; and seven had become Christians during their stay in the United States).[54] This strong Christian connection is further evidenced in an essay by O Ch'ŏnsŏk, who studied at Cornell (B.A., 1925), Northwestern (M. A., 1927), and Columbia (Ph.D., 1931). He offered detailed guidelines on how to prepare for studying in the United States. He suggested that prospective students get information from "returned students, missionaries and other Americans in Korea, the YMCA in Seoul, students currently in the United States, and the Committee on Friendly Relations among Foreign Students (division of Korea)."[55] Some of the Korean students enrolled at the alma maters of their American missionary teachers in Korea. A prominent example of this educational chain is Ohio Wesleyan University, whose alumnae included such prominent women missionaries as Lulu Frey, Mary Hillman, and Jessie Marker. Ha Nansa, mentioned earlier, became the first Korean woman to graduate from Ohio Wesleyan University, starting a long tradition of Ewha

---

[52] Ellen Widmer, "The Seven Sisters and China, 1900–1950," in *China's Christian Colleges: Cross-Cultural Connections, 1900–1950*, eds. Daniel H. Bays and Ellen Widmer (Stanford: Stanford University Press, 2009), pp. 83–105.
[53] Kramer, "International Students and U.S. Global Power in the Long 20th Century."
[54] In comparison, the percentage of Christians among Chinese students was 59.4, Japanese students, 72.8, and Indian students, 27.6. See Wheeler, et al., *The Foreign Student in America*, p. 316.
[55] O Ch'ŏnsŏk, "Miguk yuhak annae yoram" (Guidelines for Studying in the United States), *Urak'i* 4 (1930): 156–93, quoted on 185. See also Kim Hŭngjae, "Miguk yuhak" (Studying in the United States), *Tonggwang* 18 (February 1931): 66–70.

Girls' School graduates studying at Ohio Wesleyan.[56] Perhaps the most prominent Korean graduate of Ohio Wesleyan was Kim Hwallan (aka Helen Kim). She was a student at Ewha Girls' School, and with the support of her missionary mentors at Ewha, Harriett Morris, Marion Conrow, and Jeannette Walter, she enrolled at Ohio Wesleyan in 1922, where she studied religion, philosophy, and English literature. She fondly remembered those years at Ohio Wesleyan as the time when she was most enthralled with learning.[57] She received her B.A. in 1924, and she went on to earn a master's degree in philosophy from Boston University and a doctoral degree in education from Columbia University, becoming the first Korean woman to earn a PhD. Kim later became the first Korean to serve as president of Ewha Women's Professional School in 1939.

A tiny number of Korean students managed to study in countries other than Japan or the United States. Once again, the global missionary network played an important role in helping Korean students enroll in mission schools overseas. For example, in China – the third most popular country for Korean students at the time – the mission-run Suchow Women's Teachers' College and Nanjing Bible Teaching Institute hosted a large number of Korean students.[58] In particular, because Shanghai hosted the Korean Provisional Government after the March First Independence Movement, many Korean men and women went to China not only to study but to contribute to the Korean nationalist movements.[59] Like Japan, China was sometimes a stepping stone for going somewhere else for further study.[60] Yang Hanna (1893–1976) and Ch'oe Yŏngsuk (1904–1932) are examples whose unusual

---

[56] Yi Tŏkju, *Han'guk kyohoe ch'ŏŭm yŏsŏngdŭl* (The First Group of Women in Korean Churches) (Seoul: Hongsŏngsa, 2007), p. 63; Annual Reports of the Korean Woman's Conference of the Methodist Episcopal Church, 1908, p. 6.

[57] Kim Chŏngok, *Imonim Kim Hwallan* (My Aunt Kim Hwallan) (Seoul: Chŏngusa, 1977), pp. 71–73.

[58] Sin Namju, "1920-nyŏndae chisigin yŏsŏng ŭi tŭngjang kwa haeoe yuhak" (The Emergence of Women Intellectuals and Studying Overseas in the 1920s), *Yŏsŏng kwa yŏksa* 3 (2005): 1–75, quoted on 23–4.

[59] In a rare oral history of women, entitled *Changgang ilgi* (A Life History of Chŏng Chŏnghwa) (Hangmin, 1998), Chŏng recalls her time in Shanghai. According to her, there was a women's group, Taehan Puinhoe (Korean Women's Association), in Shanghai (p. 65). She thought it was largely for graduates of Ewha who were "new women" (*sin yŏsŏng*). Her description of that association was rather negative. She said: "Some of these women thought they were paving a new path because of modern education they received but their behaviors made people uncomfortable. Therefore, they were not well received by the Korean community in Shanghai." Chŏng herself might have been one of the "new women" in terms of education. Her father had urged her to go to the US for study, but she declined his advice to assist her father-in-law, Kim Kajin, and her husband Kim Ŭihan, who worked for the Korean Provisional Government in Shanghai. Her father also asked her to study in Japan, which she declined again. When she returned to Korea in 1922 (fourth time since 1920), she briefly attended a girls' school, Kŭnhwa, which was founded by Ch'a Mirisa (aka Kim Mirisa) who was educated at Scarritt College in the United States.

[60] O Ch'ŏnsŏk, "Miguk yuhaksaengsa," *Samch'ŏlli* 5, no. 1 (1933): 26–9.

stories add an even more dynamic picture of the diverse trajectories of studying overseas.

Yang Hanna (1893–1976) was born into a Christian family in Pusan, Kyŏngsang Province. She attended Ilsin High School for Girls, which was founded by Australian women missionaries affiliated with the Presbyterian Women's Missionary Union (PWMU) in Victoria.[61] In 1917 after graduating from Ilsin, she went to the Yokohama Theological Seminary. Soon after the March First Independence Movement in 1919, she moved from Yokohama to Shanghai, where she was affiliated with the Korean Provisional Government while studying at the Suzhou Women's Teachers' College, a Methodist mission school.[62] Since her status of a student made it easier for her to travel, she maintained her affiliation with Suzhou while commuting between Shanghai and Pusan to help the Korean independence movement. Yang also emerged as the leader of women's movement in Southeast Korea, founding the Pusan Yŏja Ch'ŏngnyŏnhoe (Young Women's Association of Pusan) in 1921.[63] Yang pursued further education at Ewha Women's Professional School, majoring in early childhood education and graduating in 1925. As *Tonga ilbo* reports, Yang undertook studies in Australia in 1926, the first Korean woman ever to travel to Australia to study.[64] *The Missionary Chronicle*, an Australian mission magazine, reports that on September 26, 1926, Yang Hanna arrived in Melbourne with Amy Skinner (?–1954), an Australian missionary colleague she had worked with in Pusan. Skinner had been a member of the Student Volunteer Movement affiliated with the University of Melbourne, and worked in Korea as a missionary from 1914 to 1940.[65] According to *The Missionary Chronicle*, Yang intended to first work on her English and then to prepare for her diploma program in early childhood education.[66] There is no further follow-up on Yang in missionary documents after this report; however, other evidence indicates that she was back in Korea by July 1928, at which point she

---

[61] The first group of Australian women missionaries arrived in Pusan on October 12, 1891. They were affiliated with the Presbyterian Women's Missionary Union (PWMU). Just as US missionaries had done in other parts of Korea, the PWMU led the way in women's education in the southeastern region of Korea, founding the first girls' school, Ilsin, in 1895, which started as an orphanage with three girls. For the early history of the Australian mission in Korea, see Hyaeweol Choi, "Claiming their own Space: Australian Women Missionaries in Korea, 1891–1900," *Australian Historical Studies* 48, no. 3 (2017): 416–32.

[62] *Tonga ilbo*, November 3, 1921, p. 4. Suzhou Women's Teachers' College was called in Korean, Soju kyŏnghae yŏja sabŏm hakkyo (蘇州景海女子師範學校).

[63] Yi Songhŭi, "Yang Hanna ŭi sam kwa hwaltong e kwanhan il koch'al" (A Study of the Life and Work of Yang Hanna), *Yŏsŏng yŏn'gu nonjip* 13 (2002): 5–37.

[64] *Tonga ilbo*, August 18, 1926, p. 3.

[65] Kim Sŭngt'ae and Pak Hyejin, comp., *Naehan sŏn'gyosa ch'ongnam, 1884–1984* (A Comprehensive Survey of Missionaries in Korea) (Seoul: Han'guk kidokkyo yŏksa yŏn'guso, 1994), pp. 467–8.

[66] *The Missionary Chronicle*, January 1, 1927, p. 8.

appears to have forged a career for herself as a specialist in early childhood education and social welfare, affiliated mostly with Christian groups.[67]

The story of Ch'oe Yŏngsuk is unique because she went from Korea to China and Europe via the trans-Siberian route in search of new knowledge. She was born into a Christian family in Yŏju, Kyŏnggi Province, in 1904. Like many Korean women intellectuals at that time, Ch'oe was educated at a Christian mission school, Ewha Girls' School.[68] In an essay reflecting on her education she recollects, "unlike my peers, I did not desire to go to Japan for my continued study. For some reason, I had always longed for China and wanted to go there to study."[69] Ch'oe arrived in Nanjing in 1923 and studied at Nanjing Ming De Girls' School, founded by the American North Presbyterian Church in 1884.[70] She soon joined a small Korean community centered on a Christian church. She wrote that "we sometimes went to our pastor's house and had Korean *kimch'i*. These visits remain some of my fondest memories about my stay in Nanjing."[71] During her four-year sojourn in China, Ch'oe was impressed by the Chinese women's movement, and she cut her hair short, a symbolic act of becoming a modern woman.[72] She also frequently visited Shanghai – the site of the recently established Korean Provisional Government. Korean patriots, young and old, traveled to Shanghai to assist in the goal of achieving national independence from exile. It was during this period in China that Ch'oe was deeply influenced by nationalist and socialist ideas. Ch'oe's dream went beyond Asia. She wrote:

I did not want to go back to Korea after graduating from Nanjing University. Although I knew very well that my loving parents and siblings were waiting for me, I really had no desire to return to my homeland. I was born into a humble family, and so, from the day I left Korea, I suffered financial hardships. For my four years in Nanjing, I had to work in order to pay for my tuition and living expenses. However, my passionate desire to learn more made material poverty bearable. With the same desire for learning, I decided to go to Sweden, which I had always dreamed of from the time of my childhood.[73]

---

[67] Yi, "Yang Hanna," 14.
[68] Hyaeweol Choi, *Gender and Mission Encounters in Korea: New Women, Old Ways* (Berkeley: University of California Press, 2009), pp. 86–120.
[69] Ch'oe Yŏngsuk, "Kŭriun yennal ŭi hakch'ang sidae, Sŏjŏn taehaksaeng saenghwal" (Missing our school days, my college life in Sweden), *Samch'ŏlli* 4, no. 1 (January 1932): 72–74, quoted on 72. This essay is translated in *New Women in Colonial Korea: A Sourcebook*, compiled, translated and annotated by Hyaeweol Choi (New York: Routledge, 2013), pp. 183–4.
[70] Nanjing Ming De Girls' School changed its name to Private Ming Deh Girls' School in 1912. It became Nanjing No. 5 Middle School in 1952 and was renamed as Nanjing No. 36 Middle School in the early 1970s. The school was reorganized to become Nanjing Professional School for Women in 1986. See Minnie Vautrin, *Terror in Minnie Vautrin's Nanjing: Diaries and Correspondence, 1937–38* (Champaign: University of Illinois Press, 2008), p. 232.
[71] Ch'oe, "Kŭriun yennal ŭi hakch'ang sidae," 72.   [72] *Tonga ilbo*, July 23, 1926, p. 5
[73] Ch'oe, "Kŭriun yennal ŭi hakch'ang sidae," 73. See also U Miyŏng, "Sin yŏsŏng Ch'oe Yŏngsuk non: yŏsŏng sam kwa chehyŏn ŭi kŏri" (A Study on the New Woman Ch'oe Yŏngsuk: A Woman's Life and the Distance in Representation), *Minjok munhwa yŏn'gu* 45 (2006): 293–328.

There are a few hints as to the route Ch'oe may have taken to get from China to Sweden. In his book *In Korean Wilds and Villages*, the Swedish zoologist Sten Bergman (1895–1975), who visited Korea in 1935 to gather specimens of the local flora and fauna, wrote that there were three routes to get to Asia from Sweden: via America, via the Suez Channel, and via Siberia.[74] He followed the third option, the trans-Siberian route. It appears that Ch'oe travelled the same route but in reverse to get to Sweden. Ch'oe left Shanghai by ship on July 9, 1926, and arrived in Dalian, where she was arrested by the Japanese police because she was carrying socialist books. She was not detained for very long, moving on from there to Scandinavia. Based on her own notes and the route that Bergman describes, the most likely itinerary for Ch'oe was: Shanghai–Dalian–Mukden (Shenyang)–Changchun–Harbin–Manchuria–Chita–Verchneudinsk (capital of the Buryat-Mongolian Republic)–Trans-Baikalia–Irkutsk–Taiga–Krasnojarsk–Omsk–Perm–Sverdlovsk–Moscow–Bjeloostrov (Russian frontier station)–Leningrad (St. Petersburg)–Abo–Stockholm.

On her arrival in Stockholm in the spring of 1926, Ch'oe was overwhelmed by the unfamiliarity of both the language and the customs. She describes how everything she encountered "seemed so different from what I was familiar with," and how lonely she felt. To learn Swedish, she attended a school "equivalent of a middle school in a rural area" for several months, and then she was admitted to the Department of Political Economy at Stockholm University in the fall, with the lofty ideal of serving the underprivileged back home.[75] As in China, she had to work to support her studies. She wrote: "To be sure, I had some difficult times earning the 100 *won* I needed every month to support my studies."[76] To earn money she sold pillows and cushions that she had embroidered and gave language lessons.[77]

According to an article in *Chosŏn ilbo* dated February 23, 1935, the above-mentioned Sten Bergman recalls encounters with Ch'oe, whom he met at a "Stockholm Museum" several times and through whom he learned about Korea. He added that Ch'oe "worked at the Prince's Library for a short time, filing East Asian materials."[78] The prince in question was Gustaf Adolf, who later became the King of Sweden. Ch'oe's opportunity to work for the prince appears to have come out of the fact that he had visited Korea in October 1926 as part of a trip he took around the world. The prince was a devoted amateur

---

[74] Sten Bergman, *In Korean Wilds and Villages* (London: Travel Book Club, 1938), pp. 9–20. Bergman visited Korea in 1935. In the Preface, he acknowledges the support of "His Royal Highness The Crown-Prince of Sweden" who wrote a letter of recommendation (no page number). He also acknowledges a number of Japanese officials who made his trip and stay possible.
[75] Ch'oe, "Kŭriun yennal ŭi hakch'ang sidae," 73.
[76] Ch'oe, "Kŭriun yennal ŭi hakch'ang sidae," 74.   [77] *Tonga ilbo*, November 29, 1931.
[78] *Chosŏn ilbo*, February 23, 1935, p. 2.

archaeologist, and during his tour to East Asia, he had the opportunity to visit a newly excavated royal grave site in the ancient capital, Kyŏngju, Korea. The Japanese government made arrangements so that the prince had the honor of lifting a golden crown from the grave site. Due to his ceremonial involvement in the excavation, the grave site is named Sŏbongch'ong, with the character "Sŏ" referring to Sweden.[79] After he returned to Sweden, the prince bequeathed various art objects he acquired in Korea to the Museum of Far East Antiquities, founded in 1926 and opened to the public in 1927 as a temporary exhibition.[80] After three years' preparations, the permanent exhibitions opened in 1929.[81] At that time, the Museum did not have a permanent building of its own and rented the third floor of the building that housed the Stockholm School of Economics.[82] Given Ch'oe's language proficiency in Korean, Chinese, and Swedish and the fact that she was the first "East Asian" woman student at the University, she may have been known to the prince or the Museum's director as the person best qualified to do the cataloguing.[83]

After receiving her B.A. degree from Stockholm University in 1930, Ch'oe Yŏngsuk scraped together some money to visit various foreign countries on her way back to Korea, in order "to gain a better understanding of the conditions that were playing out in those places." On her journey home to Korea, she appears to have made stops in about twenty countries, including Denmark, Germany, Italy, Greece, Turkey, Egypt, India, and Vietnam.[84] She stayed the longest in India, spending four months in the subcontinent. Her main goal there was to meet her "heroes Mohandas Gandhi [1869–1948] and Sarojini Naidu [1879–1949]," whose dedication to the Indian nationalist movement for independence resonated deeply with her. Since the Indian National Congress was in session, Ch'oe could not talk with Gandhi for long but "still felt exhilarated by the opportunity to meet him" even if only briefly, and she later wrote how she "fondly remember[ed] his emaciated face smiling at me . . . He repeatedly told me how glad he was to meet me."[85] In the

---

[79] http://www.k-heritage.tv/hp/hpContents/story/view.do?contentsSeq=754&categoryType=2 (accessed August 9, 2016).

[80] According to Eva Myrdal of the Far East Asian Antiquities staff, the Museum's "founding collection was the Neolithic, archaeological material collected by Prof Johan Gunnar Andersson in the field in China 1921–1924." Email communication with her on August 17, 2016 (Eva. Myrdal@varldskulturmuseerna.se).

[81] http://www.varldskulturmuseerna.se/en/ostasiatiskamuseet/exhibitions/previous-exhibitions/exhibitions-1929-2011/ (accessed August 15, 2016).

[82] I inquired into the possibility of Ch'oe's being a student at the Stockholm School of Economics, but I was informed that there is no record of her on any roster of former students.

[83] *Tonga ilbo*, November 29, 1931. Interestingly, Ch'oe herself never mentioned her employment related to the Prince's private library or the Museum.

[84] Chŏn Ponggwan, "Chosŏn ch'oech'o Sweden kyŏngje hakcha Ch'oe Yŏngsuk aesa" (A Sad Story of Ch'oe Yŏngsuk, the First Korean Woman Holding a Degree in Economics from Sweden), *Sin tonga* 560 (May 2006): 542–55.

[85] Ch'oe Yŏngsuk, "Kkandŭi wa Naidu hoegyŏn'gi—Indo e 4 kaewŏl ch'eryu hamyŏnsŏ" (Interviews with Gandhi and Naidu from my Stay in India), *Samch'ŏlli* 4, no. 1 (January

case of Naidu, Ch'oe actually had a number of occasions to interact with her.[86] Naidu had already been introduced to Koreans through her poetry,[87] and she became even more renowned in 1925 when she became the first woman to preside over the Indian National Congress, the key body of the independence movement in India. She was hailed in Korea as a "revolutionary woman" whose nationalist activism, along with that of Gandhi, was reported with great admiration.[88] Further, Naidu was a key figure who "galvanized Indian women's suffrage and linked it inextricably to nationalist claims on the imperial state."[89] Naidu and Ch'oe had previously met while Ch'oe was studying in Sweden, most likely during Naidu's tour of Europe in 1929.[90] Since then they had kept in close contact and had corresponded with one another. Ch'oe considered Naidu "a magnificent person" and a "trusted comrade" whose "gentle character gave her the air of a poet; her fortitude gave her the air of a political leader." Naidu encouraged Ch'oe to stay in India and work as a journalist, but Ch'oe felt obliged to return to Korea, and she arrived there in November 1931 after nine years away from home.[91]

In her short commentary in the December 1931 issue of *Tonggwang*, Ch'oe talks about her experiences in India. She reports how, when the Indians asked her about the Korean version of the Indian National Congress, she felt ashamed because there was no such national body representing the Korean populace. Despite the challenges that would be faced in establishing a people's congress in Korea, Ch'oe expressed her desire to undertake such a project. Unfortunately, her health quickly deteriorated on her return to Korea, and she passed away on April 23, 1932, less than six months after arriving back in her home country.[92]

Ch'oe's return to Korea was marked by difficulty in securing a position, a factor that may have contributed to her early death. She attempted to find employment in

---

1932): 47–9, quoted on 47–8. This essay is translated in *New Women in Colonial Korea: A Sourcebook*, pp. 180–83.

[86] Ch'oe, "Kkandŭi wa Naidu hoegyŏn'gi," 180–83.   [87] *Kaebyŏk* 25 (July 1922): 40–5.

[88] Chŏng Insŏp, "Hyŏngmyŏng yŏsŏng 'Naidu' wa Indo" (Revolutionary Woman Naidu and India), *Samch'ŏlli* 11 (January 1931): 37, 44–7.

[89] Antoinette Burton, *Dwelling in the Archive: Women Writing House, Home and History in Late Colonial India* (Oxford: Oxford University Press, 2003), p. 9.

[90] *The Mahatma and The Poetess: A selection of letters exchanged between Gandhiji and Sarojini Naidu*, compiled by E. S. Reddy and edited by Mrinalini Sarabhai; http://www.gandhiashramsevagram.org/index.php.

[91] Ch'oe, "Kkandŭi wa Naidu hoegyŏn'gi."

[92] *Chosŏn ilbo*, April 25, 1932, p. 2. There are competing reports on the cause of her death. It was rumored to be the miscarriage of a child. There is no clear evidence that this rumor warrants belief. According to *Chosŏn ilbo*, April 25, 1932, when Ch'oe arrived in India, she met a Korean man called "Ro mo" (Mr. Ro without a first name), who just returned from England, and they fell in love. For more speculation on her death, see http://premium.chosun.com/site/data/html_dir/2014/02/03/2014020301779.html. For a thoughtful discussion of Ch'oe's premature death, see also Theodore Jun Yoo, "The Biography of Ch'oe Yŏng-suk and the Politics of Gender in Colonial Korea," *Journal of Women's History* 21, no. 4 (Winter 2009): 161–3.

numerous sectors, including education and journalism, but it was all to no avail. Ultimately, she had to peddle vegetables on the street to support herself and her family. It is unclear why she was unable to secure a position that was commensurate with her training. One reason may be that her decision to study in Sweden was unusual for a Korean student at that time. That meant that there was no existing network of teachers and seniors that could assist her. In fact, the global Christian network was a catalyst in women's education and employment. Many former students went on to work at their alma maters or at other Christian organizations, and thus this global Christian network was essential for that first generation of professional women. Given that, it is interesting to note that in her writings Ch'oe rarely refers to her teachers at Ewha, her alma mater, perhaps suggesting that she remained outside the network, either coincidentally or by choice. In that regard, one might also note that Ch'oe seems to have been heavily influenced by socialism from her stay in China and her study of political economy in Sweden. In a context where evangelical missionaries and most Korean Christians were politically conservative and abhorred the growing influence of socialism among Korean youths, Ch'oe's progressive politics might have marked her as an outsider and possibly worked against her efforts to secure a job.[93]

The diverse trajectories of Korean women studying overseas show that, despite the strong influence of Japan as the primary host country, the circuit of metropole and colony was just one side of that history. There were more complex, overlapping, and wide-ranging routes of study overseas beyond that circuit. Setting aside the formidable will of individuals in pursuit of modern knowledge, what helped many pioneering women to travel overseas was often the regional and global Christian network forged through mission schools and church organizations in Korea and overseas. One of the most critical assets of belonging to this Christian network was not only the shared information and tips about studying overseas but the opportunity to receive scholarships – full or partial – without which it was difficult, if not impossible, to pursue study overseas, especially for those who came from economically disadvantaged families.

Scholarship and Financial Aid for Spirituality: Cases in the United States

For the vast majority of Korean students, arranging financial support was the most challenging part of studying overseas.[94] Julian Park, who was the Secretary for the Korean Student Federation of North America, toured colleges in 1922 to gauge the well-being of Korean students on various campuses. He

---

[93] Timothy S. Lee, *Born Again: Evangelicalism in Korea* (Honolulu: University of Hawai'i Press, 2010), pp. 60–62.

[94] O Ch'ŏnsŏk offers a detailed list of scholarship programs available in US universities in his guidelines. See O, "Miguk yuhak annae yoram," 173–6.

128 Crossing: Selfhood, Nation, and the World

noted that "almost all of our students are self supporting."[95] Many students engaged in menial work on farms, in factories, or at restaurants, and others worked as salesclerks or domestic help. Korean immigrants sometimes helped these desperate students find jobs.[96] For example, a Korean-run company in Detroit, Yuhan Chusik Hoesa (Yuhan Corporate Company), advertised something called the "student plan" in *Urak'i* through which students could purchase products at a wholesale price and resell them at a retail markup.[97]

Among women students, jobs as babysitters or housemaids were common.[98] Detailed accounts of that type of work are rare, but in her autobiography, Yim Yŏngsin (1899–1977), a graduate of Kijŏn Girls' School, a Southern Presbyterian mission school in Chŏnju, shares her experiences working as a housemaid while she was studying at the University of Southern California. She relates stories about her mishaps with common household items that she had never seen or used in Korea, including an incident in which the house "almost burned down when the mechanism of a gas stove baffled me and I searched for the trouble with a lighted match," or "the electric coffee percolator started melting on the dining-room table when I forgot to put water in it and waited patiently for the coffee to percolate." Communication in her second language was another challenge. Yim describes how one of her employers "nearly went out of her mind when I replied to her every 'Please don't do it' with a 'Yes, I will.' While it might not seem that way to the untutored ear, in the Korean language, one answers with a positive to the other person's negative. At any rate, I was fired at the end of a week."[99] While the passage of time allows her to reflect on these episodes with amusement, the need to earn income to support their study abroad and juggling time and energy between study and work added tremendous burdens to students.

Under these circumstances, the Christian network provided some level of assistance to many of the students in the form of formally established scholarships, informally arranged sponsorships, or assistance in finding employment to help them fund their studies.[100] A noteworthy example is the Committee on

---

[95] Julian Park (Secretary for Korean Students), "Report on College Visitation," *Korean Student Bulletin* 1, no. 1 (December 1922): 3.
[96] "Sosŏl morŭnŭn nara ro!," *Urak'i* 2 (1926): 130–40.
[97] "Yuhan chusik hoesa" (Detroit, Mich), *Urak'i* 2 (1926), 371.
[98] Kim Sŏngŭn, "1920-30-nyŏndae yŏja Miguk yuhaksaeng ŭi silt'ae wa insik" (The Reality and Consciousness of Women Students Studying in the United States in the 1920s and 1930s), *Yŏksa wa kyŏnggye* 72 (2009): 201–5.
[99] Louise Yim, *My Forty Years Fight for Korea* (Seoul: International Cultural Research Center, Chung-ang University, 1951), p. 166.
[100] The historian Emily Anderson describes the case of Japanese Christians residing in the United States who provided destitute Korean students with money provided by the Japanese Consulate in Chicago. These funds were designated to help solve "the Korean problem" after the March First Independence Movement. Such a case, she argues, "reveals not only the geographic reach of the Japanese empire's claim that it ruled over Koreans regardless of where they were, but

Friendly Relations among Foreign Students of the International YMCA (hereafter, the Committee), a major Christian organization that was devoted to a broad program of effective and strategic investment in the work of the foreign mission. It offered a wide range of practical assistance to foreign students, including meeting them at the steamer on their arrival at American ports; providing for their immediate needs, such as board and lodging; and helping them to connect with the college and the local YMCA and YWCA.[101] Because Korean students in the United States were almost exclusively Christian, the Committee gave special attention to them. For instance, Charles D. Hurrey, the General Secretary of the Committee, called attention to the financial challenges faced by Korean students, many of whom were forced to "abandon plans for study and to engage in manual labor for a living." He believed that these native Korean Christian students would be invaluable assets for the future of the Korea mission, but that the monetary hardship they suffered significantly undercut such a future. He even argued that it would be much more effective to invest in Korean students in the United States than to send American missionaries to Korea. He wrote:

How can the Christian people of America cooperate in turning the disappointment and despair of these students into hope and the completion of their course? Are we justified in sending more money and missionaries to Korea while the crying needs of Korean students at our doors are not met? Many of these students desire to return to their native land in Christian work, and if given the training which they seek here, their services to the Kingdom in Korea will exceed that of many missionaries; the two or three years of additional study which they require would more than balance an equal amount of time devoted by a foreign missionary to language study. Moreover, the returning Korean student is at home among his own people; he knows the depths of their hearts; the foreign missionary, on the other hand, is always a foreigner.[102]

After the 1924 Immigration Act was implemented, financial hardship became even greater. The new immigration law excluded Asian immigrants, and restricted entry to the country to "students." That designation meant they could not legally work. O Ch'ŏnsŏk estimated that nine out of ten students had to give up employment after the new law went into effect, basically

---

also of the deep anxiety that beset the state, the Government-General, and those who supported the colonization of Korea." Emily Anderson, *Christianity and Imperialism in Modern Japan: Empire for God* (London: Bloomsbury Academic, 2014), pp. 159–60.

[101] The Committee made it clear that it "has no interest or motive other than the furthering of the moral, social, and educational interests of the students" and "there is no fund set aside for the purpose of affording scholarship aid. However, if conditions so change as to render pecuniary aid, we shall feel it our duty to notify all students in regard to the matter," *Korean Student Bulletin* 1, no. 1 (December 1922): 3–4.

[102] Charles D. Hurrey, "An Urgent Message to Friends of Korean Students," *Korean Student Bulletin* 2, no. 1 (November 1923): 13. Responding to many appeals, the Committee on Friendly Relations appointed Mr. K. S. Yum (Yŏm Kwangsŏp), a graduate student at the University of Chicago, as Secretary for Korean students.

eliminating the practice of "work and study" that had evolved for the majority of Korean students in the United States.[103] The Great Depression of 1929 also had a devastating impact on Korean students, especially in financial terms. *Sinhan minbo* reported that "there has been no worse time in the past fifty years than right now for our Korean students."[104] Similarly, a Korean magazine, *Tonggwang*, alerted US-bound Korean students to the unprecedented challenges they would face in the United States as the value of Korean currency dropped to less than one-third of its earlier value.[105]

Scholarship programs were also severely curtailed during the Great Depression, although a few programs specifically designed for Asian women did continue. Two of the most important ones for Korean women were the Oregon Agricultural College's (OAC's) International Friendship Scholarship for students of home economics (see Chapter 2 for detailed introduction) and the University of Michigan's Barbour Scholarship for Oriental Women.

The Barbour scholarship was established in 1917 at the University of Michigan with a generous donation from Levi Barbour, a Michigan alumnus himself (grad. 1863).[106] Barbour was a firm believer in women's rights, writing that women "should have every facility for education and every right and privilege to exert their influence to the fullest extent." As a prominent donor to the University of Michigan, he had already contributed funding to the establishment of the campus's first women's center, the Barbour Gymnasium, and the Betsy Barbour House, a women's dormitory. Barbour was inspired to create a scholarship for "Oriental women" when he was traveling in Asia and had a chance to observe the impressive work that three Asian women graduates of the University of Michigan had done in their respective countries. Two of these alumnae – Kang Cheng (aka Ida Kahn, grad.1896) and Shih Mei-yu (aka Mary Stone, grad. 1896) – were from China and one, Tomo Inoue (grad. 1901), was from Japan.[107] All three had been trained in medicine at Michigan. Kang and Shih were brought to Michigan by their missionary teacher Gertrude Howe, a graduate of Michigan herself and another strong advocate for women's education.[108]

---

[103] O Ch'ŏnsŏk, "Miguk yuhaksaengsa." See also O Ch'ŏnsŏk's article "Miguk yuhak annae yoram."
[104] "Sinmun kumun: Miguk yuhaksaenggye sosik" (New and Old News: News from Korean Students in the US), *Tonggwang* 37 (September 1932): 13.
[105] "Konghwang kwa yuhakkye" (Depression and the World of Studying Overseas), *Tonggwang* 37 (September 1932): 13.
[106] Ruth Bordin, "Levi Lewis Barbour – Benefactor of University of Michigan Women," fol. History, Box, Barbour Scholarship for Oriental Women Committee (University of Michigan) Records, 1914–1983, Bentley Historical Library, University of Michigan (hereafter, BHL).
[107] W. Carl Rufus, "Barbour Scholars around the World" (Jan. 1937), 1, fol. History, Box, Barbour Scholarship for Oriental Women Committee (University of Michigan) Records, 1914–1983, BHL.
[108] Dana Robert, *American Women in Mission: A Social History of their Thought and Practice* (Macon: Mercer University Press, 1996), pp. 185–6.

Tomo Inoue was also the product of a missionary education, a graduate of Kwassui, a Methodist mission school for women in Japan.[109] Barbour was deeply impressed by the changes these pioneering Asian women had effected in their home countries, and he believed that their education in the United States had provided the impetus for reform in their native countries. Hoping to help other women, he proposed an initial gift of $50,000 to establish a scholarship program at Michigan specifically for "Oriental women." The scholarship program became official in 1917, offering $800 per year per student. That was quite a generous amount, given that the average yearly expenses for studying in the Midwest region of the United States at the time was approximately $640 that includes lodging, meals, books, and other incidentals.[110]

The competition for the Barbour Scholarship was stiff.[111] The scholarship program's governing body sought recommendations for talented students from Americans living and working in Asia many of whom were affiliated with Christian schools or organizations. In 1918 John R. Effinger of the College of Literature, Science and Arts at Michigan wrote to Levi Barbour that: "The [Barbour Scholarship for Oriental Women] Committee felt that if we were to have an Advisory Committee in Japan, which would be really effective and which would be able to really help us in making a wise choice, it might be to our advantage to have an American as our special representative in Japan and give to this person a [sic] Advisory Committee which might be consulted from time to time."[112] He then suggested that Mary C. Baker, who was the General Secretary of the YWCA in Yokohama, be considered as the representative.[113] Barbour approved that proposal.[114] This Advisory Committee in Japan and the Barbour Scholarship for Oriental Women Committee in Ann Arbor regularly communicated about new prospective scholarship candidates as well as the progress and troubles of students currently on scholarship. For example, one

---

[109] Rosetta Sherwood Hall, "Women Physicians in the Orient," *The Korea Mission Field* 21, no. 2 (February 1925): 42.

[110] O, "Miguk yuhak annae yoram."

[111] In records from 1939, more than one hundred applied for nine slots. W. C. Rufus, "University of Michigan Barbour Scholarships for Oriental Women, May 19, 1939," fol. Newsletters 1927–46, Box, Barbour Scholarship for Oriental Women Committee (University of Michigan) records, 1914–1983, BHL.

[112] Some word(s) seems to be missing in this quotation especially after "*person*," but the quoted passage is as it was written. A letter of November 4, 1918, to Levi L. Barbour from John R. Effinger, fol. Correspondence 1918–69, Box, Barbour Scholarship for Oriental Women Committee (University of Michigan) records, 1914–1983, BHL.

[113] A letter of November 4, 1918, to Levi L. Barbour from John R. Effinger; and "YWCA of the USA Records," fol. 9, "Reports 1918–1921," Box 335, Record Group 5, International Work, Sophia Smith Collection, Smith College.

[114] A letter of November 5, 1918, to John R. Effinger from Levi L. Barbour, fol. Correspondence 1918–69, Box, Barbour Scholarship for Oriental Women Committee (University of Michigan) records, 1914–1983, BHL.

such report discusses the case of a Japanese student who "had a rather serious love affair which apparently diverted her attention from her studies" during her first year and ultimately was not reappointed as a Barbour scholar.[115]

The appointment of W. Carl Rufus as Secretary of the Barbour Scholarship for Oriental Women Committee in 1920 also shows the far-reaching impact that the US missionary network had on the scholarship. Rufus was appointed as Secretary of the Committee in 1920, and he served in that capacity until 1946. He joined the faculty at Michigan in 1917 as a professor of astronomy. Prior to this academic appointment, he had been a missionary in Korea. He and his wife, Maude Squire, went to Korea in 1908 as missionaries and worked there until 1917. He taught mathematics and astronomy at Union College in P'yŏngyang and Chosen Christian College (now Yonsei University) in Seoul – two major mission institutions of higher education for men in colonial-era Korea. Rufus was also a member of one of the most prominent American missionary families in Korea. His sister was Ethel Underwood, who was married to Horace Horton Underwood. Ethel and Horace were both prominent missionaries in Korea in their own right, but in addition Horace's father, Horace Grant Underwood, had founded Chosen Christian College, and his mother, Lilias Horton Underwood, was a pioneering medical missionary who served Korea's royal family.[116] Rufus's decade of experience in "the Orient" gave him a background that was ideally suited for overseeing the Barbour scholarship program.[117]

Although Rufus was only one member of the Committee that selected the Barbour scholars, his career as a missionary and his extensive network within the Protestant mission in Korea played a significant role in his strong sense that Korean students should have greater access to educational opportunity. He had observed the educational system under Japanese rule, which was composed of the two separated tracks – "a lower one for the Koreans and a higher one for the Japanese," and he believed that such a segregated and discriminatory system "provided some cause for dissatisfaction on the part of the Koreans, especially their [Korean] racial pride is very sensitive and they have no reason to admit inferior mental ability."[118] He was skeptical of Japan's assimilation project that emphasized "national language [kokugo], national morals, and industrial

---

[115] Letter of W. Carl Rufus to the members of the Barbour Scholarship Advisory Committee in Japan, dated May 17, 1938, fol. Correspondence 1918–69, Box, Barbour Scholarship for Oriental Women Committee (University of Michigan) records, 1914–1983, BHL.

[116] W. Carl Rufus, "Barbour Scholars around the World" (January 1937), 3, fol. History, Box, Barbour Scholarship for Oriental Women Committee (University of Michigan) records, 1914–1983, BHL.

[117] "Proposed Minutes of the November, 1946, Faculty Meeting, College of Literature, Science, and the Arts," Box, W. C. Rufus Family, BHL; and W. Carl Rufus, "Twenty-five years of the Barbour scholarships" 1942 (reprinted from Michigan Alumnus Quarterly Review, December 19, 1942, vol. XLIX, no. 11).

[118] W. Carl Rufus, "The Japanese Educational Policy in Korea," Korea Review 2, no. 11 (Jan. 1921): 13–16, quoted on 15.

training," in an effort to turn Koreans into "loyal subjects," and he argued that the Japanese "coercive assimilation is doomed to failure."[119] He wrote that Japanese educational policy was intended to keep Koreans at the low and practical areas of study, "an intellectual diet of Japanese sweetmeats instead of a wholesome meal of universal history, literature, science and art, with a little Korean relish."[120] He argued that such an education "can scarcely be expected to produce intelligent world-citizens possessing initiative and character."[121] As noted earlier, the colonial government did establish the Keijō Imperial University (Kyŏngsŏng Cheguk Taehakkyo), in Seoul in 1924; however, the main beneficiaries of the university were Japanese expatriates and no woman was admitted. Rufus understood why, given the sheer lack of institutions of higher learning and the discriminatory educational policy of the colonial state,[122] some ambitious and capable Korean students wanted to pursue study overseas, and he argued that those aspiring students "should not be denied passports to prevent study in foreign lands."[123]

There was no local advisory committee in Korea, unlike in Japan, so Rufus's connections to missionaries serving in Korea were vital for identifying potential candidates for the scholarship. The number of Barbour scholars from Korea was relatively small compared to the number from China and Japan. In total, eleven Korean students received Barbour scholarships between 1924 and 1942.[124] Many of the Korean Barbour scholars were educated at mission schools, particularly Ewha Girls' School or Ewha Women's Professional School, the flagship Methodist mission schools for girls in Korea. In 1924 the Barbour Scholarship program awarded its first scholarship to a Korean student, Song Poksin (aka Grace Song). She received a degree in public health in 1929.[125] She was from P'yŏngyang,[126] once called "the Jerusalem of the East" because of the exceptional success of evangelical activities there. In a report published in 1925 in *The Korea Mission Field*, Rosetta Sherwood Hall (1865–1951), a prominent Methodist medical missionary, referred to Song

---

[119] Rufus, "The Japanese Educational Policy in Korea," 13–16.
[120] Rufus, "The Japanese Educational Policy in Korea," 16.
[121] Rufus, "The Japanese Educational Policy in Korea," 15.
[122] Chŏng, *Ilche ŭi taeHan'guk singminji kyoyuk chŏngch'aeksa*, 335–7.
[123] Rufus, "The Japanese Educational Policy in Korea," 16.
[124] Fol. Recipients, Box, Barbour Scholarship for Oriental Women Committee (University of Michigan) records, 1914–1983, BHL.
[125] Song did not return to Korea after completing her studies at Michigan as she married W. H. Line and helped in her husband's business. She and her husband visited Korea later and offered "motion picture lectures" that were hugely popular. See "Addresses of former Barbour fellows and scholars 1937," 6, fol. Newsletters 1927–1946 (see News Letter May 10, 1937, p. 11 and News Letter May 19, 1939, p. 9), Box, Barbour Scholarship for Oriental Women Committee (University of Michigan) records, 1914–1983, BHL.
[126] "The Levi L. Barbour Scholarships for Oriental Women," September 17, 1927, 13, Third Barbour Scholarship Newsletter 1927, Barbour Scholarship Newsletters 1927–46, BHL.

Poksin as "Dr. Song," describing her as one of twelve Korean women who "have received license to practice medicine."[127] Song had already received a medical degree from the Tokyo Women's Medical College in 1922, and as Hall mentions in her essay, Song received a Barbour Scholarship at the University of Michigan in 1924.[128] Significantly, in the same essay, Hall mentions Dr. Tomo Inoue, one of the Asian women doctors who had inspired Levi Barbour to create the Barbour Scholarship program. Hall notes: "The municipality of Osaka employs a Japanese woman physician for its factory women, and Dr. I. Tomo, one of *our* Kwassui graduates, is the advising doctor of the Peeress' School in Tokyo. Similar work should be awaiting our Korean women doctors" [emphasis added].[129] The way Hall refers to Inoue as "one of *our* Kwassui graduates" suggests a view in which all mission schools and hospitals were part of a missionary network that stretched across countries and helped share information, which, in turn, facilitated the flow of students in their pursuit of higher education overseas.

A group of Ewha graduates followed Song Poksin into the Barbour Scholarship program, including Kim Tongjun (aka Katherine Kim), who majored in English (1928–1932);[130] Meri Kim (aka Mary Kim) in music (1930–1933); Ko Hwanggyŏng (aka Evelyn Koh) in sociology (1931–1937); and Kim Sinsil in physical education (1935–1938). On completing their degrees, each of these women was recruited to join the faculty at Ewha College, and they all went on to play major roles in their respective fields. In an administrative document of the Barbour Scholarship program titled "What We Should Know About Applicants [to the Barbour Scholarship Program]," one of the questions is "What Barbour Scholars do you know or have talked with?"[131] The fact that a chain of Ewha's graduates were successful in their applications to the Barbour Scholarship program

---

[127] Rosetta Sherwood Hall (1865–1951) was a prominent Methodist medical missionary in Korea. She was an ardent advocate of medical education for Korean women. Since there was no proper medical school for women in Korea until Hall co-founded the Chosŏn Women's Medical Training Institute in 1928, some of the aspiring students were sent overseas, including to the Union Women's Medical College of Peking, which had a collaborative relationship with Christian hospitals in P'yŏngyang, and to the Tokyo Women's Medical College. See Rosetta Hall and Esther K. Pak, "Woman's Medical Work, Pyeng Yang," *The Korea Mission Field* 5 (1909): 109–11; Sonja M. Kim, *Imperatives of Care: Women and Medicine in Colonial Korea* (Honolulu: University of Hawai'i Press, 2019), pp. 65–71.

[128] Rosetta Sherwood Hall, "Women Physicians in the Orient," *The Korea Mission Field* 21, no. 2 (February 1925): 41; and Kim Sangdŏk, "Yŏja ŭihak kangsŭpso" (Medical Training Center for Women), *Ŭisahak* 2, no. 1 (1993): 80–84.

[129] Hall, "Women Physicians in the Orient," 42.

[130] Ewha 100-nyŏnsa p'yŏnch'an wiwŏnhoe, *Ewha 100-nyŏnsa* (The Hundredth History of Ewha Womans University) (Seoul: Ewha yŏja taehakkyo ch'ulp'anbu, 1994), p. 152.

[131] "What We Should Know About Applicants," fol. Correspondence 1918–69, Box, Barbour Scholarship for Oriental Women Committee (University of Michigan) records, 1914–1983, BHL.

Scholarship and Financial Aid for Spirituality 135

demonstrates how important such school ties were in the minds of the people administering the Barbour scholarships.

Tracking the paths of international students who graduated in the early-twentieth century can be a challenge. The Barbour Scholarship program stands out in terms of its systematic records of students not only during the degree program but beyond, in the form of newsletters and correspondence with former students. W. Carl Rufus wrote: "The Committee in charge of the Barbour Scholarships for Oriental Women desires to maintain correspondence with all Barbour scholars in order that the interchange of information may be mutually beneficial. We wish each one of you to know how the work in Michigan is progressing and we desire to keep informed regarding your activities since you left our midst."[132] Rufus was particularly successful in staying in touch with former students. Celia Chao, one of the recipients of the Barbour Scholarship, remembers Rufus as "one of the best correspondents I have known. He never neglected to answer a letter from any of the Barbour Scholars, however unimportant it may have seemed."[133]

Rufus kept in touch with Barbour scholars not only through correspondence and newsletters but through actual visits.[134] Rufus and his wife, Maude Squire, traveled the world in 1936, during his sabbatical. One of the chief goals was to "meet people, especially Michigan men and women, and more specifically our own Barbour scholars, 150 of whom [are] scattered around the world," and they managed to meet almost three-quarters of those former recipients. The Rufuses visited Hawai'i, Japan, Korea, the Philippines, Singapore, Indonesia, Burma, and India, getting together with former students who were active and prominent in their own professions. Rufus also learned that "Barbour clubs" had been organized among graduates in each country.[135] Korea was a stop on this world tour that the Rufuses held in "keen anticipation" because "[we] lived [in Korea] ten years and said farewell to a host of friends eighteen years ago." When they arrived in Pusan, a port city in the Southeast corner of Korea, they were greeted by Dr. Wonchul Lee (aka David Lee), a Michigan alumnus who had received a PhD in astronomy from

---

[132] "To all Barbour scholars" [Date not included], fol. Correspondence 1918–69, Box, Barbour Scholarship for Oriental Women Committee (University of Michigan) records, 1914–1983, BHL.

[133] Celia Chao, "In memoriam Prof. W. Carl Rufus," Box, W. C. Rufus Family, BHL.

[134] Rufus also served on the Advisory Committee of the Korean Student Federation of North America along with other well-known figures to Koreans, such as John Dewey, Edmund de S. Brunner, Homer B. Hulbert, and Charles D. Hurrey. *Directory of Korean Students in North America 1936–1937*, published jointly by the Social Relations Department of the Korean Student Federation of North America and the Korean Division of the Committee on Friendly Relations among Foreign Students, see p. 3; https://archive.org/details/ldpd_11381026_000 (accessed April 2, 2018).

[135] W. Carl Rufus, "Barbour Scholars around the World" (January 1937), 3, fol. History, Box, Barbour Scholarship for Oriental Women Committee (University of Michigan) records, 1914–1983, BHL.

Michigan in 1923 and was a faculty member of Chosen Christian College. The Rufuses also met former Barbour scholars, including Mary Kim (Kim Meri) and Evelyn Ko (Ko Hwanggyŏng) of Ewha Collge and Katherine Kim (Kim Tongjun) of Hamhŭng Girls School.[136]

Interestingly, some of the Barbour students listed as Korean were actually children of Korean immigrants in Hawai'i.[137] Two sisters from Hawai'i, Priscilla Choy (1925) and Martha Choy (1928), were early recipients of Barbour scholarships (see Figure 3.1). Martha Choy had a particularly illustrious career. She graduated from Honolulu Normal School and President William McKinley High School and received a Barbour Scholarship in 1928. While pursuing her M.A. at Michigan, she resided at the Martha Cook building, and served as vice-president of the same residential hall in 1930.[138] She also served on the Editorial Board of the *KSB*, a rare source available for our understanding of the realities Korean students faced in the United States.[139] Significantly, she attended the Pan-Pacific Women's Conference, held in Honolulu from August 9 to 23, 1928, as a delegate of the All Asian Association of University Women. As Fiona Paisley demonstrates, this Pan-Pacific Women's Conference was an important platform for developing international and intercultural communication among women in the Pacific region.[140] After completing her M.A. at Michigan, Choy went to China to teach at Yenching Women's College in Peking.[141] There she met Graham Chen, a medical doctor, and they married in 1934.[142] She subsequently taught at the YWCA of Peking, while her husband was "on the staff of Peiping Union Medical College, which is backed by the Rockefeller Institute."[143] According to *Barbour Scholars News* (Fall 1939), she "received an appointment from the

---

[136] Rufus, "Barbour Scholars around the World," 3; and "Michigan Alumnae (Barbour Scholars) engaged by religious institutions," fol. Recipients, Box, Barbour Scholarship for Oriental Women Committee (University of Michigan) records, 1914–1983, BHL.

[137] In comparison, there were separate categories of "Japanese American" or "Chinese American" to distinguish them from those from Japan or China. See "Permanent Record of Barbour Scholars," fol. Recipients, Box, Barbour Scholarship for Oriental Women Committee (University of Michigan) records, 1914–1983, BHL.

[138] *Michiganensian* (1929), 438; and *Michiganensian* (1930), 457.

[139] She served on the Editorial Board between 1928 and 1932.

[140] Fiona Paisley, *Glamour in the Pacific: Cultural Internationalism and Race Politics in the Women's Pan-Pacific* (Honolulu: University of Hawai'i Press, 2009). Another recipient of the Barbour scholarship, Mary Kim, attended the third Pan-Pacific Women's Conference, August 6–22, 1934. See *The Argus*, August 4, 1934, 10 and August 8, 1934, 15.

[141] "Barbour Scholarship News Letter 1933," 2; and "Barbour Scholarship News Letter 1934," 3, BHL.

[142] A letter of W. Carl Rufus to Barbour Scholars, May 7, 1935, p. 4. fol. Newsletters 1927–46, Box, Barbour Scholarship for Oriental Women Committee (University of Michigan) records, 1914–1983, BHL.

[143] News Letter May 10, 1937, 3, BHL.

Scholarship and Financial Aid for Spirituality

Figure 3.1 Barbour Scholarship recipients: Martha Choy, Katherine Kim, and Mary Kim (third, eighth, and tenth from the left in the last row), 1930–1931
Source: HS835, UM Barbour, Bentley Historical Library, University of Michigan

superintendent of instruction in Hawai'i as exchange teacher to Minnesota for this winter, a high honor never before accorded to an oriental."[144]

Formal scholarships programs, such as the Barbour Scholarship at the University of Michigan or the International Friendship Scholarships at Oregon Agricultural College (see Chapter 2), were in short supply, but they were crucial in helping Korean women obtain advanced degrees. Furthermore, on graduation, almost all the Korean recipients of those scholarships were appointed to faculty positions at Ewha Women's Professional School – the only institution of higher education for women in Korea until 1938. Those women faculty played a pioneering role in introducing modern disciplines, expanding the existing curriculum, and training the next generation of women.[145] The educational opportunities they had overseas and the positions they secured in Korea were, in large part, due to the fact that they had close ties

---

[144] Fol. Newsletters 1927–46, Box, Barbour Scholarship for Oriental Women Committee (University of Michigan) records, 1914–1983, BHL.
[145] Kim, "1920-30-nyŏndae yŏja Miguk yuhaksaeng ŭi silt'ae wa insik," 191.

with mission schools, American missionaries, and Christian community in general. They were methodically guided, encouraged, and supported by missionaries and their associates at home and abroad in finding their way to studying overseas, choosing their majors, and securing jobs. However, as discussed earlier in the case of Ch'oe Yŏngsuk, those who did not conform to the missionary expectations in terms of their religious, political, and cultural outlook faced a much harsher reality in navigating a career path on returning to Korea.

Local and National Identity Through Cosmopolitan Sensibility

Those students who went abroad to pursue advanced knowledge saw themselves as having twin functions: to absorb, translate, and adapt what they learned overseas to the specific context of Korea to help modernize and strengthen the nation; and to act as ambassadors of a sort and to introduce Korean history, culture, and politics to their host countries. In this vein, it is noteworthy that in February 1928 a group of Korean women intellectuals who were studying in the United States gathered in New York City to found the Kŭnhwahoe (Association of the Rose of Sharon) to promote the profile of Korea among the population of the United States as part of their nationalist movement. Kim Maria (1891–1944) as president, Hwang Aedŏk (1892–1971) as secretary, and Pak Indŏk (1896–1980) as outreach coordinator were the leaders of the Association. Kim Maria and Hwang Aedŏk were both attending Columbia University at the time. All three of these women had been imprisoned in 1919 for their participation in the March First Independence Movement, and the popular magazine *Samch'ŏlli* called the three "giant woman heroes who created unforgettable memories for the Korean nation."[146] This history of camaraderie in their pursuit of national independence, and their sense of duty as privileged intellectuals studying in the United States, may have motivated them to create an organization to contribute to the Korean nation, even if it was from afar, an act that could be called "long-distance nationalism," in the words of Benedict Anderson.[147] The goals of Kŭnhwahoe included (1) support of patriotic activities in the Korean community based in the United States, with the grand goal of national independence; (2) creating a sense of unity and inspiring patriotic consciousness among Korean women in the United States; and (3) aiding the public activities of the Korean American community to inform foreigners of the (colonial) situation in

---

[146] "Chosŏn yŏryu 10 kŏmul yŏlchŏn" (Biographies of Ten Great Women in Korea), *Samch'ŏlli* 3, no. 11 (November 1931): 37–9; Choi, *Gender and Mission Encounters in Korea*, pp. 155–64.
[147] Benedict R. O'G. Anderson, *Long-Distance Nationalism: World Capitalism, and the Rise of Identity Politics* (Berkeley: Centre for German and European Studies University of California, 1992).

Korea through publications and lectures.[148] The organization was rather short-lived, so it is hard to trace the specific activities in which it engaged. One might infer that the brevity of its existence had to do with the fact that the majority of students who made up its membership had to work to earn money to support their studies, and most were in the United States for only a year or two. Hwang Aedŏk reflected on her time at Columbia University as a struggling international student, saying she felt her studies and experience had been constrained by economic difficulties and also by her lack of English-language proficiency. She wrote that for every hour of work her fellow students put into their studies, she had to work ten just to keep up, and thus she did not have any free time to enjoy campus life.[149] In spite of the short life of the Kŭnhwahoe and the paucity of records about its activities, the very fact of its founding may illustrate the spirit of Korean students, their eagerness to take on leadership in the movement toward national independence, and their intermediary role in interpreting Korean history, culture, and politics for a wider audience.

In addition to organizations such as the Kŭnhwahoe, publications enabled students to fill an intermediary role between Korea and the United States. The above-mentioned journal, the *KSB*, is a noteworthy example. It was published in English and sponsored by the YMCA's Committee on Friendly Relations Among Foreign Students, which also sponsored the bulletins of other foreign student groups, including the *Filipino Student Bulletin* and the *Japanese Student Bulletin*.[150] The Christian faith-based nature of the sponsoring organization is clearly reflected in the purpose of the *KSB*. It aimed "to serve all the Korean students in this country in a way to bring them into closer contact with the Christian influence and to foster the moral and educational interests among them," and also "to deepen and widen the interest of the American Christians in Korea and her people."[151] A large portion of the content of the *KSB* was devoted to various Christian activities in which Korean students participated, including conferences of the World's Student Christian Federation and mission work in big cities such as New York or Los Angeles.[152] The *KSB* also played a key role in connecting Korean students with one another, sharing "Personal

---

[148] http://encykorea.aks.ac.kr/Contents/Index?contents_id=E0007474 (accessed June 19, 2017).
[149] Hwang Aesidŏk, "Miguk K'olŏmbia taehak: Miguk ŭi namnyŏ konghak ŭn ŏttŏk'e hana" (Columbia University in the United States: How Do Co-ed Universities Work in the United States), *Man'guk puin* 1 (1932): 53–5; Pak Hwasŏng, *Saebyŏk e oech'ida* (Shouting out at the Dawn), in *Pak Hwasŏng munhak chŏnjip* (Anthology of Pak Hwasŏng's Work) (Seoul: P'urŭn sasangsa, 2004).
[150] *Urak'i* (The Rocky) is another important magazine, published by the Korean Student Federation of North America between 1925 and 1936. Unlike the *Korean Student Bulletin*, *Urak'i* was published in Korean, and did not have any particular religious predilection.
[151] *Korean Student Bulletin* 1, no. 1 (December 1922): 1. I use the version compiled by Asia t'aep'yŏngyang kyoyuk palchŏn yŏn'gudan of the Seoul National University. See *Korean Student Bulletin* (Seoul: Sŏnin, 2000). Page numbers are on this 2000 version.
[152] *Korean Student Bulletin* 1, no. 1 (December 1922): 1, 3.

140 Crossing: Selfhood, Nation, and the World

News," celebrating accomplishments, publishing the Korean Student Directory annually, and organizing annual meetings that were held in major cities, such as Chicago, New York, or Los Angeles. Photographs from those annual meetings, where a Korean flag was displayed along with that of the United States, illustrate how the *KSB* served as a platform for enhancing Korean identity and patriotism.

Similarly, Korean students' participation in international student organizations, such as the Cosmopolitan Clubs, tended to reinforce their national identity through interactions with other foreign students from all over the world.

A photograph taken at the Candle Ceremony of the Intercollegiate Cosmopolitan Club at Columbia University (Figure 3.2) captures the ambience of these gatherings and gives us a sense of how studying overseas may have afforded a respite to foreign students whose countries were colonized.[153] What is notable about the photograph is that the Korean national flag is displayed along with the flags of Japan and many other countries, and that Korean and Japanese students stand side by side holding signs with the names of their respective home countries. Since Korea was a colony of Japan, Koreans were officially identified as subjects of Japan; however, in this cosmopolitan space, away from the colonized homeland, Korean students were able to claim their own national identity with their national flag – a symbol of sovereignty.[154]

A sense of duty to the nation is commonly detected in the feelings expressed by Korean female students. In her comment on the broader culture in the United States, Kim Meri, who studied music at the University of Michigan, wrote "I opposed jazz music, which American students seemed to love. I regretted that motion pictures embraced decadence rather than conveying *lofty ideals or concerns that people ought to have for their country*" (emphasis added).[155] When Yun Sŏngdŏk, who studied music at Northwestern University, was interviewed by the popular Korean magazine *Samch'ŏlli*, she talked about how she was at first puzzled by American women, who "pay little attention to society or nation." Rather, "their only interest seemed to be in their own happiness." She continued, "But doesn't it make sense? They live in a society that has plenty of money with excellent cultural facilities. On top of that, *they have a country* which is the strongest in the world. They must have never felt

---

[153] Harry E. Edmonds, "A New Endowment for International Friendship," fol. 68A, Box 10, series G, R62, Rockefeller Archive Center.
[154] Another important publication by Korean students in the United States, *Urak'i*, emphasizes that Korean "national" characters they want to foster should be neither "blind jingoism" (maengmok chŏk kuksujuŭi) nor "irresponsible internationalism" (much'aegim chŏk kukchejuŭi). "Urak'i chujang" (Claims by Urak'i), *Urak'i* 3 (1928): 52–8, quoted on 52.
[155] Kim Meri, "Noksaek ŭi kkum" (Dreams of Hope), *Sinin munhak* (January 1935), quoted in *Sin yŏsŏng kil wi e sŏda* (A New Woman Stands in the Street), comp. eds. Sŏ Kyŏngsŏk and U Miyŏng (Seoul: Homi, 2007), 203–7.

Identity Through Cosmopolitan Sensibility 141

Figure 3.2 The Candle Ceremony of the Intercollegiate Cosmopolitan Club, Columbia University, circa 1921
Source: Harry Edmonds, "A New Endowment for International Friendship," Educational Interests, 1921–1922 (Rockefeller Family, R62, Series G, Box 10, Folder 68A), Rockefeller Archive Center

any urgency for nation or society and thus their thinking never goes beyond the individual" (emphasis added).[156] Echoing Yun's sentiment, Kim Sŏngsil, who studied at Mount Holyoke College, shared her experience at a National Training School for the Secretary of YWCA in 1929. One of the American participants asked her whether she felt it was fortunate or unfortunate to be a Korean woman. Kim answered without hesitation that "it has been a privilege to be a Korean woman" because "if I had been born in a country like the United States, there would have been fewer opportunities for me to become a pioneer in blazing a new path. As a Korean woman I have the privilege and many more opportunities to become a pioneer in any number of different fields. Day and night, I am committed to this mission." Like Yun, Kim observes that American women seem to live an easy life with no worries about their families, their society, or their nation, and thus they pursue individual pleasure, comfort,

---

[156] "Ch'oegŭn Miguk sin yŏsŏng" (Contemporary American New Woman), Samch'ŏlli 3 (November 1929): 7–11.

luxury, and entertainment. In contrast, Korean women devote themselves to working for the people (*minjung saŏp*).[157] Being a colonized subject without a sovereign country was a defining feature in the identity of these Korean students. Given that sense of oppression and sacrifice that those Korean students felt in their own situations, the seemingly carefree, individualistic, even decadent lifestyle they witnessed in their American counterparts was a shock.

At the same time, Korean students envied the freedom that the American students felt and the seemingly unlimited possibilities in their rich, powerful country. Son Chinsil, who studied at the University of Dubuque, wrote: "[A]fter observing the American female students' lives, I conclude that American women have 'true lives' (*ch'am salda*), while Korean women have had miserable lives." To her, a true life involved intellectual, social, and physical health, and she was particularly impressed by the physical strength of American women, who enjoyed various sports. Still, the biggest impression that living in the United States left on her was in the area of "social life." Given the longstanding culture of gender separation in Korea, seeing women and men mingle freely in classrooms, libraries, and all kinds of campus activities was an eye-opening experience.[158] Another Korean student who was studying at Columbia University, under the pen name Yuam, stated: "It is the advanced status of women that particularly impresses those of us who study in the United States. One sees a stark difference between the United States and the East." The key force driving the advancement of women in the United States was the expansion of women's education at the college level. Citing scientific research studies, Yuam critiques a number of groundless assumptions embedded in the arguments against women's college education used in Korea.[159] In this way, Korean women made use of their direct experience with Americans and their culture to introduce new ways of thinking about the advancement of women.

In an interesting survey of US-based Korean students, respondents were asked what should be emulated and what should be rejected from US society and culture.[160] The things they considered worthy of emulation included advanced technology, practicality, innovation, respect for individual will,

---

[157] Kim Sŏngsil, "Chosŏn yŏja kidokkyo ch'ŏngnyŏnhoe kŭpsŏnmu," *Ch'ŏngnyŏn* 10, no. 1 (January 1930): 3–5, quoted on 3; and Chŏng, "Ilcheha Han'guk yŏsŏng ŭi Miguk yuhak kwa kŭndae kyŏnghŏm," 86–7.

[158] Son Chinsil, "Miguk yŏhaksaeng ŭi saenghwal" (The Life of American Female Students), *Urak'i* 1 (1925): 110–14.

[159] Yuam, "Miguk yŏja kodŭng kyoyuk—yŏja ŭi hyangsang chŭk kungmin ŭi hyangsang" (Higher Education for Women in the United States: Advancement of Women is Equal to Advancement of the Nation), *Tonggwang* 7 (November 1926): 10–17.

[160] "Miguk yuhaksaeng ŭi Miguk munmyŏng e taehan kamsang" (Opinions about American Civilization among Korean Students in the United States), *Urak'i* 3 (1928): 1–11; "Miguk esŏ matpon talgo ssŭn kyŏnghŏm" (Both Sweet and Bitter Experiences in the United States), *Urak'i* 4 (1930): 139–45.

human rights, especially respect for women and children, and equal opportunity for everyone. In contrast, the list of things to reject included the mentality that "money is all powerful," the indulgence of material pleasures, individualism, the entertainment industry, racism, the excessive social life, and anti-Asian sentiment.[161] It is noteworthy that racism was often singled out as one of the least pleasant aspects of life in the United States. Chang Iuk (1895–1983), a student at the University of Dubuque, wrote in 1925 that: "You might be surprised to hear that racism exists in the United States, which has been known as the pioneer of humanity, freedom, and equality, but that is the fact. ... Indeed, one might argue that racism is worse in the United States than it is in any other country."[162] Korean students also repeatedly mentioned widespread materialism in the United States, which they considered to be immoral. The most scathing criticism of US materialism and its impact on women came from Hŏ Chŏngsuk (1902–1991), a leading socialist woman, who commented on American women as follows: "Sculptors make lifeless dolls, but the capitalist civilization [of the United States] has the power to create breathing dolls [women]. In no country other than this capitalist bastion, the United States, can one see these beautiful living dolls who seem to eat money."[163] This type of representation of American women was further bolstered by the Korean print media.[164]

Interestingly, the exaggerated image of US women as self-indulgent, materialistic members of an affluent society was contrasted with the image of women in some European countries. Kim Hwallan wrote about Danish women, whom she had had a chance to observe in 1928, when she stopped in Denmark on her way to Jerusalem to attend a conference of the International Missionary Council. In reflecting on what she had seen, she describes Danish women as "unpretentious in their make-up and dress. They make their own clothes from

---

[161] Whang Kyung Koh, "America as I see It," *Korean Student Bulletin* (May–June 1935): 5–6. Koh, who was a student at the University of Michigan, points out the limitations of her impressions of America because she has "not lived in America long enough to be able to give a complete picture," and her "observations have been limited by association with a certain class or people."

[162] Chang Iuk, "Kyoyukhak kyŏnji esŏ kwanch'al hanŭn yuMi haksaeng ŭi simlisang kyŏnghŏm" (Psychological Experiences of Korean Students in the United States from the Perspective of Education), *Urak'i* 1 (1925): 28–41, quoted on 32. Chang also notes that racism is not entirely Americans' fault. He observes that Koreans' lack of proficiency in English and lack of cultural understanding may also contribute to the racist attitudes of Americans.

[163] Hŏ Chŏngsuk, "Ul chul anŭn inhyŏng ŭi yŏja guk, pukMi insanggi" (A Country of Women Who Look Like Dolls That Know How to Cry: An Observation of North America), *Pyŏlgŏn'gon* (December 1927): 75. For Hŏ's life, see Ruth Barraclough, "Red Love and Betrayal in the Making of North Korea: Comrade Hŏ Jŏng-suk," *History Workshop Journal* 77 no. 1 (Spring 2014): 86–102.

[164] An extreme case was reported in *Samch'ŏlli* of a young female student in New York who bought 120 pairs of expensive silk stockings, costing a total of $410, or 820 *won*. The report complained that ten such girls could send a country into bankruptcy. "Yŏ haksaeng ŭi sach'i" (Luxury of Girl Student), *Samch'ŏlli* 3 (November 1929): 7.

dark-colored, solid textiles. They do not seem to put any artificial decorations in their hair, simply twisting it into a bun or cutting it short or just leaving it natural," and they "seem to place a premium on practicality over vanity. If she lives in meager surroundings, she does not waste her time fantasizing about a bigger, better house; instead, she invests herself in her humble cottage, working to make it as comfortable and inviting as she can." Danish women were presented as a counterpoint to the typical image of the "New Woman," who had become the ultimate symbol of vanity. Thus, Kim presents the Danish model as a counterbalance to the stereotype of the "Western" women. Further, Kim attributes the strong minds and will of Danish women to their "conservative religious tradition and a monarchical political system." She argues that this does not mean they hold onto a "backward religious ideology" or an autocratic political system. On the contrary, she continues, the steady, solid, no-nonsense quality of Danish people stems from their pride in their own traditions, history, and culture. Therefore, far from being swayed by the fluctuating fashion of the day, Danish women felt free to select what worked best for them. Their monarchical political system did not follow the old model of the oppressive tyrant but had a novel form that valued peasants and worked to ensure their well-being. Kim goes on to make a pointed comment about the genuine gender equality she found in Danish society. There, she says, women did not need a special movement because the society made no gender distinctions or discrimination in the provision of education, civil rights, or work. Kim concludes that Danish culture "does not harbor any of the evil customs that honor men and despise women, so you cannot find any unhealthy attitudes about gender in either women or men." Kim's representation of Danish society and culture complicates the issue of modernity and gender roles on two fronts: it insists on a fluid boundary between so-called tradition and modernity, and it challenges the stereotypical image of the "Western" woman as a symbol of modern excess in fashion and materialism.[165]

In a similar vein, Pak Indŏk offered observations of Germany that complicate the notion of what is "Western" in the minds of Koreans.[166] She traveled to Germany as part of her first global speaking tour. She was particularly interested in understanding how Germany managed to fix an economy that had been devastated by World War I. During the trip, Pak visited a rural community and was deeply impressed by the industriousness of the people. She describes German women as hard-working and helpful to their husbands in working their farmland. She lauds German resourcefulness, embodied in their tendency to make full use of everything, never wasting anything. She writes: "German women are the best in

[165] Kim Hwallan, "Nae ka pon oeguk yŏsŏng" (My Observation on Foreign Women), *Kidok sinbo* (December 1928).
[166] Pak Indŏk, "Nae ka pon Togil nongch'on" (My Observations of a Rural Community in Germany), *Samch'ŏlli* 4, no. 4 (April 1932): 66–9.

the management of a household.... They do not discard old garments that have become worn but repair them again and again.... They make a budget for the household and stick to their spending plan." Mirroring Kim Hwallan's commentary about Danish society's adherence to its own tradition and deep regard for its own history and local particularities, Pak observes how German rural communities preserve their traditional pattern of small family based manufacturing rather than trying to imitate the advanced urban model of mass production. She is particularly impressed by the capacity of the rural people in Germany to evaluate a situation critically and find the best response given their particular cultural and historical circumstances, a trait she contrasts with the Korean tendency to readily abandon the "old-fashioned" and hastily adopt something new without considering its appropriateness for the Korean context.

It is significant that these comments by Kim Hwallan and Pak Indŏk are focused on "Western women" in rural Denmark and Germany. Given that the economic system in colonial Korea was predominantly agricultural, their main concern at that time was the revitalization of rural life as part of a program of advancement toward becoming a modern nation. Chapter 4 details how the Danish model for rural revitalization resonated with many Korean intellectuals, including Kim and Pak, and thus Denmark became an important model to emulate.[167] Despite the fact that it was only one-fifth the size of Korea in terms of geographic area and had only one-sixth the population, Denmark was considered a model for agriculture. Koreans looked at Denmark and saw a small, barren country that was nonetheless able to become affluent because of its excellent educational system and rural reform. The emphasis on the value of manual labor and the scientific study of agriculture in education was thought to be especially important, in that it resulted in Danish students' developing an openness to and passion for agriculture. This favorable attitude toward agriculture was contrasted with the attitudes of urban-based educated people in Korea, who esteemed the white-collar professions and looked down on the agricultural sector.[168] The direct exposure that these Korean women had to the advanced modern societies of northern Europe helped them locate Korea within the global context and also sharpened their capacity to adapt Western knowledge and practices to the particular conditions of Korea.

Conclusion

Figure 3.3 is a photograph of Kim Hwallan (third from the right in the first row) taken in 1928 at the Mount of Olives, Jerusalem, with the leaders of global

---

[167] Han Kwija, "Tenmak nongch'on sosik" (News about Agriculture in Denmark), *Nongmin saenghwal* 1 (1929): 35–6.
[168] Han, "Tenmak nongch'on sosik," 35–6.

Figure 3.3 Kim Hwallan at the International Missionary Council, Jerusalem, 1928
Source: LC-DIG-matpc-07146 (digital file from original photograph) LC-M361-888 (b&w film copy negative), G. Eric and Edith Matson Photograph Collection, Library of Congress

Christianity who attended the meeting of the International Missionary Council (hereafter, IMC). Kim was arguably the most prominent woman educator in colonial Korea at the time. A graduate of Ewha and one of the most valued protégés of American missionary teachers, she was encouraged to pursue further studies at Ohio Wesleyan University (B.A.), Boston University (M.A.), and Columbia University (PhD). The fact that she was one of six Korean delegates invited to the 1928 Jerusalem conference testifies to her stature within the Korean Christian community. The 1928 IMC was known for the emerging trend in which "a new generation was taking over."[169] One-fourth of the 230 participants "came from younger churches [in non-Western countries]," and forty-two were Asians.[170] Among important agenda items for discussion at the IMC were racism and uneven power relationships between Western missionaries

[169] Hans-Ruedi Weber, *Asia and the Ecumenical Movement 1895–1961* (London: SCM Press LTD, 1966), p. 154.
[170] Weber, *Asia and the Ecumenical Movement 1895–1961*, p. 154.

and the non-Western missionized. In her report to Korean Christians at home about her observations at the IMC, Kim highlighted the need to address racial conflict and to change the relationship between the missionaries and the missionized from a hierarchical structure to a partnership.[171] Indeed, Kim Hwallan's path to the presidency at Ewha Women's Professional School shows some tensions between the missionary desire to continue in a leadership role and Koreans' desire to take over leadership after years of training and experience.[172]

In this 1928 group photograph with IMC participants from fifty nations (see Figure 3.3), Kim's hair is bobbed (*tanbal*), a style associated with the modern "New Woman." In her autobiography, she writes that she had cut her long hair on her way to the IMC. She and her colleagues passed through Saigon, where she saw some Vietnamese laborers who had hair so long that they had to wrap it around their bodies. She couldn't help but to ask why they kept their hair so long and disheveled. When she was told that it was to keep their tradition, it struck her as being a useless adherence to custom. And then it dawned on her that she herself kept her hair long due to Korean tradition, even though she felt it was inconvenient and time-consuming to maintain. When she arrived in Marseille, the first thing she did was to have her hair cut short.[173] Kim knew that her short haircut would cause a sensation in Korean society, but she favored progress over tradition and rejected routines or practices that acted as a barrier to progress. Interestingly, she continued to dress in a Korean *hanbok*, a distinctive symbol and identifier of Korean tradition. Standing shoulder to shoulder with leading Christian men and women from all over the world, she visually embodies both tradition and modernity in this photograph.

In a significant way, the tensions between tradition and modernity are at the heart of "crossing" domestic borders. The traditional notion of women as the bearers of Korean tradition coexisted with the new expectation that women would contribute to building the modern nation. Women's travel overseas broke the traditional norm of the "inside-outside rule," but it was publicly justified by the new expectations for women in the modern era. Still, women's newly acquired mobility and the experiences that accompanied it did have limits.[174] More often than not, women sensed tensions between possibilities

---

[171] Kim Hwallan, "Yerusalem taehoe wa kŭmhu kidokkyo" (Jerusalem and the Future of Christianity), *Ch'ŏngnyŏn* 8, no. 8 (November 1928): 2–5.

[172] In his diary, Yun Ch'iho indicated growing tensions between Alice Appenzeller and Kim Hwallan. See *Yun Ch'iho ilgi*, November 2, 1933 and June 24, 1938. See also Donald N. Clark, *Living Dangerously in Korea: The Western Experience 1900–1950* (Norwalk: EastBridge, 2003), pp. 183–4.

[173] Kim Hwallan, *Kŭ pit sok ŭi chagŭn saengmyŏng* (A Little Life in that Light) (Seoul: Yŏwŏnsa, 1965), pp. 133–4.

[174] Bryna Goodman and Wendy Larson, "Introduction: Axes of Gender: Divisions of Labor and Spatial Separation," in *Gender in Motion: Divisions of Labor and Cultural Chang in Late Imperial and Modern China*, eds. Bryna Goodman and Wendy Larson (Lanham: Rowman & Littlefield Publishers, Inc., 2005), pp. 1–25.

and limitations in their transnational mobility and experiences. Those tensions are found not only in colonial regulations and in abstract ideologies, such as nationalism or individualism, but also in the women's practical everyday experiences, as expressed, for example, through choices in style of dress, hairstyle, utterance, or music. It was through those tensions that women developed a sense of colonized self, national identity, and gendered bodily practice. Furthermore, direct exposure to other societies and cultures helped them gain an even sharper perspective on the local conditions that were particular to Korea. In an essay she wrote on her way back to Korea after attending the 1928 IMC, Kim Hwallan wrote: "We are neither in the past nor in the future, neither in Europe nor in the United States. We are born right here in Korea."[175] From that specific locality and temporality, she urges the educated class of women to see clearly where they stand and what duties they have. Invoking the idea that the level of a civilization is measured by the status of the women in the society, she says that educated women in Korea have a particular obligation to lift the lowly conditions in which the vast majority of women live. She also notes that although missionary schools and organizations have helped women's education for the past forty years, it is now the duty of educated Korean women to help ordinary, underprivileged women in Korea find opportunities to learn and grow.[176] In this call to duty we can detect an emerging shift toward Korean women taking the reins from foreign missionaries in the project of enlightening women through education and social reform activities, which are the focus of Chapter 4.

---

[175] Kim Hwallan, "Chosŏn yŏhaksaeng ŭi ijung ch'aegim" (Double Duties of Korean Girl Students), *Ewha* 1 (1929): 10–12, quoted on 12.
[176] Kim, "Chosŏn yŏhaksaeng ŭi ijung ch'aegim," 11–12.

4 Labor: Searching for Rural Modernity

In 1932, the popular magazine *Samch'ŏlli* published an article about the founding of a "Women's Collective Farm" (*yŏin chiptan nongjang*).[1] The story about a group of four women undertaking such a large-scale and challenging task grabbed the attention of the Korean public. The group was led by Hwang Aedŏk (1892–1971), a Japan- and US-educated Christian woman educator and reformer.[2] They had purchased a tract of land measuring 100,000 *p'yŏng* [approximately 80 acres] in a remote village in the Suan district of Hwanghae Province in 1930. The writer of the article refers to their purchase as "the most remarkable news" in Korean women's history. The land was not fertile, but it was cheap, and the women thought they could make it arable through the use of better fertilizer and modern farming techniques. A striking feature of the women's collective farm project was to waive the traditional fees for tenancy, which had become devastatingly high for tenant farmers, until the land was made fertile again. In this project, farmers were allowed to cultivate a piece of land and harvest as much from it as they could. The goal behind this radical initiative was to motivate farmers to use their knowledge and experience to return the land to an arable state and lay the foundation for continuing productivity. The reporter of the *Samch'ŏlli* article implies that the "Women's Collective Farm" project has great potential for success, pointing out: "Wasn't it the white-clothes people [Koreans] who cultivated the barren land in Siberia? Wasn't it the Korean people who turned the vast land of Manchuria into a fertile paddy?" Ultimately, this "Women's Collective Farm" project was envisioned as something of a laboratory for rural revitalization, not only in farming but also in housing, childcare, home maintenance, education, cultural facilities, and consumer cooperatives, and the initial phase was to be followed with an expansion of the farm by purchasing more land through a "Cooperative for Collective Land Purchase" (*kongdong t'oji kumae chohap*) (see Figure 4.1).[3]

---

[1] "Simman p'yŏng p'yŏngya e kŏnsŏldoenŭn yŏin chiptan nongjang" (Women's Collective Farm Built on the Eighty Acres), *Samch'ŏlli* 4, no. 3 (March 1932): 55–7.
[2] The other three women involved in the project were Hong Aedŏk, Chang Nodŭk, and Ch'oe Ŭnsin.
[3] "Simman p'yŏng p'yŏngya e kŏnsŏldoenŭn yŏin chiptan nongjang," 55–7.

Figure 4.1 Women's collective farm
Source: *Samch'ŏlli* 4, no. 3 (March 1932): 55

Hwang's ambitious rural project in the remote village of Suan in Korea stands out because of its deep connection with American Christian women. Specifically, the members of the Woman's Christian Temperance Union (WCTU) in Scranton, Pennsylvania provided Hwang and her project with financial and moral support.

Hwang's connection with those WCTU members began in the summer of 1926, just before she enrolled at Columbia University. Like many other Korean students in the United States at that time, she had to work to support her studies.[4] Since coming to the United States in 1925 she had worked as dishwasher, a housemaid, and a peddler selling necklaces and perfume. She learned that rich people from the New York area would spend their summers outside the city, so she traveled to those locations in search of work. When she was passing through Scranton, she encountered WCTU members who had heard of the success in evangelical work in Korea and thus were eager for firsthand reports from Hwang. It would have been difficult to find a better spokesperson for the effectiveness of the mission work in Korea than Hwang, one of the most prominent graduates of Ewha Girls' School, an American Methodist mission school in Korea, and a leader in the Korean Young Women's Christian Association (YWCA), whose activities included Korea's temperance movement.[5] In addition, Hwang's activism for the national independence movement in 1919 had put her in jail twice.[6] The members of the Scranton WCTU were impressed by Hwang and decided to assist in her education. With their donation, Hwang received $60 cash per month, along with milk and eggs for two years, until she finished her studies at Columbia in 1928.[7]

After receiving her degree in 1928, Hwang wanted to learn more about rural life and agricultural practices in the United States before she returned to Korea, and thus she visited Pennsylvania State University, which had a well-regarded agriculture program. While there she took agriculture classes and had the opportunity to observe and work with American farmers.[8] She also took the opportunity to visit Scranton again. During her visit, she gave talks on Korean history and the ongoing independence movement as well as on the work of US

---

[4] According to journalist Ch'oe Ŭnhŭi, Hwang turned down a scholarship arranged by Alice Appenzeller, a missionary teacher at Ewha, to study on her own. See Ch'oe Ŭnhŭi, *Yŏsŏng ŭl nŏmŏ anak ŭi nŏul ŭl pŏtko* (Beyond the Womanly Domain, Removing the Veil of the Housewife) (Seoul: Munijae, 2003), p. 226.

[5] The Korea YWCA was founded in 1922. Hwang Aedŏk served as the President of the Korea YWCA in 1924–1925. Han'guk YWCA 80-nyŏnsa p'yŏnch'an wiwŏnhoe, *Han'guk YWCA 80-nyŏnsa* (The Eightieth History of Korea YWCA) (Seoul: Taehan YWCA Yŏnhaphoe, 2006), p. 566; Ch'ŏn Hwasuk, *Han'guk yŏsŏng kidokkyo sahoe undongsa* (The History of Social Movement of Korean Christian Women) (Seoul: Hyeansa, 2000); Yu Sŏnghŭi, "Han'guk YWCA undong ŭi silch'ŏn chŏk kidokkyo yŏsŏngjuŭi e kwanhan yŏn'gu" (A Study of Action-Oriented Christian Feminism in the Korea YWCA Movement), PhD dissertation, Seoul National University, 2013.

[6] Ch'oe, *Yŏsŏng ŭl nŏmŏ anak ŭi nŏul ŭl pŏtko*, pp. 218–25.

[7] The donation from the members of WTCU was not enough to cover her living expenses, so Hwang worked at the cafeteria of the International House. Ch'oe, *Yŏsŏng ŭl nŏmŏ anak ŭi nŏul ŭl pŏtko*, pp. 226–7; Pak Hwasŏng, *Saebyŏk e oech'ida* (Shouting Out at the Dawn), in *Pak Hwasŏng munhak chŏnjip* (Anthology of Pak Hwasŏng's Work) (Seoul: P'urŭn sasangsa, 2004), pp. 332–3.

[8] Hwang Aesidŏk, "Miguk K'olŏmbia tachak: Miguk ŭi namnyŏ konghak ŭn ŏttŏk'e hana" (Columbia University in the United States: How Do Co-ed Universities Work in the United States), *Man'guk puin* 1 (1932): 53–5, quoted on 55.

missionaries in Korea. Her talks were popular and inspirational to American church members, and many of them made donations to Hwang for her future work in Korea.[9]

On returning to Korea in January 1929, Hwang was appointed to the faculty of Hyŏpsŏng Theology Institute for Women (Hyŏpsŏng Yŏja Sinhakkyo). This appointment was possible in part because of her connection with Anna B. Chaffin (1883–1977), a long-serving missionary in Korea and the founding principal of Hyŏpsŏng. Chaffin was studying religious education at Columbia in 1927 during her furlough from her service in the Korea mission, when Hwang was also enrolled at Columbia.[10] During that time in New York, the two women shared their passion for rural development with each other, and Chaffin proposed that Hwang be placed in charge of the new program for training women leaders in rural development at Hyŏpsŏng on her return to Korea. With institutional backing from Hyŏpsŏng and the substantial funds she had raised from WCTU members in Scranton as well as contributions from like-minded Korean colleagues, Hwang was able to purchase the abovementioned land and an old house in Suan to launch her first rural development programs in 1930.

After the launch, she sent a report to the members of WCTU in Scranton delineating how their donations to her rural programs had been used.[11] This report became a catalyst for the idea of the "Esther Circle," in reference to Hwang Aedŏk, who was known in missionary circles by the name "Esther Hwang," organized by the Scranton WCTU to further support the endeavors of Hwang Aedŏk in her rural reform projects in Korea.[12] The members of the Esther Circle collected $25 to $50 a month, which they sent to Hwang. In addition, some enthusiastic members occasionally donated much larger amounts (in one case, $600). This philanthropic activity went on until the outbreak of the Asia Pacific War.[13] The ongoing funding was crucial for Hwang, allowing her to put her ideas about rural reform into practice, setting up schools and community centers to educate people in remote rural areas. She summarized her accomplishments in Suan: She had established a literacy program that was open to all villagers; she advocated abstention from drinking, smoking, and gambling for the improvement of daily life (which was, no doubt,

---

[9] Ch'oe, *Yŏsŏng ŭl nŏmŏ anak ŭi nŏul ŭl pŏtko*, p. 227.
[10] Kim Sŭngt'ae and Pak Hyejin, comp., *Naehan sŏn'gyosa ch'ongnam, 1884–1984* (A Comprehensive Survey of Missionaries in Korea) (Seoul: Han'guk kidokkyo yŏksa yŏn'guso, 1994), p. 200.
[11] Pak, *Saebyŏk e oech'ida*, p. 340. See also Kim Sŏngŭn, "1930-nyŏndae Hwang Aedŏk ŭi nongch'on saŏp kwa yŏsŏng undong" (Hwang Aedŏk's Rural Project and Women's Movement in the 1930s), *Han'guk kidokkyo wa yŏksa* 35 (November 2011): 141–80.
[12] Pak, *Saebyŏk e oech'ida*. Photographs of Mrs. E. W. Stuart and the members of the Esther Circle in Scranton. No page number indicated.
[13] Ch'oe, *Yŏsŏng ŭl nŏmŏ anak ŭi nŏul ŭl pŏtko*, pp. 214–33.

appealing to American Christian donors, especially those members of the WCTU); she was able to convince local farmers voluntarily to participate in rural development programs.[14] She set the ambitious goal of establishing one school per village (*myŏn*), echoing the Japanese colonial government's policy (*il myŏn il kyo*) of 1928.[15] Her work in rural development was expansive, stretching from Korea to Manchuria, linking some of the most remote rural communities in Korea with unexpected places and people in the United States, largely through the Christian network created by the foreign missionary enterprise, the WCTU, and local churches.[16]

Hwang was not alone in this type of work, broadly referred to in Korea as the "Rural Revitalization Movement" (nongch'on chinhŭng undong) in the 1920s and 1930s. Regardless of political orientations, a class of educated women made efforts to assist the great numbers of illiterate and impoverished Koreans living in the rural areas. In this chapter, I specifically focus on the role of Protestant Christian women intellectuals in the Rural Revitalization Movement in the 1920s and 1930s. The engagement of Hwang Aedŏk and her fellow Protestant reformers in this movement helps us expand the notion of "colonial modernity," which has primarily been associated with the idea of urban, industrial, material, and secular aspects of change. As Albert Park argues, the concept of "colonial modernity" needs to capture "a full representation of the complex experiences of life shaped by rupturing political, economic, and social forces."[17] As a way to shed new light on modernity, colonialism and nationalism, he offers an in-depth analysis of the rural movements led by faith-based groups, namely, the Korean Young Men's Christian Association (YMCA), Presbyterians, and Ch'ŏndogyo (Religion of the Heavenly Way). However, in spite of the fact that women forged important alliances with many of these faith-based groups, women's involvement in the rural movement has been underexplored. While men occupied the leadership roles, women intellectuals actively worked with women and children, who represented more than half the

---

[14] Hwang Aedŏk, "Yugo: Hwangmuji rŭl hyech'imyŏ" (Posthumous Work: Cultivating the Barren Land), *Sin yŏwŏn* (July 1972): 209–13. Cited in Kim, "1930-nyŏndae Hwang Aedŏk ŭi nongch'on saŏp kwa yŏsŏng undong," 153.

[15] *Tonga ilbo*, August 18, 1931.

[16] Hwang went to Harbin in 1935. While working as the head of Harbin branch of *Tonga ilbo*, she helped create farming communities for Korean migrants, but she did not have a chance to actually visit those sites because there frequent attacks by bandits. By the time she went to Harbin, she had been married to Pak Sun for five years. Pak grew up in Manchuria. They came back to Korea once World War II broke out. Kim, "1930-nyŏndae Hwang Aedŏk ŭi nongch'on saŏp kwa yŏsŏng undong," 159–61; Hwang Aesidŏk, "Ch'ŏngch'un kwa kyŏrhon" (Youth and Marriage), *Samch'ŏlli* (March 1933): 65–7. See also "ChaeMan tongp'o munje chwadamhoe" (Roundtable Discussion on the Problems Facing Koreans in Manchuria), *Samch'ŏlli* 5, no. 9 (September 1933): 47–51.

[17] Albert Park, *Building A Heaven on Earth: Religion, Activism, and Protest in Japanese Occupied Korea* (Honolulu: University of Hawai'i Press, 2015), p. 3.

population of rural communities, and thus it is crucial to bring women into the analysis to gain a fuller understanding of the rural reform movement and the impact of that movement on the experience of gendered modernity within the specific context of Japanese colonial rule.

In this chapter, I particularly attend to the ways in which the interdenominational, global Christian network brought people, resources, and information together in envisioning and executing these rural programs. I argue that, in response to the dire economic realities and cultural demands for the restoration of the Korean nation, Protestant women intellectuals tended to take an approach that was consciously apolitical, focusing primarily on basic literacy and practical knowledge for improving home life and family finances. Their rural projects largely centered on enlightenment (*kyemong*) and moral or spiritual cultivation (*chŏngsin suyang*), which appeared to be quite similar to the colonial government's Rural Revitalization Campaign (*Nōson shinkō undō*), which ran from 1932 to 1940.[18] However, in spite of their superficial similarity, the underlying goal of the Korean initiatives was the restoration of the nation while the colonial state's programs were designed to mobilize the colonized for the Japanese empire. It is difficult to measure the impact of the Korean Christian women's rural work, but their vision for rural development and specific reform endeavors show how gendered colonial modernity was shaped by myriad forces, including colonial state power and the global Christian missionary network.

Beholding Rural Decline

In his 1932 essay entitled "To Women Intellectuals," the male socialist Im Wŏn'gŭn (1899–1963) evokes the typical, exaggerated stereotype of the "New Woman" (*sin yŏsŏng*), dressed in the latest fashion, sweeping through the urban space in pursuit of luxury and self-indulgence. He bluntly states that he cannot identify a single case of a woman intellectual who could be called a pioneer in service of Korean women, and he urges the Korean "New Woman" to see the reality of Korea and prepare to carry out a unique historical mission (*yŏksa chŏk kwaje*), which he calls the liberation movement (*haebang undong*). Im further suggests that ignorant rural women and low-class urban "moms" are awaiting the guidance of educated women.[19]

Contrary to Im's harsh representation of the "New Woman,"[20] in reality, many women intellectuals were keenly aware of the dire conditions in Korea, especially the economic devastation that was affecting rural communities, and they often prioritized rural revitalization as the most urgent matter to tackle. In her 1925

---

[18] *Chosŏn ch'ongdokpu kwanbo* (Gazette of Government-General of Korea), September 30, 1932.
[19] Im Wŏn'gŭn, "Int'eri yŏsŏng ege" (To Women Intellectuals), *Man'guk puin* 1 (1932): 36–7.
[20] Chŏng Ch'ilsŏng, a socialist woman intellectual, laments that men "mercilessly criticize, sneer at, or look down on women as spectators," while doing "nothing to assist women."

article, "To Girl Students Returning to their Homes in the Countryside," socialist Hŏ Chŏngsuk (1902–1991) advocated prioritizing the rural enlightenment movement over the women's movement. She considered the illiterate rural population to be "potential pillars of a new society, a new world," and urged female students to go into rural areas to train women and children to read so that they could understand current affairs.[21] On her graduation in 1928 from Lucy Girls' School, a Methodist mission school, Ch'oe Yongsin (1909–1935), who became one of the best-known rural reform activists, made a cogent argument in *Chosŏn ilbo*, stating that "a society is composed of men and women.... A sound society can be constructed only when the educated woman strives to fulfill her duties and responsibilities.... Right now the first step for us [educated women] is to guide rural women ... it is our responsibility to help rural women out of ignorance."[22] In addition to the aforementioned Hwang Aedŏk, some leading Christian women intellectuals, such as Kim Hwallan (1899–1970) and Pak Indŏk (1896–1980), undertook in-depth studies of rural development in countries including Denmark, Russia, Germany, and the United States, and tried to put that knowledge into practice through the academic training they provided to the next generation as well as concrete reform projects appropriate for the Korean situation. To those who had traveled overseas, especially to the United States and Europe, the tremendous gap between Korea and advanced countries – in terms of the level of modernization, industrialization, and urbanization, living standards and educational opportunities, as well as political conditions – was critical in sharpening their awareness of the dismal condition of Korea, which was predominantly a rural economy whose decline was becoming precipitous.

Early on, many Korean intellectuals and reformers viewed the hardships in rural communities as a vital sign that the economic foundation of the nation was in crisis. Some saw a dangerous tendency that flouted the agricultural roots and spirit of the Korean nation.[23] An editorial in *Kaebyŏk* in 1923 acutely reflects the urgent sense that rural communities and their health would be essential in restoring the Korean nation. The editorial argues:

Chŏng Ch'ilsŏng, "Ŭisik chŏk kaksŏng ŭro put'ŏ: Musan puin saenghwal esŏ" (Beginning with Conscious Awakening: Life of the Proletarian Women), *Kŭnu* 1 (1929): 35–7.
[21] Hŏ Chŏngsuk, "Hyangch'on e toraganŭn yŏhaksaeng chegun ege" (To Girl Students Returning to their Homes in the Countryside), *Sin yŏsŏng* 3, no. 8 (1925): 2–5.
[22] Ch'oe Yongsin, "Kyomun esŏ nongch'on e" (From the School Gate to the Rural Community), *Chosŏn ilbo*, April 1, 1928, 3.
[23] Kim Kijŏn, "Nongch'on kaesŏn ŭi kin'gŭp tongŭi" (Urgent Matters for Discussion on the Improvement of the Rural Community), *Kaebyŏk* 5 (November 1920): 16–21. Clark Sorensen argues that the category of "peasant" was created in 1920s' colonial Korea by intellectuals. Since the modern urban sphere, which had been shaped by Western and foreign influences, could not represent "the national," the peasants and the rural were designated to represent Korean national identity and roots. Clark Sorensen, "National Identity and the Creation of the Category of 'Peasant' in Colonial Korea," in *Colonial Modernity in Korea*, eds. Gi-Wook Shin and Michael Robinson (Cambridge: Harvard University Press, 1999), p. 303.

Korea's demise will not come in its political demise. Korea's demise will not come with the destruction of its culture. The real demise of Korea will come when the peasant class is lost. The soul of Korea is its peasant class. To resuscitate Korea, we must resuscitate the peasants. To civilize Korea, we must civilize the peasants. To make Korea wealthy, we must enrich its peasants. This is Korea's unique reality.[24]

By the early 1920s, the need to address the worsening living conditions in rural areas had become urgent and unavoidable. Farmers made up close to 80 percent of the population, and given their prominence in the population the rapid deterioration of the rural economy and the growing misery in the lives of peasants were reason for alarm. Since the Japanese colonial state had launched a cadastral survey (1910–1918) and introduced various programs to increase agricultural productivity, the traditional landlord–tenant relationship had been significantly altered and the rural economy had been actively incorporated into the scheme of capitalist industrial development.[25] The colonial government's economic reforms bolstered the power of landlords while denying the customary tilling rights to peasants in the process of commercializing the agricultural sector. Although agricultural capitalism surely benefited wealthy landlords, the majority of landless peasants were perennially in debt due to high tenant fees, taxes, and rising living costs, and thus their ability to sustain themselves was threatened, especially after the Great Depression of 1929.[26] A 1931 editorial in *Tonggwang* bluntly stated that all the benefits from the rural policies of the colonial government went to large-scale, entrepreneurial landlords while

---

[24] *Kaebyŏk* 31 (January 1923): 11–32, quoted on 25.
[25] Gi-Wook Shin, "Agrarian Conflict and the Origins of Korean Capitalism," *American Journal of Sociology* 103, no. 5 (March 1988): 1309–51, quoted on 1312.
[26] Shin, "Agrarian Conflict and the Origins of Korean Capitalism"; and "Uri ege pap ŭl tago" (Give Us Food), *Tonga ilbo*, March 24, 1932, 1. Hong Pyŏngsŏn, a key leader of Korea YMCA's endeavor in the rural movements with which Korea YWCA collaborated, captured the ways in which the rural life was being devastated by its deep integration into the capitalist economy. He wrote in 1930 that: "[A]s all kinds of imported modern articles are being sold all over the country, even to the most distant mountain valleys, the living expenses of every farmer increase without his knowing it, while his yearly income from the farm remains the same, which makes it increasingly difficult to make a living ... the majority of the farmers are ignorant, own no land, have no capital to support their farming enterprise; indeed, every farmer holds debt from 50 to 300 Yen ... [E]very landowner has been turned into a tenant-farmer, and the tenant-farmers are living the lives of itinerants, emigrating to other countries or moving into the cities in order to get food." See "Survey of the Young Men's Christian Association and the Young Women's Christian Association of Korea (Seoul, Korea July 1930)," 142, 145–46, fol. 5, Box 5, series 3, Missionary Research Library Archives (hereafter, MRL) 12: Ecumenical/World Mission, YMCA and YWCA Records 1925–1945, Burke Library, Columbia University. In a report on the rural conditions in Korea in 1935, John H. Reisner, executive secretary of the Agricultural Missions Foundation of YMCA from the US, further confirmed that "most of the farmers are so enmeshed in debts that they cannot extricate themselves. Interest rates average thirty-six per cent a year and are often much higher. The sequence in thousands of cases is: debt, loss of land, discouragement, tenancy, greater debt, then utter despair." John H. Reisner, "Rural

small landholders and tenant farmers experienced a rapid decline in their livelihood.[27]

In this context, Korean reformers representing a wide range of ideological orientations – from socialism to liberal bourgeois nationalism to agrarianism and various religious faiths – turned their attention to rural communities. They were seeking ways to bring peasants out of economic misery, and, in some cases, to enhance their political consciousness or to restore beneficial Korean values for the sake of national solidarity. Leftists considered peasants to be one of the more important forces in bringing about a socialist revolution. They organized a large number of peasant associations throughout the country, providing literacy and lessons on labor and politics and helping peasants defend themselves against abuse and exploitation from landlords.[28] Bourgeois nationalists also embraced the role of peasants in modernizing Korea. Based on their firm belief in modern capitalist development, their rural campaigns largely focused on improving lives through literacy, cultural reforms, and enhanced knowledge of agriculture. Two major daily newspapers joined in the advocacy of this line of rural reform, represented by *Chosŏn ilbo*'s Literacy Movement (1929–1934) and *Tonga ilbo*'s V Narod Movement (1931–1934). In these nation-wide campaigns, large numbers of students were mobilized to travel to the countryside to provide literacy training for the rural population.[29] The Korean Language Association (Chosŏnŏ Hakhoe) also made a significant contribution to this effort by providing textbooks and organizing and presenting lectures by prominent linguists, such as Yi Yunjae (1888–1943), Ch'oe Hyŏnbae (1894–1970), and Kim Yungyŏng (1894–1969).[30]

Unlike leftist and bourgeois reformers, who firmly believed in the modernist view of linear historical development, agrarianists of diverse backgrounds took an anti-capitalist, anti-urban, anti-foreign, and anti-modern stance. They advocated a self-sufficient agrarian society with a strong emphasis on moral reconstruction, tradition, and collectivism, all of which categorically rejected the

---

Reconstruction Work in Korea, 1935," ed. Chang Kyusik, "Han'guk YMCA ŭi nongch'on chaegŏn saŏp," *Chungang saron* 29 (2009): 243–9, quoted on 245.

[27] "Nongŏp konghwang kwa nongmin ŭi mollak kwajŏng" (Depression of Agriculture and the Process of Decline of the Peasants), *Tonggwang* 20 (April 1931): 18–30.

[28] Park, *Building A Heaven on Earth*, p. 72.

[29] For instance, Hwang Sindŏk (1898–1984), a journalist working for a women's magazine *Sin kajŏng* (New Family), drew attention to the dire conditions in the rural areas where children suffer from poverty, an unhygienic environment, and absence of good children's literature or songs. She urges female students in urban areas to go to their hometown during the summer break and try to take care of those children by teaching literacy and numeracy. See Hwang Sindŏk, "Nongbŏn'gi wa nongch'on adong munje" (The Busy Time in the Rural Area and the Issues of Rural Children), *Sin kajŏng* (October 1935) [This essay is included in Ch'ugye Hwang Sindŏk sŏnsaeng kinyŏm saŏphoe, *Munŏjijiannŭn chip ŭl* (House That is not Collapsing) (Seoul: Ch'ugye Hwang Sindŏk sŏnsaeng kinyŏm saŏphoe, 1984), pp. 76–8.

[30] 3.1. yŏsŏng tongjihoe, *Han'guk yŏsŏng tongnip undongsa* (The History of Women in the Independence Movement) (Seoul: 3.1. yŏsŏng tongjihoe, 1980), 320–48.

modernist stance of the leftists and the bourgeoisie.[31] In comparison, as Albert Park demonstrates, some faith-based reform groups differentiated themselves from the agrarianists in that their reform ideas firmly centered on the rural but rejected neither capitalism nor modernity. Rather, they envisioned the new role of religion to be one that helped people adjust to rapidly changing reality by providing not only spirituality but also economic necessities in everyday life.[32]

The distinct, competing visions that Korean reformers had for rural revitalization should be understood in conjunction with the Japanese colonial policy, which was conceived and implemented in the face of declining rural stability caused by poverty and class conflict. From the perspective of the colonial government, an unstable, impoverished rural economy in Korea would be detrimental to Japan's drive for industrialization and mobilization for war in the 1930s. To address the growing problems of the rural depression and the resulting unrest, the colonial government implemented new laws that limited the power of landlords, and at the same time facilitated the mobilization of "government-sanctioned intermediary associations" that would act as a bridge between local rural communities and the state in tackling rural crisis. The sociologists Gi-Wook Shin and Do-Hyun Han have used the concept of "colonial corporatism" to understand this linkage between society and the state and demonstrate how the colonial policy on rural affairs shifted from the "Campaign to Increase Rice Production" (sanmi chŭngsik kyehoek) and landlord-based local control in the 1920s to the "Rural Revitalization Campaign" and more direct state involvement in rural affairs in the 1930s. The Rural Revitalization Campaign began in 1932 under Governor General Kazushige Ugaki. It was carried out through a close-knit administrative network of "rural revitalization committees (shinkōkai)" comprised of respected members of the local community and government officials, linking villages and counties to provinces and the central government.[33] Under the rallying cry of self-renovation (charyŏk kaengsaeng), the stated purpose of the Campaign was to enhance agricultural production, increase the availability of cash, eliminate household debt and reform everyday practice (e.g., abstaining from smoking and drinking, wearing colored clothing instead of white).[34] However, its ultimate goal was "to exert more disciplinary power and control over the peasantry" by suppressing and uprooting anti-colonial, regime-challenging

---

[31] Gi-Wook Shin, "Agrarianism: A Critique of Colonial Modernity in Korea," *Comparative Studies in Society and History* 41, no. 4 (October 1999): 784–804.
[32] Park, *Building A Heaven on Earth*.
[33] Kyung Moon Hwang, *Rationalizing Korea: The Rise of the Modern State 1894–1945* (Oakland: University of California Press, 2016), pp. 80–81.
[34] Chi Sugŏl, "Ilche ŭi kun'gukjuŭi p'asijŭm kwa 'Chosŏn nongch'on chinhŭng undong'" (Militaristic Fascism and "Rural Revitalization Campaign" of Japanese Imperial Rule), *Yŏksapip'yŏng* (May 1999): 16–36.

Beholding Rural Decline 159

peasant movements.[35] As Kyung Moon Hwang aptly puts it, colonial officials envisioned the Campaign as a "comprehensive, totalizing effort – not only to solve urgent economic problems in the rural sectors, but eventually to reorient the mind and spirit of villagers and to renovate modes of communal life, including local administration."[36]

In this Campaign by the colonial state, women were extensively organized through various women's groups (*puinhoe*). Attributing the miserable state of the rural economy to the lack of women's involvement due to the traditional custom of *naeoebŏp* ("inside-outside rule") that discouraged women working alongside men, the Campaign aimed to bring women into the public and economic arena by organizing various women's groups throughout the country and distributing practical information about collective farming, home management, hygiene, and family economy.[37]

Kajŏng chiu (Friends of the Family), the only state-sponsored (*kwanbyŏn*) magazine for rural women offers some detailed elements of the Campaign targeting rural women. Published from December 1936 to March 1941 by the Alliance of Chosŏn Credit Unions (Chosŏn Kŭmyung Chohap Yŏnhaphoe), which was founded by the colonial state in 1933 as a financial policy institute,[38] the magazine was widely disseminated, growing from a circulation of 19,500 in 1936, to 64,000 in 1938.[39] In the beginning, it aimed to provide "interesting and useful" information to rural women, who had largely remained "ignorant and unaware of the rapidly changing world";[40] however, after the outbreak of the second Sino-Japanese War, the magazine was fully utilized to promote the colonial state's policy of *naisen ittai* (Japan and Korea as one body) and *sōdōin* (total mobilization), particularly emphasizing the duties and responsibilities of women (*ch'onghu puin*) in Japanese imperial wars.[41]

In addition, the Chosŏn Kŭmyung Chohap Yŏnhaphoe offered workshops (*kangsŭphoe*), designed to provide selected women leaders from all over the country with systematic training so that they could convey their knowledge and hands-on experience to the other women in their villages. The first such workshop was held from December 16 to 23 in 1936. This training workshop was open to those who had graduated from higher common school or the equivalent and were seen to have a talent for leadership, those who had graduated from common schools and had five or more years of work experience in farming, those who currently held a leadership position in one of the credit cooperatives and had literacy in Korean, or those who had already participated in a similar

---

[35] Park, *Building A Heaven on Earth*, p. 71; Chi, "Ilche ŭi kun'gukjuŭi p'asijŭm," 16.
[36] Hwang, *Rationalizing Korea*, p. 80.   [37] *Kajŏng chiu* 1 (1936).
[38] Mun Yŏngju, "Ilche malgi kwanbyŏn chapchi 'Kajŏng chiu' (1936.12~1941.03) wa 'saeroun puin'," *Yŏksamunjeyŏn'gu* 17 (2007): 179, 184.
[39] Mun, "Ilche malgi kwanbyŏn chapchi 'Kajŏng chiu'," 185.   [40] *Kajŏng chiu* 2 (1937): 57.
[41] Mun, "Ilche malgi kwanbyŏn chapchi 'Kajŏng chiu'," 186–7.

training program. The lecturers invited to the workshop were all Japanese with the exception of one Korean speaker, Son Chŏnggyu, a teacher at Kyŏngsŏng Women's Higher Common School at the time.[42] As the editorial office of the magazine comments at the end of the report on this workshop, the participants were expected to go back to their villages and further develop women's organizations with new will, determination, and enthusiasm.[43] As a follow-up report, one of the first workshop participants, Kim Hyŏnja from Orori, near Hamhŭng in Hamgyŏng Province, was interviewed by a reporter from *Kajŏng chiu* in 1937. Kim describes what the workshop had inspired her to do. She organized a Credit Union Women's Group (Kŭmyung Chohap Puinhoe). She noted that organizing such a group was easy because there were already other women's groups in her community, such as Patriotic Women's Group (Aeguk Puinhoe) and National Defense Women's Group (Kukpang Puinhoe), implying that she made use of the existing membership of other women's groups. She also shared the content of lectures she had given at regular meetings in her community, including how the rural community would improve only when women could work alongside men, why it was important to use credit cooperatives, why superstition needed to be eliminated from rural life, and how savings and women's side-jobs (*puŏp*) could help out with family finances.[44]

In her analysis of colonial policies related to the Rural Revitalization Campaign in the 1930s, Kim Puja argues that the colonial government "discovered" the female population in the process of pursuing rural revitalization, viewing women as the key mediators in its "self-renovation" program (*charyŏk kaengsaeng*), which aimed to "regenerate the spirit of peasants," who were presumed to be lazy, ignorant, and undisciplined, and turn them into loyal, industrious, and productive members of the empire.[45] Women's education, in particular, was put at the forefront because it was believed that "educating a boy is to educate one person; however, educating a girl is to educate the entire family."[46] When equipped with modern knowledge, sound morals, and, most of all, Japanese spirit, women were considered to be the best agents for reforming the rural population and, ultimately, advancing Japanese empire.[47] Countless women's groups (*puinhoe*), set up by the colonial intermediaries throughout the country, were expected to carry out this colonial mandate. Significantly, as detailed below, Korean Christian women reformers' agenda for rural

---

[42] *Kajŏng chiu* 2 (1937): 13–17. [43] *Kajŏng chiu* 2 (1937): 17.
[44] *Kajŏng chiu* 7 (1937): 5–9.
[45] Kim Puja, *Hakkyo pak ŭi Chosŏn yŏsŏng tŭl* (Korean Women Outside the School) (Seoul: Ilchogak, 2009), see chapter 4, pp. 260–86.
[46] Kim, *Hakkyo pak ŭi Chosŏn yŏsŏng tŭl*, p. 265.
[47] To train future women leaders more systematically, Kyŏngsŏng Yŏja Sabŏm Hakkyo (Seoul Teachers' College for Women) was established in 1935 with educational goals being "*naisen*

revitalization overlapped with that of the colonial state, although it was often driven by the desire for Korean national restoration.

Envisioning Rural Modernity

The early-twentieth century saw a rapid decline in the rural economy and consequent social disintegration. In response, Korean women intellectuals engaged in rural issues more proactively beginning in the late 1920s. To be sure, there were differences in their political and cultural orientations; however, they shared a sense that there was an urgent need to provide the rural population with basic, practical programs to relieve the ongoing problems of illiteracy, lack of hygiene, and family debt. They were also unified in focusing their reform ideas on women as the linchpin in reviving the rural communities and, ultimately, the entire Korean nation. In this vein, the establishment of Kŭnuhoe (Friends of the Rose of Sharon) in 1927 was a significant historical event. As an affiliate of Sin'ganhoe (New Trunk Association, 1927–1931), which was organized as a united front movement in pursuit of national liberation, Kŭnuhoe was the first nationwide women's organization, bringing together a wide range of groups that held divergent ideological orientations, from socialism to liberal bourgeoisie and Christianity. In her discussion of the role of the Kŭnuhoe, the socialist feminist Hŏ Chŏngsuk clearly acknowledged that "Korea's economic base still lies in agriculture. The centrality of the rural economy, which had strong connections to the feudal system, means that many women remain trapped in the family systems and social traditions that were part of feudalism."[48] Some of the socialist members believed that Korean women were not yet prepared to engage in radical political activism, and thus, the focus should be on the enlightenment movement.[49] In this united front, Korea's rural crisis and women's degraded life were an important agenda for focused discussion and action. In spite of its promised role as the leading women's organization with many branches and memberships in tackling centuries-long gender oppression and improving women's lives, Kŭnuhoe soon disintegrated when bourgeoisie nationalists and

---

ittai" (Japan and Korea as One Body) and "*pudŏk*" (womanly virtue). With the outbreak of the Sino-Japanese war in 1937, the Third Chosŏn Education Act was issued in 1938, and the goal of education for women changed from "leaders of the rural development" and "good wife, wise mother" to "hwangguk sinmin" "hwanggun pyŏngsa" "hwangguk yŏsŏng" "hwangguk ŭi ŏmŏni." Kim, *Hakkyo pak ŭi Chosŏn yŏsŏng tŭl*, pp. 271–3.

[48] Hŏ Chŏngsuk, "Kŭnuhoe undong ŭi yŏksa chŏk chiwi wa tangmyŏn munje" (Historical Status and Urgent Duties of Kŭnuhoe), *Kŭnu* 1 (May 1929): 5–13. See also Nam Hwasuk, "1920-nyŏndae yŏsŏng undong esŏŭi hyŏptong chŏnsŏnnon kwa Kŭnuhoe" (Kŭnuhoe and the United Front in the Women's Movement in the 1920s), *Han'guk saron* 25 (1991): 201–49; and Chang Wŏna, "Kŭnuhoe wa Chosŏn yŏsŏng haebang t'ongil chŏnsŏn" (Kŭnuhoe and the United Front for the Liberation of Korean Women), *Yŏksamunje yŏn'gu* 42 (2019): 391–431.

[49] Ch'oe Chŏnghŭi, "Chosŏn yŏsŏng undong ŭi paljŏn kwajŏng" (The Development of the Women's Movement in Korea), *Samch'ŏlli* 3, no. 11 (1931): 94–6.

Christian women withdrew their membership because their enlightenment-centered and apolitical goals were in conflict with the directions of hard-core socialist women who prioritized political agenda focusing on social class strife.[50] Kŭnuhoe was dissolved in 1931 due to internal conflicts as well as increasing surveillance and oppression by the colonial state.

Once Kŭnuhoe had passed out of existence, Christian women's groups took over some of the functions that organization had filled. Because these groups were affiliated with mission schools and churches throughout the country, they had a solid institutional base to support the reform effort. Furthermore, they had the nationwide organization of the Korea YWCA, which was thoroughly interconnected with the World YWCA and WCTU, as well as with various other Christian organizations throughout the world. It was this local, national, and global institutional network that helped some Christian women educators and reformers undertake extensive research on rural reform models and eventually take leadership roles in the rural movement. As briefly described at the beginning of this chapter, Hwang Aedŏk's rural campaign illustrates the vital role that institutional and personal networks among Christian organizations played in launching and advancing the campaign. Below, I introduce two other prominent Christian women intellectuals, Kim Hwallan and Pak Indŏk, whose vision for rural revitalization in colonial Korea had been shaped by their transnational experiences facilitated by the global Christian network.

Kim Hwallan (aka Helen Kim) was the first Korean woman to receive a PhD degree, which she completed in 1931 at Columbia University.[51] Her doctoral thesis, entitled "Rural Education for the Regeneration of Korea," deeply engaged the contemporary concerns about the crisis in rural Korea. Her choice of topic, which preoccupied many Korean intellectuals of the time, and her approach to rural problems, which drew on ideas from disparate locations, demonstrated that the global Christian network was instrumental in this work. Prior to undertaking her doctoral studies, Kim participated in the International Missionary Council (hereafter, IMC) meeting in Jerusalem in 1928, which may well have helped shape her interest in and perspective on religion and society in relation to rural development.[52] Kim was one of six representatives from

---

[50] Kenneth Wells, "The Price of Legitimacy: Women and the Kŭnuhoe Movement, 1927–1931," in *Colonial Modernity in Korea*, eds. Gi-Wook Shin and Michael Robinson (Cambridge: Harvard University Press, 1999), pp. 191–220.

[51] Helen Kiteuk Kim, "Rural Education for the Regeneration of Korea," PhD dissertation, Columbia University, July 1931. Columbia University Rare Book & Manuscript Library.

[52] After Kim returned from the IMC meeting in Jerusalem, she began to advocate rural reform and urge young men and women to devote their time and knowledge to improving rural life. See Kim Hwallan, "1929-nyŏn ŭl mannŭn Chosŏn yŏja kidokkyo ch'ŏngnyŏnhoe" (The Korean Young Women's Christian Association in the Beginning of 1929), *Ch'ŏngnyŏn* 9, no. 1 (January 1929): 3–4; and "Nongch'on munhwa chinhŭng undong: kyoyuk munje" (Movement to Improve Rural Culture: Educational Issues), *Tonga ilbo*, January 1, 1933, 7.

Envisioning Rural Modernity 163

Korea, and was the only woman out of the six.[53] At this particular IMC meeting, "rural problems" were one of the key agenda items for discussion.[54] The IMC asserted that rural problems needed urgent attention because of the sheer size of the rural population and, more importantly, because of "the great issues of Christian civilization at stake." The Council argued that the mission had not offered the appropriate level of attention and service in rural communities. While spirituality continued to be the central tenet of Christian civilization, the IMC urged people to consider that spiritual life cannot be separated from physical, mental, and social conditions, and thus that the program of missionary work should address every aspect of human life and human relationships.[55] This focused attention on rural problems and all aspects of human life also had to do with the growing challenge to "anti-Christian" or "anti-religion" movements, which began in the early 1920s, charging that evangelical policy had failed to alleviate the pain and hardship of poverty or assist in meeting the practical needs of everyday life.[56] As a concrete and practical step for action, participants at the IMC meeting identified the "rural community" as the focus of reform efforts, and discussed various "agencies for community development" as key instruments for change.

In the IMC's discussion of the purpose of the "Christian Mission in Relation to Rural Problems in Asia and Africa," the "family and the home" was singled out as the first among the five agencies for improving "rural civilization." It was viewed as the "conserver of the race and the nursery of Christian character," and as "the basal factor of the community life." In the same discussion, it was argued that, "work for women should receive major attention and a larger range of activity be opened up for them."[57] The role women played in the "improvement of family life" was significant because they were responsible for "such

[53] Jerusalem, Minutes, 13, fol. 6, Box 4, series 4, MRL Series 12. Yu Sŏnghŭi argues that the IMC made crucial impact on the active promotion of the rural programs by the YWCA. Yu, "Han'guk YWCA undong," p. 144.
[54] "The World Mission of Christianity. Messages and Recommendations of the Enlarged Meeting of the International Missionary Council held at Jerusalem, March 24–April 8, 1928," pp. 55–63, fol. 9, Box 4, series 4, MRL Series 12. See also Kim Hwallan's brief reflection on the IMC meeting. Kim Hwallan, "Yerusalem taehoe wa kŭmhu kidokkyo" (Jerusalem and the Future of Christianity), Ch'ŏngnyŏn 8, no. 8 (November 1928): 2–5.
[55] "The World Mission of Christianity," p. 55.
[56] For example, when the World Student Christian Federation (WSCF) was held at Peking's Tsing Hwa College in 1922, an anti-Christian protest was staged outside the conference, charging WSCF with "being anti-science, narrow-minded and imperialist." Inside the conference were also tensions with respect to Christian policy in social and international affairs. Kim Hwallan was one of the Korean delegates at this WSCF conference. See Renate Howe, *A Century of Influence* (Sydney: UNSW Press, 2009), pp. 159–60. Korean intellectuals also reported on this growing anti-Christian, anti-religion movement. See Kŭmsŏng, "Pi kidokkyo tae tongmaeng sŏnŏn, chabonjuŭija ka kidokkyo rŭl poyuha nŭn kŭ imyŏn" (Declaration of the Non-Christian Alliance: Reasons for Capitalist Imperialists to Keep Christianity), *Kaebyŏk* 52 (October 1924): 56–8.
[57] "The World Mission of Christianity," p. 57.

home activities as the care of children, food, sleeping facilities, sanitation, and all that centers about the life of women and children."[58] In the end, the 1928 IMC stated:

> We desire to lay special emphasis upon the importance which attaches to the home and its service to and relationships with the community. Too frequently missionary work in rural areas neglects the woman, especially with reference to her contributions, both as an individual and as homemaker, to community welfare. Both in general and religious education of children, the mother's influence may be almost decisive. All, therefore, that has been said with reference to education applies with equal force to the selection and training of women workers in the field, and of women missionaries who are sent there.[59]

This passage indicates that, in the view of the IMC, women were "decisive" in the efforts to build a rural civilization. Kim Hwallan echoed this sentiment in her PhD dissertation, highlighting the crucial role that women played in ensuring the regeneration of the rural community, noting that "the influence of the keywoman in a village cannot be underestimated when we see whole villages making reforms under women's orders. In some cases she and not the headman may be the one person upon whom the village regeneration rests."[60]

In addition to the focused discussion about rural problems at the IMC conference, one of the invited speakers at the conference was Edmund de Schweinitz Brunner, a professor of education at Teachers College, Columbia University under whom Kim Hwallan would later study. Brunner was already well-known among Christian Koreans. For its 1928 meeting in Jerusalem, the IMC commissioned Brunner to visit Korea and examine rural conditions there to understand their impact on the work of the mission. It is quite clear that rural reform in Korea was an interest that Kim and Brunner had in common and that they knew one another's work and ideas on the subject. Indeed, Brunner wrote an "Introduction," which served as a foreword, for Kim's dissertation, and in her dissertation she cites a great deal of Brunner's report for the IMC on rural conditions in Korea.[61]

The other influential event that was significant in the development of Kim Hwallan's thinking about rural reform was a visit to Denmark, which took place during a brief European tour that she and her male colleagues undertook en route to the 1928 IMC meeting in Jerusalem.[62] Denmark's agrarian reforms had been well-known among Korean intellectuals and reformers since the early

---

[58] "The World Mission of Christianity," p. 57. [59] "The World Mission of Christianity," p. 60.
[60] Kim, "Rural Education for the Regeneration of Korea," pp. 110–11.
[61] Kim, "Rural Education for the Regeneration of Korea." In the copy of her dissertation I consulted from the Columbia University Rare Book & Manuscript Library, Brunner's "Introduction" was missing. However, it can be found in Uwŏl munjip 1, ed. Uwŏl munjip p'yŏnch'an wiwŏnhoe (Seoul: Ewha yŏja taehakkyo ch'ulp'anbu, 1979), pp. 5–6.
[62] Kim's male colleagues included the prominent Christian leaders Hong Pyŏngsŏn (1888–1967) and Sin Hŭng'u (1883–1959).

1920s.[63] Many saw the Danish program of rural reform as a model to emulate, especially such features as the Danish cooperative system, the folk high school system, and physical exercise programs.[64] But having the opportunity to witness the impact of rural reforms and directly interact with Danish reformers seems to have had a profound effect on Kim, which can be seen in her doctoral dissertation.

In her discussion of the "Danish experiment" in her dissertation, Kim notes some fundamental differences between Korea and Denmark, especially in the political and economic domains. For instance, when she discusses Danish agricultural economy, she notes:

Korea has yet to find a unique product and a world market for it, before she can expect prosperity at all comparable to that of the Danish farmers, which was made possible largely through the conversion of corn into dairy products. These in turn were exported through cooperative measures to the world market near at hand. Korea has neither the unique and standardized product nor easy access to the world market at the present time.... Another difficulty that the Danes did not have to face was that of foreign capital and control. [Unlike colonized Korea, Denmark is an independent nation and thus] Danes could invest, manage and control all the aspects of their life in their own way and according to their own will.[65]

Keenly aware of the significant differences between Denmark and Korea, especially in terms of political and economic sovereignty, she mainly tries to elicit lessons about how Denmark was able to transform itself in the face of "the threat of national death" about three-quarters of a century earlier and become a model for rural revitalization.[66] She sees the national leader, N. F. S. Grundtvig (1783–1872), as having played a heroic role in

---

[63] Yi Kit'ae introduced the Danish agricultural history and characteristics in a series of articles, entitled "Chongmal ŭi nongŏp" (Agriculture of Denmark), from June 1925 to March 1926 in Ch'ŏngnyŏn, magazine of the Korea YMCA. See also "Chŏngmalguk ŭl kuhan sahoe kyoyuk" (Social Education that Saved Denmark), Tonga ilbo June 1, 1927, 4; Pang T'aeyŏng, "Chŏngmal nongch'on kŭp kyoyuk" (Danish Rural Community and Education), Tonggwang 7 (November 1926): 28–32. For detailed analysis of the impact of the Danish model on rural reform movements in Korea, see Park, Building A Heaven on Earth, pp. 150–90. The Danish model was also influential in imperial Japan. Japanese modern historian Emily Anderson shows how the Danish model made significant impact on Japanese Christian leaders. In particular, Anderson offers a detailed analysis of the life and activism of Kashiwagi Gien (1860–1938), who was "a stubborn critic of imperialism, capitalism, and militarism," and whose vision for a "small" non-belligerent Japan "drew upon a broad and cosmopolitan set of influences," including models of Danish folk high schools and agricultural cooperatives. See Emily Anderson, Christianity and Imperialism in Modern Japan: Empire for God (London: Bloomsbury, 2014), pp. 185–216, quoted on 187.

[64] Sin Hŭng'u, "Chŏngmal esŏ pogo on kŏt" (What I Saw in Denmark), Pyŏlgŏn'gon 16/17 (December 1928): 72–73.

[65] Kim, "Rural Education for the Regeneration of Korea," p. 74.

[66] Kim, "Rural Education for the Regeneration of Korea," pp. 64–5.

raising a "new spirit" among the Danes at a crucially transformational point in Denmark. She characterizes the Danish "new spirit ... as nationalistic, democratic, and practical."[67] The "nationalistic" character of the new spirit included Grundtvig's emphasis on Danish history, language, and folk life as the foundation of what it means to be a Dane. It was also "democratic" because his vision was based on "belief in the common people" and "religious, political and academic freedom [as] a necessary condition for full human development." Grundtvig's "practical" application of his vision was embodied in the establishment of folk high schools for all and on the active role of the cooperative unions based on trust and solidarity among the peasants. In the end, Kim sees three lessons from the Danish model that could be applied to Korea, especially in the areas of education to "regenerate Korea": "the spiritual awakening as the purpose of education, the consideration of 'personality effects' in the teaching methods, and the use of indigenous culture and history as the major part of the curriculum."[68]

Kim was particularly impressed by the emphasis that the Danish model put on indigenous history, language, environment, and culture. Early on, Kim had already shown her strong belief in the value of Korean traditional cultures and advocated for the restoration of some of those values. For example, she considered Korean clothes, cuisine, and housing to be Korea's proud heritage to the world.[69] Her encounter with the Danish model, which fully cultivates its folk tradition, may thus have reinforced her belief in the power of Korea's rich cultural heritage, represented in the "recorded and unrecorded accumulations and development of four millenniums [sic] in art, literature and music, together with the customs and habits of the daily life." She argued that this rich heritage should be considered a "tremendous field as an educational background full of educational assets and opportunities."[70] Further, she made a "special mention" about the Korean language as "an asset for education" as Koreans speak one language and have a phonetic system of writing, *han'gŭl*.[71]

---

[67] Kim, "Rural Education for the Regeneration of Korea," p. 66.
[68] Kim, "Rural Education for the Regeneration of Korea," p. 74.
[69] Kim Hwallan, "Munhwa undong e taehayŏ" (About Cultural Movement), *Tonga ilbo*, February 22, 1921, 3.
[70] Kim, "Rural Education for the Regeneration of Korea," p. 20. Kim's special attention to Korea's native tradition, custom, and art was already evident in her earlier article, entitled "Culture and the Korean People," published in 1930. In it, she emphasizes the distinctiveness of Korean art and culture in comparison with Chinese, Japanese, and even the Western ones. Citing extensively from Andreas Eckardt's, *History of Korean Art*, she shows her strong sense of national pride in Korean indigenous art forms and expression that value simplicity, modesty, and fluidity. She also notes that the Korean language "is considered by the world language students to be the most perfect system of written language." See "Survey of the Young Men's Christian Association and the Young Women's Christian Association of Korea," pp. 119–22.
[71] Kim, "Rural Education for the Regeneration of Korea," p. 20.

Envisioning Rural Modernity 167

The main challenge Kim saw was that the rich traditions of Korea had been monopolized by a privileged few in the past and was currently being monopolized by the urban populace. Given that, she posed a series of questions: "How to enrich the lives of the farmers by making the cultural opportunities available to them? ... How to adjust the school curriculum that the rural children may also grow up in the best cultural environment the nation is capable of offering? What kind of education will help these people to make a normal transition from the ancient to the modern culture? Is the so-called 'modern education' a healthy movement? Or are there dangers involved?"[72] As Kim noted, these questions present "a complicated phase of the problem of rural education in Korea."[73] While the Danish model is certainly evident in her vision for rural education in Korea, she was conscientious in considering the relevance and applicability of the Danes' experiences in colonized Korea. After all, Koreans had had neither political and economic sovereignty nor cultural autonomy, unlike the Danes. Further, the Japanese colonial state's assimilation policy dictated the educational field.

In this vein, Kim makes a few proposals that educators and reformers consider to improve rural education. One of the proposals she makes in her dissertation is to make use of existing indigenous Korean schools called *kŭlbang* or *sŏdang*, which Brunner calls the "most significant and sociologically sound" proposal.[74] Before the modern system of education was introduced in Korea in the late-nineteenth century, *kŭlbang* served as the basic unit of education for boys. Almost every village had a *kŭlbang*. As the American missionary Horace H. Underwood observed: "It is still true that there was hardly a village of any size which did not have its village school [*kŭlbang*], and that the education of the time was both more esteemed and more widespread than in any European country up to comparatively recent years."[75] According to the "Government Survey of Korean Schools" (May 1929), there were 14,957 *kŭlbang* spread throughout the country, while there were only 1,505 government-recognized public and private elementary schools.[76] When the colonial government failed to provide universal education to all, the *kŭlbang* continued to serve as the most pervasive and also most economical educational agency for children in the rural community. As Kim notes, the persistence of the *kŭlbang* led the colonial authority to impose regulations on it in 1918 in order to check and control its curriculum and personnel.[77] For example, the new curriculum

---

[72] Kim, "Rural Education for the Regeneration of Korea," pp. 21–2.
[73] Kim, "Rural Education for the Regeneration of Korea," p. 22.
[74] Uwŏl munjip p'yŏnch'an wiwŏnhoe, *Uwŏl munjip* 1, p. 5; and Kim "Rural Education for the Regeneration of Korea," pp. 51–6. In her dissertation, *kŭlbang* and *sŏdang* were differently Romanized: "kulpang" and "sohtang."
[75] Cited in Kim, "Rural Education for the Regeneration of Korea," p. 51.
[76] Kim, "Rural Education for the Regeneration of Korea," p. 53.
[77] Kim, "Rural Education for the Regeneration of Korea," pp. 53–4.

guidelines required Japanese language instruction and banned the use of "prohibited or improper books" that espoused radical and anti-colonial feelings.[78] Even with the surveillance and control imposed by the colonial state, Kim describes how *kŭlbang* could potentially provide basic literacy and elemental learning for the majority of the populace, who were being denied the benefit of modern development. Furthermore, Kim envisions the centuries-old and village-based *kŭlbang* as an important vehicle for the regeneration of Korea, an already-existing mechanism for reinforcing indigenous values and heritage, in parallel to the emphasis that the Danish model placed on these.

Pak Indŏk, another well-known Christian woman intellectual, also promoted the Danish model for rural development in Korea. She visited Denmark in 1931 while on her first global speaking tour and became a strong advocate for the Danish model for rural development, especially in relation to women's work in rural areas. On her return to Korea, Pak published a book entitled *Danish Folk High School*,[79] which her colleague Sin Hŭng'u (aka Hugh Cynn) described as "the first and only work that treats the subject adequately," pointing out that it "took her much time, insight and orientation to integrate the underlying spiritual principles of the Danish movement and the dire realities of Korean situation into an adjusted whole."[80] In her preface to the book, Pak writes that visiting Denmark and learning about the Danish folk high school tradition and practice was the most precious experience she had on her first global tour.[81] Although she traveled from one country to the next in the fast-paced, jam-packed schedule, she spent the most substantial part of the trip in Denmark, meeting a variety of people, visiting Danish homes, and even attending a folk high school as a guest student. Those experiences in Denmark significantly shaped her outlook and the specific strategies she developed for Korean social reforms.

Pak's first impression of Denmark was extremely positive.[82] On the train travelling from Hamburg in Germany to Copenhagen, she observed that "it is hard to tell who is a peasant and who is an urban gentleman from their clothing.

---

[78] Kim, "Rural Education for the Regeneration of Korea," p. 54.

[79] Induk Pak (Pak Indŏk), *Danish Folk High School* (Chŏngmal kungmin kodŭng hakkyo), (Kyŏngsŏng: Chosŏn kidokkyo ch'ŏngnyŏn yŏnhaphoe, 1932).

[80] "Copied from a recent letter received from Dr. Hugh Cynn in reply to my questions about the work of Induk Pak," "Deceased folder 2," The Alumnae Center, Wesleyan College Archives. There is no date indicated, but judging from the content, this letter was written in 1932 in a later part of the year. Unlike Cynn's claim, there was an earlier publication in 1930 on Denmark's rural development, entitled *Chŏngmal nara yŏn'gu* (Study on Denmark), eds. and comps. Anna Chaffin and Ch'oe Pongsik. In this 1930 book, Hwang Aedŏk contributed a chapter on Danish cooperatives. See Yu, "Han'guk YWCA undong," p. 144.

[81] Pak, *Danish Folk High School*, p. 1.

[82] Unlike Pak, her contemporary intellectual, Pak Sŭngch'ŏl, who was studying in Germany, was not impressed by Denmark, thinking that it lagged behind in industrial development. Pak Sŭngch'ŏl, "Pukku yŏlguk kyŏnmun'gi" (Records of Observations in Northern Europe), *Kaebyŏk* 43 (January 1924): 61–8, especially 62–4.

Men and women, young and old all wear clean clothes and they all look pretty content and friendly. I had heard that in Denmark there are very few exceptionally wealthy people or very poor people and thus there is only one class. I see how true that is judging from their appearance."[83] Pak's impression of Denmark as a near ideal society with a minimal gap between the rich and the poor and between the urban and the rural was reinforced by her actual interactions with Danish people and her firsthand experience with Denmark's well-known folk high school system, which has been credited with the dramatic transformation of Denmark into a paradise for farmers.

In May 1931, Pak spent two weeks as a guest student at a folk high school, the International People's College (hereafter, IPC) in Helsingør, which was founded in 1921 by Peter Manniche (1889–1981). Pak's colleagues, including Kim Hwallan, Hong Pyŏngsŏn, and Sin Hŭng'u had already visited the IPC in 1928, on their way to Jerusalem to attend the IMC conference. Pak had direct interactions with the school's founder, Peter Manniche, and from him learned the history of the folk high school movement, which began in the early-nineteenth century. He told her that in those early days, peasants were poor, ignorant, and manipulated, but, in the present day, peasants had been transformed into well-educated, well-to-do individuals who had become highly influential in national politics. Part of that transformation, according to Manniche, was due to the folk high school movement, which radically changed the rural population in terms of their mentality, attitude, and everyday life. A reflection of the transformational impact of the movement can be seen in the fact that the once-infertile, sandy soil of Denmark had been made fertile for agricultural production.

While Manniche maintained the traditions that N. F. S. Grundtvig and Christen Kold (1816–1870), the founders of the Danish folk high school movement, had established at the schools, he also paid special attention to "looking outward – even to the whole world – rather than ... nostalgically looking back to the 'golden age' of the folk high school movement."[84] As the present-day principal of the IPC, Søren Launberg, has pointed out, although Danish identity and culture are an important component of the curriculum, they are integrated into the school's broader mission to foster "active global citizens."[85] The general profile of students at the IPC over its history indicates that, while Danes were the vast majority during the winter terms from November to March, from April to July about half the enrollment was made

---

[83] Pak Indŏk, *Segye ilchugi* (Record of the Global Tour) (Kyŏngsŏng: Chosŏn ch'ulp'ansa, 1941), pp. 106–11, quoted on p. 107.
[84] Max Lawson, *A Celebration of 75 Years of Working for Peace and International Friendship* (Helsingør: International People's College, 1996), p. 7.
[85] Interview with Søren Launberg at International People's College in Helsingør on August 26, 2016.

up of foreign students. During the regular sessions, very few Asian students were registered at the school. Between 1921 and 1931, only one Japanese and two Indian students were enrolled in the school. However, in the summers of that same decade, the "international holiday courses," which lasted only twelve days, drew about fifty Japanese, Chinese, and Egyptian students.[86] The IPC also invited international dignitaries, such as Rabindranath Tagore,[87] and frequently hosted teachers who had come from other parts of Europe and the United States to learn more about the folk high school model for possible adaptation and transplantation to their home countries.[88] International affairs and issues relating to global outlook and cosmopolitanism were regularly featured in the IPC magazine, *IHS*, and annual reports.[89]

Deeply affected by the horrors of World War I, Manniche was particularly interested in peace education and fellowship among various nationalities, combining tenets of Christianity, democracy, socialism, and anti-militarism. In his prospectus for the founding of the IPC, he wrote:

> The International People's College is to be established on the general lines of the existing Danish folk high schools, but with modifications necessary to adapt it for townsmen and for men of various nationalities.... Furthermore it is hoped that it may be possible to create and foster such an atmosphere of true fellowship – alike between student and student and between students and staff – associated with Christian frugality; sincerity and ready co-operation – as may convince not a few that between Christianity and Democracy and Socialism and between nation and nation there should be no division, but on the contrary the bond of common interest and common aims.[90]

It is noteworthy that Manniche's educational philosophy drew from various intellectual, religious, and social traditions, including Christianity and socialism. He wrote: "Socialism without Christianity is tending towards materialism and will not shrink away from using the brutal force in order to serve its ends, and a Christianity which is not concerned with society, which is not at work building up a new kingdom on earth will never be a moving force in life."[91]

---

[86] Peter Manniche, "Ten Years," *IHS*, no. 2 (Maj 1931): 6–8; *IHS*, no. 4 (December 1931): 15. (udgivet af den internationale højskoles elevforening, published by the International High School Student Union), IPC Archive. In 2016, IPC had fifteen Danish students and eighty-five international students. Interview with Søren Launberg at IPC on August 26, 2016.

[87] Tagore visited IPC in 1930. *IHS*, no. 1 (July 1930): 6.

[88] Frank Smith (Berea College), "Thoughts from America," Annual Jahresschrift Aarsskrift 1929: 13–14; and *IHS*, no. 2 (May 1931): 13.

[89] For instance, "The Conflict in Manchuria," *IHS*, no. 1 (March 1932): 1–3; J. F. Mashford, "The Spirit of Internationalism," Jahresschrift Aarsskrift, 1925: 29–30; W. H. Marwick, "The Psychology of Internationalism," Jahresschrift Aarsskrift, 1925: 21–3; and Hughes Griffith, "The British Empire and World Peace," Jahresschrift Aarsskrift, 1927: 49–52.

[90] Lawson, *A Celebration of 75 Years of Working for Peace and International Friendship*, pp. 8–9.

[91] Lawson, *A Celebration of 75 Years of Working for Peace and International Friendship*, p. 14.

Envisioning Rural Modernity   171

Manniche's "lifelong straddling of Christianity and Socialism" was reflected in the exceptional emphasis he placed on manual labor, which became a central part of the curriculum of the IPC.[92] Indeed, when Pak attended IPC as a guest student for two weeks, she was particularly impressed by the integration of manual labor into the daily curriculum.[93] In addition, Pak understood that after the political demise and economic collapse of the country in 1814, Denmark had revitalized itself to become a paradise for farmers through the "popular awakening movement" (*minjung kaksŏng undong*).[94] For her, it was that "awakening" of the people that was the key to any social movement to revive a nation. As long as people can maintain a hopeful mentality, she believed, even in the face of political or economic failure, the nation can be preserved.[95] Her ideals and practices in rural reform programs reflect this central emphasis on manual labor and mental awakening.

Kim Hwallan and Pak Indŏk had the privilege of traveling the world as students, speakers, and representatives of the Korean Christian community, which had been fostered by the global Christian network.[96] Those transnational experiences, through which they were able to observe and learn about alternative models and practices, further helped them appreciate and articulate the particular local and national conditions in Korea. In Kim's doctoral dissertation on rural education and Pak's book on Danish folk high schools, we can see an

---

[92] Lawson, *A Celebration of 75 Years of Working for Peace and International Friendship*, p. 15.
[93] Pak presents the following daily class schedule as typical for the IPC:
- 7:30 AM Singing
- 8:00–9:00 AM Foreign languages – Danish, French, German, or English
- 9:00–10:00 AM Lecture on a variety of issues, such as labor, social science, psychology, or history
- 10:00–11:00 AM Manual labor
- 11:00–12:00 AM Exercise/sports
- 12:00–2:00 PM Lunch
- 2:00–3:00 PM Drawing, mathematics, and composition
- 3:00–3:30 PM Tea time
- 3:30–4:30 PM Free discussion

Pak was deeply impressed by the emphasis that Danes placed on manual labor in the curriculum. She later adopted this emphasis on manual labor when she founded her own school, Berea in Korea, in 1962. During her first global tour, Pak visited Berea College in Louisville, Kentucky. Berea emphasized manual labor, which was in part influenced by the Danish folk high school tradition. For example, Berea's English teacher, Frank Smith visited IPS to learn more about the Danish educational system. See Pak, *Segye ilchugi*, pp. 44–7, 106–23; "Personalia," *IHS* no. 2 (Maj 1931): 13.
[94] Pak, *Danish Folk High School*, p. 114.
[95] Pak, *Danish Folk High School*, p. 115. Speaking of key principles in the rural campaign, Pak's close colleague, Sin Hŭng'u argued that mental strength was more important than rural productivity. See Sin Hŭng'u, "Nongch'on saŏp ŭi 3-dae kangnyŏng" (Three Principles in the Rural Campaign), *Ch'ŏngnyŏn* 11, no. 11 (December 1931): 3.
[96] Kim Hwallan represented Korean Christian students at the World Student Christian Federation held in Peking in 1922, participated at the IMC in Jerusalem in 1928, where she impressed other participants with her presentation on rural problems and racial tensions. Yu, *Han'guk YWCA undong*, p. 71.

intellectual journey through which each woman developed an appreciative but critical eye toward the dynamics between the local and the global and between the traditional and the modern. In the process of actively exploring new models from various places, they were forced to reconsider and reevaluate local and national situations in Korea, in an attempt to create a model that would be appropriate for contemporary Korea. A critical question to ask is whether the visions of rural reform held by Christian women intellectuals such as Kim Hwallan, Pak Indŏk, and Hwang Aedŏk could possibly coexist with the Japanese colonial state's own Rural Revitalization Campaign, or was there an inevitable clash. In the following section, we look in more detail at the participation of women reformers in the Rural Revitalization Movement, to illustrate how challenging it was for them to put their theories and proposals into practice, what institutional bases and networks they used to advance that movement and to what extent these Korean initiatives differed from the colonial state's.

"Go to the People": The Praxis of Gendered Rural Modernity

The rural campaign spearheaded by Christian women in the 1920s and 1930s was carried out mostly in connection with the Korea YWCA.[97] Founded in 1922, the YWCA was the largest Christian women's organization in Korea, and it was linked to an international network (see Figure 4.2). As a prominent global Christian women's organization, the World YWCA offered a crucial network through which Korean women leaders could travel to foreign countries for conferences or training sessions. For example, Yu Kakgyŏng (1892–1966), the first president of the Korea YWCA, participated in a YWCA training course in Shanghai in 1924.[98] Kim Hwallan was the Korean delegate at numerous international meetings, including the World YWCA meeting in Washington, DC, in 1924, as well as the IMC in Jerusalem in 1928.[99] Interacting with participants from all over the world provided Korean delegates with knowledge of various programs in advanced countries and familiarized them with the particular local and national conditions in less-developed, colonized countries. Thus the Korea YWCA was uniquely positioned to play a key role in shaping and fostering the country's rural revitalization work, equipped with both understanding of international practices and knowledge of the particular conditions in Korea.

The YWCA's rural work evolved along with that of the Korea YMCA, which launched its rural campaign in 1925 by creating the "Agricultural Division" (Nongch'onbu). Prior to 1925, the work of the YMCA and YWCA was

---

[97] Ch'ŏn, Han'guk yŏsŏng kidokkyo sahoe undongsa, pp. 50–51.
[98] Taehan YWCA yŏnhaphoe, Han'guk YWCA pan paengnyŏn (The Fiftieth History of Korea YWCA) (Seoul: Taehan YWCA yŏnhaphoe, 1976), p. 43.
[99] Taehan YWCA yŏnhaphoe, Han'guk YWCA pan paengnyŏn, pp. 44–5.

"Go to the People": The Praxis of Gendered Rural Modernity 173

Figure 4.2 Early members of the Korea YWCA
Source: Courtesy of the Korea YWCA

essentially "a city type of work in Seoul among the educated classes."[100] However, it became clear that the poverty-stricken rural districts, which constituted the largest segment of the country, needed a great deal of assistance. Christian leaders, especially Sin Hŭng'u as secretary general of the National Federation of the YMCA in Korea, were instrumental in shifting the Christian group's focus from urban areas to rural.[101] In 1924, after a series of pilot projects in villages, the YMCA outlined a rural reconstruction program, and "the first American secretaries for the program, two in number, were sent in 1925. Three Korean secretaries were also secured." Additional personnel were hired in the years that followed.[102]

The YWCA did not originally provide any rural services. Any such programs were offered through the YMCA, and those were open to men, women, and children.[103] It was not until 1928 that the YWCA launched its own

[100] Reisner, "Rural Reconstruction Work in Korea, 1935," 245.
[101] Koen de Ceuster, "The YMCA's Rural Development Program in Colonial Korea, 1925–35: Doctrine and Objectives," Review of Korean Studies 3, no. 1 (July 2000): 5–33.
[102] Reisner, "Rural Reconstruction Work in Korea, 1935," 245.
[103] Nongch'onbu, "Nongch'on e kago om" (Returning from the Rural Areas), Ch'ŏngnyŏn 5, no. 4 (April 1925): 11; and Il kija (A Reporter), "Nongch'on saŏp chorŏpsik ŭl kugyŏng hagosŏ" (After Observing the Graduation Ceremony of the Rural Project), Ch'ŏngnyŏn 6, no. 5 (May 1926): 43–5.

Agricultural Division to offer more systematic programs for girls and women.[104] About one-third of its budget in 1928 was devoted to the rural work, which was a major shift in budgetary allocation from activities to solve "social problems," such as prostitution, drinking, early marriage, and superstition, to programs for the rural population.[105]

The overall goal of the rural work was to improve the standard of living for farmers in both economic and cultural terms. To that end, the reforms implemented a range of innovations, including a variety of cooperative unions, hygienic practices, new technologies for agricultural development, cottage industries for housewives, and literacy for all.[106] Specific items in the YWCA's activities for the rural program included: the campaign to improve kitchens; the campaign for proper drainage and sewage; the campaign to control diseases; the war on flies, mosquitoes, etc.; credit unions; savings unions; cooperative buying; cooperative selling; education of farmers on the proper care of babies; Korean literacy; methods for improving seed generation, fertilizers, and farm implements; and women's avocations, such as chicken-raising, animal husbandry, silkworm husbandry, bee culture, and cultivation of flowers and vegetables.[107] The YWCA also offered itinerating lecturers, provided pamphlets, and held a modest "farmers' institute," workshops of seven to ten days where local leaders learned various rural improvement techniques.[108]

Hwang Aedŏk served as the first "trained full-time secretary" of the Agricultural Division of the Korea YWCA from 1930 to 1932.[109] As noted earlier, Hwang had trained at Columbia University (1926–1928), and, on returning to Korea, she served as the head of the Department of Rural Work Training at Hyŏpsŏng Theology School for Women. As a key leader of the rural campaign, Hwang emphasized that "Korea's rural movement is different from examples found in other countries. Korea has its own particular conditions, and we need to bear our unique situation in mind when we consider the best plan moving forward."[110] She diagnosed the current status of the rural movement in Korea as "ideologically driven rather than pragmatic with concrete plans and programs."[111] In this vein, she made it clear that she was committed to a "rural

---

[104] Yu, *Han'guk YWCA undong*, p. 144; Ch'ŏn, *Han'guk yŏsŏng kidokkyo sahoe undongsa*, pp. 48–51.
[105] Yu, *Han'guk YWCA undong*, pp. 144–5.   [106] Yu, *Han'guk YWCA undong*, p. 145.
[107] "Survey of the Young Men's Christian Association and the Young Women's Christian Association of Korea," 58–59; and Reisner, "Rural Reconstruction Work in Korea, 1935," 247.
[108] "Survey of the Young Men's Christian Association and the Young Women's Christian Association of Korea," 55–7.
[109] "Survey of the Young Men's Christian Association and the Young Women's Christian Association of Korea," 8. In this survey, the term, "Rural Committee" is used instead of "Agricultural Division." In Korean, it was called "Nongch'onbu," and for consistency, I use the "Agricultural Division" in both the YMCA and YWCA. See also Ch'ŏn, *Han'guk yŏsŏng kidokkyo sahoe undongsa*, p. 51.
[110] *Tonga ilbo*, January 1, 1930, 9.   [111] *Tonga ilbo*, January 1, 1930, 9.

enlightenment movement" (*nongch'on kyemong undong*) as the first step. By "rural enlightenment movement," she meant alleviating the rampant problem of illiteracy among the rural population through night classes and lectures. In addition, she stressed the need to establish locally based institutes that would bring farmers together in solidarity, as well as a training institute for future leaders of the rural movement.[112]

However, Hwang was fully aware of numerous challenges to carrying out the rural work effectively. Without a large contingent of paid, full-time personnel in the YWCA, the organization had to rely largely on volunteers, especially students from mission schools, who often constituted the majority of participants in the Y's regular meetings.[113] There was little communication between the National Committee and regional, city, and rural districts, and there were no YWCA rural centers.[114] Under these circumstances, it was only through the exceptional devotion of individual Koreans that some success was seen in the rural movement. High school and professional school students played a key role as volunteers in the rural programs during their summer and winter breaks from school.[115] In her capacity as the Head of the Department of Rural Work Training at Hyŏpsŏng Theology School for Women and also the general secretary of the Agricultural Division of the YWCA, Hwang had a mission to train her students to become Christian workers for rural revitalization.

Hwang's best-known disciple in the rural work was Ch'oe Yongsin (1909–1935). Ch'oe's extraordinary devotion to rural work in the village of Saemgol near Suwŏn was and has remained legendary, inspiring many of her contemporaries and as well as later rural workers. Born in South Hamgyŏng Province, near Wŏnsan, a major trading port, Ch'oe Yongsin came from an early modern pioneering family in that region. Her grandfather, Ch'oe Hyojun, established the Ch'wisŏng School in 1899, and her father, Ch'oe Ch'anghŭi, who later became principal of the Ch'wisŏng School, took a leadership role in youth, cultural, and rural movements in the region in the 1920s. In 1921 Ch'oe Ch'anghŭi took the initiative in organizing the group called Hongnonghoe, which promoted agricultural knowledge and development. Growing up in such a household, Ch'oe Yongsin had early exposure to modern reform activities, especially rural development.

Christian education also acted as a channel that led Ch'oe into the rural campaign. She received all her education at Christian mission schools, including the Lucy Girls' School in Wŏnsan, a Methodist school founded in 1903, and

---

[112] *Tonga ilbo*, January 1, 1930, 9.
[113] Ch'ŏn, *Han'guk yŏsŏng kidokkyo sahoe undongsa*, p. 51.
[114] "Survey of the Young Men's Christian Association and the Young Women's Christian Association of Korea," 9–14.
[115] Hŏ, "Hyangch'on e toraganŭn yŏhaksaeng chegun ege"; and Hwang, "Nongbŏn'gi wa nongch'on adong munje."

later Hyŏpsŏng. By the time she graduated from Lucy in 1928, she already had a clear plan to devote herself to the improvement of rural life. As mentioned earlier, on April 1, 1928, *Chosŏn ilbo* published an essay by Ch'oe in which she urged educated women to help rural women escape the dark life of illiteracy, emphasizing rural women's enlightenment as an indispensable ingredient for national development.[116] Her enrollment at Hyŏpsŏng under the supervision of Hwang Aedŏk further strengthened her will to devote herself to the rural work. In 1929, she attended the summer conference of the Korea YMCA and YWCA as the student representative from Hyŏpsŏng. Prominent Christian leaders such as Yun Ch'iho, Sin Hŭng'u, and Kim Hwallan attended the conference, at which the main agenda item for discussion was "Christianity and Peasants."[117] Some of these key Christian leaders, such as Sin Hŭng'u and Kim Hwallan, had attended the 1928 IMC in Jerusalem, where the role of Christianity in rural development was a central point of discussion, and this 1929 summer conference seems to have focused on the same topic. While studying at Hyŏpsŏng, Ch'oe took on her first rural work during the summer break in 1929, in the village of Yonghyŏn in Hwanghae Province. Unfortunately, her health declined during her stay there, but she remained so devoted to rural work that she asked to be transferred to another rural area that might be more salutary to her health.

Ch'oe was eventually sent to Saemgol (aka Ch'ŏn'gok) in Suwŏn, a village slightly less remote than Yonghyŏn, where she was officially appointed a rural worker by the YWCA in October 1931.[118] The location was chosen based on a survey conducted by the YWCA on rural conditions in the Suwŏn area. The rural work in Saemgol was sponsored by Mrs. Sherwood Eddy (aka Maud Arden Eddy), who was the director of the agricultural division of the US YWCA.[119] Unlike the majority of students, who engaged in the rural movement only during school breaks, Ch'oe committed herself completely to the rural work, becoming a full-time rural resident. At first, she faced prejudice, resistance, and indifference from the village residents, but she taught the local children a song and dance for *ch'usŏk* (fall harvest festival), and that performance convinced the villagers that the learning could have a positive impact. After receiving an initial donation from the village women's group, Ch'oe solicited additional funding by going house to house, and she ultimately succeeded in raising enough money to build a school. She taught children during the daytime and women and the

---

[116] *Chosŏn ilbo*, April 1, 1928, 3.
[117] Kim Hyŏngmok, "Ch'oe Yongsin kajok ŭi minjok undong ch'amyŏ wa yŏksa chŏk ŭiŭi" (The Participation of the Family of Ch'oe Yongsin in the Nationalist Movement and its Historical Meaning), in *The 2nd Choi Yongshin Symposium*, Ansan, November 28, 2014, pp. 20–50, quoted on p. 37.
[118] 3.1. yŏsŏng tongjihoe, *Han'guk yŏsŏng tongnip undongsa*, p. 336; and Yu, *Han'guk YWCA undong*, pp. 145–6.
[119] Taehan YWCA yŏnhaphoe, *Han'guk YWCA pan paengnyŏn*, p. 58.

"Go to the People": The Praxis of Gendered Rural Modernity   177

Figure 4.3 Korea YWCA Rural Revitalization Campaign
Source: Courtesy of the Korea YWCA

elderly at night, and she significantly reduced illiteracy through her tireless work (see Figure 4.3).[120] In 1934, she decided to pursue further education in Japan, enrolling at the Kobe Theology School for Women to major in social work, but she contracted beriberi and had to withdraw after only three months.[121]

By the time she returned to Saemgol, the YWCA's work in the Rural Revitalization Movement had shifted in its priorities. Rather than sending individual workers to reside and work in a particular location, as Ch'oe had done, the YWCA decided to train selected village women as future leaders in their own communities through workshops for a short period of time. This shift meant that the YWCA stopped providing direct funding to the villages by 1934.[122] Already in deteriorating health and without funding to support the work she found purpose in, Ch'oe Yongsin died in Saemgol in January 1935. She was a mere twenty-six years old.

---

[120] "Ko Ch'oe Yongsin yang ŭi palbaon ŏpchŏk ŭi kil" (The Path of Accomplishment of Late Ch'oe Yongsin), *Sin kajŏng* (May 1935): 56–63.
[121] Ch'oe's brother, Ch'oe Sip'ung was in Kobe in 1932, working as a member of the Chosŏn Consumer Cooperative, and it is inferred that Ch'oe Yongsin chose Kobe for study because of her brother. See Kim, "Ch'oe Yongsin kajok ŭi minjok undong ch'amyŏ wa yŏksa chŏk ŭiŭi," 39.
[122] Yu, *Han'guk YWCA undong*, p. 146.

178   Labor: Searching for Rural Modernity

In contrast to Ch'oe Yongsin's rural work in Saemgol, which was specific site-based, residential work, a much more common engagement of women reformers in rural work was itinerant, typically from Seoul to countryside, offering lectures and holding consulting sessions. Pak Indŏk was one of the most prominent itinerant rural reformers. Setting aside the question of the actual impact of elite women's rural work, what makes Pak stand out among those women reformers is the ways in which she utilized the global Christian network to a hitherto-unprecedented extent in order to support her rural campaign. In particular, she used her global speaking tours – the first between 1928 and 1931 and the second between 1935 and 1937 – to raise funds for rural revitalization in Korea.

Pak had a rough start in her rural work due to her personal circumstances. Unlike Hwang Aedŏk, who was highly respected by her contemporaries as a model woman intellectual who "has virtue (tŏk) and incredible organizing skills,"[123] Pak had already taken the highly unusual step of leaving her husband and two young daughters behind in Korea to go to the United States to study at Wesleyan College in Macon, Georgia, in 1926. On returning to Korea in 1931 after completing her studies and her first global tour, she promptly filed for divorce, taking the unprecedented step of agreeing to pay alimony to her husband in order to be let out of the unhappy marriage.[124] The Christian community that she had long been associated with did not approve of her divorce, and she was virtually ostracized.[125]

In the midst of the negative publicity about her divorce,[126] Pak's fellow Christian leader Sin Hŭng'u was one of the few who defended her and provided her with work. In his capacity as the general secretary of the Korea YMCA, Sin made arrangements for Pak to engage in Christian work, including rural outreach activities for women that were sponsored through donations from the United States. In correspondence to a donor in the United States, Sin gives a full report of Pak's activities.[127] The letter appears to have been written in response to a query from the donor about Pak's divorce, and in particular about the alimony payment. The donor wanted to know whether the money had come out of his donation. Sin responds firmly to the donor's query, stating: "Not one penny has been given to Mr. Kim [Kim Unho, Pak's former husband] either

[123] "Chosŏn yŏryu 10 kŏmul yŏlchŏn (1), Pak Indŏk, Hwang Aesidŏk yang ssi" (A Series of Ten Big Names of Outstanding Women of Korea, Part 1: Pak Indŏk and Hwang Aesidŏk), Samch'ŏlli 3, no. 11 (November 1931): 37–9, quoted on 39.
[124] Kenneth Wells, "Expanding Their Realm: Women and Public Agency in Colonial Korea," in Women's Suffrage in Asia, eds. Louise Edwards and Mina Roces (London: Routledge Curzon, 2004), p. 160.
[125] Hyaeweol Choi, "Debating the Korean New Woman: Imagining Henrik Ibsen's 'Nora' in Colonial Era Korea," Asian Studies Review 36 (March 2012): 59–77.
[126] "Pak Indŏk konggaechang: Ihon sodong e kwanhayŏ" (An Open Letter to Pak Indŏk Regarding the Fiasco of her Divorce), Sin yŏsŏng 5, no. 11 (1931): 30–35.
[127] "Copied from a recent letter received from Dr. Hugh Cynn in reply to my questions about the work of Induk Pak." Hugh Cynn is the anglo name of Sin Hŭng'u.

directly or indirectly out of the money you have been sending. And further more [sic] be assured that he will never get one penny from the committees here out of this money or any other money." Sin goes on to explain in great detail how Pak had scrupulously saved the money she had earned from her global tour (1928–1931), which had been sponsored by the Student Volunteer Movement and numerous Christian groups and individuals throughout the world. The tone of the letter is defensive, but it does provide Sin with an opportunity to highlight the value of the rural work Pak had done in spite of the personal tribulations she was undergoing at that time. For example, he mentions that Pak wrote a book, *The Danish Folk High School*, published in 1932 by the Korea YMCA, and that she was also a popular speaker at conferences and the YMCA's district institutes, where she spoke on a variety of topics, including "Youths Abroad," "Women in the West," "Danish Farmers," "Women and Folk School," "The Christian Student Movement in America, in England," "The Present Day Thoughts in the Christian Church of the West," "Jesus, our Hope," and "God, our Life." As Sin emphasizes, in all Pak's speeches, "her chief message is the new hope, courage and life in God through the Master for all of us."[128]

Sin's letter also provides a great deal of detail about the rural work carried out by Pak Indŏk.[129] Her rural work was not like the specific site-based activities that Ch'oe Yongsin undertook while residing within the rural community. Instead, Pak became an itinerant speaker, traveling from community to community, evangelizing and giving lectures. In his letter, Sin describes Pak's practice:

On the appointed day in each week she leaves immediately after lunch and goes on a trolley or bus to the end of the line at the city limit. Then she walks several miles and enters a village of anywhere from thirty to several hundred houses. There are sometimes small church buildings available, but more often only someone's inner room could be had, and if even that cannot be had, she has to make house to house calls. If a meeting place is arranged for, the women, some very old and some very young, come to meet with her. She begins with topics of common interest and gradually leads them to the new life of hope and courage. Besides this specific spiritual message she gives talks on hygiene [sic], sanitation, cottage industry, budgeting, travel, women's rights, etc. Two or three hours are spent that way, and all present including herself thoroughly enjoy and get uplifted. Where there is a church she is often asked to take the Sunday service. In the main she follows the method used by the Y.M.C.A. in its rural work.... This work is extremely useful, and now all the churches and missions are aroused to it, but as yet there are only a few who are actually doing it, and Induk [i.e., Pak Indŏk] is

---

[128] "Copied from a recent letter received from Dr. Hugh Cynn in reply to my questions about the work of Induk Pak."
[129] "Copied from a recent letter received from Dr. Hugh Cynn in reply to my questions about the work of Induk Pak."

the only one who is doing it among women with an organization whose object is to do that specific thing.[130]

Pak's rural work came at a time when the direction of the YMCA's and YWCA's rural projects had begun to shift from dispatching rural workers to work alongside the farmers to instituting "Farmers' Self-Cultivation Centers" (Nongmin Suyangso), which aimed to educate farmers to be future leaders in their own rural communities. By 1934 this policy shift led to the elimination of all financial support for village work like that conducted by Ch'oe Yongsin in Saemgol and to the reallocation of the Y's budget to activities at the farmers' self-cultivation centers.[131] According to Kim Hwallan, the idea of a self-cultivation center for rural leaders came about during the tour of Denmark in 1928. Inspired by the success in Denmark, the delegates planned to establish such a center after their return.[132] The first farmers' self-cultivation center was established in Sinch'on, Seoul, in November 1932. It was, in Yun Ch'iho's words, "a novel experiment – trying to Koreanize the Folk High School ideas of Denmark."[133] It began with fifteen trainees representing twelve provinces. The use of the word *suyang* in the name of the training center is noteworthy for two reasons. First, the Korean word is a translation of the equivalent Japanese word *shūyō* ("self-cultivation"), which the colonial authority used in its Rural Revitalization Campaign. Second, whether it was intended or not, the declared goal of "self-cultivation," "spiritual awakening," or "enlightenment" gives the impression of an apolitical organization that centered on inner and personal well-being rather than a sociopolitical agenda. Nevertheless, in spite of their seemingly apolitical goals, the Japanese colonial authority subjected this organization to the same surveillance and suspicion that it did for other groups, which caused limitations in the scope and content of activities undertaken by the farmer's self-cultivation center. Yun Ch'iho lamented: "Even here [the farmers' self-cultivation center] we are hampered by the police for we are not given freedom to teach the national history and patriotic songs of Korea."[134]

That self-cultivation center in Sinch'on was considered to be a joint operation of the YMCA and YWCA, offering annual workshops for future leaders of

---

[130] "Copied from a recent letter received from Dr. Hugh Cynn in reply to my questions about the work of Induk Pak."

[131] Yu, *Han'guk YWCA undong*, p. 146; Kim, "1930-nyŏndae Hwang Aedŏk ŭi nongch'on saŏp kwa yŏsŏng undong," 155–6. Kim argues that the success of the rural work in Saemgol, Suwŏn was due not to the YWCA but to Ch'oe Yongsin and the residents of Saemgol.

[132] Kim Hwallan, *Kŭ pit sok ŭi chagŭn saengmyŏng* (A Little Life in that Light) (Seoul: Yŏwŏnsa, 1965), pp. 134–5.

[133] *Yun Ch'iho ilgi*, November 15, 1932; Chang, "Han'guk YMCA ŭi nongch'on chaegŏn saŏp," 244.

[134] *Yun Ch'iho ilgi*, November 15, 1932.

the rural community.¹³⁵ The first workshop for women (*nongch'on puyŏ chidoja suyangso*) was held in 1934.¹³⁶ This Korean-initiated workshop took place two years before the colonial state-sponsored organization, Chosŏn Kŭmyung Chohap Yŏnhaphoe, organized its own ten-day workshop for women (*puin kangsŭphoe*) in December 1936. The main goal of the four-week workshop was to cultivate the mental fortitude of the peasant women and expand their knowledge of household management. Those who received training were expected to share their knowledge with the other women in their villages and make efforts to correct everyday practices and improve the moral and economic life in the villages.¹³⁷ Pak Indŏk, Hwang Aedŏk, and Kim Hwallan were all on the roster of speakers for the workshop.¹³⁸ Twenty participants aged eighteen to forty enrolled in the first workshop. The content of the workshop closely reflected what was laid out in Pak Indŏk's 1932 book, *Danish Folk High School*, including classes on cultivating the mind (*chŏngsin suyang*), improving knowledge for better household management and child-rearing, and undertaking economic activities to assist with family finances.

The workshop had a notable impact on participants. Below are reflections from two of the women who attended:

I learned so much. I had lived without any standard idea about the concepts of time, hygiene, children's education, economy, love, or neighborhood. I realized I wasted a lot of time.... With the full strength of my will I was determined [to gain as much information as I could from the workshop], and I learned lots of skills through hands-on practice. I will convey what I was privileged to learn to many homes in my village whenever I can. (Hŏ Kyŏngsin from Hongch'ŏn, Kangwŏn Province)

My greatest wish in life was to put my hair up and wear high heels. I thought changing my appearance like that was what I needed to do to become a great woman. But I realized [through the workshop] that that was all vanity. I learned that I could be an active member of the community with a respectable character even within the rural

---

¹³⁵ Ch'ŏn, *Han'guk yŏsŏng kidokkyo sahoe undongsa*, pp. 57–8; and Hong Pyŏngsŏn, "Chŏngmal kungmin kodŭng hakkyo sik nongmin suyangso che 4-hoe saeng mojip e taehayŏ" (Regarding the Recruitment of Participants in the Farmers' Self-Cultivation Center that Modeled After the Danish Folk High School), *Ch'ŏngnyŏn* 15, no. 7 (October 1935): 12–13.

¹³⁶ Yun Ch'iho relays some gossip, suggesting that Kim Hwallan "is jealous of the too close attentions which Dr. H.C. [Hugh Cynn] pays to P.I.D. [Pak Indŏk]. He wrote in his diary on December 16, 1932: "with wife went to Miss Pak In Duk's Sunday Children Hall to hear her report of the work she has been doing for and among the village women. The new room just finished can seat 100 children. It was filled by men and women who are more or less in sympathy with the work of Miss P.I.D. She is certainly a talented woman. Most of the Ewha ladies – Miss Appenzeller to begin with – were there. Miss Helen Kim was conspicuous by her absence. Gossips say H.K. is jealous of the too close attentions which Dr. H.C. pays to P.I.D. P.I.D. has been ostracized by many for her having divorced her husband. But had she not done it, she would have been so buried either in the drudgeries or pleasures of her domestic life, that she could never have been able to go out and about to promote the welfare of rural women. God may have a great work for her to do."

¹³⁷ Kim, "1930-nyŏndae Hwang Aedŏk ŭi nongch'on saŏp kwa yŏsŏng undong," 157–8.

¹³⁸ *Kidok sinbo*, April 11, 1934. Cited from Kim, "1930-nyŏndae Hwang Aedŏk ŭi nongch'on saŏp kwa yŏsŏng undong," 156.

home.... I am determined to work for women and families who did not have the opportunity I had. (Pak Chŏngsuk from Wŏnju, Kangwŏn Province)[139]

Workshops for future women leaders in the rural community were an expedient option at a time when funding and personnel were scarce. And it was under these circumstances that Pak Indŏk once again demonstrated her ingenious skills for fund-raising to support her rural work. Pak was invited again by the US Student Volunteer Movement to speak at their quadrennial convention in January 1936, in Indianapolis, Indiana.[140] Around that same time she was also invited to speak at the 1936 Chain of Missionary Assemblies in Florida.[141] Just as she had done during her first global tour (1928–1931), Pak maximized the opportunity that these invitations presented and successfully extended her tour from November 1935 to September 1937 through her Christian friends' network while raising funds to support her rural work in Korea. During her tour she traveled about 80,000 miles and gave 642 presentations at "colleges and universities, high schools, churches, men's civic organizations, and women's clubs."[142] The main subject matter of her lectures was "the deplorable condition of farmers and their families in Korea." She would use her observations from traveling in the rural areas and describe Koreans' efforts at rural revitalization. She shared how she "had learned that one of the best ways to help raise spiritual and economic standards was first to provide help in a physical way. Since our farms were small, tractors were not practical but oxen or cows were needed to plow and to use as beasts of burden.... I usually ended my talks by saying that one co-operative cow on a Korean farm could do far more effective work than a thousand words."[143] Her talks proved to be very popular and compelling to her audiences. Pak was able to raise enough funds to purchase several cows that could be shared by farmers in the region.[144]

By the time Pak came back to Korea in September 1937, the second Sino-Japanese War had already broken out and the circumstances in Korea were rapidly changing. Japan's policy toward imperialization (*kōminka*) under the slogan "Japan and Korea as one body" (*naisen ittai*) was having a significant impact on everyday life. For example, new government regulations discouraged the study and use of Korean and required Japanese as the language of instruction in

---

[139] *Chosŏn chungang ilbo*, April 1, 1934. Cited from Kim, "1930-nyŏndae Hwang Aedŏk ŭi nongch'on saŏp kwa yŏsŏng undong," 158.
[140] She was one of the platform speakers at the convention where she "asserted in the course of her address that Christianity has brought much joy and happiness to the village women in Korea." "Eleven Koreans Attend Student Volunteer Convention," *The Korean Student Bulletin* (December – January 1935–1936): 3.
[141] Induk Pahk, *September Monkey* (New York: Harper & Brothers, 1954), p. 182.
[142] Pahk, *September Monkey*, p. 186.   [143] Pahk, *September Monkey*, pp. 186–7.
[144] In homage to the assistance these donors provided, the cows were named after the donor or the donor's hometown. Pahk, *September Monkey*, pp. 182–8.

"Go to the People": The Praxis of Gendered Rural Modernity 183

schools.[145] As Pak later recalled, "the most startling thing about the Korea to which I came back in September, 1937, was that I could not understand what the people, including my own daughters, were saying; nor could I make myself understood as everybody was speaking Japanese."[146] In addition, the Japanese Government-General subjected all Korean associations or organizations, including religious assemblies, to more restrictions than ever before. Shortly after Pak returned to Korea, she initiated a Bible study class for college men and women in her church in Seoul, but such classes were soon banned because Koreans "were not allowed to group a number of young people together under the sanction of a church for fear things other than religion might be discussed." Moreover, since Japanese was not used in the class, they were "violating another of the national pressures."[147] Furthermore, the Korea YMCA leadership began to urge its fellow Christians to adhere to the policy of *naisen ittai* and support soldiers on the battlefield.[148]

Under these circumstances, with gifts from her American friends and supporters, Pak managed to build two cottages in Yanggok, near Kimp'o in Kyŏnggi Province – one as a training center for rural women leaders, and the other as a teachers' residence. It was there in Yanggok that she first conducted classes for women from the surrounding villages.[149] She would commute from Seoul to Yanggok on the days when she taught classes. These were mostly in the winter months, when farmers had more free time. Other than that, not much information is available about this training program, which did not last long. As the Pacific War intensified and fuel became scarce, it was increasingly difficult for Pak to make the 30-mile commute by bus to Yanggok from Seoul. But perhaps more crucially, the village authorities in Yanggok requested that she shut down her cottages, presumably because of pressure from the Japanese authorities. She sold the cottages, and with those funds she established an institute for girls, Tŏkhwa Yŏsuk, in Seoul in 1941.[150] Though it is beyond the scope of this book, Pak closely worked with leading Japanese settlers in establishing Tŏkhwa Yŏsuk, and her advocacy for Japan began in earnest, ultimately earning her the label of a "collaborator."[151]

---

[145] Chŏng Chaech'ŏl, *Ilche ŭi taeHan'guk singminji kyoyuk chŏngch'aeksa* (The History of Educational Policy under Japanese Colonial Rule in Korea) (Seoul: Ilchisa, 1985), pp. 354–63, 423–32.
[146] Pahk, *September Monkey*, p. 194. For *kokugo* (national language) policy during the kōminka period, see Christina Yi, "National Language, Imperialization, and the Gendered Aporia of Empire," *positions* 24, no. 4 (November 2016): 813–37.
[147] Pahk, *September Monkey*, p. 195.
[148] Ku Chaok, "Chungdae siguk e chehaya" (In the Critical Political Times), *Ch'ŏngnyŏn* 17, no. 9 (September 1937): 2; and Hong Pyŏngsŏn, "Kungmin chŏngsin ch'ongdongwŏn kwa ch'onghu huwŏn" (Total Mobilization of People's Spirit and War Support from the Rear), *Ch'ŏngnyŏn* 6 (October 1938): 7.
[149] Pahk, *September Monkey*, pp. 195–6.   [150] Pahk, *September Monkey*, pp. 197–8.
[151] One of Pak's speeches in her support of Japanese imperial war is "Tonga yŏmyŏng kwa pando yŏsŏng" (The Dawn of Asia and Korean Women), *Tae tonga* 14, no. 3 (1942): 90–92.

Pak certainly demonstrated exceptional talents as a fund-raiser in the United States for her rural work. She was uniquely suited for undertaking the task not only because she was a very popular speaker, which was certainly an essential ingredient, but also because she was extraordinarily diligent in making and maintaining a professional and personal network of individuals and organizations overseas, which helped her multiply her opportunities to speak and raise funds. As a result, unlike other rural workers, Pak was unusually well-funded by patrons in the United States, who donated to support her rural projects. Unfortunately, for all of Pak's talent at fund-raising for her rural projects, there was little of substance left in the aftermath. To be sure, hostile political circumstances, especially after the second Sino-Japanese War, hindered progress in the rural work. Even the colonial state-sponsored rural campaign was transformed into a mechanism for total mobilization to support Japan's imperial wars.[152] However, the fact that she never based herself in the rural community, choosing to commute from her home in Seoul to the rural communities as an itinerant lecturer, significantly lessened the impact that she left on the rural movement and fueled the suspicion that urban-based intellectuals were unfit "outsiders" rather than true crusaders for the well-being of peasants.[153]

In this vein, Pak's rural work was placed in stark contrast with that of Ch'oe Yongsin in literary works of the time. On her death in January 1935, Ch'oe Yongsin was commemorated in the leading daily newspaper *Tonga ilbo* as a "pioneer of the V Narod Movement" in Korea, a key figure who had fully dedicated her time, energy, and will to the rural movement. The newspaper urged "intelligentsia women" to follow her example of self-sacrifice for the betterment of the nation.[154] The prominent male writer Sim Hun (1901–1936) wrote a popular novel, *Evergreen* (*Sangnoksu*), inspired by Ch'oe's life and work. Serialized in *Tonga ilbo* from September 10, 1935 to February 15, 1936, the novel tells the story of a group of young intellectuals devoted to revitalizing rural communities. Some of the characters in the novel are clearly based on actual people.[155] In particular,

---

[152] Chi, "Ilche ŭi kun'gukjuŭi p'asijŭm"; Mun, "Ilche malgi kwanbyŏn chapchi 'Kajŏng chiu'."
[153] There were common criticisms of "rural leaders" who did not actually work in the rural community along with peasants but acted as rural leaders. In his essay, Sin Hŭng'u made a counter argument that not all rural leaders need to be peasants themselves and that some could contribute to the rural movement with their vision and knowledge. He cited Danish pioneers, such as N. F. S. Grundtvig, who transformed the rural life not as a peasant but a pastor and spiritual leader. See Sin Hŭng'u, "Nongch'on chidoja sibi e taehayŏ" (Regarding the Controversy about Rural Leaders), *Ch'ŏngnyŏn* 12, no. 8 (September 1932): 3.
[154] *Chosŏn chungang ilbo*, March 3–4, 1935, 4.
[155] In his essay, Clark Sorensen traces the origin of the "peasant literature" proposed by Yi Sŏnghwan in 1925 in the literary journal Chosŏn ŭi mundan. See Clark Sorensen, "National Identity and the Creation of the Category of "Peasant" in Colonial Korea," in *Colonial Modernity in Korea*, eds. Gi-Wook Shin and Michael Robinson (Cambridge: Harvard University Press, 1999), p. 303. Later, the Korean Peasant Society (Chosŏn nongminsa) published the journal *Chosŏn nongmin* (December 1925–June 1930). The Korean Peasant Society was organized by intellectuals who were involved in the journal *Kyebŏk*. And *Kyebŏk*

the protagonist, Ch'ae Yŏngsin, a selfless and devoted rural worker, is modeled on Ch'oe Yongsin. The Ch'ae character is presented in sharp contrast to the character Paek Hyŏn'gyŏng, the general manager of the Korea YWCA, an elite woman educated in the United States. Paek is a stereotype of the "intellectual" rural reformer who claims to be a "friend" of the peasant women but nonetheless places an unbridgeable gulf between herself and the peasants through her Western-style clothing and manners.[156] While Ch'ae is repeatedly referred to as an "angel" in the novel, Paek is depicted as hypocritical, self-indulgent, and very Westernized in her lifestyle, speech, and attitude. Paek lives in Seoul in a "culture house" (*munhwa chut'aek*), referring to a Western-style brick house, where she enjoys life's pleasures, such as night tours on the Han River. With her luxurious urban lifestyle, Paek is the antithesis of Ch'ae, who lives in a rundown thatched-roof house in a remote village and works to exhaustion for the villagers. The male protagonist of the novel, Pak Tonghyŏk, criticizes the hypocrisy he sees in the way Paek undertakes for the peasants and the rural movement during the day, but every evening goes back to the city to indulge herself in the urban lifestyle of luxury.

The author of the novel never indicated that the character of Paek was based on an actual person; however, it may very well be that Paek is supposed to represent Pak Indŏk. Similar in character to "Paek," Pak was a woman educated in the United States who became a leading figure in the rural movement, serving as the executive secretary of the Rural Work Department of the General Board of the Methodist Church.[157] Further, the author's description of Paek's "culture house" is strikingly close to the home of Pak Indŏk, which is referred to as a "culture house" in an interview she gave to the popular magazine *Samch'ŏlli*.[158] Parallel to the portrayal of Paek as a "Westernized woman" in the novel, the interview shows some markers of "Western influences" on Pak Indŏk. For example, her responses to the reporter's questions are peppered with English. Readers are told that she plays piano or Hawai'ian guitar in her leisure time. She describes herself as physically active, enjoying hiking, swimming, and skating. The description of Pak's Western-style house, lifestyle, and attitude are uncannily similar to those of the character of Paek Hyŏn'gyŏng in *Evergreen*. Interestingly, the interview was published in *Samch'ŏlli* in August 1935. Shortly after its appearance, the novel *Evergreen* was serialized in *Tonga ilbo*, from September 10, 1935 to February 15, 1936, and it seems reasonable to infer that the character of Paek in *Evergreen* may

was run by the members of the Ch'ŏndogyo (Religion of the Heavenly Way). Yi Tonhwa is one of the key members of *Kyebŏk*.

[156] Yi Man'gyu, "Chosŏn samdae chonggyo konggwaron, kidokkyohoe ŭi kong kwa kwa," *Kaebyŏk* sin'gan 1 (November 1934): 27–31, 42, quoted on 30.

[157] "Copied from a recent letter received from Dr. Hugh Cynn in reply to my questions about the work of Induk Pak."

[158] *Samch'ŏlli* 7, no. 7 (August 1935): 82–5.

well have been inspired by Pak Indŏk and the portrayal of her informed by the interview in *Samch'ŏlli*.

Whether or not *Evergreen*'s contrasting portrayals of a rural-based reformer and an urban-based reformer are valid, it is important to understand such a novel in historical context. Sim's novel belongs to the genre of "peasant literature" (*nongmin sosŏl*), which was very popular in the 1930s; earlier examples include Yi Kwangsu's novel *Hŭk* (*Soil*), which was serialized in *Tonga ilbo* in 1932, and Yi Kiyŏng's novel *Kohyang* (*Hometown*), which was serialized in *Chosŏn ilbo* from 1933 to 1934. This genre of peasant literature incorporated an explicit didactic message about idealized modern womanhood by contrasting rural activists like Ch'oe Yongsin with the New Woman (*sin yŏsŏng*) in urban areas. As noted elsewhere, I purposely use the singular term "New Woman" to refer to the image constructed by (male) hegemonic discourses, in order to distinguish it from the plural term "New Women" when referring to actual historical figures.[159] In the view of these male writers, the ideal woman is often someone who sacrifices personal pleasure and dedicates herself completely to work for the nation and the poor peasants, as represented by Ch'ae Yŏngsin in *Evergreen*, or who becomes a factory worker, as in the figure of Insun in Yi Kiyŏng's novel *Hometown*.[160] In contrast, the New Woman embodies the opposite of the idealized woman who sacrifices for others. As Yi Kwangsu puts it in his novel *Soil*, "ten years ago [new] women talked about the moralistic stuff like patriotism and ideals, but those are now thrown into garbage."[161]

To be sure, some New Women may have fit this stereotype. The problem lies in the often exaggerated and oversimplified representation of the imagined New Woman, which, in turn, leads to a dismissal of the contributions of actual New Women to the rural movement, no matter how fleeting that contribution may have been. As a leading feminist whose divorce had scandalized Korean society, Pak Indŏk's "Westernized" behavior and lifestyle made her vulnerable to further criticism, as if being "Westernized" could not be compatible with patriotism in general and rural reform in particular.[162] Such public perceptions contributed to the condemnation of women intellectuals' vision for rural work

---

[159] Hyaeweol Choi, *New Women in Colonial Korea: A Sourcebook* (London: Routledge, 2013), p. 3. See also Chandra Talpade Mohanty, "Under Western Eyes: Feminist Scholarship and Colonial Discourses," *Feminist Review* 30 (Autumn 1988): 61–88, quoted on 62.

[160] Yi Kyŏngnan, "1930-nyŏndae nongmin sosŏl ŭl t'onghae pon 'singminji kŭndaehwa' wa nongmin saenghwal" ("Colonial Modernity" and Peasant Life Reflected in Peasant Literature in the 1930s), in *Ilche ŭi singmin chibae wa ilsang saenghwal*, ed. Yonsei University kukhak yŏn'guwŏn (Seoul: Hyean, 2004), pp. 404–5.

[161] See Yi Kwangsu, *Hŭk* (Seoul: Munhak kwa chisŏngsa, 2005), pp. 282–3.

[162] The perceived incomparability between feminism and nationalism was not unique in Korea. As feminist historian Sue Morgan summarizes, "all too often nationalist discourses have castigated feminism as antithetical to national independence." Sue Morgan, ed., *The Feminist History Reader* (London: Routledge, 2006), p. 33.

and to the dismissal of their interest in pursuing it as frivolous, hypocritical, or even useless.

Conclusion

Under the economic and sociocultural exigencies of rural Korea in the 1920s and 1930s, Protestant women intellectuals and students participated in the movement to restore the rural community and by extension the Korean nation. Their primary directive was "enlightenment" as the pathway to improving farmers' lives. With the vast majority of the rural population mired in illiteracy, deprivation and poverty, those elite women believed that the rural work in Korea at that particular moment should prioritize "enlightenment" rather than emphasize particular ideologies or resort to lofty, abstract ideals. Accordingly, their rural programs focused on basic literacy and numeracy training, practical knowledge about nutrition and disease prevention, side-jobs to help with family finances and use of various cooperatives. Improving domestic family life was particularly important as part of the rural enlightenment movement and contributed to empowering women as they gained more knowledge about nutrition, hygiene, family budgeting, and childrearing. Economic independence was another key lesson as the rural work encouraged women to take side-jobs to help with family finances. Through these programs, leaders of the rural work stressed the indispensable role women played in nourishing the family, enriching the family coffers, and contributing to a healthier, more stable community. In a broader context, women's participation in and contributions to the development of rural communities were seen as one of the linchpins in restoring Korea.

It is significant to note that the ultimate goal of "enlightenment," "self-cultivation," and "mental awakening" advocated by Protestant women intellectuals in their rural movement appeared in line with the colonial state's Rural Revitalization Campaign, which also emphasized "mental awakening" and "self-cultivation" in order to create "friendly feelings and hearty cooperation between Japanese and Koreans" and "sympathy, harmony, and mutual help between officials and the people."[163] In her research on rural youths in Japan and its colonies, Sayaka Chatani offers the insight that "[w]ith regard to the goal of formulating an image of rural youth as pillars of modern society, *anticolonial forces and colonial officials were in an unintended collaborative relationship,*" and *shūyō* (self-cultivation, K: *suyang*) as the basic principle in guiding youth groups was "a code for depoliticization and developing discipline."[164] This "unintended collaborative relationship" hinged on the

---

[163] Shin and Robinson, *Colonial Modernity in Korea*, p. 8.
[164] Sayaka Chatani, *Nation-Empire: Ideology and Rural Youth Mobilization in Japan and Its Colonies* (Ithaca: Cornell University Press, 2018), pp. 125, 194. Emphasis added.

seemingly depoliticized goal of enlightenment or self-cultivation, although one may suspect that Korean reformers' discourse on enlightenment might have impregnated their covert goals, such as nationalist consciousness and resistance to colonial rule. The absence of an overt political agenda in Protestant women intellectuals' rural campaign enabled them to carry out their mission even though they still faced constraints from the colonial authority. Perhaps, more importantly, as reflected in the feedback of those peasant women who participated in the farmers' self-cultivation workshop, what peasant women were most interested in was practical knowledge and skills that could actually help them improve the lives and communities.

Another prominent feature of Protestant women intellectuals' rural campaign was the fact that the international Christian network was instrumental in launching and maintaining the endeavors of Korean women intellectuals' in rural revitalization. As shown in the cases of Hwang Aedŏk and Pak Indŏk, personal connections and fund-raising with US church groups helped these educated Korean women secure funding to carry out their rural work, although such funding was "earmarked" for the ultimate goal of the spread of Christianity. Those connections were part of a much greater network that included the US foreign missions, the Woman's Christian Temperance Union, the Student Volunteer Movement, and the World YMCA and YWCA. This network enabled and fostered encounters between Korean and American women, creating a bridge that linked peasants in remote villages in Korea with white middle-class women in the United States and beyond. The YWCA was one of the most visible parts of this network, with local, regional, and international levels of organization. Similar to the Korea YMCA's rural work, the Korea YWCA was "international in character and outlook."[165] Its key leaders were inspired by foreign models, especially Danish and US examples, but tried to adapt what they had learned and observed in those countries to the particular conditions found in Korea. Kim Hwallan's doctoral thesis succinctly illustrates this mindfulness about the need to adapt foreign practices to the local conditions. There was also a deep awareness that the rich heritage of Korean culture could be a mechanism for restoring Korea and helping people live the best possible lives despite the disruptive transition to modernity and stringent colonial oppression.[166] Financial constraints and the rapidly changing political situation, especially after the second Sino-Japanese War, curtailed and eventually eliminated women's rural work. Nevertheless, their discourse on the necessity of rural revitalization and their concrete proposals and actions, which

---

[165] de Ceuster, "The YMCA's Rural Development Program in Colonial Korea."
[166] Kim, "Rural Education for the Regeneration of Korea," pp. 116–18.

emphasized basic practical knowledge along with renewed appreciation for Korea's native culture, showed their goals and struggles in pursuit of a locally sensible modernity – one that was inspired, facilitated, and empowered by transnational encounters but was still rooted in native traditions and naked realities of rural Korea.[167]

---

[167] Helen Schneider's work on educated Chinese women's engagement in rural work shows a similar pattern in that they "indigenized or localized foreign knowledge about how to reform families originally learned from their missionary teachers." Helen Schneider, "Raising the Standards of Family Life: Ginling Women's College and Christian Social Service in Republican China," in *Divine Domesticities: Christian Paradoxes in Asia and the Pacific*, eds. Hyaeweol Choi and Margaret Jolly (Canberra: ANU Press, 2014), pp. 113–39, quoted on p. 114.

Conclusion

The first feminist magazine, *Sin yŏja* (*New Woman*), was founded in 1920. Its founding as well as its demise only one year later were emblematic of some of the major features of the gender politics to come – namely, Christian connections, a transnational outlook, and an interrupted project of modernity. Leading figures in founding and running the magazine included Kim Wŏnju (aka Kim Iryŏp, 1896–1971), Na Hyesŏk (1896–1948), Pak Indŏk (1897–1980), Sin Chullyŏ (1898–1980), and Kim Hwallan (1899–1970). All except Na were graduates of Ewha Girls' School, the flagship Methodist mission school for girls, and pursued advanced learning in Japan or the United States. *Sin yŏja* distinguished itself from previous women's magazines by assembling an editorial and administrative staff comprised entirely of women, except for a single male advisor, Yang Uch'on. In congratulatory remarks at the founding of *Sin yŏja*, Alice Appenzeller (1885–1950), the principal of Ewha Girls' School, called it "the first magazine which they [women] can call their very own."[1] Indeed, *Sin yŏja* was "their very own" in the sense that the magazine gave women an outlet through which they could put forward their own voices, expressing their views instead of being represented, judged, or admonished by Korean men or Western missionaries. Deploring the inhumane treatment of women for thousands of years and joining the "outcry of humankind" for reform (*kaejo*) after World War I, the magazine literally and symbolically opened the era for the New Woman (*sin yŏsŏng*) with a profound sense of historical agency in asserting the ideas, visions, and sensibilities of women themselves.[2]

From its inception, *Sin yŏja* invited women of any social standing to contribute, stating that the magazine belonged to all Korean women (*Chosŏn yŏja chŏnch'ae ŭi kŏt*) and was not the exclusive property of the members of the editorial board (*p'yŏnjip tongin*).[3] Thus, in the face of the general denial of basic human rights for women, the magazine offered the opportunity for any woman to voice publicly her daily experiences and concerns that arose from

---

[1] Alice Appenzeller, "Ch'uk Sin yŏja" (Congratulations to *Sin yŏja*), *Sin yŏja* 1 (1920): 10–11.
[2] *Sin yŏja* 1 (1920): 2–3. [3] *Sin yŏja* 2 (1920): 64.

Conclusion

those experiences. In addition, the spirit and content of the magazine were transnational in the sense that the editorial team was keenly aware of the rapidly changing world, especially the political, intellectual, and cultural trends in the aftermath of World War I. One way it gave its readers a view into the larger world was to translate many pieces of foreign literature. *Sin yŏja* carried "aphorisms and dictums, anecdotes, jokes, and myths and legends of Western origin, all functioning to widen the literary and cultural horizons of readers beyond the narrow confines of Korea."[4] The magazine strove to make known to female readers the remarkable accomplishments of women in ancient history, as well as the distinguished careers of contemporary women worldwide, so that readers would awaken to their own potential as free, independent, and capable beings.

It is also important to note, however, that *Sin yŏja* was inconsistent in putting forward the globally circulated feminist agenda. The literary scholar Ji-Eun Lee offers an analysis of the content of the magazine that demonstrates how its progressive outlook often seems circumscribed. For one thing, the magazine never openly advocated some key items in the feminist agenda, such as legal or political rights. Its vision for new womanhood "was much more moderate and centered on more practical and mundane elements."[5] For example, an article entitled "Discussion on Women's Social Responsibility" talks about the role of women in transforming society, but its practical advice centers on a woman's role as a housewife and a mother in managing her house work, aided by modern scientific knowledge about hygiene, nutrition, and childcare. The article also details women's responsibility to "avoid pride in oneself, be prudent and humble, obey men, and put learning into practice."[6] In a nutshell, "old forms and ideas can reappear and remain highly valued under a new veneer."[7] In this vein, the overall tone and strategy of the magazine is captured in the cartoon in Figure 5.1.

The cartoon depicts the daily life of Kim Iryŏp, the founder of *Sin yŏja*, drawn by her fellow feminist Na Hyesŏk. Kim and Na were two of the most prominent feminists in early-twentieth-century Korea.[8] They were fiercely outspoken, challenging the patriarchal social norms and practices and forcefully advocating for women's rights. These two women also led exceptionally dramatic personal lives that embodied their aspirations for modern womanhood

---

[4] Yung-Hee Kim, "In Quest of Modern Womanhood: Sinyŏja, A Feminist Journal in Colonial Korea," *Korean Studies* 37 (2013): 44–78, quoted on 73.

[5] Ji-Eun Lee, *Women Pre-Scripted: Forging Modern Roles through Korean Print* (Honolulu: University of Hawai'i Press, 2015), p. 102.

[6] Lee, *Women Pre-Scripted*, p. 99.   [7] Lee, *Women Pre-Scripted*, p. 102.

[8] Yu Chinwŏl, *Kim Iryŏp ŭi Sin yŏja yŏn'gu* (A Study of Sin yŏja by Kim Iryŏp) (Seoul: P'urŭn sasang, 2006); Jin Y. Park, *Women and Buddhist Philosophy: Engaging Zen Master Kim Iryŏp* (Honolulu: University of Hawai'i, 2017); and Sŏ Chŏngja, comp., *Chŏngwŏl Ra Hyesŏk chŏnjip* (Anthology of Chŏngwŏl Ra Hyesŏk) (Seoul: Kukhak charyowŏn, 2001).

Figure 5.1 New woman
Panel 1 She makes full use of the limited time given to her, reading until midnight
Panel 2 She composes poems while cooking
Panel 3 She thinks about the successful future of *Sin yŏja* while mending clothes
Panel 4 She works on an article throughout the night until dawn
Source: *Sin yŏja* 4 (1920): 53–6

and simultaneously reflected the harsh criticism and backlash each faced throughout her adult life. In a significant way, the cartoon represents the beginning of their feminist movement, signaling the heated debates that

Conclusion 193

would take place on "old" and "new" womanhood in the 1920s. In this portrayal of Kim's daily routine, she is "burdened with several tasks" that combine her household duties, e.g., cooking and sewing, with her role as the editor of *Sin yŏja*.[9] The cartoon clearly represents an emergent, hybrid womanhood combining the "old" womanhood that was centered on domestic duties with the new roles for women in the public sphere as writers, editors, and artists. It was this fluid, dynamic, and paradoxical space between old norms and new ideals, and between compliance and resistance that women had to navigate in their lives and work.

In the same issue in which this cartoon appears, there is an "announcement" (*yego*) advertising the next issue (volume 5) of the magazine, scheduled to appear in the following year, 1921. The *yego* announces that volume 5 will carry a translation of the work by the "famous writer from northern Europe who is most authoritative regarding the woman question (*puin munje*)."[10] This "famous writer from northern Europe" refers to Henrik Ibsen and the work that was translated was his play, *A Doll's House*, which had become a global sensation after its first performance in Copenhagen in 1879.[11] The play struck a chord that resonated across national and cultural boundaries,[12] and Korea was no exception. It was Na Hyesŏk who initiated the popularization of Nora, the protagonist of the play, as an icon of new womanhood in colonial Korea when she referred to Nora as one of the "ideal women" in an essay that she wrote in 1914 while studying Western painting at Joshibijutsu Daigaku in Japan. At that time, the Japanese feminist magazine, *Seitō* (Blue Stockings, 1911–1916), was highly influential in shaping the discourse on gender politics, and Ibsen's work was a common feature of that heated debate.[13] The influence that *Seitō* and its leading feminists, such as Hiratsuka Raichō and Yosano Akiko, had on Na is evident in her essay.[14] As I discussed in Chapter 1, the global popularity of *A Doll's House* and the character of Nora signaled an exhilarating shift toward women's liberation, but there was, at the same time, deep anxiety about the far-reaching impact that liberation would have on women and family. Unfortunately, the planned publication of *A Doll's House* in Korean translation

---

[9] *Sin yŏja* 4 (1920): 53–6.   [10] *Sin yŏja* 4 (1920): 57.
[11] Joan Templeton, *Ibsen's Women* (Cambridge: Cambridge University Press, 1997); Julie Holledge, "Addressing the Global Phenomenon of A Doll's House: An Intercultural Intervention," *Ibsen Studies* 8, no. 1 (2008): 13–28.
[12] The first mention of Ibsen in Korea was in Ch'oe Namsŏn's (1890–1957) Korean translation of the Japanese author Uchimura Kanzō's (1861–1930) "The Goal of the Study of Geography" in a magazine, *Sonyŏn* (Youth), in 1909. For the reception of *A Doll's House* in East Asia, see Saburo Sato, "Ibsen's Impact on Novelist Shimazaki Tōson," *Comparative Literature Studies* 33, no. 1 (1996): 75–81; Kamaluddin Nilu, (2008) "A Doll's House in Asia: Juxtaposition of Tradition and Modernity," *Ibsen Studies* 8, no. 2 (2008): 112–29.
[13] Jan Bardsley, *The Bluestockings of Japan: New Woman Essays and Fiction from Seitō, 1911–1916* (Ann Arbor: Center for Japanese Studies, University of Michigan, 2007).
[14] Na Hyesŏk, "Isangjŏk puin" (Ideal Woman), *Hakchigwang* 3 (December 1914): 13–14.

in *Sin yŏja* never came to fruition. The magazine had to be shut down due to financial difficulties. A Korean translation of Ibsen's play was eventually published in serialized form in *Maeil sinbo*, the Japanese colonial state-run newspaper, in 1921 at the urging of the editorial staff of *Sin yŏja*.[15] If it had been published in *Sin yŏja*, it could have helped further advance the magazine's original mission to awaken (*kaksŏng*) Korean women by introducing new perspectives. Still, the fact that the *Sin yŏja* editorial board took the initiative to bring *A Doll's House* to a Korean audience firmly shows that the pioneering women of *Sin yŏja* were actively engaged in the transnational flow and consumption of ideas.

In this book, I have taken a transnational perspective in examining the formation of modern gender norms and practices in Korea under Japanese colonial rule. Building on previous studies that illuminate the intersecting dynamics of the forces of nationalism, colonialism, and modernity in reshaping gender ethics and practices, this book further complicates those dynamics by investigating the influence of non-colonial Western powers, especially the United States, in shaping discourse on and experience of women. There is no question that Japan as Korea's colonizer exerted powerful influences in sociopolitical, legal, administrative, economic, and medical domains. However, the colonial state's cultural hegemony, especially in the domains of gender norms and practices, is complicated for at least two reasons. One is that, unlike the examples of Euro-American colonization in history, in this case, the colonizer (Japan) and the colonized (Korea) had "racial, cultural and religious affinities."[16] More specifically, for centuries they had shared Confucian-prescribed gender norms, some of which were considered backward and oppressive in the Euro-centric discourse of "civilization and enlightenment" in late-nineteenth century Japan and Korea. Given this distinctive history, the binary juxtaposition of the colonizer as superior and the colonized as inferior did not work for gender relations. The other is related to the fact that Japan was a latecomer in Euro-centric imperial system, so Japan was "socially and culturally kept outside it."[17] In this vein, as various chapters of the book demonstrate, Japanese models or references to modern domesticity or gender relations are surprisingly scarce in Korean print media. Instead, Euro-American models and sources prevailed, in part because Koreans perceived the original source of modernity, including modern womanhood, as being in the West. Thus, I have argued in this book that Japan's colonial power and its

---

[15] *Maeil sinbo*, January 23, 1921.

[16] Jin-kyung Park, "Picturing Empire and Illness: Biomedicine, Venereal Disease and the Modern Girl in Korea under Japanese Colonial Rule," *Cultural Studies* 28, no. 1 (2014): 108–41, quoted on 108.

[17] Jordan Sand, "Subaltern Imperialists: The New Historiography of the Japanese Empire," *Past and Present* 225, no. 1 (2014): 273–88, quoted on 275.

cultural hegemony in gender relations should be understood against the background of the existence of Euro-American cultural influences as non-colonial powers that had begun even before Korea was colonized by Japan in 1910. In particular, Protestant Christian missionaries, who began to arrive in Korea from 1884, were one of the key conveyors of Western modernity and made a lasting impact on the shape of modern gender relations.

In an effort to move beyond the nexus of metropole and colony, I have specifically focused on the flow of ideas, people, materials, and images to investigate the roles that transnational encounters played in the evolution of modern gender ideology, domestic practices, a sense of locality in the modern world, and the newly found space in the public and global sphere. The analysis has centered on the role of the global Protestant Christian network in constructing modern womanhood. Diverging from the conventional understanding of modernity as leading to greater "secularization," this book puts forward the thesis that Protestant Christianity, introduced in Korea in the late-nineteenth century, was one of the key facilitators enabling women to experience the modern. In my use of the terms "modernity" or "the modern," I do not mean a singularly defined concept but rather what constituted the modern in people's own narratives and experience. In Koreans' perceptions, the Western missionaries were viewed as the bearers of advanced civilization embodied especially in the modern institutions of education and medicine. In this vein, Christianity, civilization, and "the West" all blurred together into a single idea associated with modernity.

In this book, I have used the concept of "Protestant modernity" as a heuristic device to unpack the complex dynamics that shaped modern gender ideology and practices. I define "Protestant modernity" as an ideology that upholds the linear historical movement toward modernity in material and technological aspects but that also places the moral and spiritual role of Christianity at the core of that enterprise. A key element of the concept is the coexistence of the spiritual and the secular. For Korean women, conversion to Christianity was instrumental for gaining access to "secular modernity" in the form of modern education, scientific home management, economic independence, opportunities to travel, and a new lifestyle, all of which were facilitated through missionary organizations and personal networks. Emphasizing the intertwined dynamics between religious faith and secular/material experiences, this book makes the case that religion should be seriously considered in the discussion of "colonial modernity" and illustrates how the global Christian network played a critical part in fashioning modern gender relations within and beyond the constraints of the Japanese colonial state.

In my analysis, I have not ignored the impact of the colonial governance. Rather, I have attended to gender politics as it emerged under the jurisdiction of the Japanese colonial authority but within the context of powerful influences of

Euro-American cultures throughout the world. I suggest that modern gender relations in Korea were constructed through the dynamic interaction of Japanese colonial policies with the continuing legacy of Confucian tradition, or what might be more appropriately labelled the re-Confucianization of gender relations adjusted for the new era, and the rising influence of popular Western modernity. As detailed in Chapter 1, the most powerful gender ideology in twentieth-century Korea, "wise mother, good wife" (*hyŏnmo yangch'ŏ*), emerged from diverse roots: gender norms and practices drawn from the Confucian ideal of "womanly virtue," the Meiji gender ideology of *ryōsai kenbo*, and the Victorian notion of true womanhood. Commonly understood as the "traditional" gender norm of Korea from the Chosŏn dynasty, "wise mother, good wife" was, in fact, a modern construct that came out of colonial and transcultural influences at the turn of the twentieth century. Significantly, the ideology was decidedly not "modern," as it lacked emphasis on selfhood, political equality, or legal rights – key components of modernity and emerging feminist thought. Still, it helped women expand the scope of their lives and the work of mothers and wives under the banner of the "modern home" and "modern family." Home was not simply the site of conventional domestic duties. It was recreated as a space where women could exercise power and authority, and there was an acknowledgment of the value of women having scientific learning and household management skills for the betterment of the family and by extension the nation. In this way new, modern practices were brought into alignment with the old norms. In other words, what seemed to be *modern* served the maintenance and revision of an inherently conservative gender ideology. I will discuss the resilience of patriarchy below, but the power and influence of the "wise mother, good wife" still reverberates in contemporary South Korea. The "*new* wise mother, good wife" is expected to be physically attractive, well-informed for the sake of her children's education, and financially savvy in order to enhance family wealth. Those qualifications, updated for the present time, did not, however, signal any significant shift in the core ideas of the traditional gendered domain, which remained largely unchanged.[18]

Transnational influences were also manifest in everyday material practices in the "modern home," as discussed in Chapter 2. As with gender ideology, the image of the modern home was created from many sources. The Protestant missionaries' Western-style brick houses outfitted with imported household furnishings were objects of deep curiosity and fascination, presenting myriad "modern" items – clocks, rugs, wallpaper, sewing machines, rocking chairs,

---

[18] The Japanese historian Koyama Shizuko echoes a similar trend in Japan when she argues that "the notion of 'good wife' and 'wise mother' remains very much the prevailing expectation today." Koyama Shizuko, *Ryōsai Kenbo: The Educational Ideal of "Good Wife, Wise Mother" in Modern Japan*, trans. Stephen Filler (Boston: Brill 2013), quoted on p. 7.

organs. These were household accoutrements that were well beyond the means of the vast majority of Koreans, but they nevertheless inspired new ideas and images of the modern home.

The 1915 Home Exhibition in Seoul organized by the Japanese colonial government was a presentation of the scientifically designed "modern home" on a much larger scale. Koreans in cities and rural communities alike were strongly encouraged by Japanese colonial offices to see the models presented at the Exhibition and reform their own homes. And yet the models presented were not primarily Japanese. The exhibition prominently featured Western models and designs, reflecting Japan's desire to show its prowess in achieving "modernity" by demonstrating how quickly and thoroughly it had caught up with Euro-American countries. Interestingly, the exhibition staged in Seoul was almost identical to one in Tokyo several months earlier, for which there was an accompanying booklet entitled "The Ideal Home" (*Risō no katei*). In that booklet, Japanese experts criticized conventional houses in Japan for their lack of rationality, functionality, and conduciveness to family bonding. These traits were at the core of modernity, and any home that lacked them was viewed as inadequate for the modern era. However, such criticisms were nowhere to be found in the media coverage of the 1915 Home Exhibition in Seoul. Instead, the Seoul exhibition showcased Japan's status as a modern nation on a par with Euro-American countries. In doing so, the Japanese colonial power unwittingly revealed its *cultural* marginality by adopting Western models within the presumed hierarchy among imperial powers.

Given this, it is perhaps no mystery why Japanese models of home and domesticity were conspicuously absent in Korean print materials. Popular magazines from that time disproportionally feature Euro-American houses and domestic practices. These practices were frequently introduced and interpreted by Korean elites who had seen modern homes and family relations in person during their stays and travel in Europe and the United States. The influence of the United States in shaping modern domesticity in Korea is particularly evident in the establishment of home economics as a discipline at Ewha Women's Professional School. Again, the US foreign missionary network was instrumental. The network sponsored the travel of Ava Milam, a home economist from Oregon Agricultural College (OAC), when she toured East Asia. She would go on to help establish home economics throughout East Asia as well as overseeing the training of future Asian home economists at OAC through a scholarship program specifically designed to support Asian woman students. Milam's far-reaching impact continued in postcolonial Korea through training more home economists and offering assistance with reconstruction of home economics after World War II (see Figure 5.2). She was bestowed an Award for Distinguished Service in 1968 by Yonsei University where her former student, Ch'oe Isun, was

Figure 5.2 Ava Milam with her Korean students during her visit to South Korea in 1948
Source: Ava Milam Clark Papers, Oregon State University Libraries Special Collections & Archives Research Center

Dean of the College of Home Economics.[19] In a significant way, the US missionary work was a consistently powerful force in shaping "modern domesticity" in Korea from the late-nineteenth century through the Japanese colonial era and into postcolonial South Korea.

Gender norms and the material practices embedded in modern domesticity were the result of "border crossing" in both the literal and the figurative sense – between nations, between the old and the new, between tradition and modernity, between native culture and foreign culture, and between the individual and

[19] "Yonsei University in Korea Bestows Award for Distinguished Service," Box 106, Folder, "Milam Clark, Ava B," Ava Milam Clark Papers, Oregon State University Libraries Special Collections & Archives Research Center.

the collective. One of the most radical changes that Korean women experienced in the modern era was leaving home to receive an education. In a relatively short period of time, women went from being relegated to the private sphere of the home to gaining modern knowledge at formal educational institutions. A small minority even crossed national borders to pursue higher degrees. They traveled not only to Japan, the most common destination for study, but also to China, North America, Europe, and Australia. Many of these women came from very humble family origins, and they emerged as a new class of elite women. By crossing domestic borders within and beyond the circuit of the metropole and the colony in pursuit of modern knowledge, they paved the way for women to enter modern professions in fields such as home economics, medicine, nursing, music, arts, education, sociology, and religion. These border crossings were not merely about intellectual endeavors; it was also deeply emotional, material, and intercultural. Here again, the global Christian network played a crucial role by bringing students into Christian schools, giving them information on admission policies and living conditions overseas, providing full or partial scholarships, and offering social assistance, often through religious organizations, which comprised informal networks that helped them adjust to their new academic and cultural environments. This global Christian network also enabled a few prominent Korean women to travel the world as public speakers or representatives at international Christian conferences.

The transnational experiences those elite women had as students, speakers, and travelers provided them with the impetus for rethinking gender norms related to family, work, the materiality of everyday life, and bodily practices, as well as to the nation. Ironically, their direct exposure to foreign societies and cultures sharpened their sense of locality as well as their own national and racial identities. In other words, these Korean women intellectuals became even more aware than before of the drastically different conditions in colonized Korea after their own unmediated interactions with people and institutions in Euro-American and Asian societies. On returning to Korea, their sharpened sense of local and national conditions was put to work in social and educational reforms. Chapter 4 discussed the Rural Revitalization Movement, with many local projects spearheaded by these women. While it is hard to measure the extent of the impact they had at that time, it is important to recognize that their international experience, fostered by global Christian organizations, provided them with intellectual, institutional, and financial resources that enabled them to envision and carry out projects to improve the lives of Korean peasants in the late 1920s and 1930s. In particular, the Danish model gained a passionate following among Korean reformers. Although the historical, political, and economic circumstances were drastically different in Korea compared to those found in Denmark, the Danish emphasis on national history, language, cultural traditions, and religion, as well as the high value placed on the work done by peasants and manual laborers, became key guidelines for rural revitalization in Korea. The participation of women reformers in this rural program was often channeled into "woman's work," which was centered on improving the lives of women and children by reforming the family through the application of scientific and hygienic knowledge and rational and efficient governance. In this "woman's work," women reformers envisioned the domestic sphere as the foundation for building a healthy nation fostered by the morality and resourcefulness of women.

In this book, I have tried to bring to light the voices and experiences of elite Korean women by analyzing the ways in which they selected, resisted, or appropriated both native and foreign ideas and practices in constructing modern gender relations under Japanese colonial rule. As was the case elsewhere, the "woman question" that emerged in late-nineteenth-century Korea was an integral part of the nationalist project to build a modern nation-state. In that project, women were portrayed as backward, ignorant, and oppressed, in contrast to the portrayal of the presumably advanced Western women as "secular, liberated and in control of their own lives."[20] To overcome the backwardness that was signified by the despicable treatment of women under the "doctrine of inferiority of women," Korean male pundits advocated for the education of women.[21] Nonetheless, male-dominant public discourse also displayed alarmed concern about "educated women" who were too "modernized," "Westernized," or "Americanized." To say that someone was "Westernized" generally meant that she had lost touch with tradition and national authenticity. In Korea, a view had developed in which women were expected to be the foundation of the nation in their capacity as mothers of the next generation. Given their centrality in the future development of an independent Korea, women becoming "Westernized" caused deep anxiety, regardless of whether it reflected reality. This is one reason why it is imperative, in the discussion of modern gender relations, to investigate what "the West" was in the perceptions of Koreans, in tandem with Japanese colonial dominance.

Setting aside the complexity and diversity of "the West," it is clear that the way Koreans perceived "the West" was profoundly connected to the idea of modernity. In this book, I have highlighted Protestant missionary groups as one of the key agencies representing "the West." They largely came from the United States, Canada, the United Kingdom, and Australia, with US

---

[20] Dorothy Ko points out how the "identification of women with backwardness and dependency acquired a new urgency in the May Fourth-New Culture period (1915–27)" and argues that "the deep-seated image of the victimized 'feudal' women has arisen in part from an analytical confusion that mistakes normative prescriptions for experienced realities." See Dorothy Ko, *Teachers of the Inner Chambers* (Stanford: Stanford University Press, 1994), pp. 1–3.

[21] Yun Ch'iho, *Yun Ch'iho ilgi* (Diary of Yun Ch'iho), December 12, 1893.

missionaries being the largest and most influential group. It is important to note that evangelical missionaries were deeply concerned about the impact of modern secular forces that they thought would result in a "decadent" lifestyle, immorality, and, most importantly, loss of religious faith. While prioritizing evangelization, however, what they did went beyond their religious mission. They provided various services in modern education, medicine, and social welfare programs as part of their evangelical efforts and also in response to the pressure of the local people. As a result, as Ruth Brouwer argues: "[A]t the same time that Christianity was being jettisoned by many self-conscious moderns in the West, it was serving as a modernizing vehicle among various colonized and non-Western people."[22] The religion-based "modern" institutions that missionaries founded – schools, clinics, and social service centers – contributed significantly to the image of the West and Christianity that was being amalgamated with the idea of modernity. In fact, the impact of US missionary groups on the formation of modern institutions and values is unparalleled. As Ian Tyrrell observes: "A large part of American expansion took the form not of political or even economic penetration but of the spread of institutions and cultural values. The most obvious examples of cultural penetration were the missionary groups."[23]

When it comes to women's history, the legacy of the Protestant missionaries has been central in understanding the intellectual, cultural, and institutional roots that shaped modern womanhood in Korea. As has been illustrated in each of the preceding chapters, it was often the global Christian network that facilitated the flow of ideas, materials, and people. Rather than "Westernizing" them, I have argued, Korean women's border-crossing experiences sharpened their sense of their own national and racial identity. Some of those elite women I have examined in this book tended to make a conscious effort to emphasize Korea's "traditional heritage" and the question of relevance of foreign ideas to local conditions in Korea. In a significant way, their national identity was *transnationally* articulated.[24]

One prominent example of this dynamic is the politics of clothing. The common stereotype Koreans had of women who had been educated overseas was that they were fully "Westernized."[25] Their Western-style dress was taken

---

[22] Ruth Compton Brouwer, *Modern Women Modernizing Men* (Vancouver: UBC Press, 2002), p. 3.
[23] Ian Tyrrell, *Woman's World/Woman's Empire: The Woman's Christian Temperance Union in International Perspective, 1880–1930* (Chapel Hill: University of North Carolina Press, 1991), p. 2.
[24] Chih-ming Wang, *Transpacific Articulations: Student Migration and the Remaking of Asian America* (Honolulu: University of Hawai'i, 2013), p. 20.
[25] Chong Bum Kim, "Preaching the Apocalypse in Colonial Korea: The Protestant Millennialism of Kil Sŏn-ju," in *Christianity in Korea*, eds. Robert E. Buswell Jr. and Timothy S. Lee (Honolulu: University of Hawai'i Press, 2006), p. 149. Kim makes a brief note that "wholesale Westernization" can be found only in "the elite" especially those who "went to study in the United States."

as a marker of being unpatriotic and self-indulgent. In truth, however, while studying overseas, the vast majority of Korean women chose to wear *hanbok*, the traditional Korean dress, especially on formal occasions when photographs were taken.

Ch'oe Isun (Figure 5.3) was featured in a full page of the Oregon Agricultural College school yearbook, *The Beaver*. In that portrait she wears the traditional *hanbok*, and the accompanying text says of her: "The best-liked of foreign students ... described as 'unobtrusive but sweet and very friendly' by her Snell Hall friends ... she is proud of her native land."[26] A group photograph of Barbour Scholarship recipients at the University of Michigan shows Kim Meri and Ko Hwanggyŏng in *hanbok* (Figure 5.4).[27] For her graduation ceremony at the University of Stockholm, Ch'oe Yŏngsuk also wore a *hanbok* (Figure 5.5).[28] Certainly one can find photographs of Korean women students dressed in Western clothing,[29] but it seems that Korean women students most often wore *hanbok* for their college yearbooks, graduation albums, club activities, and social meetings.

The *hanbok* was a marker of Korean identity. It instantly signified these women as Korean, and, by extension, it helped distinguish Korean traditions from those other cultures. Wearing a *hanbok* may have been a conscious choice that Korean women made to demonstrate their national authenticity, but it should be noted that Korean male students in the United States, for example, didn't seem to feel compelled to reflect their national origin through their clothing, for they uniformly dressed in Western suits. In *The Birth of the Modern World*, Chris Bayly points out that men adopted the Western or modern dress code very quickly. He calls it "conforming to standards." For example, in 1780, "the most powerful men in the world were dressed in a large variety of different types of garment.... By 1914, a growing number of the most important men operating in public arenas wore Western-style clothes wherever they lived."[30]

Women did not make similar choices in their clothing. Despite the modern changes, women continued to be associated with the domestic and the traditional. The Western suit that Korean men wore was decidedly a public bodily act to associate themselves with modernity, privilege, and power. For women, however, adopting Western bodily practices in fashion and hairstyles invited

---

[26] *The Beaver 1937*, Ava Milam Clark Papers, Oregon State University Archives, Corvallis, Oregon.
[27] A photograph of 1932–33, fol. 1931–1940, Box, Barbour Scholarships for Oriental Women Committee photograph series, the Bentley Historical Library, University of Michigan.
[28] *Tonga ilbo*, November 29, 1931.
[29] For example, in a group photograph with the members of the Philosophy Club at Wesleyan College, Pak Indŏk is dressed in Western-style clothing. "Deceased folders" for Pahk, Mrs. Induk, AB. 1928, The Alumnae Center, Wesleyan College.
[30] C. A. Bayly, *The Birth of the Modern World 1780–1914* (Malden: Blackwell Publishing, 2004), pp. 12–19, quoted on 13.

Figure 5.3 Ch'oe Isun
Source: *The Beaver* (1937), Ava Milam Clark Papers, Oregon State University Libraries Special Collections & Archives Research Center

public scrutiny.[31] Not only Korean male pundits but foreign missionaries in Korea held similar views on women's sartorial choices. In his 1906 essay "Women's Rights in Korea," Homer Hulbert (1863–1949), an American missionary, condemned Korean women's attempts to "imitate the foreigner" by wearing the "distastefully coordinated Western style dress" in their desire to be liberated, to be educated, and to speak up.[32] This comment reflects the broad tendency of Western men as well as Korean male intellectuals to frown on "oriental women" who opted for Western clothing, hairstyles, or ways of speech. Given the broader discursive field in which the words, bodies, and

---

[31] For the politics of Western/native dress code from a comparative perspective, see Margot Badran, "Gendering the Secular and Religious in Modern Egypt: Woman, Family, and Nation," in *Religion, the Secular, and the Politics of Sexual Difference*, eds. Linell E. Cady and Tracy Fessenden (New York: Columbia University Press, 2013), p. 107.

[32] Homer Hulbert, "Women's Rights in Korea," *Korea Review* 6, no. 2 (February 1906): 51–9.

Figure 5.4 Barbour Scholarship recipients: Kim Meri and Ko Hwanggyŏng (third and eighth from the left in the first row), 1933–1934
Source: HS838, UM Barbour, photograph by Rentschler, Bentley Historical Library, University of Michigan

Figure 5.5 Ch'oe Yŏngsuk
Source: *Tonga ilbo*, November 29, 1931

lives of women were intensively scrutinized, Korean female students' choice of the *hanbok* may be understood as a distinctively gendered bodily practice.

Wearing a *hanbok*, however, does not mean that these women intellectuals conformed to the male-dominant discourse. Some women strategically embodied "Koreanness" by wearing the *hanbok* and emphasizing Korean aesthetics and traditions as the foundation of modern Korea, effectively undermining the exaggerated image of the foreign-educated woman as running away from tradition and Koreanness. It is important to understand that when these women emphasized "tradition," they did not mean all elements of "tradition," for they certainly criticized certain oppressive customs imposed on women for centuries. Rather, they were attempting to strike a delicate balance between the native and the foreign in envisioning a new Korea. Those who traveled overseas were in a position to compare Korea with other societies. They also gained a realistic understanding of Western societies through direct exposure to those societies and their people. Reports and comments of these Korean sojourners reveal that, while they appreciated foreign models and practices if they were relevant for Korea, they were also critical of sociocultural features of Western societies, such as excessive materialism, racism, and lack of national consciousness.

Not only the West but other colonized countries served as sources of inspiration as well as offering a standard against which to measure Korea. When Ch'oe Yŏngsuk traveled to India in 1931, on her way back to Korea after completing her studies in Sweden, she could not help but think of the sorry destiny of India having gone from being one of the most fabulous ancient civilizations, along with China and Egypt, to being a colony of "a mere island country" (Britain).[33] Yet when she herself attended the Indian National Congress, she was very impressed by the unity of the Indians under prominent national leaders such as Gandhi and Naidu, and wondered why Korea did not have such a national body to unite and represent Koreans under Japanese colonial rule.[34]

When we attend to the voices of the elite women discussed in this book, through their writings, photographs, and biographies, we see that their individual choices in life and work were interwoven with the changing national politics and the globally interlinked forces and agencies of their time. Those forces, both visible and invisible, penetrated the very essence of everyday domestic life, daily routines, dietary habits, disciplinary training, and people's general outlook on life, society, and the world. In particular, globally connected Christian organizations facilitated the movement of people, ideas, and material

---

[33] "Indo yuram" (Traveling in India), *Chosŏn ilbo*, February 3, 1932.
[34] "Indo yuram" (Traveling in India), *Chosŏn ilbo*, February 4, 1932; and Ch'oe Yŏngsuk, "Taejung ŭi tan'gyŏl" (Unity of the Populace), *Tonggwang* 29 (December 1931): 71.

cultures, contributing to the multilayered contours of modern gender relations. It is not easy to measure the extent to which the global Christian network emancipated or constrained women. What is certain is that it provided women with unprecedented opportunities to become educated, work as professionals, and even travel globally as students or speakers, paving new pathways to modernity. At the same time, the conservative gender ideology and hierarchy embedded in the Christian community – both local and global – tended to constrict the women's choices in life. In a significant way, women's lives were caught between a new space that offered them emancipation and the continuing practices of patriarchal domination.

The questions raised in this book point to specific historical moments in colonial Korea; however, they also go hand in hand with a broader, enduring question: How has patriarchy adjusted so as to sustain itself at different historical times? In her 2017 book, *The Big Push: Exposing and Challenging the Persistence of Patriarchy*, Cynthia Enloe argues that patriarchy is far from "passé" or "yesterday." She writes: "Patriarchy is as current as Brexit, Donald Trump, and nationalist political parties. It is as *au courant* as Twitter, hedge funds, and weaponized drones. Patriarchy is not old-fashioned; it is as hip as football millionaires and Silicon Valley start-ups."[35] The very fact that people shy away from using the term "patriarchy," she argues, contributes to its continuing survival. She then proposes the concept of "sustainable patriarchy" as an analytical tool for "exposing the ways patriarchal systems are being perpetuated."[36]

The present book is in line with the urge expressed by Enloe and other feminist scholars to probe how patriarchal norms and practices were challenged, adjusted, modernized, and even reinforced within a particular historical and sociopolitical context. As evidenced in myriad examples of misogynistic violence throughout the contemporary world (including the latest incidents revealed by the "#MeToo Movement"), the deep roots and systems of patriarchy have been kept alive. In this book, I have traced how the undercurrents of patriarchal norms and relationships persisted in the face of modern transformations prior to and during Japanese colonial rule in Korea. Focusing on the role of the global Christian network in shaping modern gender relations in Korea, this book shows the ways in which resilient patriarchy remains at work at the intersections of the local, national, and global, with constant adjustments to the particular historical context. New openings for women were compromised by old norms in Korea, but women also sometimes appropriated old norms in paving new paths to modernity.

---

[35] Cynthia Enloe, *The Big Push: Exposing and Challenging the Persistence of Patriarchy* (Berkeley: University of California Press, 2017), p. 15.
[36] Enloe, *The Big Push*, p. 17.

Conclusion

In writing and rewriting the history of gender relations in modern Korea, an immediate challenge is the sheer lack of archival materials. This is not merely a matter of relevant materials not existing. It is a matter of the politics of archives and how to interpret the meaning of the presence or absence of extant sources. In her book, *The Fantasy of Feminist History*, Joan Scott writes:

> The pursuit of knowledge in the archive is a highly individualized task, but it's not lonely. The researcher surrounds herself with the whispering souls she conjures from the material she reads. If she's a good reader, she listens, too, for silences and omissions.... The challenge ... is that the texts don't speak for themselves; the whispers are heard only through a process of translation, and the very words – spoken or written – carry different meanings in each of their iterations. The dead don't come back to life as they were, but as we represent them.[37]

While visiting numerous archives in search of *any* trace of Korean women at home (Korea) and overseas (the United States, Japan, China, Sweden, Denmark, Germany, and Australia), I sometimes felt the exhilaration of finding rare, fascinating sources that gave me clues about the realities faced by these women. At other times, I was disappointed by the striking dearth of tangible, traceable records. The very paucity of archival records often stimulated further questions in an effort to connect the scattered dots in order to make sense of the sketch that was emerging.[38] While the book provides some of those realities and experiences, many more questions remain to be further investigated: What did these women experience and aspire to do while growing up in colonial Korea? What might it have meant to become "modern" when they were expected (or expected themselves) to be the bearers of Korean tradition? For those who traveled overseas, what was it like when they encountered people, places, customs, languages, institutions, religions, food, and clothing that were unfamiliar and far removed from previous experiences? What were their experiences on returning home after completing study overseas?[39] What is gathered, contemplated, and given value as history in this book is just the tip of the iceberg. There is a vast gendered history of modern Korea still to be discovered, reinterpreted, and brought to life. As Rita Felski reminds us in *The Gender of Modernity*, the "history of the modern is thus not yet over; in a very real sense, it has yet to be written."[40]

---

[37] Joan Wallach Scott, *The Fantasy of Feminist History* (Durham: Duke University Press, 2011), p. 145.

[38] Scott, *The Fantasy of Feminist History*, p. 147.

[39] Very few sources are available that help us understand the homecoming experiences of women intellectuals in colonial Korea. Na Hyesŏk's recollection is one of the few extant records. Literary works published at that time do give us some glimpse into the complex emotional currents those returnees contended with after they came back to Korea from studying overseas. See Na Hyesŏk, "Ah, chayu ŭi P'ari ka kŭriwŏ" (Missing the Freedom of Paris), *Samch'ŏlli* 4, no. 1 (January 1932): 43–6; Theodore Jun Yoo, *It's Madness: The Politics of Mental Health in Colonial Korea* (Oakland: University of California Press, 2016), pp. 94–9.

[40] Rita Felski, *The Gender of Modernity* (Cambridge: Harvard University Press, 1995), p. 212.

Bibliography

Archival sources

The Alumnae Center, Wesleyan College, Macon, Georgia
Ava Milam Clark Papers, Oregon State University Libraries Special Collections & Archives Research Center
Bentley Historical Library, University of Michigan
Butler Library, Columbia University Archival Collections, Columbia University
Chosŏn ch'ongdokpu kwanbo (Gazette of Government-General of Korea), Han'guksa teit'a peisŭ, Kuksa p'yŏnch'an wiwŏnhoe
Chungang Yŏja Kodŭng Hakkyo, Seoul, Korea
Doshisha Women's College, Kyoto, Japan
General Commission on Archives and History, The United Methodist Church, Drew University, Madison, New Jersey
Howard Gotlieb Archival Research Center, Boston University Archive, Boston University
Induk University, Seoul, Korea
International People's College Archives, Helsingør, Denmark
Japan Women's University, Tokyo, Japan
Kinjo Women's College, Nagoya, Japan
Korea YWCA, Seoul, Korea
Korean Film Archive
Korean Heritage Library, University of Southern California
Kwangju Sup'ia Yŏja Kodŭng Hakkyo Library, Kwangju, Korea
Missionary Research Library Archives, Burke Library, Union Theological Seminary, New York
Östasiatiska Museet (Museum of Far Eastern Antiquities), Stockholm, Sweden
Presbyterian Historical Society, Philadelphia, Pennsylvania
Rockefeller Archive Center, Sleepy Hollow, New York
Scarritt-Bennett Center, Nashville, Tennessee
Shanghai American School, Shanghai, People's Republic of China
Shanghai Korean Provisional Government, Shanghai, People's Republic of China
Shanghai Municipal Archives, Shanghai, People's Republic of China
Special Collections and University Archives, Vanderbilt University
Stockholm University Registrar, Stockholm, Sweden
Swedish National Archives (Riksarkivet), Stockholm, Sweden
Tongnae Yŏja Kodŭng Hakkyo (formerly Ilsin Girls' School), Pusan, Korea

Tsuda University, Kodaira, Japan
Yun Ch'iho ilgi (Diary of Yun Ch'iho), Kuksa p'yŏnch'an wiwŏnhoe, Kwach'ŏn, Korea

Newspapers and magazines

Argus, The
Chasŏn puinhoe chapchi
Cheguk sinmun
Chosŏn ilbo
Ch'ŏngnyŏn
Ewha
Hakchigwang
Heathen Woman's Friend
IHS (published by the Internationale Højskoles Elevforning, Denmark)
Kaebyŏk
Kaebyŏk sin'gan
Kajŏng chapchi
Kajŏng chiu
Kidok sinbo
Kiho hŭnghakhoe wŏlbo
Korea Mission Field
Korea Review
Korean Repository
Korean Student Bulletin
Kŭnu
Kŭrisŭdo sinmun
Kyŏngsŏng ilbo
Maeil sinbo
Man'guk puin
Mansebo
Michiganensian
Missionary Chronicle
Nongmin saenghwal
Pusan ilbo
Pyŏlgŏn'gon
Samch'ŏlli
Seitō
Sin kajŏng
Sin tonga
Sin yŏja
Sin yŏsŏng
Sinhak wŏlbo
Sinhan minbo
T'aegŭk hakpo
Taehan hŭnghakbo
Taehan hyŏphoe hoebo

Taehan ilbo
Taehan maeil sinbo
Tonga ilbo
Tonggwang
Tongnip sinmun
Urak'i
Uri chip
Uri ŭi kajŏng
Woman's Missionary Friend
Yŏja chinam
Yŏsŏng

Books and Articles

3.1. yŏsŏng tongjihoe. *Han'guk yŏsŏng tongnip undongsa* (The History of Women in the Independence Movement). Seoul: 3.1. yŏsŏng tongjihoe, 1980.

Aguiar, Marian. *Tracking Modernity: India's Railway and the Culture of Mobility.* Minneapolis, MN: University of Minnesota Press, 2011.

Ahn, Katherine. *Chosŏn ŭi ŏdum ŭl palk'in yŏsŏngdŭl* (Awakening the Hermit Kingdom: Pioneer American Women Missionaries in Korea), trans. Kim Sŏngung. Seoul: P'oiema, 2009.

"AHR Conversation: On Transnational History." *American Historical Review* 111, no. 5 (December 2006): 1441–64.

An, T'aeyun. "Singminji e on cheguk ŭi yŏsŏng: Chae Chosŏn Ilbon yŏsŏng Tsuda Setsuko rŭl t'onghaesŏ pon singminjuŭi wa chendŏ" (A Japanese Woman in Korea: Gender and Colonialism as Seen through the Eyes of a Korea-based Japanese Woman, Tsuda Setsuko). *Han'guk yŏsŏnghak* 24, no. 4 (2008): 5–33.

Singmin chŏngch'i wa mosŏng (Colonial Politics and Motherhood). P'aju: Han'guk haksul chŏngbo, 2006.

Anderson, Benedict R. O'Gorman. *Long-Distance Nationalism: World Capitalism, and the Rise of Identity Politics.* Berkeley, CA: Centre for German and European Studies, University of California, 1992.

Anderson, Emily, ed. *Belief and Practice in Imperial Japan and Colonial Korea.* Singapore: Palgrave Macmillan, 2017.

"Introduction: Empire of Religions: Exploring Belief and Practice in Imperial Japan and Colonial Korea," in *Belief and Practice in Imperial Japan and Colonial Korea*, ed. Emily Anderson. Singapore: Palgrave Macmillan, 2017, xvii–xxviii.

Christianity and Imperialism in Modern Japan: Empire for God. London: Bloomsbury, 2014.

"The Annexation of Korea to Japan." Editorial Comment. *American Journal of International Law* 4, no. 4 (1910): 923–25.

Ardis, Ann L. *New Women, New Novels: Feminism and Early Modernism.* New Brunswick, NJ: Rutgers University Press, 1990.

Asad, Talal. *Formations of the Secular: Christianity, Islam, Modernity.* Stanford, CA: Stanford University Press, 2003.

Genealogies of Religion: Discipline and Reasons of Power in Christianity and Islam. Baltimore, MD: Johns Hopkins University Press, 1993.

Asia t'aep'yŏngyang kyoyuk palchŏn yŏn'gudan of the Seoul National University. *Korean Student Bulletin.* Seoul: Sŏnin, 2000.

Atkins, E. Taylor, "Colonial Modernity," in *Routledge Handbook of Modern Korean History*, ed. Michael J. Seth (London: Routledge, 2016), pp. 124–40.

Austin, Herbert Henry. *A Scamper Through the Far East.* London: E. Arnold, 1909.

Badran, Margot. "Gendering the Secular and Religious in Modern Egypt: Woman, Family, and Nation," in *Religion, the Secular, and the Politics of Sexual Difference*, eds. Linell E. Cady and Tracy Fessenden. New York: Columbia University Press, 2013, pp. 103–20.

Baird, Annie. *Daybreak in Korea: a Tale of Transformation in the Far East.* New York: Fleming H. Revell Company, 1909.

Inside Views of Mission Life. Philadelphia, PA: Westminster Press, 1913.

Baker, Don. "A Slippery, Changing Concept: How Korean New Religions Define Religion." *Journal of Korean Religions* 1, no.1/2 (September 2010): 57–92.

"Creating the Sacred and the Secular in Colonial Korea." Unpublished paper presented at a workshop on Secularism in Japan, held at University of Oslo, Norway, June 19, 2015.

Ballantyne, Tony and Antoinette Burton, eds. *Bodies in Contact: Rethinking Colonial Encounters in World History.* Durham, NC: Duke University Press, 2005.

Bardsley, Jan. *The Bluestockings of Japan: New Woman Essays and Fiction from Seitō, 1911–1916.* Ann Arbor, MI: Center for Japanese Studies, University of Michigan, 2007.

Barlow, Tani, "Debates over Colonial Modernity in East Asia and Another Alternative." *Cultural Studies* 26, no. 5 (2012): 617–44.

ed. *Formations of Colonial Modernity in East Asia.* Durham, NC: Duke University Press, 1997.

Barraclough, Ruth. "Red Love and Betrayal in the Making of North Korea: Comrade Hŏ Jŏng-suk." *History Workshop Journal* 77, no. 1 (Spring 2014): 86–102.

Bayly, C. A. *The Birth of the Modern World 1780–1914.* Malden, MA: Blackwell Publishing, 2004.

Bays, Daniel H. and Ellen Widmer, eds. *China's Christian Colleges: Cross-Cultural Connections, 1900–1950.* Stanford, CA: Stanford University Press, 2009.

Bennett, Judith. "Feminism and History." *Gender & History* 1, no. 3 (Fall 1989): 251–72.

Bergman, Sten. *In Korean Wilds and Villages.* London: Travel Book Club, 1938.

Bernstein, Gail Lee, ed. *Recreating Japanese Women, 1600–1945.* Berkeley, CA: University of California Press, 1991.

Brouwer, Ruth Compton. *Modern Women Modernizing Men: The Changing Missions of Three Professional Women in Asia and Africa, 1902–69.* Vancouver: University of British Columbia Press, 2002.

Brown, Arthur J. *The Mastery of the Far East: The Story of Korea's Transformation and Japan's Rise to Supremacy in the Orient.* New York: Charles Scribner's Sons, 1919.

Buell, Raymond Leslie. "Again the Yellow Peril." *Foreign Affairs* 2, no. 2 (December 15, 1923): 295–309.

Burton, Antoinette. "Archive Stories: Gender in the Making of Imperial and Colonial Histories," in *Gender and Empire*, ed. Philippa Levine. New York: Oxford University Press, 2004, pp. 281–93.
 Dwelling in the Archive: Women Writing House, Home, and History in Late Colonial India. Oxford: Oxford University Press, 2003.
 "Colonial Encounters in Late-Victorian England: Pandita Ramabai at Cheltenham and Wantage 1883–6." *Feminist Review* 49 (Spring 1995): 29–49.
Buskirk, J. D. Van. "The Composition of Typical Korean Diets." *Japan Medical World* 4, no. 6 (June 1924): 1–4.
Cady, Linell E. and Tracy Fessenden, eds. *Religion, the Secular, and the Politics of Sexual Difference*. New York: Columbia University Press, 2013.
Calhoun, Craig. "Rethinking Secularism." *Hedgehog Review* 12, no. 3 (2010): 35–48.
Campbell, Elizabeth M. *After Fifty Years: a Record of the Work of the P.W.M.U. of Victoria*. Melbourne: Spectator Publishing, 1940.
Caprio, Mark E. *Japanese Assimilation Policies in Colonial Korea, 1910–1945*. Seattle, WA: University of Washington Press, 2009.
Carrier, James G. "Occidentalism: The World Turned Upside-down." *American Ethnologist* 19, no. 2 (May 1992): 195–212.
Casanova, José. *Public Religions in the Modern World*. Chicago, IL: University of Chicago Press, 1994.
Chai, Alice Yun. "Women's History in Public: 'Picture Brides' of Hawai'i." *Women's Studies Quarterly* 16, no. 1/2 (Spring–Summer 1988): 51–62.
Chakrabarty, Dipesh. "The Difference—Deferral of a Colonial Modernity: Public Debates on Domesticity in British Bengal," in *Tensions of Empire: Colonial Cultures in a Bourgeois World*, eds. Frederick Cooper and Ann Laura Stoler. Berkeley, CA: University of California Press, 1997, pp. 373–405.
Chandra, Vipan. *Imperialism, Resistance, and Reform in Late Nineteenth-Century Korea: Enlightenment and the Independence Club*. Berkeley, CA: Institute of East Asian Studies, University of California, 1988.
Chang, Hyun Kyong. "Musical Encounters in Korean Christianity: A Trans-pacific Narrative." PhD diss., UCLA, 2014.
Chang, Iuk. "Kyoyukhak kyŏnji esŏ kwanch'al hanŭn yuMi haksaeng ŭi simlisang kyŏnghyŏm" (Psychological Experiences of Korean Students in the United States from the Perspective of Education). *Urak'i* 1 (1925): 28–41.
Chang, Kyusik. "Christianity and Civil Society in Colonial Korea: The Civil Society Movement of Cho Man-sik and the P'yŏngyang YMCA against Japanese Colonialism," in *Encountering Modernity: Christianity in East Asia and Asian America*, eds. Albert L. Park and David K. Yoo. Honolulu: University of Hawai'i Press, 2014, pp. 119–39.
 "Han'guk YMCA ŭi nongch'on chaegŏn saŏp" (Rural Development Project of the Korea YMCA). *Chungang saron* 29 (2009): 243–49.
Chang, Migyŏng. "Kŭndae Ilbon susin kyogwasŏ e nat'anan yŏsŏng ŭi kŭndaesŏng kwa pan-kŭndaesŏng" (The Modern and Anti-modern Nature of Womanhood Reflected in Ethics Textbooks in Modern Japan). *Ilbon'ŏ munhak* 25 (2005): 219–37.
Chang, Tusik. "Ilsang sok ŭi yŏnghwa" (Films in Everyday Life), in *Kŭndae Han'guk ŭi ilsang saenghwal kwa midia* (Everyday Life and Media in Modern Korea), ed. Tan'guk taehakkyo tongyang yŏn'guso. Seoul: Minsogwŏn, 2008, pp. 121–52.

Chang, Wŏna. "Kŭnuhoe wa Chosŏn yŏsŏng haebang t'ongil chŏnsŏn" (Kŭnuhoe and the United Front for the Liberation of Korean Women). *Yŏksamunje yŏn'gu* 42 (2019): 391–431.
Chatani, Sayaka. *Nation-Empire: Ideology and Rural Youth Mobilization in Japan and Its Colonies*. Ithaca, NY: Cornell University Press, 2018.
Chaudhuri, Nupur and Margaret Strobel, eds. *Western Women and Imperialism*. Bloomington, IN: Indiana University Press, 1992.
Chi, Sugŏl. "Ilche ŭi kun'gukjuŭi p'asijŭm kwa 'Chosŏn nongch'on chinhŭng undong'" (Militaristic Fascism and "Rural Revitalization Campaign" of Japanese Imperial Rule). *Yŏksapip'yŏng* (May 1999): 16–36.
Ching, Leo. "Yellow Skin, White Masks: Race, Class, and Identification in Japanese Colonial Discourse," in *Trajectories: Inter-Asia Cultural Studies*, ed. Kuan Hsing Chen. New York: Routledge, 1998, pp. 65–86.
Chizhova, Ksenia. "Bodies of Texts: Women Calligraphers and the Elite Vernacular Culture in Late Chosŏn Korea (1392–1910)." *Journal of Asian Studies* 77, no. 1 (February 2018): 59–81.
Cho, Heekyoung. *Translation's Forgotten History: Russian Literature, Japanese Mediation, and the Formation of Modern Korean Literature*. Cambridge, MA: Harvard University Press, 2016.
Ch'oe, Ŭnhŭi. *Yŏsŏng ŭl nŏmŏ anak ŭi nŏul ŭl pŏtko* (Beyond the Womanly Domain, Removing the Veil of the Housewife). Seoul: Munijae, 2003.
Ch'oe, Yunjŏng. "Sŭwit'ŭ hom e taehan hwansang kwa kŭndae adong munhak e nat'anan mosŏng" (The Study on the Illusion of "A Sweet Home" and Motherhood in Modern Children's Literature). *Han'guk adong munhak yŏn'gu* 23 (2012): 225–55.
Choi, E. Soon. "A Plan for Adapting Principles of Child Development to Meet the Needs of Korean Children." M.S. thesis, Oregon State Agricultural College, 1937.
Choi, Hyaeweol. "Transpacific Aspiration toward Modern Domesticity in Japanese Colonial-era Korea." *Journal of Women's History* 30, no. 4 (Winter 2018): 60–83.
"Claiming Their Own Space: Australian Women Missionaries in Korea, 1891–1900." *Australian Historical Studies* 48, no. 3 (August 2017): 416–32.
"The Home as a Pulpit: Domestic Paradoxes in Early Twentieth-Century Korea," in *Divine Domesticities: Christian Paradoxes in Asia and the Pacific*, eds. Hyaeweol Choi and Margaret Jolly. Canberra: ANU Press, 2014, pp. 29–55.
New Women in Colonial Korea: A Sourcebook. London: Routledge, 2013.
"Debating the Korean New Woman: Imagining Henrik Ibsen's 'Nora' in Colonial Era Korea." *Asian Studies Review* 36 (March 2012): 59–77.
"In Search of Knowledge and Selfhood: Korean Women Studying Overseas in Colonial Korea." *Intersections: Gender and Sexuality in Asia and the Pacific* 29 (May 2012); http://intersections.anu.edu.au/issue29/choi.htm.
Gender and Mission Encounters in Korea: New Women, Old Ways. Berkeley, CA: University of California Press, 2009.
"A New Moral Order: Gender Equality in Korean Christianity," in *Religions of Korea in Practice*, ed. Robert E. Buswell Jr.. Princeton, NJ: Princeton University Press, 2006, pp. 409–20.
"Christian Modernity in Missionary Discourse from Korea, 1905–1910." *East Asian History* 29 (June 2005): 39–68.

"Women's Literacy and New Womanhood in Late Choson Korea." *Asian Journal of Women's Studies* 6, no. 1 (2000): 88–115.
Choi, Hyaeweol and Margaret Jolly, eds. *Divine Domesticities: Christian Paradoxes in Asia and the Pacific*. Canberra: ANU Press, 2014.
Choi, Kyeong-Hee. "Neither Colonial nor National: The Making of the 'New Woman' in Pak Wansŏ's 'Mother's Stake 1'," in *Colonial Modernity in Korea*, eds. Gi-Wook Shin and Michael Robinson. Cambridge, MA: Harvard University Press, 1999, pp. 221–47.
Ch'ŏn, Hwasuk. *Han'guk yŏsŏng kidokkyo sahoe undongsa* (History of the Social Movement of Korean Christian Women). Seoul: Hyean, 2000.
Chŏn, Migyŏng. "1920–30-nyŏndae hyŏnmo yangch'ŏ e kwanhan yŏn'gu" (A Study of Wise Mother and Good Wife in the 1920s and 1930s). *Han'guk kajŏng kwalli hakhoeji* 22, no. 3 (2004): 75–93.
Chŏn, Ponggwan. "Chosŏn ch'oech'o Sweden kyŏngje hakcha Ch'oe Yŏngsuk aesa" (A Sad Story of Ch'oe Yŏngsuk, the First Korean Woman Holding a Degree in Economics from Sweden). *Sin Tonga* 560 (May 2006): 542–55.
Chŏng, Chaech'ŏl. *Ilche ŭi taeHan'guk singminji kyoyuk chŏngch'aeksa* (The History of Educational Policy under Japanese Colonial Rule in Korea). Seoul: Ilchisa, 1985.
Chŏng, Chinsŏng. "Minjok mit minjokjuŭi e kwanhan Han'guk yŏsŏnghak ŭi nonŭi: Ilbon kun wianbu munje rŭl chungsim ŭro" (A Debate on Nation and Nationalism in Korean Feminism: The Issue of Comfort Women during the Japanese Colonial Era). *Han'guk yŏsŏnghak* 15, no. 2 (1999): 29–53.
Chŏng, Chŏnghwa. *Changgang ilgi* (Diary of Changgang). Seoul: Hangminsa, 1998.
Chŏng, Chuhŭi. "Kŭndae chŏk chugŏ konggan kwa chip ŭi sasang" (Modern Residential Space and Ideas about House). PhD diss., Yonsei University, 2012.
Chŏng, Hyejung. "Ch'ŏng mal Min ch'o Chungguk yŏsŏng ŭi Ilbon Miguk yuhak" (Chinese Women's Studying in Japan and the United States in Late Qing and Early Republican Eras). *Ihwa sahak yŏn'gu* 39 (2009): 101–33.
Chŏng, Kyŏngsuk. *"Taehan cheguk malgi yŏsŏng undong ŭi sŏnggyŏk yŏn'gu"* (Characteristics of the Women's Movements in the Late Taehan Empire). PhD diss., Ewha Womans University, 1989.
Chŏng, Pyŏngjun. "Ilcheha Han'guk yŏsŏng ŭi Miguk yuhak kwa kŭndae kyŏnghŏm" (Korean Women's Studying in the United States and Their Experience of Modernity under Japanese Rule). *Ihwa sahak yŏn'gu* 39 (2009): 29–99.
Chou, Wan-yao. "The Kōminka Movement in Taiwan and Korea: Comparisons and interpretations," in *The Japanese Wartime Empire, 1931–1945*, eds. Peter Duus, Ramon H. Myers, and Mark R. Peattie. Princeton, NJ: Princeton University Press, 1996, pp. 40–68.
Ch'ugye Hwang Sindŏk sŏnsaeng kinyŏm saŏphoe. *Munŏjijiannŭn chip ŭl* (House That is not Collapsing). Seoul: Ch'ugye Hwang Sindŏk sŏnsaeng kinyŏm saŏphoe, 1984.
Chung, Wan Kyu. "An Analysis and Evaluation of Beginning Piano Methods Used in Korea." PhD diss., Texas Tech University, 1992.
Church, Marie E. and Mrs. R. L. Thomas. *The One Who Went and the One She Found*. Woman's Foreign Missionary Society, 1929.
Clark, Donald N. *Living Dangerously in Korea: The Western Experience 1900–1950*. Norwalk, CT: EastBridge, 2003.

Cohn, Bernard S. *Colonialism and Its Forms of Knowledge*. Princeton, NJ: Princeton University Press, 1996.

Cooper, Frederick and Ann Laura Stoler, eds. *Tensions of Empire*. Berkeley, CA: University of California Press, 1997.

Copeland, Rebecca. "All Other Loves Excelling: Mary Kidder, Wakamatsu Shizuko and Modern Marriage in Meiji Japan," in *Divine Domesticities: Christian Paradoxes in Asia and the Pacific*, eds. Hyaeweol Choi and Margaret Jolly. Canberra: ANU Press, 2014, pp. 85–112.

Cott, Nancy. *The Bonds of Womanhood: "Woman's Sphere" in New England, 1780–1835*. New Haven, CT: Yale University Press, 1977.

Curthoys, Ann and Marilyn Lake, eds. *Connected Worlds: History in Transnational Perspective*. Canberra: ANU E Press, 2005.

Davis, Natalie Zemon. *The Return of Martin Guerre*. Cambridge, MA: Harvard University Press, 1984.

de Ceuster, Koen. "The YMCA's Rural Development Program in Colonial Korea, 1925–35: Doctrine and Objectives." *Review of Korean Studies* 3, no. 1 (July 2000): 5–33.

Deuchler, Martina. "Propagating Female Virtues in Chosŏn Korea," in *Women and Confucian Cultures in Premodern China, Korea, and Japan*, eds. Dorothy Ko, Jahyun Kim Haboush, and Joan R. Piggott. Berkeley, CA: University of California Press, 2003, pp. 142–69.

The Confucian Transformation of Korea: A Study of Society and Ideology. Cambridge, MA: Harvard University Press, 1992.

DeVries, Jacqueline. "Rediscovering Christianity after the Postmodern Turn." *Feminist Studies* 31, no. 1 (Spring 2005): 135–55.

Duara, Prasenjit. "The Discourse of Civilization and Pan-Asianism." *Journal of World History* 12, no. 1 (2001): 99–130.

Duncan, John. "The Naehun and the Politics of Gender," in *Creative Women of Korea: The Fifteenth through the Twentieth Centuries*, ed. Young-Key Kim-Renaud. Armonk, NY: M. E. Sharpe, 2004, pp. 26–57.

Enloe, Cynthia. *The Big Push: Exposing and Challenging the Persistence of Patriarchy*. Berkeley, CA: University of California Press, 2017.

Eskildsen, Robert. *Transforming Empire in Japan and East Asia: The Taiwan Expedition and the Birth of Japanese Imperialism*. Singapore: Palgrave Macmillan, 2019.

"Of Civilization and Savages: The Mimetic Imperialism of Japan's 1874 Expedition to Taiwan." *American Historical Review* 107, no. 2 (April 2002): 388–418.

Ewha 70-nyŏnsa p'yŏnjip wiwŏnhoe. *Ewha 70-nyŏnsa* (The Seventieth History of Ewha). Seoul: Ewha Womans University Press, 1956.

Ewha 100-nyŏnsa p'yŏnch'an wiwŏnhoe. *Ewha 100-nyŏnsa* (The 100th History of Ewha). Seoul: Ewha Womans University Press, 1994.

Faison, Elyssa. *Managing Women: Disciplining Labor in Modern Japan*. Berkeley, CA: University of California Press, 2007.

Felski, Rita. *The Gender of Modernity*. Cambridge, MA: Harvard University Press, 1995.

Flemming, Leslie A., ed. *Women's Work for Women: Missionaries and Social Change in Asia*. Boulder, CO: Westview Press, 1989.

Frankl, John. *Han'guk munhak e nat'anan oeguk ŭi ŭimi* (The Meaning of the Foreign Reflected in Korean Literature). Seoul: Somyŏng, 2008.

Garon, Sheldon. *Molding Japanese Minds: The State in Everyday Life*. Princeton, NJ: Princeton University Press, 1997.

"Women's Groups and the Japanese State: Contending Approaches to Political Integration, 1890–1945." *Journal of Japanese Studies* 19, no. 1 (1993): 5–41.

Gilmore, George. *Korea from Its Capital*. Philadelphia, PA: The Presbyterian Board of Publication, 1892.

Goldman, Emma. *Anarchism and Other Essay*. New York and London: Mother Earth Publishing Association, 1911.

Goodman, Bryna and Wendy Larson. "Introduction: Axes of Gender: Divisions of Labor and Spatial Separation," in *Gender in Motion: Divisions of Labor and Cultural Chang in Late Imperial and Modern China*, eds. Bryna Goodman and Wendy Larson. Lanham, MD: Rowman & Littlefield Publishers, Inc., 2005.

Graham, Gael. *Gender, Culture, and Christianity: American Protestant Mission Schools in China 1880–1930*. New York: Peter Lang, 1995.

Grimes, Etta Belle. "Applied Home Economics in Korea." *Journal of Home Economics* 17 (January 1925): 36–7.

Guterl, Matthew Pratt. "Comment: The Futures of Transnational History." *American Historical Review* 118, no. 1 (2013): 130–39.

Haboush, Jahyun Kim, ed. *Epistolary Korea: Letters in the Communicative Space of the Chosŏn, 1392–1910*. New York: Columbia University Press, 2009.

"Filial Emotions and Filial Values: Changing Patterns in the Discourse of Filiality in Late Chosŏn Korea." *Harvard Journal of Asiatic Studies* 55, no. 1 (June 1995): 129–77.

ed. and trans. *The Memoirs of Lady Hyegyŏng: The Autobiographical Writings of a Crown Princess of Eighteenth-Century Korea*. Berkeley, CA: University of California Press, 1995.

Haenig, Huldah A. "From West Gate to East Gate." *Woman's Missionary Friend* 43, no. 1 (January 1911): 9–11.

Haggis, Jane. "Ironies of Emancipation: Changing Configurations of 'Women's Work' in the 'Mission of Sisterhood' to Indian Women." *Feminist Review* 65 (Summer 2000): 108–26.

Hall, Rosetta Sherwood. "One New Life in the Orient." *Woman's Missionary Friend* 28, no. 12 (June 1897): 342–3.

Han, Hŭisuk, "Yŏhakkyo nŭn ŏpsŏtta, kŭrŏna kyoyuk ŭn chungyo haetta" (There was no Girl's School, but Education was Important), in *Chosŏn yŏsŏng ŭi ilsaeng* (Lives of Chosŏn Women), ed. Kyujanggak han'gukhak yŏn'guwŏn. P'aju: Kŭrhangari, 2010, pp. 214–41.

Han, Sanggwŏn. *Ch'a Mirisa chŏnjip I and II* (Compiled Works of Ch'a Mirisa I and II). Seoul: Tŏksŏng yŏja taehakkyo Ch'a Mirisa yŏn'guso, 2009.

Han'guk yŏsŏng yŏn'guso yŏsŏngsa yŏn'gusil, ed. *Uri yŏsŏng ŭi yŏksa* (Our Women's History). Seoul: Ch'ŏngnyŏnsa, 1999.

Han'guk yŏsŏngsa p'yŏnch'an wiwŏnhoe. *Han'guk yŏsŏngsa 2* (History of Korean Women 2). Seoul: Ewha yŏdae ch'ulp'anbu, 1972.

Han'guk YWCA 80-nyŏnsa p'yŏnch'an wiwŏnhoe. *Han'guk YWCA 80-nyŏnsa* (The Eightieth History of Korea YWCA). Seoul: Taehan YWCA Yŏnhaphoe, 2006.

Hansen, Karen Transberg, ed. *African Encounters with Domesticity*. New Brunswick, NJ: Rutgers University Press, 1992.

Harkness, Nicholas. *Songs of Seoul: An Ethnography of Voice and Voicing in Christian South Korea*. Berkeley, CA: University of California Press, 2014.

Häussler, Sonja. "Kyubang Kasa: Women's Writings from the Late Chosŏn," in *Creative Women of Korea: The Fifteenth Through the Twentieth Centuries*, ed. Young-Key Kim-Renaud. Armonk, NY: M. E. Sharpe, 2004, pp. 142–62.

Haynes, Emily Irene. "Union Academy School and Evangelistic Work on Pyeng Yang District." Annual Report of the Korea Woman's Conference of the Methodist Episcopal Church, 1910.

Henning, Joseph. *Outposts of Civilization: Race, Religion, and the Formative Years of American-Japanese Relations*. New York: New York University Press, 2000.

Henry, Todd A. *Assimilating Seoul: Japanese Rule and the Politics of Public Space in Colonial Korea, 1910–1945*. Berkeley, CA: University of California Press, 2014.

Hill, A. and M. Deacon. "The Problem of Surplus Women in the Nineteenth Century: Secular and Religious Alternatives," in *A Sociological Year Book of Religion in Britain*, no. 5, ed. D. Martin. London: SCM Press, 1972, pp. 87–102.

Hill, Patricia R. *The World Their Household: The American Woman's Foreign Mission Movement and Cultural Transformation, 1870–1920*. Ann Arbor, MI: University of Michigan Press, 1985.

Hŏ, Tonghyŏn. "Chosa sich'aldan (1881) ŭi Ilbon kyŏnghŏm e poinŭn kŭndae ŭi t'ŭkching" (Characteristics of Modernity Experienced in Japan by the Korean Inspection Group). *Han'guk sasangsa hakhoe* 19 (2002): 507–37.

Hŏ, Ŭn. *Ajikto nae kwi en Sŏgando param sori ka* (I Still Hear the Sound of the Wind in Sŏgando). Seoul: Chŏngusa, 2008. (First published 1995.)

Hoganson, Kristin. "Cosmopolitan Domesticity: Importing the American Dream, 1865–1920." *American Historical Review* 107, no. 1 (2002): 55–83.

Holledge, Julie. "Addressing the Global Phenomenon of A Doll's House: An Intercultural Intervention." *Ibsen Studies* 8, no. 1 (2008): 13–28.

Hong, Jeesoon. "Christian Education and the Construction of Female Gentility in Modern East Asia." *Religions* 10, no. 467 (2019). 10.3390/rel10080467.

Hong, Ji Yeon and Christopher Paik. "Colonization and Education: Exploring the Legacy of Local Elites in Korea." *Economic History Review* (2017): 1–27.

Hong, Yanghŭi. "Sin Saimdang, 'hyŏnmo yangch'ŏ' ŭi sangjing i toeda" (Sin Saimdang Becomes the Symbol of "Wise Mother, Good Wife"), in *Sin Saimdang, kŭ nyŏ rŭl wihan pyŏnmyŏng* (Sin Saimdang: In Her Defense), eds. Ko Yŏnhŭi, Yi Kyŏnggu, Yi Sugin, and Hong Yanghŭi. Seoul: Tasan Kihoek, 2016, pp. 166–213.

"Singminji sigi hojŏk chedo wa kajok chedo ŭi pyŏnyong" (Transformation of the Family System through the Family Registrar during the Japanese Colonial Era). *Sahak yŏn'gu* 79 (2005): 167–205.

"Ilche sigi Chosŏn ŭi yŏsŏg kyoyuk: hyŏnmo yangch'ŏ kyoyuk ŭl chungsim ŭro" (Korean Women's Education during the Japanese Colonial Era: With a Focus on Education for Wise Mother and Good Wife). *Han'gukhak nonjip* 35 (2001): 219–57.

Howard, Keith. *True Stories of the Korean Comfort Women: Testimonies*. New York: Cassell, 1995.

Howe, Renate. *A Century of Influence*. Sydney: UNSW Press, 2009.

Hu Ying. *Tales of Translation: Composing the New Woman in China, 1899–1918*. Stanford, CA: Stanford University Press, 2000.
Huber, Mary Taylor and Nancy Lutkehaus, eds. *Gendered Missions: Women and Men in Missionary Discourse and Practice*. Ann Arbor, MI: University of Michigan Press, 1999.
Huh, Donghyun. Trans. Vladimir Tikhonov. "The Korean Courtiers' Observation Mission's Views on Meiji Japan and Projects of Modern State Building." *Korean Studies* 29 (2005): 30–54.
Hulbert, Homer. "Women's Rights in Korea," *Korea Review* 6, no. 2 (February 1906): 51–9.
Hunter, Jane. *The Gospel of Gentility: American Women Missionaries in Turn-of-the-Century China*. New Haven, CT: Yale University Press, 1984.
Hutchison, William R. "A Moral Equivalent for Imperialism: Americans and the Promotion of 'Christian Civilization,' 1880–1910," in *Missionary Ideologies in the Imperial Era: 1880–1920*, eds. Torben Christensen and William R. Hutchison. Aarhus: Forlaget Aros, 1982, pp. 167–77.
Hwang, Kyung Moon. *Rationalizing Korea: The Rise of the Modern State 1894–1945*. Oakland, CA: University of California Press, 2016.
A History of Korea. London: Palgrave Macmillan, 2010.
Hyun, Theresa. *Writing Women in Korea: Translation and Feminism in the Colonial Period*. Honolulu: University of Hawai'i Press, 2004.
Im, Sŏkchae, ed. *Ŏmma p'umsok adŭl maŭm sok* (In Mom's Embrace, in Son's Mind). Seoul: Yonsei University Press, 2007.
Iriye, Akira. *Global and Transnational History: The Past, Present, and Future*. Basingstoke: Palgrave Macmillan, 2013.
Jager, Sheila Miyoshi. *Narratives of Nation Building in Korea: A Genealogy of Patriotism*. Armonk, NY: M. E. Sharpe, 2003.
Jakobsen, Janet and Ann Pelligrini, eds. *Secularisms*. Durham, NC: Duke University Press, 2008.
Judge, Joan. *Republican Lens: Gender, Visuality, and Experience in the Early Chinese Periodical Press*. Stanford, CA: Stanford University Press, 2015.
The Precious Raft of History: The Past, the West, and the Woman Question in China. Stanford, CA: Stanford University Press, 2008.
"Talent, Virtue, and the Nation: Chinese Nationalisms and Female Subjectivities in the Early Twentieth Century," *American Historical Review* 106, no. 3 (June 2001): 765–803.
Kajŏng taehak. *Ewha kajŏnghak 50-nyŏnsa* (The Fiftieth History of Home Economics at Ewha). Seoul: Ewha yŏja taehakkyo kajŏng taehak, 1979.
Kal, Hong. "Modeling the West, Returning to Asia: Shifting Politics of Representation in Japanese Colonial Expositions in Korea." *Comparative Study of Society and History* 47, no. 3 (July 2005): 507–31.
Kang, Kyong-ae, *From Wonso Pond: A Colonial-period Korean Novel, through the Eyes of its Working-Class Heroes*, trans. Samuel Perry. New York: Feminist Press, 2009.
Kang, Naehŭi. "Yŏngŏ kyoyuk kwa yŏngŏ ŭi sahoe chŏk wisang" (English Education and the Social Status of the English Language), in *Singminji ŭi ilsang, chibae wa kyunyŏl* (Everyday Life in Colony, Dominance and Fissure), eds. Kong Cheuk and Chŏng Kŭnsik. Seoul: Munhwagwahaksa, 2006, pp. 401–32.

Kaplan, Amy. "Manifest Domesticity." *American Literature* 70, no. 3 (1998): 581–606.

Kawamoto, Aya. "Han'guk kwa Ilbon ŭi hyŏnmo yangch'ŏ sasang" (Ideology of Wise Mother and Good Wife in Korea and Japan), in *Mosŏng ŭi tamnon kwa hyŏnsil* (Discourse on Motherhood and its Reality), ed. Sim Yŏnghŭi Seoul: Nanam Ch'ulp'an, 1999, pp. 221–44.

Kelly, Arlene Woods. *Educational Institution for Women 1889–1989*. Nagoya: Kinjo Gakuin, 1989.

Kendall, Laurel and Mark Peterson, eds. *Korean Women: View from the Inner Room*. New Haven, CT: East Rock Press, 1983.

Kerber, Linda. "The Republican Mother: Women and the Enlightenment—An American Perspective." *American Quarterly* 28, no. 2 (Summer 1976): 187–205.

Kim, Chinsong. *Sŏul e ttansŭhol ŭl hŏhara* (Permit Dance Halls in Seoul). Seoul: Hyŏnsil munhwa yŏn'gu, 1999.

Kim, Chong Bum. "Preaching the Apocalypse in Colonial Korea: The Protestant Millennialism of Kil Sŏn-ju," in *Christianity in Korea*, eds. Robert E. Buswell Jr. and Timothy S. Lee. Honolulu: University of Hawai'i Press, 2006, pp. 149–66.

Kim, Ch'ŏl. *Pokhwasulsa tŭl: sosŏl ro ingnŭn singminji Chosŏn* (The Ventriloquists: Reading Colonial Korea through Fiction). Seoul: Munhak kwa chisŏngsa, 2008.

Kim, Chŏngok. *Imonim Kim Hwallan* (My Aunt Kim Hwallan). Seoul: Chŏngusa, 1977.

Kim, Dong Hoon. *Eclipsed Cinema: The Film Culture of Colonial Korea*. Edinburgh: Edinburgh University Press, 2017.

Kim, Hanmee Na. "'America' in Colonial Korea: A Vantage Point for Capitalist Modernity." *positions* 26, no. 4 (November 2018): 647–85.

Kim, Helen Kiteuk. "Rural Education for the Regeneration of Korea." PhD diss., Columbia University, 1931.

Kim, Hwallan. *Kŭ pit sok ŭi chagŭn saengmyŏng* (A Little Life in that Light). Seoul: Yŏwŏnsa, 1965.

"Namsŏng ŭi pansŏng ŭl ch'ok ham" (Urging Men to Critically Reflect on Themselves), *Sin yŏja* 4 (June 1920): 38–40.

Kim, Hwansoo Ilmee. *The Korean Buddhist Empire: A Transnational History, 1910–1945*. Cambridge, MA: Harvard University Press, 2018.

Kim, Hyegyŏng. *Singminji ha kŭndae kajok ŭi hyŏngsŏng kwa chendŏ* (Gender and the Formation of the Modern Family under Colonial Rule). Seoul: Ch'angbi, 2006.

Kim, Hyŏngmok. "Ch'oe Yongsin kajok ŭi minjok undong ch'amyŏ wa yŏksa chŏk ŭiŭi" (The Participation of the Family of Ch'oe Yongsin in the Nationalist Movement and its Historical Meaning), in *The 2nd Choi Yongshin Symposium, Ansan*, November 28, 2014.

Kim, Jaeeun. *Contested Embrace: Transborder Membership Politics in Twentieth-Century Korea*. Stanford, CA: Stanford University Press, 2016.

Kim, Jisoo. *The Emotions of Justice: Gender, Status, and Legal Performance in Chosŏn Korea*. Seattle, WA: University of Washington Press, 2017.

Kim, Jungwon. "'You Must Avenge on My Behalf': Widow Chastity and Honour in Nineteenth-Century Korea." *Gender & History* 26, no. 1 (2014): 128–46.

Kim, Key-Hiuk. *The Last Phase of the East Asian World Order: Korea, Japan, and the Chinese Empire, 1860–1882*. Berkeley, CA: University of California Press, 1980.

Kim, Kwangmin. "Korean Migration in Nineteenth-Century Manchuria: A Global Theme in Modern Asian History," in *Mobile Subjects: Boundaries and Identities* in *Modern Korean Diaspora*, ed. Wen-hsin Yeh. Berkeley, CA: Institute of East Asian Studies, 2013, pp. 17–37.

Kim, Kyŏngil. *Yŏsŏng ŭi kŭndae, kŭndae ŭi yŏsŏng* (Modernity of Women, Women of Modernity). Seoul: P'urŭn yŏksa, 2004.

Kim, Michael. "Mothers of the Empire: Military Conscription and Mobilisation in Late Colonial Korea," in *Gender Politics and Mass Dictatorship: Global Perspectives*, eds. Jie-Hyun Lim and Karen Petrone. Basingstoke: Palgrave Macmillan, 2011, pp. 193–212.

Kim, Myŏngsŏn. "1915-nyŏn Kyŏngsŏng kajŏng pangnamhoe chŏnsi chut'aek ŭi p'yosang" (Representation of "Modern Housing" Exhibited at Home Exposition of *Keijō* in 1915). *Taehan kŏnch'ukhoe nonmunjip* 28, no. 3 (2012): 155–64.

Kim, Puja. *Hakkyo pak ŭi Chosŏn yŏsŏng tŭl* (Korean Women Outside the School). Seoul: Ilchogak, 2009.

Kim, Sangdŏk. "Yŏja ŭihak kangsŭpso" (Medical Training Workshop for Women). *Ŭisahak* 2, no. 1 (1993): 80–84.

Kim, Sŏng'u. "Saeroun tosijut'aek ŭi hyŏngsŏng kwa saenghwal ŭi pyŏnhwa" (The Formation of New Urban Housing and Changes in Life), in *Ilche ŭi singmin chibae wa ilsang saenghwal* (Japanese Colonial Control and Everyday Life), ed. Yonsei University kukhak yŏn'guwŏn. Seoul: Hyean, 2004, pp. 75–115.

Kim, Sŏngŭn. "1930-nyŏndae Hwang Aedŏk ŭi nongch'on saŏp kwa yŏsŏng undong" (Hwang Aedŏk's Rural Project and Women's Movement in the 1930s). *Han'guk kidokkyo wa yŏksa* 35 (November 2011): 141–80.

"1920–30-nyŏndae yŏja Miguk yuhaksaeng ŭi silt'ae wa insik" (The Reality and Consciousness of Women Students Studying in the United States in the 1920s and 1930s). *Yŏksa wa kyŏnggye* 72 (2009): 183–238.

Kim, Sonja M. *Imperatives of Care: Women and Medicine in Colonial Korea*. Honolulu: University of Hawai'i Press, 2019.

"Kang Kyŏngae: Introduction and Translations of 'The Path Chosŏn Women Must Tread,' 'Two Hundred Yen for My Manuscript,' and 'On Leaving Kando, a Farewell to Kando'," in *Imperatives of Culture: Selected Essays on Korean History, Literature, and Society from the Japanese Colonial Era*, eds. Christopher P. Hanscom, Walter K. Lew, and Youngju Ryu. Honolulu: University of Hawai'i Press, 2013, pp. 132–53.

Kim, Sujin. "Chŏnt'ong ŭi ch'angan kwa yŏsŏng ŭi kungminhwa: Sin Saimdang ŭl chungsim ŭro" (The invention of Tradition and the Nationalization of Women with a Focus on Sin Saimdang). *Sahoe wa yŏksa* 80 (2008): 215–55.

"1920–30-nyŏndae sin yŏsŏng tamnon kwa sangjing ŭi kusŏng" (Excess of the Modern: Three Archetypes of the New Woman and Colonial Identity in Korea, 1920s to 1930s). PhD diss., Seoul National University, 2005.

Kim, Sun Joo and Jungwon Kim, comp. and trans. *Wrongful Deaths: Selected Inquest Records from Nineteenth-Century Korea*. Seattle, WA: University of Washington Press, 2014.

Kim, Sunjŏn and Chang Migyŏng. "'Pot'ong hakkyo susinsŏ' rŭl t'onghae pon yŏsŏng myosa" (Portrayal of Women Reflected in "Book of Moral Education for Common School"), in *Cheguk ŭi singminji susin* (Empire's Moral Cultivation of the Colonized), ed. Kim Sunjŏn. Seoul: Cheiaenssi, 2008, pp. 305–24.

Kim, Sŭngt'ae, ed. *Ilche kangjŏmgi chonggyo chŏngch'eksa charyojip* (A Sourcebook of the Religious Policies during the Japanese Colonial Era). Seoul: Han'guk kidokkyo yŏksa yŏn'guso, 1996.

Kim, Sŭngt'ae and Pak Hyejin, comp. *Naehan sŏn'gyosa ch'ongnam, 1884–1984* (A Comprehensive Survey of Missionaries in Korea). Seoul: Han'gukkidokkyo yŏksa yŏn'guso, 1994.

Kim, Susie Jie Young. "The Ambivalence of 'Modernity': Articulation of New Subjectivities in Turn of the Century Korea." PhD diss., University of California Los Angeles, 2002.

Kim, Wŏn'gŭk et al. *Singminji chisigin ŭi kaehwa sasang yuhakki* (Records of Studying Overseas and Enlightenment Thoughts of Intellectuals in Colonial Korea). Seoul: T'aehaksa, 2005.

Kim, Yongbŏm. *Munhwa saenghwal kwa munhwa chut'aek: kŭndae chugŏ tamnon ŭl toedoraboda* (Culture Life and Culture House: Reflecting about the Discourse on Modern Housing). Seoul: Sallim, 2012.

Kim, Yunsŏng. "1920–30-nyŏndae Han'guk sahoe ŭi chonggyo wa yŏsŏng tamnon: 'misin t'ap'a' wa 'hyŏnmo yangch'ŏ' rŭl chungsim ŭro" (Religion and Gender Discourse in 1920s and 1930s Korea: With a Focus on "Eradication of Superstition" and "Wise Mother, Good Wife"). *Chonggyo munhwa pip'yŏng* 9 (2008): 164–90.

Kim, Yung-Chung. *Women of Korea: A History from Ancient Times to 1945*. Seoul: Ewha Womans University Press, 1979.

Kim, Yung-Hee. "In Quest of Modern Womanhood: Sinyŏja, A Feminist Journal in Colonial Korea." *Korean Studies* 37 (2013): 44–78.

"Under the Mandate of Nationalism: Development of Feminist Enterprises in Modern Korea, 1860–1910." *Journal of Women's History* 7, no. 4 (1995): 120–36.

Kim, Yunsŏn. "Cheguk sinmun e nat'anan Miguk yuhak kwa yuhaksaeng kisŏ (p'yŏnji) yŏn'gu" (A Study of Korean Students Studying in the United States and Their Correspondences Reflected in Cheguk sinmun). *Ŏmun yŏn'gu* 38, no. 1 (Spring 2010): 309–33.

Kimura, Mitsuhiko. "Standards of Living in Colonial Korea: Did the Masses Become Worse off or Better off under Japanese Rule?" *Journal of Economic History* 53, no. 3 (September 1993): 629–52.

Ko, Dorothy. *Teachers of the Inner Chambers*. Stanford, CA: Stanford University Press, 1994.

Ko, Yŏnhŭi, Yi Kyŏnggu, Yi Sugin, and Hong Yanghŭi. *Sin Saimdang, kŭ nyŏ rŭl wihan pyŏnmyŏng* (Sin Saimdang, in her Defense). Seoul: Tasan kihoek, 2016.

Kokumin shinbunsha, ed. *Risō no katei* (Ideal Home). Tokyo: Kokumin shinbunsha, 1915.

Kŏmyŏl yŏn'guhoe. *Singminji kŏmyŏl: chedo, t'eksŭt'ŭ, silch'ŏn* (Censorship in Colonial Korea: System, Text, Practice). Seoul: Somyŏng ch'ulp'an, 2011.

Kono, Kimberly. *Romance, Family and Nation in Japanese Colonial Literature*. New York: Palgrave Macmillan, 2010.

Koyama Shizuko. *Ryōsai Kenbo: The Educational Ideal of "Good Wife, Wise Mother" in Modern Japan*, trans. Stephen Filler. Boston, MA: Brill, 2013.

Kramer, Paul A. "International Students and U.S. Global Power in the Long 20th Century." *The Asia-Pacific Journal*, 3-3-10, January 18, 2010 (online journal).

Kuksa p'yŏnch'an wiwŏnhoe. *Sŏgu munhwa wa ŭi mannam* (Encounters with Western Cultures). Kwach'ŏn: Kyŏngin munhwasa, 2010.

Kwon, Insook. "Feminists Navigating the Shoals of Nationalism and Collaboration: The Post-Colonial Korean Debate over How to Remember Kim Hwallan." *Frontiers: A Journal of Women Studies* 27, no. 1 (2006): 39–66.

Kwok, Pui-lan. *Postcolonial Imagination & Feminist Theology*. Louisville, KY: Westminster John Knox Press, 2005.

Chinese Women and Christianity 1860–192. Atlanta, GA: Scholars Press, 1992.

Kyujanggak han'gukhak yŏn'guwŏn, ed., *Chosŏn yŏsŏng ŭi ilsaeng* (Lives of Chosŏn Women). P'aju: Kŭrhangari, 2010.

Lake, Marilyn. "Nationalist Historiography, Feminist Scholarship, and the Promise and Problems of New Transnational Histories: The Australian Case." *Journal of Women's History* 19, no. 1 (Spring 2007): 180–86.

Lawson, Max. *A Celebration of 75 Years of Working for Peace and International Friendship*. Helsingør: International People's College, 1996.

Lee, Chulwoo. "Modernity, Legality, and Power in Korea under Japanese Rule," in *Colonial Modernity in Korea*, eds. Gi-Wook Shin and Michael Robinson. Cambridge, MA: Harvard University Press, 1999, pp. 21–51.

Lee, Helen J. S. "Eating for the Emperor: The Nationalization of Settler Homes and Bodies in the Kōminka Era," in *Reading Colonial Japan: Text, Context, and Critique*, eds. Michele M. Mason and Helen J. S. Lee. Stanford, CA: Stanford University Press, 2012, pp. 159–77.

Lee, Hyunjung and Younghan Cho. "Introduction: Colonial Modernity and Beyond in East Asian Contexts." *Cultural Studies* 26, no. 5 (2012): 601–16.

Lee, Ji-Eun. *Women Pre-Scripted: Forging Modern Roles through Korean Print*. Honolulu: University of Hawai'i Press, 2015.

Lee, Ki-baik. *A New History of Korea*. trans. Edward W. Wagner with Edward J. Shultz. Seoul: Ilchogak, 1984.

Lee, Peter, ed. *Sourcebook of Korean Civilization*, vol. 2, *From the Seventeenth Century to the Modern Period*. New York: Columbia University Press, 1996.

Lee, Timothy S. *Born Again: Evangelicalism in Korea*. Honolulu: University of Hawai'i Press, 2010.

Levine, Philippa, ed. *Gender and Empire*. Oxford: Oxford University Press, 2007.

Lew, Young Ick. "A Historical Overview of Korean Perceptions of the United States: Five Major Stereotypes." *Korea Journal* 44, no. 1 (Spring 2004): 109–51.

Lie, John. *Zainichi (Koreans in Japan): Diasporic Nationalism and Postcolonial Identity*. Berkeley, CA: University of California, 2008.

Lim, Sungyun. *Rules of the House: Family Law and Domestic Disputes in Colonial Korea*. Oakland, CA: University of California Press, 2019.

Locher-Schoten, Elsbeth. "Morals, Harmony, and National Identity: 'Companionate Feminism' in Colonial Indonesia in the 1930s." *Journal of Women's History* 14, no. 4 (Winter 2003): 38–58.

Mackie, Vera. *Feminism in Modern Japan*. Cambridge: Cambridge University Press, 2003.

Maliangkay, Roald. "Dirt, Noise, and Naughtiness: Cinema and the Working Class during Korea's Silent Film Era." *Asian Ethnology* 70, no. 1 (2011): 1–31.

Mann, Susan. *The Talented Women of the Zhang Family*. Berkeley, CA: University of California Press, 2007.
Marran, Christine L. *Poison Woman: Figuring Female Transgression in Modern Japanese Culture*. Minneapolis, MN: University of Minnesota Press, 2007.
Masuzawa, Tomoko. *The Invention of World Religions: Or, How European Universalism Was Preserved in the Language of Pluralism*. Chicago, IL: University of Chicago Press, 2005.
Matthews, Glenna. *"Just a Housewife": The Rise and Fall of Domesticity in America*. New York: Oxford University Press, 1987.
McClintock, Anne. *Imperial Leather: Race, Gender, and Sexuality in the Colonial Contest*. New York: Routledge, 1995.
Midgley, Clare, ed. *Gender and Imperialism*. Manchester: Manchester University Press, 1998.
Milam, Ava. *Adventures of a Home Economist*. Corvallis, OR: Oregon State University Press, 1969.
Mohanty, Chandra Talpade. "Under Western Eyes: Feminist Scholarship and Colonial Discourses." *Feminist Review* 30 (Autumn 1988): 61–88.
Molony, Barbara, Janet Theiss, and Hyaeweol Choi. *Gender in Modern East Asia: An Integrated History*. Boulder, CO: Westview, 2016.
Molony, Barbara and Kathleen Uno, eds. *Gendering Modern Japanese History*. Cambridge, MA: Harvard University Press, 2005.
Morgan, Sue, ed. *The Feminist History Reader*. London: Routledge, 2006.
Moose, Jacob Robert. *Village Life in Korea*. Nashville, TN: Publishing House of the M. E. Church South, Smith & Lamar, Agents, 1911.
Morris, Harriett. *The Art of Korean Cooking*. Rutland, VT: Charles E. Tuttle Company, 1959.
Mouer, Elizabeth Knipe. "Women in Teaching," in *Women in Changing Japan*, eds. Joyce Lebra, Joy Paulson, and Elizabeth Powers. Stanford, CA: Stanford University Press, 1976, pp. 157–90.
Mun, Yŏngju, "Ilche malgi kwanbyŏn chapchi 'kajŏng chiu'' (1936.12~1941.03)wa 'saeroun puin'," *Yŏksamunjeyŏn'gu* 17 (2007): 179–201.
Muta, Katsue. "Kajok, sŏng kwa yŏsŏng ŭi yangŭisŏng" (Family, Sexuality and the Duality of Woman), in *Tong Asia ŭi kŭndaesŏng kwa sŏng ŭi chŏngch'ihak* (The Modernity of East Asia and the Politics of Sexuality), ed. Han'guk yŏsŏng yŏn'guwŏn. Seoul: P'urŭn Sasang, 2002, pp. 127–42.
Myers, Ramon H. and Mark R. Peattie, eds. *The Japanese Colonial Empire, 1895–1945*. Princeton, NJ: Princeton University Press, 1984.
Nam, Hwasuk. "1920-nyŏndae yŏsŏng undong esŏŭi hyŏptong chŏnsŏnnon kwa Kŭnuhoe" (Kŭnuhoe and the United Front in the Women's Movement in the 1920s). *Han'guk saron* 25 (1991): 201–49.
Nilu, Kamaluddin. "A Doll's House in Asia: Juxtaposition of Tradition and Modernity." *Ibsen Studies* 8, no. 2 (2008): 112–29.
No, Chisŭng. "'Na Ungyu yŏnghwa ŭi kwan'gek tŭl hogŭn musŏng yŏnghwa kwan'gek e taehan han yŏn'gu" (A Study on the Change of Spectatorship and the Meaning of the Na Ungyu's Films from the Late 1920s to the Late 1930s). *Sanghŏ hakpo* 23 (2008): 185–224.

Noble, Mattie Wilcox. *The Journals of Mattie Wilcox Noble*. General Commission on Archives and History, The United Methodist Church, Drew University, Madison, New Jersey.
   comp. *Victorious Lives of Early Christians in Korea*. Seoul: Christian Literature Society, 1927.
Nolte, Sharon H. and Sally Ann Hastings. "The Meiji State's Policy Toward Women, 1890–1910," in *Recreating Japanese Women, 1600–1945*, ed. Gail Lee Bernstein. Berkeley, CA: University of California Press, 1991, pp. 151–74.
Oak, Sung-Deuk. "The Indigenization of Christianity in Korea: North American Missionaries' Attitudes towards Korean Religions, 1884–1910." PhD diss., Boston University, 2002.
Oh, Se-mi. "Letters to the Editor: Women, Newspapers, and the Public Sphere in Turn-of-the-Century Korea," in *Epistolary Korea: Letters in the Communicative Space of the Chosŏn, 1392–1910*, ed. Jahyun Kim Haboush. New York: Columbia University Press, 2009, pp. 157–67.
Oppenheim, Robert. *An Asian Frontier: American Anthropology and Korea, 1882–1945*. Lincoln, NE: University of Nebraska Press, 2016.
Paek, Okgyŏng. "Kŭndae Han'guk yŏsŏng ŭi Ilbon yuhak kwa yŏsŏng hyŏnsil insik: 1910-nyŏn dae rŭl chungsim ŭro" (Korean Women's Studying in Japan and their Viewpoints on Reality in the 1910s). *Ihwa sahak yŏn'gu* 39 (2009): 1–28.
Pahk, Induk. *September Monkey*. New York: Harper & Brothers, 1954.
Paisley, Fiona. *Glamour in the Pacific: Cultural Internationalism and Race Politics in the Women's Pan-Pacific*. Honolulu: University of Hawai'i Press, 2009.
   Loving Protection?: Australian Feminism and Aboriginal Women's Rights 1919–1939. Carlton: Melbourne University Press, 2000.
Pak, Ch'ansŭng. "1920-nyŏndae toIl yuhaksaeng kwa kŭ sasang chŏk tonghyang" (The Ideological Trends of Korean Students Studying in Japan in the 1920s). *Han'guk kŭnhyŏndae yŏn'gu* 30 (2004): 99–151.
   "1910-nyŏndae toIl yuhak kwa yuhak saenghwal" (Korean Students Studying in Japan in the 1910s and their Lives in Japan). *Yŏksa wa tamnon* 34 (2003): 113–39.
   "1890-nyŏndae huban kwanbi yuhaksaeng ŭi toIl yuhak" (Government-sponsored Students Studying in Japan in Late 1890s). *Kŭndae kyoryusa wa sangho insik* 1 (2001): 75–128.
   Han'guk kŭndae chŏngch'i sasangsa yŏn'gu (A Study of the History of Modern Political Thought in Korea). Seoul: Yŏksa pip'yŏngsa, 1993.
Pak, Chinyŏng. "Chungguk munhak mit Ilbon munhak pŏnyŏk ŭi yŏksasŏng kwa sangsangyŏk ŭi chŏppyŏn" (Historicity and Imagination of Chinese and Japanese Literature Translations). *Tongbang hakchi* 164 (December 2013): 259–85.
   Pŏnyŏk kwa pŏnan ŭi sidae (The Age of Translation and Adaptation). Seoul: Somyŏng ch'ulp'an, 2011.
Pak, Hwasŏng. *Saebyŏk e oech'ida* (Shouting out at the Dawn), in *Pak Hwasŏng munhak chŏnjip* (Anthology of Pak Hwasŏng's Work). Seoul: P'urŭn sasangsa, 2004.
Pak, Indŏk. *Segye ilchugi* (Record of the Global Tour). Kyŏngsŏng: Chosŏn ch'ulp'ansa, 1941.
   Chŏngmal kungmin kodŭng hakkyo (Danish Folk High School). Kyŏngsŏng: Chosŏn kidokkyo ch'ŏngnyŏn yŏnhaphoe, 1932.

Pak, Sŏnmi. *Kŭndae yŏsŏng cheguk ŭl kŏch'ŏ Chosŏn ŭro hoeyu hada* (Modern Women Return to Korea via Empire). Seoul: Ch'angbi, 2007.

Pak, Yongok. *Kim Maria*. Seoul: Hongsŏngsa, 2003.

Pang-White, Ann A., ed. and trans. *The Confucian Four Books for Women: A New Translation of the Nü Sishu and the Commentary of Wang Xiang*. Oxford: Oxford University Press, 2018.

Park, Albert L. *Building A Heaven on Earth: Religion, Activism, and Protest in Japanese Occupied Korea*. Honolulu: University of Hawai'i Press, 2015.

Park, Albert L. and David K. Yoo, eds. *Encountering Modernity: Christianity in East Asia and Asian America*. Honolulu: University of Hawai'i Press, 2014.

Park, Alyssa M. *Sovereignty Experiments: Korean Migrants and the Building of Borders in Northeast Asia, 1860–1945*. Ithaca, NY: Cornell University Press, 2019.

Park, Hyun Ok. *Two Dreams in One Bed: Empire, Social Life, and the Origins of the North Korean Revolution in Manchuria*. Durham, NC: Duke University Press, 2005.

"Ideals of Liberation: Korean Women in Manchuria," in *Dangerous Women: Gender and Korean Nationalism*, eds. Elaine H. Kim and Chungmoo Choi. New York, Routledge, 1998, pp. 229–48.

Park, Jin Y. *Women and Buddhist Philosophy: Engaging Zen Master Kim Iryŏp*. Honolulu: University of Hawai'i Press, 2017.

Park, Jin-Kyung. "Yellow Men's Burden: East Asian Imperialism, Forensic Medicine, and Conjugality in Colonial Korea." *Acta Koreana* 18, no. 1 (June 2015): 187–207.

"Picturing Empire and Illness: Biomedicine, Venereal Disease and the Modern Girl in Korea under Japanese Colonial Rule." *Cultural Studies* 28, no. 1 (2014): 108–41.

Park, Julian. "Report on College Visitation." *Korean Student Bulletin* 1, no. 1 (December 1922): 3.

Park, Sunyoung. "Rethinking Feminism in Colonial Korea: Kang Kyŏngae and 1930s Socialist Women's Literature." *positions* 21, no. 4 (2013): 947–85.

Patterson, Wayne. *The Ilse: First-Generation Korean Immigrants in Hawai'i, 1903–1973*. Honolulu: University of Hawai'i Press, 2000.

Peltonen, Matti. "Clues, Margins, and Monads: The Micro-Macro Link in Historical Research." *History and Theory* 40 (October 2001): 347–59.

Peterson, Mark. "Women without Sons: A Measure of Social Change in Yi Dynasty Korea," in *Korean Women: View from the Inner Room*, eds. Laurel Kendall and Mark Peterson. New Haven, CT: East Rock Press, 1983, pp. 33–44.

Pratt, Mary Louise. *Imperial Eyes: Travel Writing and Transculturation*. London: Routledge, 1992.

Predelli, Line Nyhagen, and Jon Miller. "Piety and Patriarchy: Contested Gender Regimes in Nineteenth-Century Evangelical Missions," in *Gendered Missions: Women and Men in Missionary Discourse and Practice*, eds. Mary Taylor Huber and Nancy C. Lutkehaus. Ann Arbor, MI: University of Michigan Press, 1999, pp. 67–112.

Presner, Todd. *Mobile Modernity: Germans, Jews, Trains*. New York: Columbia University Press, 2007.

Prieto, Laura. "Bibles, Baseball and Butterfly Sleeves: Filipina Women and American Protestant Missions, 1900–1930," in *Divine Domesticities: Christian Paradoxes in*

Asia and the Pacific, eds. Hyaeweol Choi and Margaret Jolly. Canberra: ANU Press, 2014, pp. 367–96.

Reeves-Ellington, Barbara. "Embracing Domesticity: Women, Mission, and Nation Building in Ottoman Europe, 1832–1872," in *Competing Kingdoms: Women, Mission, Nation, and the American Protestant Empire, 1812–1960*, eds. Barbara Reeves-Ellington, Kathryn Kish Sklar, and Connie A. Shemo. Durham, NC: Duke University Press, 2010, pp. 269–92.

Reeves-Ellington, Barbara, Kathryn Kish Sklar, and Connie A. Shemo, eds. *Competing Kingdoms: Women, Mission, Nation, and the American Protestant Empire, 1812–1960*. Durham, NC: Duke University Press, 2010.

Robert, Dana. "The 'Christian Home' as a Cornerstone of Anglo-American Missionary Thought and Practice," in *Converting Colonialism: Visions and Realities in Mission History, 1706–1914*, ed. Dana Robert. Grand Rapids, MI: William B. Eerdmans Publishing Company, 2008, pp. 134–65.

American Women in Mission: A Social History of Their Thought and Practice. Macon, GA: Mercer University Press, 1996.

Robertson, Claire C. and Nupur Chaudhuri, "Editors' Note: Revising the Experiences of Colonized Women: Beyond Binaries." *Journal of Women's History* 14, no. 4 (Winter 2003): 6–14.

Robinson, Michael. *Korea's Twentieth-Century Odyssey: A Short History.* Honolulu: University of Hawai'i Press, 2007.

Cultural Nationalism in Colonial Korea, 1920–1925. Seattle, WA: University of Washington Press, 1988.

Rose, Barbara. *Tsuda Umeko and Women's Education in Japan.* New Haven, CT: Yale University Press, 1992.

Rufus, W. Carl. "The Japanese Educational Policy in Korea." *Korea Review* 2, no. 11 (January 1921): 13–16.

Ryang, J. S. "Foreword," in *Fifty Years of Light*, prepared by the Missionaries of the Woman's Foreign Missionary Society of the Methodist Episcopal Church in Commemoration of the Completion of Fifty Years of Work in Korea. Seoul, 1938.

Ryu, Dae Young. "Understanding Early American Missionaries in Korea (1884–1910): Capitalist Middle-Class Values and the Weber Thesis." *Archives de sciences sociales des religions* 113 (January–March 2001): 93–117 (online).

Sand, Jordan. "Subaltern Imperialists: The New Historiography of the Japanese Empire." *Past and Present* 225, no. 1 (November 2014): 273–88.

House and Home in Modern Japan: Architecture, Domestic Space, and Bourgeois Culture, 1880–1930. Cambridge, MA: Harvard University Press, 2003.

Sato, Saburo. "Ibsen's Impact on Novelist Shimazaki Tōson." *Comparative Literature Studies* 33, no. 1 (1996): 75–81.

Schlereth, Thomas. *Victorian America: Transformations in Everyday Life, 1876–1915.* New York: HarperCollins, 1991.

Schmid, Andre. *Korea between Empires 1895–1919.* New York: Columbia University Press, 2002.

"Colonialism and the 'Korea Problem' in the Historiography of Modern Japan: A Review Article." *Journal of Asian Studies* 59, no. 4 (2000): 951–76.

Schneider, Helen. "Raising the Standards of Family Life: Ginling Women's College and Christian Social Service in Republican China," in *Divine Domesticities: Christian*

Paradoxes in Asia and the Pacific, eds. Hyaeweol Choi and Margaret Jolly. Canberra: ANU Press, 2014, pp. 113–39.
— *Keeping the Nation's House: Domestic Management and the Making of Modern China*. Vancouver: UBC Press, 2011.
— "The Professionalization of Chinese Domesticity: Ava B. Milam and Home Economics at Yenching University," in *China's Christian Colleges: Cross-Cultural Connections, 1900–1950*, eds. Daniel H. Bays and Ellen Widmer. Stanford, CA: Stanford University Press, 2009, pp. 125–46.
Scott, Joan Wallach. *The Fantasy of Feminist History*. Durham, NC: Duke University Press, 2011.
Scranton, W. B. "Report of Pastor, Baldwin Chapel and Ewa Hak Tang—1893." Minutes of the Ninth Annual Meeting of the Korea Mission of the Methodist Episcopal Church, 1893.
Seat, Karen K. *"Providence Has Freed Our Hands": Women's Missions and the American Encounter with Japan*. Syracuse, NY: Syracuse University Press, 2008.
Shin, Gi-Wook. "Agrarianism: A Critique of Colonial Modernity in Korea." *Comparative Studies in Society and History* 41, no. 4 (October 1999): 784–804.
— "Agrarian Conflict and the Origins of Korean Capitalism." *American Journal of Sociology* 103, no. 5 (March 1998): 1309–51.
Shin, Gi-Wook and Michael Robinson, eds. *Colonial Modernity in Korea*. Cambridge. MA: Harvard University Press, 1999.
Shin, Gi-Wook and Michael Robinson. "Introduction: Rethinking Colonial Korea," in *Colonial Modernity in Korea*, eds. Gi-Wook Shin and Michael Robinson. Cambridge: Harvard University Press, 1999, pp. 1–18.
Shin, Michael D. "Yi Kwang-su: The Collaborator as Modernist Against Modernity." *Journal of Asian Studies* 71, no. 1 (February 2012): 115–20.
Shohat, Ella. "Area Studies, Transnationalism, and the Feminist Production of Knowledge." *Signs* 26, no. 4 (Summer 2001): 1269–72.
Sievers, Sharon L. *Flowers in Salt: The Beginnings of Feminist Consciousness in Modern Japan*. Stanford, CA: Stanford University Press, 1983.
Simonsen, Jane. "'Object Lessons': Domesticity and Display in Native American Assimilation." *American Studies* 43, no. 1 (Spring 2002): 75–99.
Sin, Chiyŏng. *Pu/chae ŭi sidae: kŭndae kyemonggi mit singminjigi Chosŏn ŭi yŏnsŏl, chwadamhoe* (The Age of Absence: Speeches and Roundtable Talks of Korea during the Enlightenment and Colonial Periods). Seoul: Somyŏng, 2012.
Sin, Namju. "1920-nyŏndae chisigin yŏsŏng ŭi tŭngjang kwa haeoe yuhak" (The Emergence of Women Intellectuals and Studying Overseas in the 1920s). *Yŏsŏng kwa yŏksa* 3 (2005): 1–75.
Sin, Tongwŏn. "Ilche kangjŏmgi yŏ ŭisa Hŏ Yŏngsuk ŭi sam kwa ŭihak" (Life and Works of Hŏ Yŏngsuk, the First Female Medical Practitioner). *Ŭisahak* 21, no. 1 (2012): 25–66.
Singh, Maina Chawla. *Gender, Religion, and "Heathen Lands": American Missionary Women in South Asia (1860s-1940s)*. New York: Garland Publishing, Inc., 2000.
Sinha, Mrinalini. "Gender and Nation," in *Women's History in Global Perspective*, ed. Bonnie Smith. Urbana, IL: University of Illinois Press, 2004, pp. 229–74.
Smart, Barry. "Modernity, Postmodernity and the Present," in *Theories of Modernity and Postmodernity*, ed. Bryan S. Turner. London: Sage, 1990, pp. 14–30.

Smith, Robert. "Making Village Women into 'Good Wives and Wise Mothers' in Prewar Japan." *Journal of Family History* (Spring 1983): 70–84.
Sŏ, Chŏngja, comp. *Chŏngwŏl Ra Hyesŏk chŏnjip* (Works of Chŏngwŏl Ra Hyesŏk). Seoul: Kukhak charyowŏn, 2001.
Sŏ, Kyŏngsŏk and U Miyŏng, eds. *Sin yŏsŏng kil wi e sŏda* (A New Woman Stands in the Street). Seoul: Homi, 2007.
Soh, C. Sarah. *The Comfort Women: Sexual Violence and Postcolonial Memory in Korea and Japan*. Chicago, IL: University of Chicago Press, 2009.
Song, Jee Eun Regina. "The Soybean Paste Girl: The Cultural and Gender Politics of Coffee Consumption in Contemporary South Korea." *Journal of Korean Studies* 19. no.2 (2014): 429–48.
Song, Yŏnok. "Chosŏn 'sin yŏsŏng' ŭi naesyŏnŏllijŭm kwa chendŏ" (Gender and Nationalism of the "New Woman" in Korea), in *Sin yŏsŏng* (New Women), ed. Mun Okp'yo. Seoul: Ch'ŏngnyŏnsa, 2003, pp. 83–117.
Sorensen, Clark. "National Identity and the Creation of the Category of 'Peasant' in Colonial Korea," in *Colonial Modernity in Korea*, eds. Gi-Wook Shin and Michael Robinson. Cambridge, MA: Harvard University Press, 1999, pp. 288–310.
Stark, Rodney. *Bearing False Witness: Debunking Centuries of Anti-Catholic History*. West Conshohocken, PA: Templeton Press, 2016.
Stoler, Ann Laura. *Carnal Knowledge and Imperial Power: Race and the Intimate in Colonial Rule*. Berkeley, CA: University of California Press, 2002.
Struck, Bernhard, Kate Ferris, and Jacques Revel. "Introduction: Space and Scale in Transnational History." *International History Review* 33, no. 4 (December 2011): 573–84.
Sup'ia 100-nyŏngsa kanhaeng wiwŏnhoe. *Sup'ia 100-nyŏnsa 1908–2008* (The Hundredth History of Sup'ia). Kwangju: Kwangju Sup'ia yŏja chung kodŭng hakkyo, 2008.
Taehan YWCA yŏnhaphoe. *Han'guk YWCA pan paengnyŏn* (The Fiftieth History of Korea YWCA). Seoul: Taehan YWCA yŏnhaphoe, 1976.
Taylor, Charles. *Modern Social Imaginaries*. Durham, NC: Duke University Press, 2004.
Taylor, Sandra. "Abby M. Colby: The Christian Response to a Sexist Society." *New England Quarterly* 52, no. 1 (March 1979): 68–79.
Templeton, Joan. *Ibsen's Women*. Cambridge: Cambridge University Press, 1997.
Thelen, David. "The Nation and Beyond: Transnational Perspectives on United States History." *Journal of American History* 86, no. 3 (December 1999): 965–75.
Thornber, Karen. *Empire of Texts in Motion: Chinese, Korean, and Taiwanese Transculturations of Japanese Literature*. Cambridge, MA: Harvard University Press, 2009.
Thorne, Susan. *Congregational Missions and the Making of an Imperial Culture in Nineteenth-Century England*. Stanford, CA: Stanford University Press, 1999.
——— "Missionary-Imperial Feminism," in *Gendered Missions: Women and Men in Missionary Discourse and Practice*, eds. Mary Taylor Huber and Nancy Lutkehaus. Ann Arbor, MI: University of Michigan Press, 1999, pp. 39–66.
Tikhonov, Vladimir. "Masculinizing the Nation: Gender Ideologies in Traditional Korea and in the 1890s-1900s Korean Enlightenment Discourse." *Journal of Asian Studies* 66, no. 4 (2007): 1029–65.

Tocco, Martha. "Made in Japan: Meiji Women's Education," in *Gendering Modern Japanese History*, eds. Barbara Molony and Kathleen Uno. Cambridge, MA: Harvard University Press, 2005, pp. 39–60.

Tongnip undongsa charyojip (The History of Independence Movement: Sourcebook), available at http://e-gonghun.mpva.go.kr.

Tsurumi, E. Patricia. "Colonial Education in Korea and Taiwan," in *The Japanese Colonial Empire, 1895–1945*, eds. Ramon H. Myers and Mark R. Peattie. Princeton, NJ: Princeton University Press, 1984, pp. 275–311.

Tyrrell, Ian. *Reforming the World: The Creation of America's Moral Empire*. Princeton, NJ: Princeton University Press, 2010.

"What is Transnational History?" A paper given at the Ecole des Hautes Etudes en Sciences Sociale, Paris, January 2007.

"New Comparisons, International Worlds: Transnational and Comparative Perspectives." *Australian Feminist Studies* 16, no. 36 (2001): 355–61.

Woman's World/Woman's Empire: The Woman's Christian Temperance Union in International Perspective, 1880–1930. Chapel Hill. NC: University of North Carolina Press, 1991.

U, Miyŏng. "Sin yŏsŏng Ch'oe Yŏngsuk non: yŏsŏng sam kwa chehyŏn ŭi kŏri" (A Study on the New Woman Ch'oe Yŏngsuk: A Woman's Life and the Distance in Representation). *Minjok munhwa yŏn'gu* 45 (2006): 293–328.

Uchida, Jun. *Brokers of Empire: Japanese Settler Colonialism in Korea, 1876–1945*. Cambridge, MA: Harvard University Press, 2011.

Uwŏl munjip p'yŏnch'an wiwŏnhoe. *Uwŏl munjip* 1 (Works of Uwŏl). Seoul: Ewha Womans University Press, 1979.

Vautrin, Minnie. *Terror in Minnie Vautrin's Nanjing: Diaries and Correspondence, 1937–38*.Urbana, IL: University of Illinois Press, 2008.

Veer, Peter van der, ed. *Conversion to Modernities: The Globalization of Christianity*. New York: Routledge, 1996.

Wagner, Ellasue. *Korea: The Old and the New*. New York: Fleming H. Revell Company, 1931.

Walsh, Judith E. *Domesticity in Colonial India*. Lanham. MD: Rowman and Littlefield Publishers, 2004.

Walter, Jeannette. *Aunt Jean*. Boulder, CO: Johnson Publishing Company, 1968.

Wang, Chih-ming. *Transpacific Articulations: Student Migration and the Remaking of Asian America*. Honolulu: University of Hawai'i Press, 2013.

Wang, Zheng. *Women in the Chinese Enlightenment: Oral and Textual Histories*. Berkeley, CA: University of California Press, 1999.

Weber, Hans-Ruedi. *Asia and the Ecumenical Movement 1895–1961*. London: SCM Press Ltd, 1966.

Wells, Kenneth M. "Expanding their Realm: Women and Public Agency in Colonial Korea," in *Women's Suffrage in Asia*, eds. Louise Edwards and Mina Roces. London: Routledge Curzon, 2004, pp. 152–69.

"The Price of Legitimacy: Women and the Kŭnuhoe Movement, 1927–1931," in *Colonial Modernity in Korea*, eds. Gi-Wook Shin and Michael Robinson. Cambridge, MA: Harvard University Press, 1999, pp. 191–220.

New God, New Nation: Protestants and Self-Reconstruction Nationalism in Korea, 1896–1937. North Sydney: Allen & Unwin Pty Ltd, 1990.

Welter, Barbara. "She Hath Done What She Could: Protestant Women's Missionary Careers in Nineteenth-Century America." *American Quarterly* 30, no. 5 (Winter 1978): 624–38.
Wheeler, W. Reginald, Henry H. King, and Alexander B. Davidson, eds. *The Foreign Student in America*. New York: Association Press, 1925.
Widmer, Ellen. "The Seven Sisters and China, 1900–1950," in *China's Christian Colleges: Cross-Cultural Connections, 1900–1950*, eds. Daniel H. Bays and Ellen Widmer. Stanford, CA: Stanford University Press, 2009, pp. 83–105.
Woollacott, Angela. *Race and the Modern Exotic: Three "Australian" Women on Global Display*. Clayton: Monash University Publishing, 2011.
"Postcolonial Histories and Catherine Hall's Civilising Subjects," in *Connected Worlds*, eds. Ann Curthoys and Marilyn Lake. Canberra: ANU Press, 2006, pp. 63–74.
To Try Her Fortune in London: Australian Women, Colonialism, and Modernity. Oxford: Oxford University Press, 2001.
Yang, Lianfen. "The Absence of Gender in May Fourth Narratives of Women's Emancipation: A Case Study of Hu Shi's *The Greatest Event in Life*." *New Zealand Journal of Asian Studies* 12, no. 1 (June 2010): 6–13.
Yang, Yoon Sun. *From Domestic Women to Sensitive Young Men: Translating the Individual in Early Colonial Korea*. Cambridge, MA: Harvard University Press, 2017.
"Enlightened Daughter, Benighted Mother: Yi Injik's Tears of Blood and Early Twentieth-Century Korean Domestic Fiction." *positions* 22, no. 1 (Winter 2014): 103–30.
Ye, Weili. *Seeking Modernity in China's Name: Chinese Students in the United States, 1900–1927*. Stanford, CA: Stanford University Press, 2002.
Yi, Christina. "National Language, Imperialization and the Gendered Aporia of Empire." *positions* 24, no. 4 (November 2016): 813–37.
Yi, Hwayŏng et al. *Han'guk kŭndae yŏsŏng ŭi ilsang munhwa* (The Everyday Life and Culture of the Korean Modern Woman), vol. 8. Seoul: Kukhak charyowŏn, 2004.
Yi, Kisŏ. *Kyoyuk ŭi kil, sinang ŭi kil* (Path to Education, Path to Faith). Seoul: Puksanch'ek, 2012.
Yi, Kwangnin. *Han'guk kaehwasa yŏn'gu* (A Study of the History of Korean Enlightenment). Seoul: Ilchogak, 1981.
Yi, Kwangsu. *Hŭk* (Soil). Seoul: Munhak kwa chisŏngsa, 2005.
Chaesaeng (Rebirth). Seoul: Uri munhaksa, 1996.
Yi, Kyŏnga and Chŏn Pongŭi. "1920–1930-nyŏndae kyŏngsŏngbu ŭi munhwajut'aekchi kaebal e taehan yŏn'gu" (A Study of the Development of the District of Culture Houses in Seoul in the 1920s and 1930s). *Taehan'gŏnch'ukhakhoe nonmunjip* 22, no. 3 (March 2006): 191–200.
Yi, Kyŏngnan. "1930-nyŏndae nongmin sosŏl ŭl t'onghae pon 'singminji kŭndaehwa' wa nongmin saenghwal" ("Colonial Modernity" and Peasant Life Reflected in Peasant Literature in the 1930s), in *Ilche ŭi singmin chibae wa ilsang saenghwal* (Japanese Colonial Control and Everyday Life), ed. Yonsei University kukhak yŏn'guwŏn. Seoul: Hyean, 2004.
Yi, Paeyong, Son Sŭnghŭi, Mun Sukchae, and Cho Kyŏngwŏn. "Han'guk kidokkyo yŏsŏng kyoyuk ŭi sŏnggwa wa chŏnmang—Ihwa Yŏja Taehakkyo rŭl chungsim

ŭro" (Accomplishment and Prospect of Korean Christian Education for Women—with a Focus on Ewha Womans University). *Ihwa sahak yŏn'gu* 27 (2000): 9–36.
Yi, Sanggyŏng. *In'gan ŭro salgo sipta* (I Want to Live as a Human Being). Seoul: Han'gilsa, 2000.
——— ed. *Na Hyesŏk chŏnjip* (The Complete Works of Na Hyesŏk). Seoul: T'aehaksa, 2000.
Yi, Songhŭi. "Yang Hanna ŭi sam kwa hwaltong e kwanhan il koch'al" (A Study of the Life and Work of Yang Hanna). *Yŏsŏng yŏn'gu nonjip* 13 (2002): 5–37.
Yi, Sŏngmi. "Sin Saimdang: The Foremost Woman Painter of the Chosŏn Dynasty," in *Creative Women of Korea: The Fifteenth through the Twentieth Centuries*, ed. Young-Key Kim-Renaud. Armonk, NY: M. E. Sharpe, 2004, pp. 58–77.
Yi, Sugin. "Sin Saimdang tamnon ŭi kyebohak (1) kŭndae ijŏn" (The Genealogy of the Discourse on Sin Saimdang in Pre-modern Korea). *Chindan hakpo* 106 (2008): 1–31.
——— trans. *Yŏ sasŏ* (The Four Books for Women). Seoul: Yŏiyŏn, 2003.
Yi, Sunt'ak. *Ch'oegŭn segye ilchugi* (Record of the Recent Global Tour). Kyŏngsŏng: Hansŏng tosŏ chusik hoesa, 1934.
Yi, Tŏkju. *Han'guk kyohoe ch'ŏŭm yŏsŏngdŭl* (The First Group of Women in Korean Churches). Seoul: Hongsŏngsa, 2007.
Yim, Louise. *My Forty Years Fight for Korea*. Seoul: International Cultural Research Center, Chung-ang University, 1951.
Yoo, Theodore Jun. *It's Madness: The Politics of Mental Health in Colonial Korea*. Oakland, CA: University of California Press, 2016.
——— "The Biography of Ch'oe Yŏng-suk and the Politics of Gender in Colonial Korea." *Journal of Women's History* 21, no. 4 (Winter 2009): 161–3.
——— *The Politics of Gender in Colonial Korea: Education, Labor, and Health, 1910–1945*. Berkeley, CA: University of California Press, 2008.
——— "The 'New Woman' and the Politics of Love, Marriage and Divorce in Colonial Korea." *Gender and History* 17, no. 2 (August 2005): 295–324.
Yu, Chinwŏl. *Kim Iryŏp ŭi Sin yŏja yŏn'gu* (A Study of Sin Yŏja by Kim Iryŏp). Seoul: P'urŭn sasang, 2006.
Yu, Kilchun. *Sŏyu kyŏnmun* (Observations of my Travels to the West), trans. Hŏ Kyŏngjin. Seoul: Hanyang Ch'ulp'an, 1995.
Yu, Sŏnghŭi. "Han'guk YWCA undong ŭi silch'ŏn chŏk kidokkyo yŏsŏngjuŭi e kwanhan yŏn'gu" (A Study of Action-oriented Christian Feminism in the Korea YWCA Movement). PhD diss., Seoul National University, 2013.
Yun, Chŏngnan. "19 segi mal 20 segi ch'o chae Chosŏn Ilbon yŏsŏng ŭi chŏngch'esŏng kwa Chosŏn yŏsŏng kyoyuk saŏp: kidokkyo yŏsŏng Fuchizawa Noe (1850–1936) rŭl chungsimŭro" (The Identity and Educational Work of Japanese Women in Colonial Korea in the late Nineteenth and Early Twentieth Centuries with Focus on Fuchizawa Noe). *Yŏksa wa kyŏnggye* 73 (2009): 137–72.
Yun, Kŏnch'a. *Han'guk kŭndae kyoyuk ŭi sasang kwa undong* (The Ideology of Korean Modern Education and its Social Movements), trans. Sim Sŏngbo. Seoul: Ch'ŏngsa, 1987.

Index

#Me Too Movement, 206

105 Incident (in 1911), 22

Addams, Jane, 2
Africa, 11, 163
agrarianism, 157–58
Allen, Young J., 43–44
Alliance of Chosŏn Credit Union (Chosŏn Kŭmyung Chohap Yŏnhaphoe), 159–60
American Home Economics Association, 101
An Sogyŏng, 94–95
Anglo-Chinese Southern Methodist School, 43–44
Aoyagi Tsunatarō, 6
Appenzeller, Alice, 147n.172, 151n.4, 181n.136, 190
architecture, 28; in Chosŏn, 54; western-style, 76–77, 83–87, 93–95. *See also* culture house
archives, mission, 32; politics of, 30–33, 207
Art of Korean Cooking, The, 98
Asia, 11, 27, 29, 35, 205; morality in, 92
assimilation, 23, 27–28, 49, 56, 132–33, 167
Australia, 2, 18, 25n.102, 29, 33, 90, 113, 199–200, 207; missionaries from, 39, 122

Baird, Annie, 56–57, 60–63, 78–81
Bank of Korea, 36
Barbour, Levi, 130–31
Barbour Scholarship for Oriental Women, 130–7, 202, 204
Beecher, Catherine, 17
biopolitics, 17
birth control, 1, 27
Bishop, Henry, 83
border-crossing, 18, 109, 113, 147, 198–99, 201
Britain, 1–2, 205
Brown, Arthur, 77
Brunner, Edmund de Schweinitz, 164
budan seiji, see mudan chŏngch'i

Buddhism, 17, 21
bunka seiji, see munhwa chŏngch'i

cadastral land survey, 156
Campaign to Increase Rice Production, 158
Canada, 2, 90, 200
Ch'a Mirisa, 112
Ch'ae Mansik, 68
Chaesaeng (Rebirth), 93–94
Chaffin, Anna B., 152
Chang Iuk, 143
Chasŏn puinhoe chapchi, 46, 59–60
chastity, 44, 65, 71
Cheguk sinmun, 46
child custody, 1
childrearing, 59–61, 88–91, 96, 103–105, 181
China, 2–3, 10, 12, 33, 40, 43, 47, 90, 98, 100, 111–13, 120–24, 127, 130, 136, 199, 205
Ch'oe Isun (aka E Soon Choi), 102, 104–5, 197–98, 202–3
Ch'oe Yongsin, 155, 175–78, 180, 184–86
Ch'oe Yŏngsuk, 1, 33, 121, 123–27, 138, 202, 204–5
Ch'oegŭn segye ilchugi (Record of the Recent Global Tour), 118
Ch'ŏndogyo (Religion of the Heavenly Way), 153
Chŏng Ch'ilsŏng, 50, 154n.20
Chosa Sich'aldan (Korean Couriers' Observation Mission), 3
Chosen Christian College (now Yonsei University), 118, 132, 136
Chosŏn dynasty, 7, 9, 31, 36, 40–41, 49, 196; women's education in, 44–45, 47–48
Chosŏn Pangnamhoe (1929), 86–87
Choy, Martha, 136
Chu Yosŏp, 52
chubu (house mistress), 64, 71, 96
civilization, 40, 53; Christian, 53–54, 163; discourse on, 5, 44, 103; gender and, 41–44, 47; Western, 3–5, 11, 20–21, 42, 77, 91, 117

232

Index

civilization and enlightenment (*munmyŏng kaehwa*), 20, 42–43, 47, 111, 194
collaborators (*ch'inilp'a*), 28, 109, 183
Colonial Modernity in Korea, 5–6
colonialism, Dutch, 19; Euro-American, 16, 20, 74, 194; and legal impact on women, 9. *See also* imperialism
Committee on Friendly Relations among Foreign Students of the International YMCA, 120, 128–29, 139
companionate feminism, 19
concubine, 69, 112
Confucianism, and politics of knowledge, 38; Chinese, 7; gender ethics in, 7–8, 28, 40–49, 54–55, 65, 72, 194; re-Confucianization, 196
Conrow, Marion, 121
contact zone, 7, 30, 55, 81
converts, 10, 15, 22–24, 32, 82, 120; agency of the, 23–24, 79–81; women, 13, 25, 63
Cosmopolitan Clubs, 140–41
cradle roll parties, 79–80
culture house (*munhwa chut'aek*), 86–88, 93–95, 185. *See also* house and home
culture life (*munhwa saenghwal*), 81–82, 88–89, 107

Danish folk high schools, 165, 168–71, 179–81
Denmark, 33, 125, 143, 155, 164–66, 168–71, 180, 207; Danish models for rural reform, 16, 144–45, 165–71; women in, 143–5
diet, 27, 205; balanced, 88, 102; Korean, 101–2, 105; Western, 77, 98
divorce, 1, 65–67, 71, 92, 109, 178, 186
Doll's House, A, 66–69, 109, 193–94
domesticity, and feminism, 55–56; discourse of, 42, 74, 90; during the Pacific War, 105; imperialism and, 17, 34–35; in curriculum, 57–59, 96–98; middle-class, 17; modern, 29, 48, 55, 59, 61, 74–76, 81, 90, 93, 96, 104, 107–8; Victorian notion of, 25, 28, 39, 41, 53–55

East Asia, 9–10, 43, 124–25; gender ideology in, 40–41, 47; home economics in, 98–101, 197
Edict of Korean Education, 48
Edo period, 7; women's education in, 49
education, at mission schools, 11–12, 23–25, 41, 51–52, 57–60, 90, 96–98, 115–16, 120; college, 52, 113–4, 142; enrollments, 26, 50, 90n.64; during the Chosŏn dynasty, 44–45; overseas, 12, 19, 121, 134, 137–38, 140, 202; under Japanese rule, 27, 51–52, 114, 132–33
employment, 1, 15, 128, 137–38; difficulty in, 126–27
enlightenment (*kyemong*), 114, 154–55, 161–62, 194; rural, 174–76, 180, 187–88
equality, 143, 196; class, 6; gender, 6, 21, 39, 104, 144
Esther Circle, 152
Europe, 1–2, 10, 29–30, 35, 44–45, 76, 90–91, 109, 111, 113, 117, 123, 143, 155, 164, 167, 170, 197, 199
Ewha Girls' School (Ewha Haktang), 7, 51, 57, 97, 112, 116, 120–21, 123, 127, 133–34, 151, 190
Ewha Women's Professional School (Ewha Yŏja Chŏnmun Hakkyo), 95, 97–98, 197, 102–7, 122, 134, 136–37, 147
Expedition to Taiwan (in 1874), 5

family, 9, 19, 28, 44; Christian, 46; instability of the, 66–71; modern, 59, 64, 89, 92, 196; missionary, 64; nuclear, 39, 89; patriarchal, 61; proletarian, 50
Farmers' Self-Cultivation Center (Nongmin Suyangso), 180. *See also* Rural Revitalization Campaign
fashions, 68–69, 144–45, 147–48; politics of clothing, 201–205; Western-style, 2, 69, 100
feminism, 18, 38, 191–93, 206–7; companionate, 19; domestic, 55–56; postcolonial, 14, 30–32
femininity, discourse of, 8
filial piety, 44
films, 68–71; Hollywood, 2
France, 1, 92n.72
Frey, Lulu, 57, 96, 120

gaichi (colony), 8
Gandhi, Mohandas, 125–26, 205
gender ideology, 9, 19, 24, 27, 28, 37, 56, 61, 72, 195–96, 206; localized, 41; Meiji, 41–42, 48; middle class, 50–51; Victorian, 25, 39, 42. *See also* wise mother, good wife
Germany, 33, 91, 125; women in, 144–5, 155, 207
Ginling College (in Nanjing), 99n.101, 120
Government-General of Korea, 22, 32
Gramsci, Antonio, 5
Great Depression of 1929, 130, 156
Green Flag Association (Ryokki renmei), 106
Grundtvig, N. F. S., 165–69
Gustaf VI Adolf, King of Sweden, 124–5

Ha Nansa, 112, 120
Hale, Sarah Josepha, 17
Hall, Rosetta Sherwood, 119, 133–4

hanbok (Korean dress), 147, 202, 205. *See also* fashions
han'gŭl (Korean vernacular), 46, 166
Hansŏng Kodŭng Yŏhakkyo, 45, 47–48
Hawai'i, Korean immigrants in, 119–20, 136–7
hegemony, cultural, 4–8, 75, 194–5
Hillman, Mary, 120
Hiratsuka Raichō, 2, 193
Hŏ Chŏngsuk, 143, 155, 161
Hŏ Yŏngsuk, 88–89
hojŏk (household-registry system), 9
home economics (*kasa*), 13, 28–29, 47, 51, 59, 75, 85, 91; Department of, 95–105
Home Exhibition (Kajŏng Pangnamhoe), 28, 83–87, 107, 197
Home Management House, 103–104
house and home, 73–74; Christian, 54; concept of, 74–75; inner quarters of, 18; interior, 78; Japanese style, 75, 83, 85–86; missionary, 28, 76–83; sweet home, 64, 73, 83–84, 88–89, 93. *See also* culture house
Hulbert, Homer, 203
Hurrey, Charles D., 129
Hwang Aedŏk (aka Hwang Aesidŏk), 1, 138–39, 149–53, 155, 174–76, 181, 188
Hwang Sindŏk, 52, 58–59
hygiene, 47, 59–60, 88, 93, 96, 103, 159, 161, 181, 191
hyŏnmo yangch'ŏ, *see* wise mother, good wife
Hyŏpsŏng Theology Institute for Women, 152, 174–76

Ibsen, Henrik, 67–68, 109, 193–94
ie (household), 9
Ilsin High School for Girls, 122
Immigration Act (1924), 99, 129–30
imperialism, and evangelical Christianity, 20–23; characteristics of Japanese, 4–7, 11–12, 22–23, 42, 75, 87, 105–6, 159, 182–83; culture in, 6; American, 11, 17, 20; gender and, 10–11, 55, 74, 93; Japanese settlers in Korea, 6, 11, 87; mimetic, 5; subaltern, 4–5
India, 1–2, 10, 125–26, 205
Indian National Congress, 125–6, 205
indigenization, of Western knowledge, 76, 99–101, 104–5
individualism, 19, 67, 143, 148
individuality, 91, 103–4
Indonesia, women in, 19
Inhyŏng ŭi chip ŭl nawasŏ (*After the Doll's House*), 68
Inoue Hideko, 86
Inoue Tomo, 130–1

Inside-outside rule (*naeoebŏp*), 110, 147, 159
International Friendship Scholarship, 99–105
International Missionary Council, 12, 143, 146, 162–4
International People's College (in Helsingør), 169–171; enrollments of foreign students in, 169–70
Itō Chūta, 85–86

Japan, American-run mission schools in, 115–6; as a mediator, 116–7; Christians in, 23; studying in, 115–7; women of, 8. *See also* imperialism
jokunsho (instructional texts for girls), 49

kajŏng (governing the household), 49, 64–65
Kajŏng chapchi, 46, 59, 96
Kajŏng chiu, 159–60
Kajŏng Pangnamhoe, *see* Home Exhibition
Kang Cheng (aka Ida Kahn), 130
Kang Kyŏngae, 92–93
katei (home), 75
Katei hakurankai, 85–86
Keijō Imperial University (Kyŏngsŏng Cheguk Taehakkyo), 106, 114, 133
Kijŏn Girls School, 128
Kim Hamna (aka Hannah Kim), 91, 102–4
Kim Hwallan (aka Helen Kim), 62, 121, 143–8, 155, 169, 172, 176, 180–1, 190; PhD dissertation of, 162–8, 188
Kim Maria, 62, 138
Kim Meri (aka Mary Kim), 134, 136, 140, 202, 204
Kim Sedŭi, 63–64
Kim Sinsil, 134
Kim Sŏngsil, 141
Kim Tongjun (aka Katherine Kim), 134, 136
Kim Ŭnhŭi, 50
Kim Wŏnju (aka Kim Iryŏp), 72, 190–1
Kinjo Gakuin, 116
Kishida Toshiko, 7
Ko Hwanggyŏng (aka Evelyn Koh), 106, 134, 136, 202, 204
kokumin (national subject), 48
Kokumin shinbun, 85
Kold, Christen, 169
Kollontai, Alexandra, 2
kōminka (imperialization), 27–28, 75, 90, 105–6, 182–3
Korea mission, by the Japanese, 22–23
Korea YMCA, in support of *naisen ittai*, 183; rural work of, 172, 176, 179, 188. *See also* Young Men's Christian Association

Index

Korea YWCA, rural work of, 162, 172–8. *See also* Young Women's Christian Association
Korean Industrial Exhibition (Chosŏn Mulsan Kongjinhoe), 83
Korean Provisional Government (in Shanghai), 121–3
Korean Student Bulletin, 119, 136, 139–40
Korean Student Federation of North America, 119, 127
koseki, see hojŏk
ku yŏsŏng (old-fashioned woman), 52, 61
kŭlbang (village schools), 167–8
kungmin (national subjects), 49
Kŭnhwahoe (Association of the Rose of Sharon), 138–9
Kŭnuhoe (Friends of the Rose of Sharon), 161–2
Kwassui Women's College, 116, 131, 134
Kyŏngsŏng ilbo, 83

liangqi xianmu, 40–41, 47. *See also* wise mother, good wife
literacy, 32, 50, 68, 168; movement, 152, 154, 157, 159, 161, 174–7, 187
Lucy Girls School, 155, 175
Luxemburg, Rosa, 2
Lyon, Mary, 2

Maeil sinbo, 67, 83, 85, 194
Manchuria, 29n.115, 80, 124, 149, 153
Manchurian Incident, 27
Manniche, Peter, 169–71
March First Independence Movement, 22, 109, 115, 121–2, 138
marriage, 1, 62, 66, 71; companionate, 73; early, 174
microhistory, 34
Milam, Ava, 98–105
Mimong (Illusive Dream), 68–71
missionaries, 11, 61, 164; against Westernization, 100–1; Australian, 122; impact of women, 9, 51–55, 107, 119–20; married women, 62–64; unmarried women, 61–62
modern social imaginaries, 34
modernity, 34–35, 70, 82; colonial, 5; gender and, 46, 53, 59, 67–68, 110, 144, 147; Japanese representations of, ix, 83–85, 107; religion and, 20–25, 158; rural, 161–72; secular, 24, 195; Western, i, ix–x, 91, 93, 114, 117, 195–7
Moose, Jacob Robert, 73
Morris, Harriett, 98, 103, 121

motherhood, 38, 58–59, 66, 71–72, 89–90, 93; 'empire of the mother,' 54, 90n.66
Mott, John R., 2
mudan chŏngch'i (Military Rule), 26
munhwa chŏngch'i (Cultural Rule), 22, 26–27
munmyŏng kaehwa, see civilization and enlightenment
Museum of Far East Antiquities, 125
music, 82–83, 199

Na Hyesŏk, 64–67, 116, 190–3
Naehun (Instructions for Women), 44
Naidu, Sarojini, 2, 125–6, 205
naisen ittai (Japan and Korea as One Body), 27, 105–6, 159, 182–3
namnyŏ yubyŏl (distinction between man and woman), 54
Nanjing Bible Teaching Institute, 121
Nanjing Ming De Girls' School, 123
nationalism, ix; 14–18, bourgeois, 157; gender and, 18–19, 46, 67, 138–48, 186n.162, 194
New Woman, 31–32, 52, 64, 67, 71–72, 186; Christian, 62
Nihon genji kyōiku (*Contemporary Japanese Education*), 47
Noble, Mattie, 63, 79
novels, 31, 68, 93–94, 184–6
Nü sishu (The Four Books for Women), 44–45
nutrition, 59, 89, 98, 101–3

O Ch'ŏnsŏk, 120, 129
object lessons, 75n.11, 79, 83, 85
Ohio Wesleyan University, 112, 120–1, 146
Oregon Agricultural College, 98–105, 130
oryun (Five Moral Imperatives), 8

Pacific War, The, 105–6
Pak Esther (aka Kim Chŏmdong), 119
Pak Indŏk (aka Induk Pahk), 66–67, 138, 144–5, 190; fund-raising overseas, 182; rural revitalization campaign, 155, 162, 168–72, 178–86
Pan-Pacific Women's Conference, 136
patriarchy, 38, 42, 61, 65, 191, 196, 206; in crisis, 24, 38, 40, 72
Payne, John Howard, 83
Peace Memorial Exhibition (1922), 86
peasant literature (*nongmin sosŏl*), 186
Petition for a Girls' School, 45
Philippines, 11, 32
polytheism, 81
postcolonialism, theories of, 6–7; and feminism, 14, 30–31

Presbyterian Women's Missionary Union (in Victoria, Australia), 122
print media, 8, 27, 46, 65–66, 72, 87, 90–93, 117, 143, 194
Protectorate of Japan, 3, 47
Protestant modernity, 15–25, 27–28
pubu yubyŏl (distinction between husband and wife), 8
pudŏk (womanly virtue), 28, 37, 47–49; during the Chosŏn dynasty, 41, 49
Pusan Yŏja Ch'ŏngnyŏnhoe, 122

Qing China, 40, 44

racial politics, 4, 7–8, 12, 18, 23, 30, 74, 132, 199
racism, 143, 146–7, 205
religion, 21, 59–61; and modernity, 15, 20–25; anti-, 163; gender and, 63–64, 79; legitimate or pseudo, 21
Risō no katei (*The Ideal Home*), 85
Rothweiler, Louise, 97
Rufus, W. Carl, 132–7
Rural Revitalization Campaign, 6, 153, 172, 177; Japanese colonial government's, 154, 158–61
Russia, 1, 2, 124, 155
Russo-Japanese War (1904–1905), 4, 10
ryōsai kenbo (good wife, wise mother), 9, 28, 40–41, 47–50, 55, 72, 196. See also *hyŏnmo yangch'ŏ*

Sangnoksu (*Evergreen*), 99–104
Scholarship, 109, 111–4, 119, 127–38, 184–6, 197–9, 202
Scranton, Mary F., 51
Scranton, William, 54
Secularization, ix, 21, 23–24, 195
Segye ilchugi (*Record of the Global Tour*), 110
Seitō (*Blue Stockings*), 193
Self Help Department, 57
self-cultivation (J: *shūyō*, K: *suyang*), 180, 187–8
self-renovation (*charyŏk kaengsaeng*), 160
separate spheres, 12, 19, 53, 55
September Monkey, 110
shamanism, 60–61
Shih Mei-yu (aka Mary Stone), 130
shijuku (private academies), 7
Shinto, 21, 27
Sim Hun, 184
Sin Hŭng'u (aka Hugh Cynn), 168
Sin kajŏng (magazine), 59, 83
sin kajŏng (new family), 64, 83
Sin Saimdang, representations of, 36–39
sin sosŏl (new fiction), 46, 111
Sin yŏja (magazine), 72, 190–4
Sin yŏsŏng (magazine), 59
sin yŏsŏng, see New Woman
Sinhak wŏlbo, 46
Sinhan minbo, 119, 130
Sino-Japanese War (1894–1895), 4, 10
Sino-Japanese War (1937–1945), 27, 105, 159, 184, 188
Skinner, Amy, 122
Snook, Velma, 57
Sŏbongch'ong, 125
Socialism, 50, 68, 92, 123, 127, 143, 155, 157, 161–2, 170–1
Sohye, Queen, 44
Son Chinsil, 142
Son Chŏnggyu, 160
Song Poksin (aka Grace Song), 133–4
South Korea, 31n.118, 196, 198
Sŏyu kyŏnmun (*Observations of my Travels to the West*), 43
Stockholm University, 1, 124–5
Student Volunteer Movement, 12, 109, 122, 179, 182, 188
studying overseas, 19, 27, 120–2, 127, 140, 202; colonial government's policy in, 114–5; government-sponsored, 111; in Japan, 17, 111
Sungŭi Yŏhakkyo (in P'yŏngyang), 52, 57
superstition, 41, 55, 57, 59–61, 160, 174
Sup'ia Girls School, 116
susin (morality), 8–9, 56
Suzhou Women's Teachers' College, 121–2
Sweden, 1–2, 33, 123–7, 205, 207

Taehan Empire (1897–1910), 45
Tagore, Rabindranath, 119, 170
tanbal (bobbed hair), 123, 147
terakoya (local schools), 7
Terauchi Masatake, 22
textbooks, colonial-era, 8
Tŏkhwa Yŏsuk, 183
Tokutomi Sohō, 85
Tokyo Women's Medical College, 88, 134
Tonga ilbo, 64, 91, 184
tongdo sŏgi (Eastern Way, Western Method), 43
Tongnip sinmun, 46
translation, Japanese, 3; of foreign literature, 2, 17, 90n.68, 193–4; of foreign terms, 73, 93
Transnationality, 2, 5, 12–14, 16–19
Travel, overseas, 43, 74, 109–11, 113, 118; trans-Siberian route, 123–4. See also studying overseas

Traveling Secretary of the Student Volunteer Movement of the United States, 109
Tsuda Eigaku Juku, 116
Tsuda Setsuko, 106
Tsuda Umeko, 116

Ugaki Kazushige, 158
Underwood, Horace G., 51–52
Underwood, Horace H., 119, 132, 167
Underwood, Lillias Horton, 82
Union College (in P'yŏngyang), 132
United States, 120; as a Protestant Republic, 54; as a symbol of modernity, 117–8; criticism about, 143; universities in, 117–8, 120–1; women's education in, 140–2
University of Michigan, 130–7
Urak'i, 92, 119, 128
US Army Military Government in Korea (1945–1948), 110

V Narod Movement, 157

Wagner, Ellasue, 58, 60, 73
Walter, Jeannette, 121
Wanguo gongbao, 43–44
Wesleyan College, 1, 109, 178
West, the, 3–4, 6, 12, 41, 43, 75, 91, 117, 195, 201; perception of, 10, 200; womanhood in, 67
westernization, 100, 200–2
Wilson, Woodrow, 22
wise mother, good wife (*hyŏnmo yangch'ŏ*), 19, 28, 36–37, 64, 67, 70–71; critique of, 50–51, 65; educational emphasis on, 48; terminology of, 40–41, 47; transcultural construction of, 42, 55–61
woman question, the, 40, 46, 193, 200
Woman's Christian Temperance Union (WCTU), 12, 150–1, 188
Woman's Foreign Missionary Society, 54

woman's work for woman, 12, 25, 53–55, 61–62, 71
women, converts, 13, 15, 23–25, 63, 82; elite, 34, 92, 114, 178, 185, 187, 199, 201, 205; "heathen," 54–55, 60; indigenous, 30–32; international solidarity of, 10; middle class, 48, 50–51, 54, 69, 83; organizations (*puinhoe*), 159–60; proletarian (*musan puin*), 50; undesirable, 68; writing in the Chosŏn dynasty, 31
World Student Christian Federation, 2, 12

Yang Chusam (aka J. S. Ryang), 54–55
Yang Hanna, 121–3
yangbu hyŏnbu (good husband, wise father), 65
Yanggyu Ŭisuk, 47
yellow peril, 99
Yenching University, 98
Yi I, 36
Yi Ik, 45
Yi Injik, 46
Yi Kwangsu, 58, 88, 93–94, 186
Yi Man'gyu, 13–14
Yi Sunt'ak, 118
Yim Yŏngsin, 128
Yŏ sasŏ (The Four Books for Women), 44–45
Yŏja chinam, 46, 96
Yŏngjo, King, 44
Yosano Akiko, 2, 193
Yoshimura Toratarō, 47
Yŏsŏng (magazine), 59
Young Men's Christian Association (YMCA), 2, 119–20, 129, 139, 153, 172–3, 176, 178–80, 183, 188
Young Women's Christian Association (YWCA), 12, 52, 100, 119, 129, 131, 136, 141, 151, 162, 172–7, 180, 188
Yu Kilchun, 43
Yu Kwansun, 36
Yun Ch'iho, 43–44, 176, 180
Yun Sŏngdŏk, 140–1

CPSIA information can be obtained
at www.ICGtesting.com
Printed in the USA
LVHW021552270721
693842LV00005B/470